Pages listed are first occurrences.

2

Topography of a bird

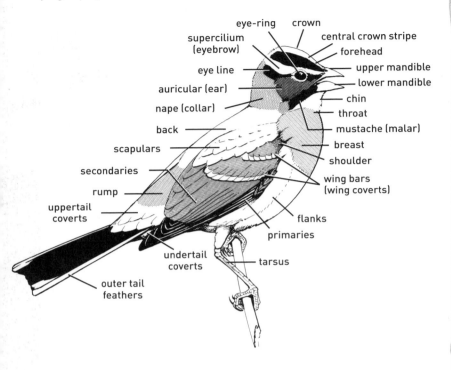

eye-ring
crown
supercilium (eyebrow)
central crown stripe
forehead
eye line
upper mandible
auricular (ear)
lower mandible
nape (collar)
chin
back
throat
scapulars
mustache (malar)
secondaries
breast
rump
shoulder
uppertail coverts
wing bars (wing coverts)
flanks
primaries
undertail coverts
tarsus
outer tail feathers

Undersurface of wing

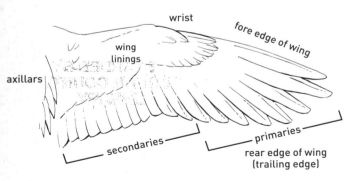

wrist
fore edge of wing
wing linings
axillars
secondaries
primaries
rear edge of wing (trailing edge)

On the upper surface of the secondaries, some waterfowl have a bright-colored patch, called a *speculum.*

PETERSON FIELD GUIDE
TO
BIRDS
of Eastern and Central
North America

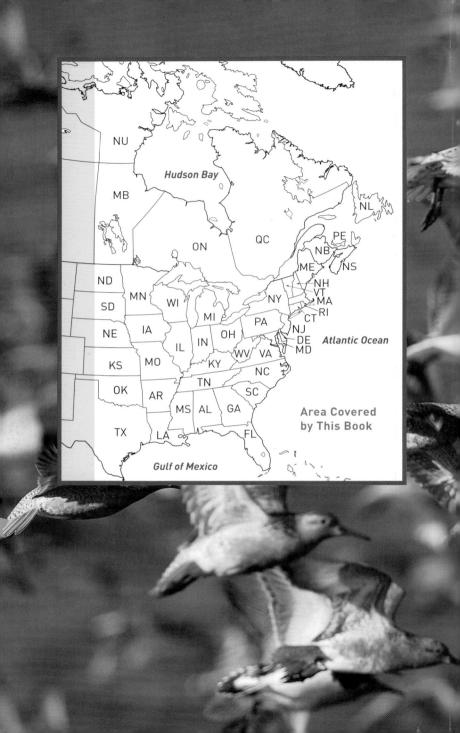

NU

Hudson Bay

MB

NL

ON

QC

PE

NB

ME

NS

ND

MN

WI

NY

NH

VT

MA

RI

SD

IA

MI

PA

CT

NE

IL

IN

OH

NJ

DE

WV

VA

MD

Atlantic Ocean

KS

MO

KY

NC

OK

AR

TN

SC

MS

AL

GA

Area Covered
by This Book

TX

LA

FL

Gulf of Mexico

PETERSON FIELD GUIDE
TO
BIRDS
of Eastern and Central North America

SIXTH EDITION

ROGER TORY PETERSON

HOUGHTON MIFFLIN HARCOURT
BOSTON   NEW YORK   2010

WITH CONTRIBUTIONS FROM
Michael DiGiorgio
Paul Lehman
Michael O'Brien
AND
Jeffrey A. Gordon
Larry Rosche
Bill Thompson III

Photographs by Jeffrey A. Gordon

Key to photographs: i: Scarlet Tanager; ii–iii: Red Knots and Ruddy Turnstones;
vi: Prairie Warbler; vii: Purple Sandpiper; ix: Brown-headed Nuthatch; xii:
Arctic Tern; xiii: Red-winged Blackbird; xv: Blue Grosbeak; xvi: Horned Lark;
1: Northern Bobwhite; 14–15: American Coots; 334–335: Anhinga;
336: Marsh Wren; 424: Northern Gannet; 433: Barn Swallow

www.hmhbooks.com

PETERSON FIELD GUIDES and PETERSON FIELD GUIDE SERIES are registered
trademarks of Houghton Mifflin Harcourt Publishing Company.

Library of Congress Cataloging-in-Publication Data

Peterson field guide to birds of eastern and central North America / Roger Tory
Peterson ; with contributions from Michael DiGiorgio . . . [et al.]. — 6th ed.
p. cm.
Rev. ed. of: Field guide to the birds of eastern and central North America /
Roger Tory Peterson and Virginia Marie Peterson. c2002.
Includes index.
ISBN 978-0-547-15246-2
1. Birds — North America.   I. Peterson, Roger Tory, 1908–1996   II. Peterson, Roger
Tory, 1908–1996. Field guide to the birds of eastern and central North America.
QL681.P45 2009
598.0973—dc22
2009037681

Book design by Anne Chalmers

Printed in China

SCP 10 9 8 7 6 5 4 3 2 1

THE LEGACY OF AMERICA'S GREAT NATURALIST AND CREATOR
of this field guide series, Roger Tory Peterson, is preserved through
the programs and work of the Roger Tory Peterson Institute of Natural History (RTPI), located in his birthplace of Jamestown, New
York. RTPI is a national nature education organization with a mis-
sion to continue the legacy of Roger Tory Peterson by promoting the
teaching and study of nature and to thereby create knowledge of and
appreciation and responsibility for the natural world. RTPI also pre-
serves and exhibits Dr. Peterson's extraordinary collection of art-
work, photography, and writing.

You can become a part of this worthy effort by joining RTPI. Simply call RTPI's membership department at 800-758-6841 ext. 226,
fax 716-665-3794, or e-mail members@rtpi.org for a free one-year
membership with the purchase of this book. Check out our award-
winning website at www.enaturalist.org. You can link to all our programs and activities from there.

CONTENTS

Foreword ix
Editor's Note xiii
Introduction 1

PLATES

FOREWORD

Sometime in my early teens I became intensely interested in bird watching. True, I had already spent a significant amount of time watching and learning about birds — not surprising, given the household in which I was raised — but it grew into an extremely focused pursuit. I spent countless hours wandering woods and slogging through salt marshes near our home in Old Lyme, Connecticut, searching for new birds. In the process, I managed to wear out several copies of the Peterson Field Guide — and I had a great time. I also acquired a much deeper understanding of my surroundings. I think most people get their start in natural history this way. In fact, I can remember someone assuring me that, at one time, virtually all the heads of the top environmental organizations in this country got their starts with a Peterson Field Guide in hand.

Being able to recognize and identify birds is crucial to our awareness of the world around us. My father used the comings and goings of birds as both a biological clock and a litmus test for the condition of the environment. The arrival and departure of migrating birds signaled to him changes in both weather and climatic conditions. The increase or decrease in the population of certain species gave him insight into the overall health of the environment — changes for either good or ill. As his friend Bob Lewin once noted, "Roger was always interested in numbers." Whether it was counting the number of moths on our screen door or the number of flamingos on a lake in Africa, the results were equally significant.

Dad always likened the process of writing a field guide to serving a prison sentence. The projects are always lengthy, and the spatial and visual constraints pronounced. Unlike stream of consciousness, field guide writing seems more akin to composing a telegram — fitting the maximum amount of information into a minimal amount of space. Likewise, the illustration can never be free and loose; it must always be tightly controlled, showing the essence of the bird in question. In both these endeavors, Dad excelled. Someone once confided to me that Dad's rendition of a robin was not only a robin, but the perfect robin. Somehow he was able to convey a bird outside of a specific moment in time and place: the robin idealized, with feathers neatly patterned and plump. His results were all the more remarkable when one watched how they were achieved. He worked mostly from memory, using only a dry, beat-up specimen of the bird for details of anatomy and occasionally a photograph or two. Somehow he was able to piece together an image of the bird as it should have been. Not just any robin, but all robins.

Dad's innovative approach was the product of a rich variety of influences. He was born in Jamestown, a small town in upstate New York known primarily for farming and light manufacture. His first foray into art was encouraged by his seventh-grade schoolteacher, and much of what he learned about birds was either self-taught or picked up from those around him. His family could not afford to send him to college, so he put himself through art school in New York City instead. This was fortuitous, as his time in New York shaped much of what was to come. There he found inspiration from such luminaries in the birding world as Louis Agassiz Fuertes and Ludlow Griscom, and he fell in with a group of avid young birders who called themselves the Bronx County Bird Club, many of whom went on to prominent careers in the biological sciences.

In 1929, Bill Vogt, Bronx County Bird Club member and editor of *Audubon* magazine's precursor, *Bird-Lore,* suggested that Dad combine his expertise in art and bird identification to create a field guide. This was at a time when definitive identification was more often made with a shotgun and dissecting knife than a pair of binoculars. The Peterson system of identification, relying on arrows to point out differences in similar-looking species, seems both simple and obvious in hindsight. At the time, however, it was an enormous innovation. Suddenly the average person could confidently identify the birds around him with just a pair of binoculars and one small book. Birding went from being the slightly odd pursuit of an eccentric few to being one of the largest spectator sports in America today. The repercussions have been enormous.

Each of Dad's many skills and talents was noteworthy in and of itself, but pieced together, they made him truly unique. His skills as an artist were unquestioned. His early artistic training caused him to emphasize the visual rather than the technical—an especially useful trait when trying to design an identification guide for the uninitiated. At the same time, he was a lifelong student of birds and had a tremendous reservoir of technical information. Many consider him to have been one of the finest field naturalists of his era. His writing style was simple, direct, and entertaining, reducing complex information to the essential bones without losing a certain lyrical quality, synthesizing scattered information into original observation.

Less frequently mentioned, but well known to his peers, was his extraordinarily acute sense of hearing. Yale University School of Medicine tested his hearing late in his life and found it to be exceptional — well into the 99th percentile of human capability — allowing him to register frequencies far above the norm. Bird walks with him were always a source of wonder. He was forever hearing and identifying distant birds that the rest of us could barely discern. I am still amazed by his uncanny ability to render bird calls into written English so that they're immediately recognizable. Overlaying all this was his incredible focus. For 70 or more years, his single overriding pleasure was the pursuit and identification of birds, to which he brought inspirational energy, skill, and enthusiasm.

In the foreword to the fifth edition of *A Field Guide to the Birds of Eastern and Central North America,* Robert Bateman referred to Dad's lifework as causing ever-expanding "ripples on a pond." This is apt. More than anything else, Dad thought of himself as a teacher. His greatest wish was to pass along his love of birds and the outdoors, to imbue the rest of us with the same sense of wonder and environmental responsibility that he himself derived from watching birds. His childhood interest, like mine, had morphed into something larger. While birds always remained his focus, they were the most visible aspect of a much greater ecological system. For him, they acted as the early warning system for the overall condition of the environment. By opening up the world of birds through his field guides, he hoped our relationship with nature would shift from one of exploitation to one of stewardship. In this, he has had more than a little success. With each new field guide owner, our world becomes a little richer, a little more full of promise. It may indeed be as Bateman says: "Roger Tory Peterson's life has been one of the most important lives of the last 100 years."

—LEE ALLEN PETERSON

EDITOR'S NOTE

In the past 75 years, ever since Roger Tory Peterson's pioneering *Field Guide to the Birds* changed the way we look at birds and jump-started the environmental movement, many birders have grown up using their Peterson Field Guide, and the book holds a special place in their hearts. Today, however, there are more field guides than ever, and more on the way. The Peterson guide is still set apart by its original concept. The Peterson Identification System is a powerful tool, just as useful and easy to understand today as it was when the first Peterson Field Guide was published. In 2008, we honored the centennial of Roger Peterson's birth with a new edition combining eastern and western North America. It was not simply a commemoration but a useful, up-to-date resource. This new edition for eastern North America is based on the considerable updating that was done for the North American guide and additionally incorporates changes introduced in the Fiftieth Supplement to the American Ornithologists' Union *Check-List of North American Birds,* released in 2009.

Revisions include an update of the taxonomy (to include, for example, splits, such as Canada and Cackling geese, and name changes, such as Oldsquaw to Long-tailed Duck). Birds newly recorded in North America, such as Fea's Petrel, Black-tailed and Yellow-legged gulls, and La Sagra's Flycatcher, are included. The text has been revised to accurately reflect our current knowledge of birds. The range maps are all new. The art has been updated where necessary. New paintings were done for birds that didn't previously occur in North America and for figures that Peterson painted over or discarded as he adapted the plates from one book to another. For some birds, the information we have about them is better than what was available when Peterson was painting, so a few of his paintings have been replaced with new ones; others have been digitally enhanced.

Peterson was an innovator. If he were a young bird watcher today, there's a good chance he would be at the forefront of new birding technology. In this book, we've included a URL (www.petersonfield

guides.com) where readers can access a set of video podcasts that are easy to use, educational, and fun. These supplements to the book cover key individual species, popular groupings of birds, and such topics as how to use range maps, identification basics, and bird topography. Jeffrey Gordon and Bill Thompson III created the video podcasts, which we hope will enhance your enjoyment of birds and bird watching.

When Roger Tory Peterson died, we lost a uniquely talented artist and naturalist. He had a profound influence on a vast number of young naturalists, however, who have devoted their lives to birds and other animals, the environment, education, art, and other vocations and avocations. The team of expert birders who brought a wealth of knowledge to the creation of the *Peterson Field Guide to Birds of North America* worked diligently to enhance Peterson's legacy while ensuring that all of the content was current and highly useful for today's birder. Paul Lehman and Bill Thompson III revised all the text. Michael O'Brien painted the new species, laid out the plates, directed the digital work, and consulted editorially. Paul Lehman supplied the information for the new range maps, graphic artist Larry Rosche created the maps digitally, and Marshall Iliff reviewed them all. Michael DiGiorgio did the digital enhancements of the art and executed the layout of the plates digitally. Kimball Garrett reviewed and revised some of the voice descriptions.

For this sixth edition of the *Peterson Field Guide to Birds of Eastern and Central North America,* Michael O'Brien took on the bulk of the work, creating plate-by-plate species lists, fine-tuning the text for eastern North America, and reviewing the plates. Paul Lehman reviewed the text and updated the range maps. Michael DiGiorgio painstakingly executed the digital layout of the plates. At Houghton Mifflin Harcourt, Anne Chalmers, Teresa Elsey, Katrina Kruse, Jill Lazer, Sara Shaffer, and Taryn Roeder all played critical roles in producing this book.

At a time when environmental concerns are paramount, it's essential that we as readers revisit the sources that inspired and deepened our appreciation of the natural world. Roger Tory Peterson's voice is for the generations, and it's with tremendous pride that we present it to you, revitalized and as relevant as always.

—LISA A. WHITE

PETERSON FIELD GUIDE

TO

BIRDS

of Eastern and Central
North America

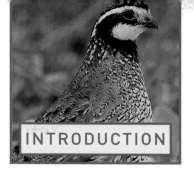

INTRODUCTION

How to Identify Birds

Veteran birders will know how to use this book. Beginners, however, should spend some time becoming familiar in a general way with the illustrations. The plates, for the most part, have been grouped in taxonomic sequence. However, in cases where there is a great similarity of shape and action, similar-appearing birds may be grouped outside their strict taxonomic order. This should aid in field identification and not frustrate the true taxonomist to any great degree.

Birds that could be confused are grouped together when possible and are arranged in identical profile for direct comparison. The arrows point to outstanding field marks, which are explained opposite. The text also gives aids such as voice, actions, and habitat, not visually portrayable, and under a separate heading discusses species that might be confused. The general range is not described for most species in the text. The annotated three-color range maps in the back of the book (pp. 338–423) provide detailed range information. Thumbnail versions of the maps also appear next to the species accounts for quick reference.

In addition to the plates of birds normally found in the region covered in this field guide, there are also plates depicting accidentals from Eurasia, the sea, and the Tropics, as well as some of the exotic escapes that are sometimes seen.

What Is the Bird's Size?

Acquire the habit of comparing a new bird with some familiar "yardstick"—a House Sparrow, robin, pigeon, etc.—so that you can say to yourself, "Smaller than a robin, a little larger than a House Sparrow." The measurements in this book represent lengths in inches (with centimeters in parentheses) from bill tip to tail tip of specimens on their backs as in museum trays. For species that show considerable size variation, a range of measurements is given. For less variable species, only one measurement is given.

What Is Its Shape?
Is it plump like a starling (left) or slender like a cuckoo (right)?

What Shape Are Its Wings?
Are they rounded like a bobwhite's (left) or sharply pointed like a Barn Swallow's (right)?

What Shape Is Its Bill?
Is it small and fine like a warbler's (1), stout and short like a seed-cracking sparrow's (2), dagger-shaped like a tern's (3), or hook-tipped like a bird of prey's (4)?

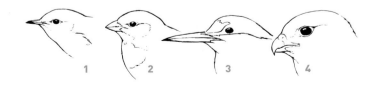

What Shape Is Its Tail?

Is it deeply forked like a Barn Swallow's (1), square-tipped like a Cliff Swallow's (2), notched like a Tree Swallow's (3), rounded like a Blue Jay's (4), or pointed like a Mourning Dove's (5)?

How Does It Behave?

Does it cock its tail like a wren or hold it down like a flycatcher? Does it wag its tail? Does it sit erect on an open perch, dart after an insect, and return as a flycatcher does?

Does It Climb Trees?

If so, does it climb upward in spirals like a creeper (left), in jerks like a woodpecker (center) using its tail as a brace, or go down headfirst like a nuthatch (right)?

How Does It Fly?

Does it undulate (dip up and down) like a flicker (1)? Does it fly straight and fast like a dove (2)? Does it hover like a kingfisher (3)? Does it glide or soar?

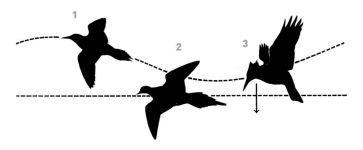

Does It Swim?

Does it sit low in the water like a loon (1) or high like a gallinule (2)? If a duck, does it dive like a scaup or a scoter (3) or dabble and upend like a Mallard (4)?

Does It Wade?

Is it large and long-legged like a heron or small like a sandpiper? If one of the latter, does it probe the mud or pick at things? Does it teeter or bob?

What Are Its Field Marks?

Some birds can be identified by color alone, but most birds are not that easy. The most important aids are what we call field marks, which are, in effect, the "trademarks of nature." Note whether the breast is spotted as in a thrush (1), streaked as in a thrasher (2), or plain as in a cuckoo (3).

Tail Pattern

Does the tail have a "flash pattern"—a white tip as in the Eastern Kingbird (1), white patches in the outer corners as in the Eastern and Spotted towhees (2), or white sides as in the juncos (3)?

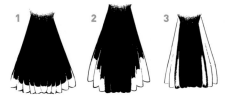

Rump Patch

Does it have a light rump like a Cliff Swallow (1) or flicker (2)? Northern Harrier, Yellow-rumped Warbler, and several shorebirds also have distinctive rump patches.

Eye Stripes and Eye-ring

Does the bird have a stripe above, through, or below the eye, or a combination of these stripes? Does it have a striped crown? A ring around the eye, or "spectacles"? A "mustache" stripe? These details are important in many small songbirds.

Wing Bars

Do the wings have light wing bars or not? Their presence or absence is important in recognizing many warblers, vireos, and flycatchers. Wing bars may be single or double, bold or obscure.

Wing Pattern

The basic wing pattern of ducks (shown below), shorebirds, and other water birds is very important. Notice whether the wings have patches (1) or stripes (2), are solidly colored (3), or have contrasting black tips.

Bird Songs and Calls

Using sounds to identify birds can be just as useful as using visual clues. In fact, in many situations, birds are much more readily identified by sound than by sight. The species accounts here include a brief entry on voice, with interpretations of these songs and calls, in an attempt to give birders some handle on the vocalizations they hear. Authors of bird books have attempted, with varying success, to fit songs and calls into syllables, words, and phrases. Musical notations, comparative descriptions, and even ingenious systems of symbols have also been employed. To supplement this verbal interpretation, there are recording collections available for nearly every region of the world and for individual groups of birds. The *Peterson Birding by Ear* CDs provide a step-by-step method for learning how to develop your listening and identification skills. Preparation in advance for particular species or groups greatly enhances your ability to identify them. Some birders do a majority of their birding by ear, and there is no substitute for actual sounds—for getting out into the field and tracking down the songster and committing the song to memory. However, an audio library is a wonderful resource to return home to when attempting to identify a bird heard in the field. Many such collections can now be taken into the field on digital audio devices. *Caution:* If using recordings to attract birds, limit the number of playbacks, and do not use them on threatened species or in heavily birded areas.

Bird Nests

The more time you spend in the field becoming familiar with bird behavior, the more skilled you'll become at finding bird nests. It is as exciting to keep a bird nest list as it is to keep a life list. Remember, if you happen to find a nest during the breeding season, leave the site as undisturbed as possible. Back away, and do not touch the nest, eggs, or young birds. Often squirrels, raccoons, and several other mammals, grackles, and cowbirds are more than happy to have you "point out" a nest and will raid it if you disrupt the site or call attention to it. Many people find young birds that have just left the nest and may appear to be alone. Usually they are not lost but are under the watchful eye of a parent bird and are best left in place rather than scooped up and taken to a foreign environment. In the winter, nest hunting can be great fun and has little impact, as most nests will never be used again. They are easy to see once the foliage is gone, and it can be a challenge to attempt to identify the maker. Books such as *A Field Guide to Birds' Nests* and *A Field Guide to Western Birds' Nests*, both in the Peterson Field Guide series, will expand your ornithological expertise.

Conservation

Birds undeniably contribute to our pleasure and quality of life. But they also are sensitive indicators of the environment, a sort of "ecological litmus paper," and hence more meaningful than just chickadees and cardinals that brighten the suburban garden, grouse and ducks that fill the sportsman's bag, or rare warblers and shorebirds that excite the field birder. The observation and recording of bird populations over time lead inevitably to environmental awareness and can signal impending changes.

To this end, please help the cause of wildlife conservation and education by contributing to or taking part in the work of the following organizations: **The Nature Conservancy** (4245 North Fairfax Drive, Suite 100, Arlington, VA 22203; www.nature.org), **National Audubon Society** (700 Broadway, New York, NY 10003; www.audubon.org), **Defenders of Wildlife** (1130 17th Street NW, Washington, DC 20036; www.defenders.org), **Roger Tory Peterson Institute of Natural History** (311 Curtis Street, Jamestown, NY 14701; www.rtpi.org), **National Wildlife Federation** (11100 Wildlife Center Drive, Reston, VA 20190; www.nwf.org), **World Wildlife Fund** (1250 24th Street NW, PO Box 97180, Washington, DC 20090; www.wwf.org), **Cornell Laboratory of Ornithology** (159 Sapsucker Woods Road, Ithaca, NY 14850; www.birds.cornell.edu), **Ducks Unlimited** (One Waterfowl Way, Memphis, TN 38120; www.ducks.org), **BirdLife International** (Wellbrook Court, Girton Road, Cambridge CB3 0NA, U.K.; www.birdlife.org), **Partners in Flight** (www.partnersinflight.org), **American Bird Conservancy** (PO Box 249, The Plains, VA 20198; abcbirds.org), as well as your local land trust and natural heritage program and your local Audubon and ornithological societies and bird clubs. These and so many other groups that have come into the forefront of bird conservation in the last 20 years merit your support.

The Maps and Ranges of Birds

The ranges of many species have changed markedly over the past 50 or more years. Some species are expanding because of protection given them, changing habitats, bird feeding, or other factors. Some "increases" may simply be the result of more field-guide-educated birders being in the field, helping to more thoroughly document bird populations and distributions. Other avian species have diminished alarmingly and may have been extirpated from major parts of their range. The primary culprit here has been habitat loss, although other factors such as increased competition or predation from other species may sometimes be involved. Species that are in serious decline in North America run the gamut, from Ivory Gull to Lesser Prairie-Chicken and Loggerhead Shrike to Bewick's Wren, Rusty Blackbird, and Red Knot.

Successful introductions of some species, such as Trumpeter Swan and Eurasian Collared-Dove, have resulted in self-sustaining, growing populations (the latter was introduced to the Bahamas, then arrived in the U.S. on its own). And a good number of additional vagrant species — out-of-range visitors from faraway lands — continue to be found (such as a Red-footed Falcon in Massachusetts). Some species that were formerly thought to occur only exceptionally have, over the past several decades, become much more regular visitors (such as Lesser Black-backed Gull) and sometimes even local breeders (such as Clay-colored Thrush). It is not always certain if such changes in status are the result of actual population increases or if they merely reflect better observer coverage and advances in field identification skills.

Range maps need to be of sufficient size to denote adequate detail and to include written information on such topics as population trends and extralimital occurrences. Thus, the range maps in this guide have been purposely placed near the back of the book where they can be reproduced in a large size not possible in the main body of the text. The maps are organized taxonomically, following the order published by the American Ornithologists' Union. In addition, thumbnail versions of the same maps are placed in the main text next to the species accounts to provide a quick overview of a species' range without needing to turn the page. The key to the range maps is located on page 337 and also on the inside of the front cover, for quick reference.

Range maps don't depict how abundant a particular species is within its range. The following list defines terms of abundance used throughout the book. The definitions presume you're in the habitat and season in which a species would occur.

Common: Always or almost always encountered daily, usually in moderate to large numbers.

Fairly common: Usually encountered daily, generally not in large numbers.

Uncommon: Occurs in small numbers and may be missed on a substantial number of days.

Scarce: Present only in small numbers or difficult to find within its normal range.

Rare or very rare: Annual or probably annual in small numbers but still largely within its normal range.

Casual: Beyond its normal range; occurs at somewhat regular intervals but usually less frequently than annually.

Accidental: Beyond its normal range; one record or a very few records.

Vagrant: Beyond its normal range.

Local: Limited geographic range within the U.S. and Canada.

Introduced: Not native; deliberately released.

Exotic: Not native; either released or escaped. A term used especially for species that are present in limited numbers and may or may not be breeding. Other species, such as House Sparrow and European Starling, were also introduced but are so well established that, in the sense used here, they are no longer considered exotic.

Unestablished exotic: Nonnative releasee or escapee that does not have a naturalized breeding population, though some may be breeding in very localized areas.

Habitats

Gaining a familiarity with a wide range of habitats will greatly enhance your overall knowledge of the birds in a specific region, increase your skills, and add to your enjoyment of birding. It is unlikely you will ever see a meadowlark in an oak woodland or a Wood Thrush in a meadow. Birders know this, and if they want to go out to run up a large day list, they do not remain in one habitat but shift from site to site based on time and species diversity for a given type of habitat.

A few birds do invade habitats other than their own at times, especially on migration. A warbler that spends the summer in Maine might be seen, on its journey through Florida, in a palm. In cities, migrating birds often have to make the best of it, like the American Woodcock found one morning on the window ledge of a New York City office. Strong weather patterns can also alter where a bird happens to appear. Hurricanes, for example, can be a disaster for many species. As these violent storms sweep over the ocean, the eye can often "vacuum" up oceanic species that seek shelter in its calmness. Upon reaching land, these normally offshore species are faced with an entirely strange habitat and account for sightings such as a Yellow-nosed Albatross heading up the Hudson River, a White-tailed Tropicbird in downtown Boston, and numbers of storm-petrels on an inland reservoir in Virginia.

Most species, however, are quite predictable for the major portion of their lives, and for the birder who has learned where to look, the rewards are great.

To start, familiarize yourself with individual habitat types. Become familiar with the dominant plant types that are indicators — for example, oak-beech woods, grass-shrub meadows, salt- or freshwater wetlands — and keep accurate records of what species you find in each. In a short time you will have a working knowledge of the predominant species in each habitat, and this will help you with identification by allowing you to anticipate what might be found there.

The seasonal movements of birds at your sites will provide an overview of migrant species that come through at a given time and will be a reference point for future visits during these migration periods. A forest dotted with migrant warblers in spring may revert to relative quiet accented by the repetitive calls of a Red-eyed Vireo or the drawn-out call of an Eastern Wood-Pewee in midsummer.

Be sure not to overlook cities and towns, where well-adapted species can be found. Peregrine Falcons have shown remarkable adaptability, nesting on strategic ledges in the walled canyons of many cities. The fertile grounds for hunting Rock Pigeons and European Starlings seem to suit this raptor quite well.

Ecotones are edges where two habitat types interface — a forest and a shrub meadow, for example. As this is not a gradual change, ecotones offer habitat for species from both of the adjoining areas and are therefore rich in bird life.

The changes in habitat over the years will also affect your favorite birding areas. Fields turn to shrubby lots and then woodlands. Bobwhite and meadowlarks may move on, but Indigo Buntings and Field Sparrows establish themselves. This dynamic is normal in the natural world. However, humankind's alterations to this process have had a great impact. Forest fragmentation is an example. As land development continues, it is affecting numerous species. A sudden disruption has a more drastic effect than a slow change, which allows for adaptation. As we divide up habitat with roadways, we have created a greater edge effect, and this allows Brown-headed Cowbirds to penetrate into forest areas where they would not have ventured in the past. They now parasitize many more species than before, and such parasitization is leading to marked declines in total numbers of many species. This forest fragmentation is also affecting the success rate of nestling fledging by increasing the numbers of some predators and by altering prime habitat requirements for obtaining food to raise the young.

Some species are obligates to a specific habitat type, and searching these areas greatly improves your chances of finding such birds. These include Golden-crowned Kinglet nesting in coniferous woodlands and Kirtland's Warbler in Michigan, which breeds only in jack pine woodlands of a specific height. Even in migration, many species remain faithful to selected habitats, such as waterthrushes along watercourses. Running or dripping water has proven to be an important attractant for migrating land birds, and in areas where fresh water is scarce, a water drip can be a gold mine for migrant warblers and other passerines.

Subspecies and Geographic Variation

Many species of birds inhabit wide geographic areas. The Savannah Sparrow *(Passerculus sandwichensis),* for example, breeds throughout North America, from Mexico north into Alaska. In such a wide-ranging species, there are geographic subsets within the population that show distinct local plumage patterns and song variants. When the distinct geographic forms of a species reach a point when the population is dominated by individuals that are recognizably different from typical individuals of the "parent" species, the local group is formally designated a subspecies of the parent species. The subspecies is named by attaching a third, subspecific name to the scientific name of the species. Thus, the pale Savannah Sparrow of Sable Island, NS (wintering along the Atlantic Coast) is called *Passerculus sandwichensis princeps,* to distinguish that form from another subspecies. (In this case, it is also known by the common name "Ipswich" Sparrow.) With at least 14 recognizable subspecies, the Savannah Sparrow ranks high among North American birds in the number of its geographic varieties.

Often a subspecific group is so distinct from the parent species that several members can be easily recognized in the field by bird watchers. A good example of this is the Dark-eyed Junco *(Junco hyemalis)*. With 12 subspecies, at least 5 are easily discerned: the "Oregon," "Pink-sided," "White-winged," "Slate-colored," and "Grayheaded" (of these, only "Slate-colored" and "Oregon" are regular in the East). For the birder, identification of subspecies can add greater challenges to birding and, when documented, valuable information, especially when subspecies are reclassified to full species status. Such has been the case, for example, with the splitting of Sharp-tailed Sparrow *(Ammodramus audacutus)* into Saltmarsh Sparrow *(A. caudacutus)* and Nelson's Sparrow *(A. nelsoni)*. The differences between Bicknell's Thrush *(Catharus bicknelli)* and Gray-cheeked Thrush *(C. minimus)* illustrate how subtle the field marks can be between species and why they had been relegated to subspecific status. The shifting of this line between subspecies and species is ongoing. Recording data on location and numbers can prove helpful in completing a picture of a species' distribution or even a new species that has been overlooked.

In this edition, species that have distinct subspecies that are easily recognized, such as Yellow-rumped Warbler *(Dendroica coronata)* and Dark-eyed Junco, have been represented. When in the field, challenge yourself to discern the subspecies. It will increase your visual and listening skills and add a new level of understanding and enjoyment of birds.

PLATES

Geese, Swans, and Ducks Family Anatidae

Web-footed waterfowl. **RANGE:** Worldwide.

Geese

Large, gregarious waterfowl; heavier bodied, longer necked than ducks; bills thick at base. Noisy in flight; some fly in lines or V formations. Sexes alike. Geese are more terrestrial than ducks, often grazing. **FOOD:** Grasses, seeds, waste grain, aquatic plants.

GREATER WHITE-FRONTED GOOSE　　　　　Uncommon M3
Anser albifrons (see also p. 22)
28 in. (71 cm). No other wild goose in our area has *yellow* or *orange* feet. Gray-brown with *pink* bill; Greenland breeding subspecies has *orange-yellow* bill and darker head and neck. *Adult* with *white patch on front of face* and variable *black bars* on belly. *Immature:* Dusky with pinkish bill, yellow or orange feet. May be confused with some domestic barnyard geese. **VOICE:** High-pitched tootling, *kah-lah-a-luk,* in chorus. **HABITAT:** Marshes, prairies, agricultural fields, lakes, bays; in summer, tundra.

SNOW GOOSE　　　　　　　　　　　　Locally common M4
Chen caerulescens (see also p. 22)
White morph: 25–33 in. (64–84 cm). *White* with *black primaries.* Head often rust-stained from feeding in muddy or iron-rich waters. Bill pink with black "lips." Feet pink. Base of bill curves back slightly toward eye. *Immature:* Pale gray; dark bill and legs. Dark morph ("Blue" Goose): 25–30 in. (64–76 cm): Dark with *white head.* Intermediates with white morph of Snow are frequent. *Immature:* Similar to young Greater White-fronted Goose, but feet and bill *dark.* **VOICE:** Loud, nasal, double-noted *houck-houck,* in chorus. **SIMILAR SPECIES:** Ross's Goose. **HABITAT:** Marshes, grain fields, ponds, bays; in summer, tundra.

ROSS'S GOOSE *Chen rossii* (see also p. 22)　　　Uncommon M5
23 in. (58 cm). Like a small Snow Goose, but neck shorter, head rounder (steeper forehead). Bill with *gray-blue or purple-blue base,* stubbier (with *vertical border* between base and facial feathering), *lacking distinctive "grinning black lips";* warts at bill base difficult to see. *Immature:* Whiter than young Snow Goose. Rare "Blue" morph shows more extensively dark neck, whiter wing patches than "Blue" Snow Goose. Hybrids with Snow Goose occur. **VOICE:** Higher than Snow, suggesting Cackling Goose. **SIMILAR SPECIES:** Snow Goose. **HABITAT:** Same as Snow Goose.

GREATER WHITE-FRONTED GOOSE

immature

adult

adult

adult

immature

SNOW GOOSE dark morph
("Blue" Goose)

adult

adult

ROSS'S GOOSE

immature

adult

Snow

intergrade
between dark
and white
morphs

SNOW
GOOSE
white morph

Ross's

Snow

BRANT *Branta bernicla* (see also p. 22)　　　**Locally common M6**
24–26 in. (59–66 cm). A small black-necked goose. Has white stern, conspicuous when it upends, whitish flanks, and band of white on neck (absent in immature). Travels in large irregular flocks. Eastern subspecies, "Pale-bellied" Brant *(B. b. hrota)*, has *light belly, less contrasty flanks, and two separated neck patches.* Pacific Coast subspecies, "Black" Brant *(B. b. nigricans),* a very rare visitor to East Coast, has dark belly and complete white band across foreneck. **VOICE:** Throaty *cr-r-r-ruk* or *krr-onk, krrr-onk.* **SIMILAR SPECIES:** Foreparts of Canada and Cackling geese not black to waterline, and those species have large white face patch. Brant is more strictly coastal. **HABITAT:** Salt bays, estuaries; in summer, tundra.

BARNACLE GOOSE *Branta leucopsis*　　　**Vagrant**
26–27 in. (66–69 cm). Similar in size to Brant. Has white sides and black chest to waterline, strongly contrasting with white belly. Note white face encircling eye. Back distinctly barred. Some reports likely represent escapees. **VOICE:** Like Snow Goose, but higher-pitched, doglike barks. **SIMILAR SPECIES:** Canada Goose larger and brown-bodied (not gray), lacks barring, has dark face. Brant has all-dark head. **RANGE:** Casual winter visitor from Greenland and Europe to Atlantic Coast; accidental farther west. Provenance of some birds in question. **HABITAT:** Ponds, lakes; grazes in fields, often with Canada Geese.

CACKLING GOOSE *Branta hutchinsii*　　　**Uncommon M7**
23–32 in. (58–81 cm). Recently elevated to full-species rank separate from very similar Canada Goose. **VOICE:** High, cackling *yel-lik.* **SIMILAR SPECIES:** Told from Canada by smaller size, shorter neck, smaller, rounder head (steeper forehead), stubbier bill, and higher-pitched voice. Distinction between larger Cacklings and smaller Canadas subtle. **HABITAT:** Lakes, marshes, fields; in summer, tundra. Seen as often with flocks of Snow Geese as with Canadas.

CANADA GOOSE *Branta canadensis* (see also p. 22)　　　**Common M8**
30–43 in. (76–109 cm). The most widespread goose in N. America. Note black head and neck, or "stocking," that contrasts with pale breast and *white chin strap.* Flocks travel in strings or in Vs, "honking" loudly. Substantial variation in size and neck length exists among populations. **VOICE:** Deep, musical honking or barking, *ka-ronk* or *ka-lunk.* Small subspecies (and Cackling Goose) have higher-pitched calls. **SIMILAR SPECIES:** Cackling Goose. **HABITAT:** Lakes, ponds, bays, marshes, fields. Resident in many areas, frequenting parks, lawns, golf courses.

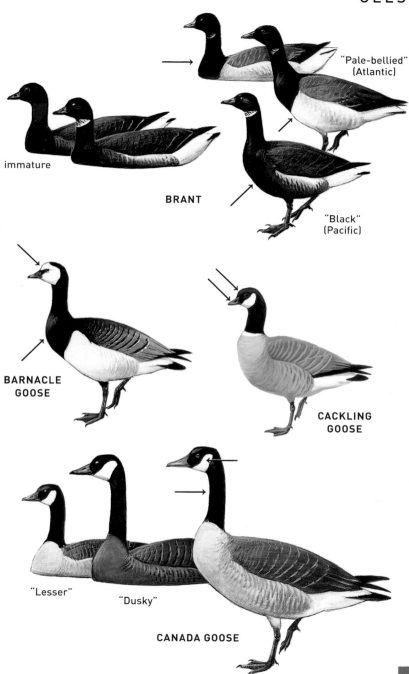

"Pale-bellied"
(Atlantic)

immature

BRANT

"Black"
(Pacific)

BARNACLE
GOOSE

CACKLING
GOOSE

"Lesser"

"Dusky"

CANADA GOOSE

Swans

Huge, long-necked all-white swimmers. Young are pale gray-brown. Sexes alike. Feed by immersing head and neck or by "tipping up." **FOOD:** Aquatic plants, seeds.

MUTE SWAN *Cygnus olor*   Fairly common, local M9

60 in. (152 cm). Introduced from Europe. Often swims with S curve in neck; wings often arched over back. *Black-knobbed orange bill* tilts down. Wingbeats make a "whooshing" sound. *Immature:* Dingy, with pinkish bill. **VOICE:** Not mute but makes hissing sounds, weak bugling. **HABITAT:** Ponds, fresh and salt; coastal lagoons, salt bays.

TUNDRA SWAN   Uncommon to locally common M11

Cygnus columbianus (see also p. 22)

52–53 in. (132–135 cm). Our most widespread native swan. Often heard long before a high-flying flock can be spotted. Bill *black,* usually with *small yellow basal spot. Immature:* Dingy, with mostly pinkish bill. **VOICE:** Mellow, high-pitched cooing: *woo-ho, woo-woo, woo-ho.* **SIMILAR SPECIES:** Trumpeter and Mute swans. **HABITAT:** Lakes, large rivers, bays, estuaries, grain fields; in summer, tundra.

TRUMPETER SWAN *Cygnus buccinator*   Uncommon, local M10

58–60 in. (147–152 cm). Larger than Tundra Swan, with longer, heavier, *all-black bill,* which has *straight ridge* recalling Canvasback. Black on lores wider, *embracing eyes* and lacking yellow spot (some Tundras also lack this spot). Bill base forms *V* shape on forehead. *Immature:* Keeps dusky body color later into first spring and summer than does Tundra. **VOICE:** *Deeper, more nasal calls* than Tundra Swan. **HABITAT:** Lakes, ponds, large rivers; in winter, also bays, grain fields, marshes.

Whistling-Ducks

Formerly called "tree ducks," these long-necked, long-legged waterfowl are closely related to geese. Named for their high-pitched calls. Gregarious. **FOOD:** Seeds of aquatic plants and grasses.

FULVOUS WHISTLING-DUCK   Uncommon, local M2

Dendrocygna bicolor (see also p. 42)

20 in. (51 cm). Note *tawny body,* dark back, *pale side stripes, black underwings, white band* on rump. **VOICE:** Squealing slurred whistle, *ka-whee-oo.* **SIMILAR SPECIES:** Black-bellied Whistling-Duck, female Northern Pintail. **HABITAT:** Freshwater marshes, ponds, irrigated land. Seldom perches in trees.

BLACK-BELLIED WHISTLING-DUCK   Locally common M1

Dendrocygna autumnalis

21 in. (53 cm). Rusty with *black belly,* bright *coral red* bill, pink legs. Broad *white wing patch. Immature:* Has gray bill and legs. **VOICE:** Four- or five-part high-pitched squealing whistle. **HABITAT:** Ponds, freshwater marshes; often nests in manmade boxes; frequently perches in trees.

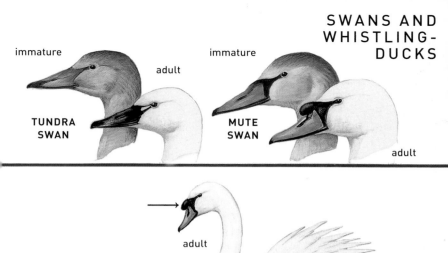

immature

adult

TUNDRA SWAN

immature

adult

MUTE SWAN

adult

MUTE SWAN

adult

immature

TUNDRA SWAN

TRUMPETER SWAN

adult

Fulvous Whistling-Duck

FULVOUS WHISTLING-DUCK

Black-Bellied Whistling-Duck

BLACK-BELLIED WHISTLING-DUCK

Geese and Swans in Flight

CANADA GOOSE *Branta canadensis*   p. 18

BRANT *Branta bernicla*   p. 18
Small; black head and neck, white stern.

GREATER WHITE-FRONTED GOOSE *Anser albifrons*   p. 16
Adult: Gray-brown neck, black bars or splotches on belly.
Immature: Dusky, with light bill and feet.

TUNDRA SWAN *Cygnus columbianus*   p. 20
Very long neck. *Adult:* Plumage entirely white.

SNOW GOOSE (WHITE MORPH) *Chen caerulescens*   p. 16
Adult: White with black primaries.

SNOW GOOSE (DARK MORPH, "BLUE" GOOSE)   p. 16
Chen caerulescens
Adult: Dark body, white head.
Immature: Dusky, with dark bill and feet.

ROSS'S GOOSE *Chen rossii*   p. 16
Smaller, slightly shorter necked and shorter billed than Snow
Goose.

Many geese and swans fly in line or V formation.

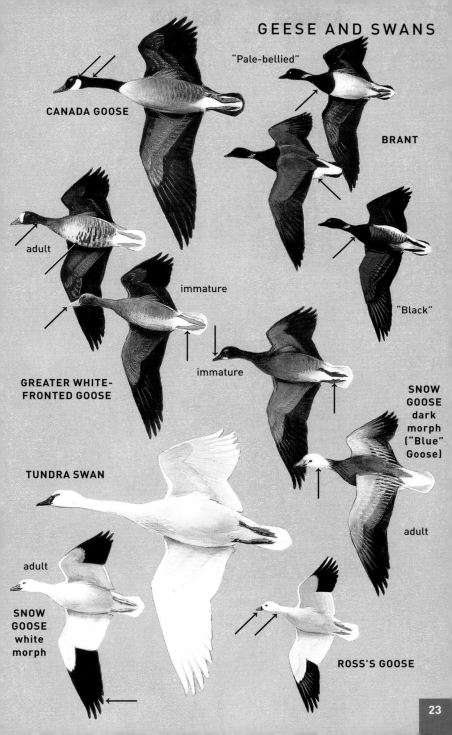

GEESE AND SWANS

"Pale-bellied"

CANADA GOOSE

BRANT

adult

immature

"Black"

immature

GREATER WHITE-FRONTED GOOSE

SNOW GOOSE dark morph ("Blue" Goose)

TUNDRA SWAN

adult

adult

SNOW GOOSE white morph

ROSS'S GOOSE

23

DABBLING DUCKS

Feed by dabbling and upending; sometimes feed on land. Take flight directly into air. Most species have an iridescent speculum on secondaries above. Sexes not alike; in midsummer, males molt into drab "eclipse" plumage, usually resembling females. **FOOD:** Aquatic plants, grain, small aquatic life, insects.

MUSCOVY DUCK *Cairina moschata*   Scarce, local
Male 32 in. (81 cm); female 28 in. (66 cm). Black, gooselike duck with large white wing patch and underwing coverts. *Male:* Bare, knobby, red face. *Female:* Duller, may lack facial knobs. Domestic Muscovies vary in pattern; often show much white. **VOICE:** Usually silent. Occasionally utters a soft quack or hiss. **RANGE:** Native of tropical America (Mex. to n. Argentina). Recent colonizer of lower Rio Grande Valley, TX. Feral populations well established in FL and near Brownsville, TX. **HABITAT:** Freshwater ponds and backwaters; wooded river corridors of Rio Grande in TX.

WOOD DUCK *Aix sponsa* (see also p. 40)   Fairly common M12
18–19 in. (45–49 cm). Highly colored; often perches in trees. In flight, white belly contrasts with dark breast and wings. Note also the long, almost square, dark tail; short neck; and angle at which bill points downward in flight. *Male:* Bizarre face pattern, sweptback crest, and rainbow iridescence unique. In eclipse, more like female but with brighter bill and suggestion of breeding head pattern. *Female:* Dull-colored; note dark crested head and *white eye patch*. **VOICE:** Male, hissing *jeeeeeeb*, with rising inflection. Female, a loud, rising squeal, *oo-eek*, and sharp *crrek, crrek*. **HABITAT:** Wooded swamps, rivers, ponds, marshes.

EURASIAN WIGEON *Anas penelope*   Rare M14
19–20 in. (48–51 cm). *Male:* Note *red-brown* head, *buff* crown. A *gray-sided* wigeon with rufous-pinkish breast. *Female:* Very similar to female American Wigeon, but in many Eurasians head is tinged with *rust* or *orange-buff;* in others it is not. Surest point is dusky (not white) axillars, or "wingpits." **VOICE:** Male, a long whistle, *wheeee-oo.* Female, a purr or quack. **HABITAT:** Same as American Wigeon, with which it is usually found.

AMERICAN WIGEON   Fairly common M15
Anas americana (see also p. 40)
19–20 in. (48–51 cm). In flight, recognized by *large white patch on forewing.* (Similarly placed blue patch of Northern Shoveler and Blue-winged Teal often appears whitish.) When swimming, rides high, picking at water like a coot. Often grazes on land. *Male:* Warm brownish; head pale gray with green eye patch. Note *white crown* (nicknamed "Baldpate"). *Female:* Brown; gray head and neck; whitish belly and forewing. **VOICE:** Male, a three-part whistled *whooa whee-whew.* Female, *qua-ack.* **SIMILAR SPECIES:** Told from female Gadwall and Northern Pintail by whitish patch on forewing, small bluish bill. See Eurasian Wigeon. **HABITAT:** Marshes, lakes, bays, fields, grass.

DABBLING DUCKS

adults

domestic
variation

**MUSCOVY
DUCK**

♀

♂ in eclipse
(summer)

WOOD DUCK

♂

♂

♀

**EURASIAN
WIGEON**

♂

♀

AMERICAN WIGEON

SILHOUETTES OF DUCKS ON LAND

dabbling ducks
(dabblers)

sea and bay
ducks (divers)

mergansers
(divers)

Ruddy Duck
(diver)

whistling-ducks
(dabblers)

25

GADWALL *Anas strepera* (see also p. 40)　　　Fairly common　M13
19–20 in. (48–51 cm). *Male: Gray* with brown head, *black rump, white speculum.* When swimming, wing patch may be concealed. Belly white, feet yellow. *Female:* Brown, mottled, with *white speculum,* yellow feet, orange sides on dark bill. **VOICE:** Male, a low, reedy *bek;* a whistling call. Female, a nasal quack. **SIMILAR SPECIES:** Female told from female Mallard by steeper forehead, wing pattern, more nasal call. **HABITAT:** Lakes, ponds, marshes.

AMERICAN BLACK DUCK　　　　　　　Fairly common　M16
Anas rubripes (see also p. 42)
22–23 in. (55–58 cm). A dusky duck that flashes *white wing linings* in flight. Note violet wing patch with thin white trailing edge. Sexes similar. Hybridizes with Mallard. **VOICE:** Similar to Mallard. **SIMILAR SPECIES:** Mallard, Mottled Duck. **HABITAT:** Marshes, bays, estuaries, ponds, rivers, lakes.

MOTTLED DUCK *Anas fulvigula*　　　　Fairly common　M18
22–23 in. (55–58 cm). Like a pale brownish version of American Black Duck. Note tan head, unstreaked buffy throat, and unmarked yellow bill with *dark spot at base of "lips."* Sexes similar. Darker than female Mallard and lacking black on bill and broad white border to speculum. **VOICE:** Very similar to Mallard's. **SIMILAR SPECIES:** American Black Duck, Mallard. **HABITAT:** Marshes, ponds.

MALLARD *Anas platyrhynchos* (see also p. 42)　　　Common　M17
22–23 in. (55–59 cm). *Male:* Note *green head, white neck ring,* grayish body, chestnut chest, white tail, blue speculum. *Female:* Mottled brown with *whitish tail.* Dark bill patched with orange, feet orange. In flight, shows white bar *on both sides* of blue speculum. **VOICE:** Male, *yeeb;* a low *kwek.* Female, boisterous quacking. **SIMILAR SPECIES:** Female Gadwall, American Black Duck, Mottled Duck. **HABITAT:** Marshes, wooded swamps, grain fields, ponds, rivers, lakes, bays, city parks.

"MEXICAN" MALLARD *Anas platyrhynchos diazi*　Uncommon, local
20–21 in. (51–54 cm). This subspecies of Mallard was formerly regarded as a distinct species called Mexican Duck. Intergrades with Mallard are frequent. Both sexes very similar to female Mallard but darker overall with grayish brown tail, thinner speculum borders; male's bill yellowish. **RANGE:** Resident in Mex. north to U.S. border, just reaching our area along Rio Grande in sw. TX. **HABITAT:** Ponds.

NORTHERN PINTAIL　　　　　　　　Fairly common　M22
Anas acuta (see also p. 40)
Male 25–26 in. (63–66 cm); female 20–21 in. (51–54 cm). *Male:* Slender, slim-necked, with long, *needle-pointed tail.* A conspicuous *white point* runs onto side of dark head. *Female:* Mottled brown; note slender neck, *gray bill.* In flight both sexes show a *single light border* on rear edge of speculum. **VOICE:** Male, a double-toned whistle: *prrip, prrip;* wheezy notes. Female, a low *quack.* **SIMILAR SPECIES:** Compare female's overall shape and bill with those of other dabbling ducks. **HABITAT:** Marshes, prairies, ponds, lakes, salt bays.

dabbling ducks tip up

DABBLING DUCKS

GADWALL

♂ ♀

dabbling ducks spring directly from the water

MOTTLED DUCK

♀ ♂

AMERICAN BLACK DUCK

♂ (female similar)

"MEXICAN" MALLARD

♀

MALLARD

♂

NORTHERN PINTAIL

♀

♂

BLUE-WINGED TEAL
Fairly common M19

Anas discors (see also p. 40)

15–16 in. (38–41 cm). A half-sized dabbling duck. *Male:* Note *white facial crescent* and large *chalky blue* patch on *forewing.* Molting males hold eclipse plumage late in year, resemble females. *Female:* Brown, mottled; dark eye line; partial eye-ring; pale loral spot; blue on forewing. **VOICE:** Male, quiet whistled peeping notes. Female, a high quack. **SIMILAR SPECIES:** Cinnamon and Green-winged teal. **HABITAT:** Ponds, marshes, mudflats, flooded fields.

CINNAMON TEAL *Anas cyanoptera*
Scarce M20

16–17 in. (41–43 cm). *Male:* A small, *dark chestnut* duck with large chalky blue patch on forewing. Adult has *red eye,* which it retains in eclipse plumage. In flight suggests Blue-winged Teal. *Female:* Very similar to female Blue-winged but tawnier; bill slightly larger (more shoveler-like), face pattern duller. *Juvenile:* Even more similar to female Blue-winged, with slightly smaller bill, somewhat bolder face pattern than adult female Cinnamon. **VOICE:** Like Blue-winged. **HABITAT:** Marshes, freshwater ponds, flooded fields. Just reaches our area on Great Plains.

NORTHERN SHOVELER
Fairly common M21

Anas clypeata (see also p. 40)

18–19 in. (46–49 cm). The long *spoon-shaped bill* gives this duck a front-heavy look. When swimming, it sits low, with bill angled toward or in water, straining water. *Male: Rufous* belly and sides; *white breast;* pale blue patch on forewing; orange feet. *Female:* Brown. Note large spatulate bill, blue-gray forewing patch, white tail, orange feet. Bill color variable. **VOICE:** Male, a soft *thup-thup.* Female, short quacks. **SIMILAR SPECIES:** Cinnamon Teal. **HABITAT:** Marshes, ponds, sloughs; in winter, also salt bays.

GREEN-WINGED TEAL
Common M23

Anas crecca (see also p. 40)

14–15 in. (36–39 cm). Teal are small, fly in tight flocks. Green-wingeds lack light wing patches (speculum *deep green*). *Male:* Small, compact, gray with brown head (a green head patch shows in sunlight). On swimming birds, note *vertical white mark* near shoulder, butter-colored streak near tail. *Female:* A small speckled duck with *green* speculum, *pale sides of undertail coverts.* Eurasian subspecies *(A. c. crecca),* a very rare winter visitor along Atlantic Coast, has horizontal rather than vertical white stripe above wing, bolder light borders to eye patch. Female similar to American subspecies. **VOICE:** Male, a high, froglike *dreep.* Female, a sharp *quack.* **SIMILAR SPECIES:** Female Blue-winged and Cinnamon teal slightly larger and larger-billed, have light blue wing patches; in flight, males show dark belly. Green-winged has white belly, broader dark border to underwing. **HABITAT:** Marshes, bays, mudflats, flooded fields.

BLUE-WINGED TEAL

♂   ♀

♂   ♀

CINNAMON TEAL

♀

♂

NORTHERN SHOVELER

GREEN-WINGED TEAL

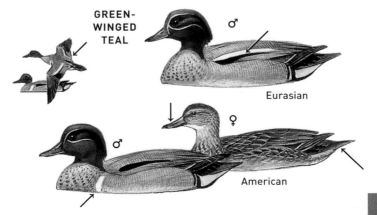

♂

Eurasian

♂   ♀

American

DIVING DUCKS

Often grouped into "sea ducks" and "bay ducks," but many are found on lakes and rivers and breed in marshes. All dive; dabbling ducks rarely do. Legs close to tail; hind toe with a paddlelike flap (lacking in dabblers). Must patter across surface of water while getting airborne. Sexes not alike. **FOOD:** Small aquatic animals and plants. Seagoing species eat mostly mollusks and crustaceans.

CANVASBACK *Aythya valisineria* (see also p. 46)   Uncommon M24
21–22 in. (53–56 cm). *Male:* Very white looking, with black chest and *chestnut red* head sloping into *long blackish* bill. *Female:* Pale grayish brown, with *long, sloping head profile.* **VOICE:** Male, in courtship, cooing notes. Female, raspy *krrrr.* **SIMILAR SPECIES:** Redhead. **HABITAT:** Lakes, salt bays, estuaries; in summer, marshes and lakes.

REDHEAD *Aythya americana* (see also p. 46)   Uncommon M25
19–20 in. (48–51 cm). *Male:* Gray; black chest and *round rufous head.* *Female:* Brown overall with round head. Both sexes have *gray* wing stripe. **VOICE:** Male, in courtship, a harsh catlike *meow;* a deep purr. Female, soft *krrr* notes. **SIMILAR SPECIES:** Canvasback has sloping forehead; male paler. See female Ring-necked Duck, scaup. **HABITAT:** Lakes, salt bays, estuaries; in summer, marshes and ponds.

RING-NECKED DUCK   Fairly common M26
Aythya collaris (see also p. 46)
17–17½ in. (43–46 cm). *Male:* Note *black back, vertical white mark* before wing. *Female:* Very dark with peaked crown, light eye-ring, light ring on bill. Both sexes with gray wing stripe. **VOICE:** Female a quacking growl: *arrp-arrp-arrp.* Male in courtship gives a low-pitched whistle. **SIMILAR SPECIES:** Female Redhead paler with rounder crown. Female scaup have distinct white face and wing patches. **HABITAT:** Wooded lakes, ponds; in winter, also rivers, bays.

GREATER SCAUP *Aythya marila* (see also p. 46)   Common M27
18–18½ in. (46–48 cm). Very similar to Lesser Scaup. Both sexes slightly larger, with more gently rounded or flat-topped head, bill slightly wider with larger black tip (nail), and *white wing stripe longer,* extending onto primaries. *Male:* Whiter on sides than Lesser; head glossed mainly with green rather than purple. *Female* (not shown): Averages slightly paler brown than Lesser; identify by size, shape, and wing stripe. **VOICE:** Male, in display, soft, wheezy whistles. Female, raspy *scaup-scaup.* **SIMILAR SPECIES:** Lesser Scaup, Ringnecked Duck, Redhead. **HABITAT:** Lakes, rivers, bays, estuaries, nearshore ocean waters; in summer, tundra and taiga ponds.

LESSER SCAUP *Aythya affinis* (see also p. 46)   Common M28
16½–17 in. (42–44 cm). Both sexes with *peaked rear crown* (in relaxed pose only; flatter when active) and wing stripe *restricted to secondaries.* *Male:* Head glossed with purple. Flanks finely barred. *Female:* Dark brown, with white patch near bill. **VOICE:** Male, in display, a soft whistle. Female, a loud *scaup.* **SIMILAR SPECIES:** Greater Scaup, Ringnecked Duck, Redhead. **HABITAT:** Lakes, bays, estuaries, nearshore ocean waters; in summer, marsh and taiga ponds.

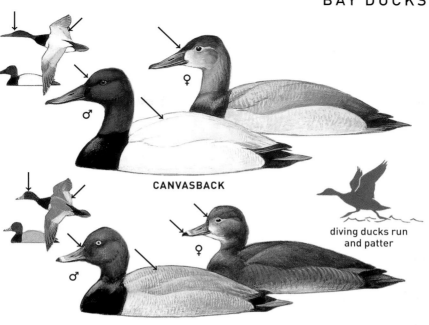

CANVASBACK

diving ducks run
and patter

♂

♀

REDHEAD

♂

♀

RING-NECKED DUCK

Lesser

Greater

eater

Lesser

♂

♀

GREATER SCAUP

♂

LESSER SCAUP

COMMON GOLDENEYE
Fairly common M37

Bucephala clangula (see also p. 46)

18½–19 in. (47–49 cm). *Male:* Note large, *round white spot* before eye. White looking, with black back and puffy, green-glossed head that appears black at a distance. In flight, short-necked; wings whistle or "sing," show large white patches. *Female:* Gray, with white collar and dark brown head; wings with large square white patches that may show on closed wing. **VOICE:** Wings "whistle" in flight. Courting male has harsh nasal double note, suggesting *pee-ik* of Common Nighthawk. Female, a harsh *gaak*. **SIMILAR SPECIES:** Barrow's Goldeneye. Male scaup have black chest. Male Common Merganser long, low, with different bill. **HABITAT:** Forested lakes, rivers; in winter, also lakes, salt bays, seacoasts.

BARROW'S GOLDENEYE *Bucephala islandica*
Scarce M38

18 in. (46 cm). *Male:* Note *white facial crescent.* Similar to Common Goldeneye, but blacker above; head glossed with *purple* (not green); nape puffier; shows *dark "spur"* on shoulder toward waterline. *Female:* Similar to female Common; head slightly darker, with steeper forehead and suggestion of puffy nape, bill shorter and more triangular, less white in wing. Bill may become all *orangey yellow,* often a good field mark but subject to seasonal change. Female Common Goldeneye often has band of yellow on bill. **VOICE:** Usually silent. Courting male, a grunting *kuk, kuk.* Female near nest, a soft *coo-coo-coo.* Wings of both species whistle in flight. **SIMILAR SPECIES:** Common Goldeneye, Bufflehead. **HABITAT:** Wooded lakes, ponds; in winter, lakes and rivers, protected coastal waters.

BUFFLEHEAD *Bucephala albeola* (see also p. 46)
Common M36

13½–14 in. (34–36 cm). Small. *Male:* Mostly white with black back; puffy head with *large, bonnetlike white patch.* In flight, shows large white wing patch. *Female:* Dark and compact, with *white cheek spot,* small bill, smaller wing patch. **VOICE:** Male, in display, a hoarse rolling note. Female, a harsh *ec-ec-ec.* **SIMILAR SPECIES:** Male Hooded Merganser has spikelike bill, dark sides. See female Black Scoter and nonbreeding adult male Ruddy Duck. See also Long-tailed Duck. **HABITAT:** Lakes, ponds, rivers; in winter, also salt bays.

RUDDY DUCK
Fairly common M42

Oxyura jamaicensis (see also p. 46)

15 in. (38 cm). Small, chubby; note *white cheek* and dark cap. Often cocks long tail upward. Flight "buzzy." Can barely walk on land. *Breeding male:* Rusty red with white cheek, black cap, large, strikingly *blue* bill. *Nonbreeding male:* Gray with *white cheek,* gray bill. *Female:* Similar to nonbreeding male, but duskier cheek crossed by dark line. **VOICE:** Courting male, a sputtering *chick-ik-ik-ik-k-k-kurrrr,* accompanied by head bobbing. **SIMILAR SPECIES:** Female Bufflehead, Black Scoter, Masked Duck (rare). **HABITAT:** Freshwater marshes, ponds, lakes; in winter, also salt bays, harbors.

COMMON GOLDENEYE

breeding ♀
(winter/
spring)

nonbreeding ♀
(summer/fall)

BARROW'S GOLDENEYE

BUFFLEHEAD

breeding ♂

nonbreeding ♂

RUDDY DUCK

KING EIDER
Rare to uncommon M29
Somateria spectabilis (see also p. 44)
22 in. (56 cm). *Male:* Note *black back* and protruding *orange bill-shield. Female:* Warm brown, weak eye-ring and thin stripe curving down behind eye, flanks barred with crescent-shaped marks. Note facial profile and dark bill. *Immature male:* Dusky, with light breast, *orangey* bill. **VOICE:** Courting male, a low crooning phrase. Female, grunting croaks. **SIMILAR SPECIES:** Common Eider larger, with flatter head profile, longer bill-lobe before eye; male Common has *white* back, female has evenly barred flanks, grayer bill. Immature male Common has grayish bill, often some white on back. **HABITAT:** Rocky coasts, ocean. Nests on tundra.

COMMON EIDER
Fairly common M30
Somateria mollissima (see also p. 44)
24–25 in. (61–64 cm). This bulky, long-necked duck is oceanic, living in flocks near shoals. *Male:* Note *black belly and white back.* Forewing and back white; head white with black crown, greenish nape. *Female:* Large, brown, *closely barred, with pale eyebrow;* long, flat facial profile. *Immature male:* At first brownish, becoming dusky with some white on breast and back. **VOICE:** Male, a moaning *ow-ooo-urr.* Female, a grating *kor-r-r.* **SIMILAR SPECIES:** King Eider. Female scoters smaller, lack heavy dark barring of female eiders. Compare eclipse male eider in flight with White-winged Scoter. **HABITAT:** Rocky coasts, shoals; in summer, also islands, tundra.

HARLEQUIN DUCK
Uncommon M31
Histrionicus histrionicus (see also p. 44)
16–17 in. (41–44 cm). A smallish, dark sea duck with a long tail. *Male:* Spectacularly patterned: slaty with chestnut sides and odd white patches and spots. *Female:* A small dusky duck with three round white spots on each side of head; no wing patch. *Immature male:* Similar to female. **VOICE:** Usually silent. Male, a squeak; also *gwa gwa gwa.* Female, *ek-ek-ek-ek.* **SIMILAR SPECIES:** Female Bufflehead has white wing patch and only one face spot. Female scoters larger, with larger bills. **HABITAT:** Turbulent mountain streams in summer; rocky coastal waters in winter.

LONG-TAILED DUCK (OLDSQUAW)
Fairly common M35
Clangula hyemalis (see also p. 44)
Male 21–22 in. (53–56 cm); female 16 in. (41 cm). The only sea duck combining much *white on body and unpatterned dark wings.* Male has pink on bill. It flies in bunched, irregular flocks, rocking side to side as it flies. *Nonbreeding male:* Note needlelike tail, pied pattern, dark cheek. *Breeding male:* Dark with white flanks and belly. Note white eye patch. *Nonbreeding female:* Dark unpatterned wings, white face with dark cheek spot. *Breeding female:* Similar but darker. *Immature:* Lacks long tail feathers. **VOICE:** Talkative; a musical *ow-owdle-ee* or *owl-omelet.* **SIMILAR SPECIES:** Bufflehead. In flight, sometimes confused with alcids because of white body, dark wings, and rapid wing-beats. **HABITAT:** Ocean, harbors, large lakes; in summer, tundra pools and lakes.

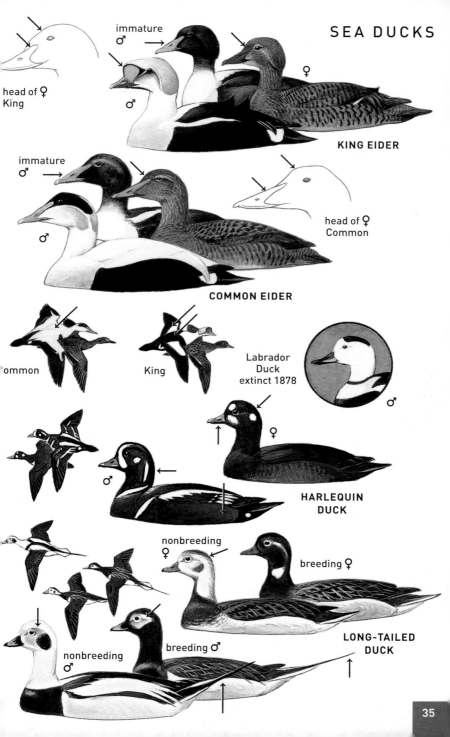

SEA DUCKS

head of ♀ King

immature ♂

♀

KING EIDER

♂

immature ♂

head of ♀ Common

COMMON EIDER

common

King

Labrador Duck extinct 1878

♂

♀

♂

HARLEQUIN DUCK

nonbreeding ♀

breeding ♀

nonbreeding ♂

breeding ♂

LONG-TAILED DUCK

SCOTERS

Scoters are heavy, blackish sea ducks seen in large flocks along ocean coasts. They often fly in thin line formation. They are usually in flocks, either single species or mixed, so look them over carefully. Scoters are usually silent but during courtship and mating may utter low whistles, croaks, or grunting noises; wings whistle in flight. **FOOD:** Mainly mollusks, crustaceans.

WHITE-WINGED SCOTER Uncommon to fairly common M33
Melanitta fusca (see also p. 44)
21 in. (53 cm). White-winged, largest of the three scoters, has a long bill feathered to nostril. On water, white wing patch is often barely visible or fully concealed (wait for bird to flap or fly). *Male:* Black, with a "teardrop" of white near eye; bill orange with black basal knob. *Female:* Sooty brown, with white wing patch and two light oval patches on face (sometimes obscure; patches more pronounced on young birds). **VOICE:** Usually silent. **SIMILAR SPECIES:** Other scoters. **HABITAT:** Salt bays, ocean; in summer, lakes.

SURF SCOTER Fairly common M32
Melanitta perspicillata (see also p. 44)
19–20 in. (48–51 cm). The "skunkhead-duck." *Male:* Black, with *white patches* on crown and nape. Heavy, sloping bill patterned with orange, black, and white. *Female:* Dusky brown; dark crown; two light spots on each side of head (sometimes obscure; more evident on young birds), one mostly vertical, the other more horizontal. **VOICE:** Usually silent. A low croak; grunting sounds. **SIMILAR SPECIES:** Female White-winged Scoter, slightly larger overall, has more extensive feathering on bill, more horizontal, oval face patches, and white wing patch (may not show until bird flaps). Black Scoter has rounder head profile (more like Redhead, whereas Surf Scoter more like Canvasback) and has more silvery flight feathers; female and immature have entirely pale cheeks. **HABITAT:** Ocean, salt bays; in summer, lakes.

BLACK SCOTER Fairly common M34
Melanitta nigra (see also p. 44)
18½–19 in. (47–48 cm). *Male:* An all-black sea duck. Bright *orange-yellow knob* on bill ("butter nose") is diagnostic. In flight, underwing shows two-toned effect (silvery gray and black), more pronounced than in other two scoters. *Female:* Sooty; *entirely light cheeks* contrast with dark cap. **VOICE:** Usually silent. Male, melodious cooing notes. Female, growls. **SIMILAR SPECIES:** Some young male Surf Scoters may lack head patches and appear all black, but they have round black spot at base of higher-sloping bill. Female and immature scoters of other two species have smaller light spots on side of head, not entirely pale cheeks. Female Black Scoter may suggest nonbreeding adult male Ruddy Duck. **HABITAT:** Seacoasts, bays; in summer, tundra and taiga ponds.

scoters fly in line or V formation

Surf

SCOTERS (SEA DUCKS)

Black

White-winged

immature

♂

♀

WHITE-WINGED SCOTER

♂

♀

immature
♂

SURF SCOTER

immature
♂

♂

♀

BLACK SCOTER

diving ducks (sea ducks and bay ducks) raft on water, skitter when taking wing

MERGANSERS

Long-lined, slender-bodied diving ducks with spikelike bill, saw-edged mandibles. Most species have a crest. In flight, bill, head, neck, and body are on a horizontal axis. Sexes not alike. **FOOD**: Chiefly fish.

COMMON MERGANSER
Fairly common M40

Mergus merganser (see also p. 40)

24–25 in. (62–64 cm). In flight, lines of these slender ducks follow the winding courses of rivers. Whiteness of adult males and merganser shape (bill, neck, head, and body held horizontally) identify this species. *Male:* Note long whitish body, black back, green-black head. Bill and feet red; breast tinged rosy peach. *Female and immature:* Gray with crested rufous head contrasting with white chin and clean white chest; large square white wing patch. **VOICE**: Male, in display, low staccato croaks. Female, a guttural *karr.* **SIMILAR SPECIES**: Female Red-breasted Merganser very similar to female Common. Note distinct cut-off of rusty head and neck from breast in Common; this is diffuse in Red-breasted. Female mergansers, which are rusty-headed, suggest male Canvasback or Redhead, but those have black chest, no crest, different bill. **HABITAT**: Wooded lakes, ponds, rivers; in winter, open lakes, rivers, rarely coastal bays.

RED-BREASTED MERGANSER
Common M41

Mergus serrator (see also p. 40)

22½–23 in. (56–58 cm). *Male:* Rakish; black head glossed with green and *crested;* breast at waterline dark rusty, separated from head by *wide white collar;* bill and feet red. *Female and immature:* Gray, with crested, dull rusty head that *blends* into color of neck; large white wing patch; red bill and feet. **VOICE**: Usually silent. Male, a hoarse croak. Female, *karr.* **SIMILAR SPECIES**: Male Common Merganser whiter, without collar and breast-band effect; lacks crest. In female Common, white chin and chest *sharply delineated* from brighter rufous head and pale gray body. Common's bill slightly thicker at base. **HABITAT**: Woodland and coastal lakes, open water; in winter, also bays, tidal channels, nearshore ocean waters.

HOODED MERGANSER
Uncommon to fairly common M39

Lophodytes cucullatus (see also p. 40)

17–18 in. (43–46 cm). *Male:* Note vertical *fan-shaped white crest,* which may be raised or lowered. Breast white, with two black bars on each side. Wing with white patch; *flanks rusty brown. Female:* Recognized as a merganser by silhouette and spikelike bill; known as this species by its small size, dusky look, and *dark head, bill, and chest.* Note loose *tawny crest.* **VOICE**: In display, low grunting or croaking notes. **SIMILAR SPECIES**: Male Bufflehead chubbier, with *white* sides. Other female mergansers larger and *grayer,* with rufous head, reddish bill. In flight, wing patch and silhouette separate female Hooded Merganser from female Wood Duck. **HABITAT**: Wooded lakes, ponds, rivers; in winter, also tidal channels, protected bays.

MERGANSERS

mergansers fly with bill, head, body, and tail on the same horizontal axis

saw-edged mandibles of merganser

♂ ♀

COMMON MERGANSER

♂ ♀

RED-BREASTED MERGANSER

♂ crest down

♀

♂ in eclipse

♂ crest up

HOODED MERGANSER

Common

Red-breasted

Hooded

39

FLIGHT PATTERNS OF DABBLING DUCKS

Note: Only males are diagnosed below. Although females are unlike the males, their wing patterns are quite similar. The names in parentheses are common nicknames used by hunters.

NORTHERN PINTAIL (SPRIG) *Anas acuta*   p. 26
Underside: Needle tail, white breast, thin neck.
Topside: Needle tail, neck stripe, single thin white border on speculum.

WOOD DUCK *Aix sponsa*   p. 24
Underside: White belly, dusky wings, long square tail.
Topside: Stocky; long dark tail, white border on dark wing.

AMERICAN WIGEON (BALDPATE) *Anas americana*   p. 24
Underside: White belly, pointed dark tail.
Topside: Large white shoulder patch.

NORTHERN SHOVELER (SPOONBILL) *Anas clypeata*   p. 28
Underside: Dark belly, white breast, white tail, spoon bill.
Topside: Large pale bluish shoulder patch, spoon bill.

GADWALL *Anas strepera*   p. 26
Underside: White belly, white underwing.
Topside: White patch on rear edge of wing.

GREEN-WINGED TEAL *Anas crecca*   p. 28
Underside: Small; light belly, dark head, broad dark borders to underwing.
Topside: Small, dark-winged; green speculum.

BLUE-WINGED TEAL *Anas discors*   p. 28
Underside: Small; dark belly, narrow dark borders to underwing.
Topside: Small; large chalky blue shoulder patch.

upper wing of a dabbling duck showing the iridescent speculum (secondaries)

NORTHERN
PINTAIL

WOOD
DUCK

♂

DABBLING DUCKS IN FLIGHT

♂

↑ Underside

♀

♂

♀

AMERICAN
WIGEON

♀

NORTHERN
SHOVELER

♂

♀

♂

♂

GADWALL

GREEN-
WINGED
TEAL

BLUE-
WINGED
TEAL

♀

♂

Topside

♂

♀

NORTHERN
PINTAIL

WOOD
DUCK

♂

♀

AMERICAN
WIGEON

♀

NORTHERN
SHOVELER

♂

♂

♀

GADWALL

GREEN-
WINGED
TEAL

♀

BLUE-
WINGED
TEAL

41

FLIGHT PATTERNS OF DABBLING DUCKS AND MERGANSERS

Note: Only males are diagnosed below. Although most females are unlike the males, their wing patterns are quite similar. Mergansers have a distinctive flight silhouette. Duck hunters often call mergansers "sheldrakes" or "sawbills."

MALLARD *Anas platyrhynchos*   p. 26
Underside: Dark chest, light belly, white neck ring, white tail.
Topside: Dark head, neck ring, two white borders on bluish speculum.

AMERICAN BLACK DUCK *Anas rubripes*   p. 26
Underside: Dark body, white wing linings.
Topside: Dark body, paler head, purplish speculum lacks forward border.

FULVOUS WHISTLING-DUCK *Dendrocygna bicolor*   p. 20
Underside: Tawny, with blackish wing linings.
Topside: Dark, unpatterned wings; white band on rump.

COMMON MERGANSER *Mergus merganser*   p. 38
Underside: Merganser shape; dark head, white body, white wing linings.
Topside: Merganser shape; white chest, large white wing patches.

RED-BREASTED MERGANSER *Mergus serrator*   p. 38
Underside: Merganser shape; dark chest band, white collar.
Topside: Merganser shape; dark chest, large white wing patches.

HOODED MERGANSER *Lophodytes cucullatus*   p. 38
Underside: Merganser shape; dusky wing linings.
Topside: Merganser shape; small white wing patches.

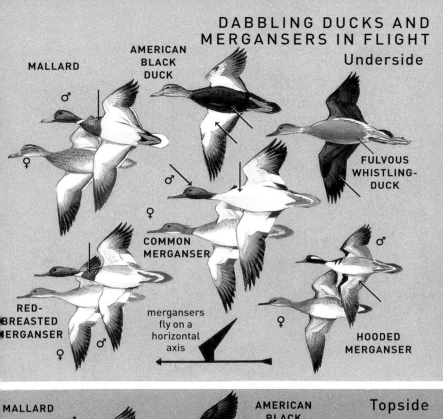

DABBLING DUCKS AND MERGANSERS IN FLIGHT
Underside

MALLARD

AMERICAN BLACK DUCK

♂

♀

FULVOUS WHISTLING-DUCK

COMMON MERGANSER

♂

RED-BREASTED MERGANSER

♀

♂

mergansers fly on a horizontal axis

HOODED MERGANSER

♀

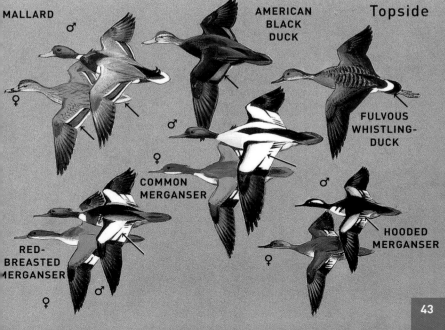

MALLARD

♂

♀

AMERICAN BLACK DUCK

Topside

FULVOUS WHISTLING-DUCK

♂

COMMON MERGANSER

♀

♂

HOODED MERGANSER

RED-BREASTED MERGANSER

♀

♂

Flight Patterns of Diving Ducks

Note: Only males are diagnosed below.

LONG-TAILED DUCK (OLDSQUAW) *Clangula hyemalis*   p. 34
Underside: Dark unpatterned wings, white belly.
Topside: Dark unpatterned wings, much white on body.

HARLEQUIN DUCK *Histrionicus histrionicus*   p. 34
Underside: Solid dark below, white head spots, small bill. Tail appears squared off, similar to that of a Wood Duck.
Topside: Dark with white marks, small bill, long tail.

SURF SCOTER *Melanitta perspicillata*   p. 36
Underside: Black body, white head patches (not readily visible from below), sloping forehead.
Topside: Black body, white head patches, sloping forehead.

BLACK SCOTER *Melanitta nigra*   p. 36
Underside: Black plumage, paler flight feathers, rounded forehead.
Topside: All-dark plumage. Body slightly smaller and pudgier than Surf Scoter's, rounded forehead.

WHITE-WINGED SCOTER *Melanitta fusca*   p. 36
Underside: Black body, white wing patches.
Topside: Black body, white wing patches.

COMMON EIDER *Somateria mollissima*   p. 34
Topside: White back, white forewing, black belly.

KING EIDER *Somateria spectabilis*   p. 34
Topside: Whitish foreparts, black rear parts.

HARLEQUIN
DUCK

♂

♀

LONG-
TAILED
DUCK

♀

♂

♀

♂

♀

♂

SURF
SCOTER

♀

BLACK
SCOTER

WHITE-WINGED
SCOTER

♂

♀

♂

♀

LONG-
TAILED
DUCK

♀

♂

COMMON
EIDER

♂

KING EIDER

HARLEQUIN DUCK

♂

♀

♂

♀

BLACK
SCOTER

SURF
SCOTER

♂

♀

WHITE-
WINGED
SCOTER

45

FLIGHT PATTERNS OF DIVING DUCKS, ETC.

Note: Only males are diagnosed below. The first five all have a black chest. The names in parentheses are common nicknames used by hunters.

CANVASBACK *Aythya valisineria* p. 30
Underside: Black chest, long profile.
Topside: White back, long profile. Lacks contrasty wing stripe of next four species.

REDHEAD *Aythya americana* p. 30
Underside: Black chest, roundish rufous head.
Topside: Gray back, broad gray wing stripe.

RING-NECKED DUCK *Aythya collaris* p. 30
Underside: Not safe to tell from scaup overhead; gray wing stripe sometimes evident.
Topside: Black back, broad gray wing stripe.

GREATER SCAUP (BLUEBILL) *Aythya marila* p. 30
Underside: Black chest, white stripe showing through wing.
Topside: Broad white wing stripe (extending onto primaries).

LESSER SCAUP (BLUEBILL) *Aythya affinis* p. 30
Topside: Wing stripe.

COMMON GOLDENEYE (WHISTLER) *Bucephala clangula* p. 32
Underside: Dark wing linings, white wing patches, rounded dark head.
Topside: Large white square wing patch, short neck, dark head.

RUDDY DUCK *Oxyura jamaicensis* p. 32
Underside: Stubby; white face, dark chest, long tail.
Topside: Small; dark with white cheeks, long tail.

BUFFLEHEAD (BUTTERBALL) *Bucephala albeola* p. 32
Underside: Like a small goldeneye; note head patch.
Topside: Small; large wing patches, white head patch.

Silhouettes of Ducks on Land

dabbling ducks (dabblers)   sea and bay ducks (divers)   mergansers (divers)   Ruddy Duck (diver)   whistling-ducks (dabblers)

DIVING DUCKS IN FLIGHT

CANVASBACK

REDHEAD

RING-NECKED DUCK

Underside

GREATER SCAUP

COMMON GOLDENEYE

RUDDY DUCK

BUFFLEHEAD

Topside

CANVASBACK

REDHEAD

RING-NECKED DUCK

GREATER SCAUP

COMMON GOLDENEYE

RUDDY DUCK

wing of LESSER SCAUP

BUFFLEHEAD

STRAY WATERFOWL

GARGANEY *Anas querquedula*   **Vagrant**
15½ in. (38 cm). *Male:* Broad white eyebrow stripe, silvery shoulder patch (in flight). *Female:* Told from Blue-winged and Cinnamon teal by bolder face pattern (shared by Green-winged Teal), gray legs, paler primaries (in flight), and bold white borders on speculum. **RANGE:** Casual visitor from Eurasia; many records from East Coast, fewer inland.

MASKED DUCK *Nomonyx dominicus*   **Vagrant**
13–13½ in. (33–34 cm). *Male:* Rusty body with black face, blue bill. Stiff tail feathers held upright at times. *Female:* Buffy with two distinct face stripes, barred back. **SIMILAR SPECIES:** Ruddy Duck. **RANGE:** Very rare, irregular visitor from Mex. and Caribbean to TX and FL; accidental elsewhere. **HABITAT:** Ponds, marshes with dense vegetation. Often hidden.

TUFTED DUCK *Aythya fuligula*   **Regular vagrant**
16½–17 in. (41–43 cm). *Male:* Differs from male Ring-necked Duck in having thin wispy crest, entirely *white* sides, and *white* (not gray) wing stripe; from scaup, by black back, wispy crest. *Female:* May have faint trace of tuft. Darker back, usually less white on face than female scaup; lacks eye-ring of female Ring-necked; eyes yellow. **VOICE:** Similar to Ring-necked Duck. **RANGE:** Regular winter visitor from Eurasia to NL; very rare elsewhere along Atlantic Coast; casual inland. **HABITAT:** Sheltered ponds, bays, reservoirs. Usually with scaup.

UNESTABLISHED EXOTICS

SMEW *Mergellus albellus*   **Provenance in question**
(Eurasia) 16 in. (41 cm). Scattered reports in East; some probably escapees.

CHINESE GOOSE *Anser cygnoides*   **Exotic**

EGYPTIAN GOOSE *Alopochen aegyptiacus*   **Exotic**

BAR-HEADED GOOSE *Anser indicus*   **Exotic**

GRAYLAG GOOSE *Anser anser*   **Provenance in question**

WHITE-CHEEKED PINTAIL   **Provenance in question**
Anas bahamensis
(West Indies) 17 in. (43 cm). Numerous reports from FL; scattered records elsewhere. Most birds are likely escapees.

MANDARIN *Aix galericulata*   **Exotic**

COMMON SHELDUCK *Tadorna tadorna*   **Exotic**

RUDDY SHELDUCK *Tadorna ferruginea*   **Provenance in question**

STRAY WATERFOWL

GARGANEY ♂ ♀

MASKED DUCK ♂ ♀

TUFTED DUCK ♂ ♀

UNESTABLISHED EXOTICS

CHINESE GOOSE

SMEW ♂ ♀

EGYPTIAN GOOSE

WHITE-CHEEKED PINTAIL ♂

GRAYLAG GOOSE

BAR-HEADED GOOSE

MANDARIN ♀ ♂

COMMON SHELDUCK ♂

RUDDY SHELDUCK ♂

CURASSOWS AND GUANS Family Cracidae

Tropical forest birds with long tails. Only one species reaches extreme s. U.S. **FOOD:** Insects, fruit, leaves, seeds. **RANGE:** New World Tropics.

PLAIN CHACHALACA *Ortalis vetula*   Fairly common, local M43
22 in. (56 cm). A large olive-brown bird shaped somewhat like a half-grown turkey with a small head. Long, rounded, pale-tipped tail, bare red throat. Difficult to observe; best found in morning when calling raucously from treetops. **VOICE:** Alarm a harsh chickenlike cackle. Characteristic call a raucous three-syllabled *cha-ca-lac,* repeated in chorus, especially in morning and evening. **SIMILAR SPECIES:** Greater Roadrunner. **HABITAT:** Woodlands, tall brush, well-vegetated residential areas.

GALLINACEOUS, OR CHICKENLIKE, BIRDS (TURKEYS, PHEASANTS, GROUSE, PARTRIDGES, AND OLD WORLD QUAIL)
Family Phasianidae

Often called "upland game birds." Turkeys are very large, with wattles and fan-like tail. Pheasants (introduced) have long pointed tail. Grouse are plump, chickenlike birds, without long tail. Partridges (of Old World origin) are intermediate in size between grouse and quail. Quail are the smallest. **FOOD:** Insects, seeds, buds, berries. **RANGE:** Nearly worldwide.

WILD TURKEY *Meleagris gallopavo*   Fairly common M55
Male 46–47 in. (117–120 cm); female 36–37 in. (91–94 cm). A stream-lined version of barnyard turkey, with rusty instead of white tail tips. *Male:* Head naked; bluish with red wattles, intensified in display. Tail erected like a fan in display. Bronzy iridescent body; barred wings (primaries and secondaries); prominent "beard" on breast. *Female and immature:* Smaller, with smaller and duller head; less iridescent; less likely to have a beard. **VOICE:** "Gobbling" of male like domestic turkey's. Alarm *pit!* or *put-put!* Flock call *keow-keow.* Hen clucks to her chicks. **HABITAT:** Woods, mountain forests, wooded swamps, field edges, clearings. Reintroduced in many areas, and such birds are adapting well to being near people.

RING-NECKED PHEASANT   Uncommon to fairly common M47
Phasianus colchicus
Male 31–33 in. (79–84 cm); female 21–23 in. (53–59 cm). A large chickenlike bird introduced from Eurasia. Note long pointed tail. Runs swiftly; flight strong, takeoff noisy. *Male:* Highly colored and *iridescent,* with *scarlet wattles* on face and *white neck ring* (not always present). *Female:* Mottled brown, with *long pointed tail.* **VOICE:** Crowing male gives loud double squawk, *kork-kok,* followed by brief whir of wings. When flushed, harsh croaks. Roosting call a two-syllable *kutuck-kutuck,* etc. **SIMILAR SPECIES:** See prairie-chickens and Sharp-tailed Grouse. **HABITAT:** Farms, fields, marsh edges, brush, grassy roadsides. Periodic local releases for hunting.

♂

♂ display

♀

WILD TURKEY

PLAIN CHACHALACA

♂

♀

♀

♂

RING-NECKED PHEASANT

51

WILLOW PTARMIGAN *Lagopus lagopus*   Fairly common M50

15 in. (39 cm). Willow and Rock ptarmigans are fairly similar. In breeding season, Willows are variable, but most males are chestnut brown, redder than any Rock; females are warm buffy brown that can overlap brown of Rock. White of wings retained all year and, in flight, contrast with summer body plumage. Nonbreeding white overall with black tail, the latter retained year-round. There is much variation between various molts. **VOICE:** Deep raucous calls. Male, a staccato crow, *kwow, kwow, tobacco, tobacco*, etc., or *go-back, go-back.* **SIMILAR SPECIES:** Rock Ptarmigan always has smaller and more slender bill that lacks strong curve on ridge shown by Willow. In winter, male Rock has *black mark* between eye and bill, lacking in both sexes of Willow. Habitats overlap, but Rock tends to prefer higher, more barren hills. **HABITAT:** Tundra, willow scrub, muskeg; in winter, sheltered valleys at slightly lower altitudes.

ROCK PTARMIGAN *Lagopus muta*   Uncommon M51

14 in. (36 cm). Breeding male is usually browner or grayer than breeding Willow Ptarmigan, lacking rich chestnut around head and neck. Some Rocks may be paler or darker than shown here. Females of the two species are similar, but Rock has smaller bill. Nonbreeding white male Rock has *black mark* between eye and bill. This is absent in most females, which may be told from female Willow by Rock's smaller bill. **VOICE:** Croaks, growls, cackles; usually silent. **SIMILAR SPECIES:** Willow Ptarmigan. **HABITAT:** Tundra, above timberline in mountains (to lower levels in winter); also near sea level in bleak tundra of northern coasts.

RUFFED GROUSE *Bonasa umbellus*   Uncommon M48

17 in. (43 cm). Note short crest, bold flank bars, and fan-shaped tail with broad black band near tip. A large chickenlike bird of brushy woodlands, usually not seen until it flushes with a startling whir. Two color morphs occur: "rusty" with rufous tail and "gray" with gray tail. Rusty birds more common in southern parts of range, gray birds more common northward. **VOICE:** Sound of drumming male suggests a distant motor starting up. Low muffled thumping starts slowly, accelerating into a whir: *Bup . . . bup . . . bup . . . bup . . . bup bup up r-rrrrr.* **SIMILAR SPECIES:** Sharp-tailed and Spruce grouse. **HABITAT:** Ground and understory of deciduous and mixed woodlands.

SPRUCE GROUSE *Falcipennis canadensis*   Scarce M49

16–17 in. (41–43 cm). Look for this *tame,* dark grouse in deep coniferous forests of North. *Male:* Sharply defined *black breast,* with some white spots or bars on sides and *chestnut band* on tip of tail. Comb of erectile red skin above eye is visible at close range. *Female:* Dark rusty or grayish brown, thickly barred, and with black-and-white spotting below; tail short and dark, with rusty tip. **VOICE:** Female, call an accelerating, then slowing, series of *wock* notes; also cluck notes. Wing flutter from male's courtship display may sound like distant rumble of thunder. **SIMILAR SPECIES:** Ruffed Grouse. **HABITAT:** Coniferous forests, jack pines, muskeg, blueberry patches.

PTARMIGANS AND GROUSE

WILLOW PTARMIGAN

nonbreeding

nonbreeding

♀

♂

♂

breeding

breeding ♀

spring

ROCK PTARMIGAN

♂ nonbreeding

♀

♂

nonbreeding ♂

breeding ♀

breeding

♂ display

RUFFED GROUSE

gray morph

rusty morph

♂ ♀

SPRUCE GROUSE

♂ display

SHARP-TAILED GROUSE
Uncommon M52

Tympanuchus phasianellus

17 in. (43 cm). A pale, speckled-brown grouse of prairies and brushy draws. Note *short pointed tail,* which in display or flight shows *white* at sides. Slight crested look. Marked below by dark bars, spots, and chevrons. Displaying male has yellow eye combs and inflates *purplish* neck sacs. **VOICE:** Cackling *cac-cac-cac,* etc. Courting note a single low *coo-oo,* accompanied by quill-rattling, foot-shuffling. **SIMILAR SPECIES:** Prairie-chickens have *rounded, dark* tail and are more barred, rather than spotted, below. Female Ring-necked Pheasant has *long pointed* tail. Ruffed Grouse has banded, *fan-shaped* tail and black neck ruff. **HABITAT:** Prairies, agricultural fields, forest edges, clearings, coulees, open burns and clear-cuts in coniferous and mixed forests.

GREATER PRAIRIE-CHICKEN
Uncommon, local M53

Tympanuchus cupido

17 in. (43 cm). A henlike bird of prairies. Brown, heavily barred. Note *rounded dark tail* (black in male, barred in female). Courting males in communal "dance" inflate orange neck sacs, show off orangey yellow eye combs, and erect black hornlike neck feathers. **VOICE:** "Booming" male in dance makes a hollow *oo-loo-woo,* suggesting sound made by blowing across a bottle mouth. **SIMILAR SPECIES:** Lesser Prairie-Chicken. Sharp-tailed Grouse, often called "Prairie-Chicken," slightly paler overall, has more spots or chevrons on underparts, and has more pointed, white-edged tail. Female Ring-necked Pheasant slightly larger, has long pointed tail. **HABITAT:** Native tallgrass prairie, now very localized; agricultural land.

LESSER PRAIRIE-CHICKEN
Scarce, local M54

Tympanuchus pallidicinctus

16 in. (41 cm). A small, pale brown prairie-chicken; best identified by range. Male's neck sacs are dull *purplish* or *plum colored* (not yellow-orange as in Greater Prairie-Chicken). Breast barring usually paler and thinner than Greater's. **VOICE:** Male's courtship "booming" not as rolling or loud as Greater Prairie-Chicken's. Both sexes give clucking, cackling notes. **SIMILAR SPECIES:** Greater Prairie-Chicken, Sharp-tailed Grouse. **HABITAT:** Sandhill country (sage and bluestem grass, oak shrublands).

SHARP-TAILED GROUSE

♂

♂ display

GREATER PRAIRIE-CHICKEN

♂

♂ display

LESSER PRAIRIE-CHICKEN

♂

♂ display

GRAY PARTRIDGE *Perdix perdix* Uncommon M46
12½–13 in. (32–34 cm). Introduced from Europe. A rotund gray-brown partridge, larger than a quail; note short *rufous tail, rusty face,* chestnut bars on sides. Male has dark U-shaped splotch on belly. **VOICE:** Loud, hoarse *kar-wit, kar-wit.* **SIMILAR SPECIES:** Northern Bobwhite. **HABITAT:** Cultivated land, hedgerows, bushy pastures, meadows.

CHUKAR *Alectoris chukar* Exotic
13½–14 in. (34–36 cm). A popular game bird from Asia. Recently released or escaped birds occasionally seen in the East. Like a large quail; gray-brown with *bright red legs and bill;* light throat bordered by clean-cut black "necklace." Sides *boldly barred.* Tail *rufous.* **VOICE:** Series of raspy *chucks;* a sharp *wheet-u.* **SIMILAR SPECIES:** Gray Partridge. Red-legged Partridge *(Alectoris rufa),* an occasional escapee, is similar but has streaked breast.

NEW WORLD QUAIL Family Odontophoridae

Quail are smaller than grouse. Sexes alike or unlike. **FOOD:** Insects, seeds, buds, berries. **RANGE:** Nearly worldwide.

SCALED QUAIL *Callipepla squamata* Uncommon, local M44
10 in. (25 cm). A pale grayish quail (sometimes called "Blue Quail") of arid country, with scaly markings on breast and back. Note *short bushy white crest,* or "cotton top," a common nickname for this species. Runs; often reluctant to fly. **VOICE:** Guinea hen–like *che-kar* (also interpreted as *pay-cos*). **HABITAT:** Shrub-grasslands, brush, arid country.

NORTHERN BOBWHITE Uncommon, declining M45
Colinus virginianus
9½–10 in. (24–26 cm). A small, rotund fowl, near size of a meadowlark. Ruddy, barred and striped, with short dark tail. Male has conspicuous white throat and white eyebrow stripe; in female these are buff. **VOICE:** Clearly whistled *Bob-white!* or *poor, Bob-whoit!* Covey call *ko-loi-kee?* answered by *whoil-kee!* **SIMILAR SPECIES:** Ruffed Grouse larger with fanlike tail. Gray Partridge. **HABITAT:** Farms, brushy open country, fencerows, roadsides, open woodlands. Recent hunting releases fairly widespread.

INTRODUCED GAME BIRDS AND QUAIL

GRAY PARTRIDGE

♂

CHUKAR

♂

Red-legged Partridge for comparison

SCALED QUAIL

♂

♀

♂

NORTHERN BOBWHITE

LOONS Family Gaviidae

Large, long-bodied swimmers with daggerlike bill; dive from surface or sink. Thrash along water on takeoff. Airborne, loons are slower and more hunchbacked than most ducks. Large webbed feet project beyond stubby tail. Seldom on land except at nest. Sexes alike. Immatures more scaly above than nonbreeding adults. **FOOD:** Small fish, crustaceans, other aquatic life. **RANGE:** Northern parts of N. Hemisphere.

RED-THROATED LOON *Gavia stellata* Common M56

25 in. (64 cm). Note slim snakelike head and neck, thin, slightly *upturned bill, often uptilted head.* Often flies with neck drooped. *Breeding:* Plain brown back, gray head, *rufous throat patch. Nonbreeding:* Slimmer than other loons with paler, spotted upperparts; adult has extensively white neck and face; first winter has smudgy gray neck. **VOICE:** When flying, a repeated *kwuk.* Guttural ptarmigan-like calls on breeding grounds; also falsetto wails. **SIMILAR SPECIES:** Other loons, Western and Clark's grebes. **HABITAT:** Nearshore ocean, bays, estuaries; in summer, tundra lakes.

PACIFIC LOON *Gavia pacifica* Rare M57

25–26 in. (64–66 cm). Smaller than Common Loon, with slightly thinner straight bill, often puffier look to head. *Breeding: Pale gray nape.* Back divided into four checkered patches. *Nonbreeding:* Note sharp, straight separation of dark and white on neck. Dark feathering around eye. **VOICE:** Deep, barking *kwow;* falsetto wails, rising in pitch. Silent away from breeding grounds. **SIMILAR SPECIES:** Nonbreeding adult Red-throated Loon also has straight separation of dark and white on neck but shows much more white. Other loons, grebes. **HABITAT:** Ocean, bays, large lakes; in summer, tundra lakes and sloughs.

COMMON LOON *Gavia immer* Common M58

31–32 in. (78–81 cm). Large, long-bodied, low-swimming; bill *stout,* daggerlike. In flight shows large, trailing feet. *Breeding:* Black head and bill. *Checkered back,* broken white necklace. *Nonbreeding:* Note *irregular or broken (half-collared) neck-pattern. Pale "eyelids."* **VOICE:** In breeding season, falsetto wails, weird yodeling, maniacal quavering laughter; at night, a tremulous *ha-oo-oo.* In flight, a barking *kwuk.* Usually silent in nonbreeding season. **SIMILAR SPECIES:** Other loons and cormorants. **HABITAT:** In summer, lakes, tundra ponds; in winter, larger lakes, bays, ocean.

YELLOW-BILLED LOON *Gavia adamsii* Vagrant M59

34–35 in. (86–89 cm). Similar to Common Loon, but bill *pale ivory* (sometimes with darker base) and slightly uptilted: straight above, slightly angled below. In nonbreeding plumage, slightly *paler* head and neck than Common, usually with small *dark ear patch.* **SIMILAR SPECIES:** Bill of nonbreeding Common Loon is somewhat pale, but culmen (upper ridge) is *dark to tip* (outer half of bill is pale in Yellow-billed). **HABITAT:** In summer, tundra lakes; in winter, casual vagrant at inland lakes.

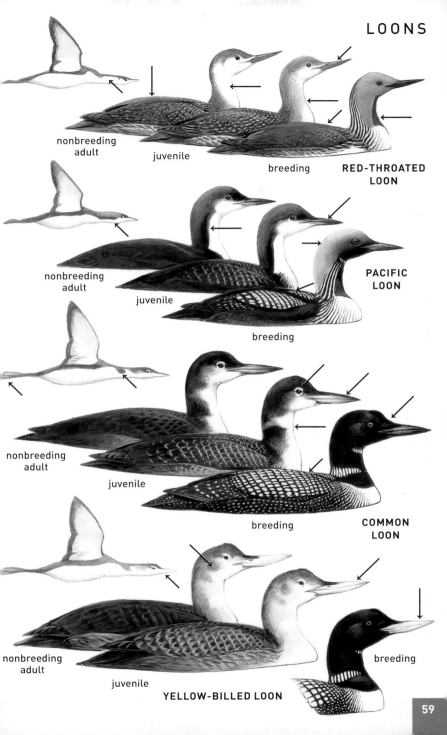

LOONS

nonbreeding adult

juvenile

breeding

RED-THROATED LOON

nonbreeding adult

juvenile

breeding

PACIFIC LOON

nonbreeding adult

juvenile

breeding

COMMON LOON

nonbreeding adult

juvenile

breeding

YELLOW-BILLED LOON

GREBES Family Podicipedidae

Ducklike divers with flat, lobed toes; thin neck; tailless look. All but Pied-billed Grebe have white wing patches, pointed bills. Sexes alike. Most young have striped heads. FOOD: Small fish, other aquatic life. RANGE: Worldwide.

PIED-BILLED GREBE *Podilymbus podiceps*   Fairly common M61
13–13½ in. (33–34 cm). A small brown diver with "chicken bill," puffy white stern. *Breeding: Black throat patch* and *ring* around pale bill. *Nonbreeding:* Lacks black markings. VOICE: Song *kuk-kuk-cow-cow-cow-cowp-cowp-cowp;* also a sizzling whinny and sharp *kwah.* HABITAT: Ponds, lakes, marshes; in winter, also salt bays and estuaries.

HORNED GREBE *Podiceps auritus*   Fairly common M62
13½–14 in. (34–36 cm). *Breeding: Golden ear patch* and *chestnut neck.* *Nonbreeding:* Black cap *clean-cut to eye level;* white foreneck, thin straight bill. VOICE: Loud *gamp,* trills on breeding grounds. Usually silent in nonbreeding season. SIMILAR SPECIES: Eared Grebe. HABITAT: Lakes, ponds, coastal waters.

EARED GREBE *Podiceps nigricollis*   Uncommon M64
12½–13 in. (32–33 cm). Note peaked crown, skinny neck, and slightly upturned, all-dark bill. *Breeding: Wispy golden ear tufts, black neck.* *Nonbreeding:* Dark cap extends *below eye,* neck usually dusky. VOICE: On breeding grounds, a musical *poo-ee-chk.* HABITAT: Prairie lakes, ponds; in winter, open lakes, coastal bays and estuaries.

RED-NECKED GREBE *Podiceps grisegena*   Uncommon M63
18–19 in. (46–49 cm). A largish grebe. *Breeding: Long rufous neck, light cheek,* black cap. *Nonbreeding:* Grayish with white crescent on neck; *yellowish* on bill. In flight, double wing patch. VOICE: Loud braying on breeding grounds. SIMILAR SPECIES: Loons, mergansers. HABITAT: Lakes, ponds; in winter, large lakes, salt water.

LEAST GREBE *Tachybaptus dominicus*   Uncommon, local M60
9½ in. (24 cm). Smaller, darker than Pied-billed Grebe, with white wing patches (usually concealed), puffy undertail coverts, slender *black bill, golden eyes.* VOICE: A chattering whinny. HABITAT: Ponds and lake edges.

WESTERN GREBE   Uncommon, local M65
Aechmophorus occidentalis
25 in. (64 cm). A large slate-and-white grebe with long neck. Bill long, greenish yellow with dark ridge. Black of cap extends *below eye.* VOICE: Loud, reedy *crik-crick.* SIMILAR SPECIES: Clark's Grebe, loons. HABITAT: Rushy lakes; in winter, large lakes, bays, coasts.

CLARK'S GREBE *Aechmophorus clarkii*   Scarce, local M66
25 in. (64 cm). Very similar to Western Grebe. *White surrounds eye;* bill orange-yellow. VOICE: Single-noted *creet* or *criik.* HABITAT: Similar to Western.

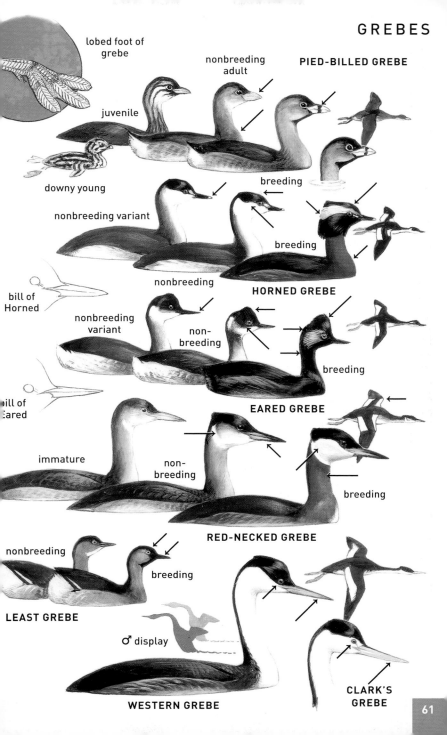

GREBES

lobed foot of grebe

PIED-BILLED GREBE

nonbreeding adult

juvenile

downy young

breeding

nonbreeding variant

HORNED GREBE

nonbreeding

bill of Horned

nonbreeding variant

nonbreeding

breeding

bill of Eared

EARED GREBE

immature

nonbreeding

breeding

RED-NECKED GREBE

nonbreeding

breeding

LEAST GREBE

♂ display

WESTERN GREBE

CLARK'S GREBE

SHEARWATERS AND PETRELS
Family Procellariidae

Gull-like birds of open sea that glide low over waves (usually with wings more stiffly extended than shown here). They often bank, or arc, up and down like a roller coaster, particularly in strong winds. Typically fly with several flaps and then a glide. Wings narrower than those of gulls. Shearwaters and petrels, along with albatrosses and storm-petrels, have tubelike external nostrils on bill, so are often called "tubenoses." **FOOD:** Fish, squid, crustaceans, ship refuse. **RANGE:** Oceans of world. Most species rarely seen from our mainland shores.

NORTHERN FULMAR
Uncommon to fairly common M67

Fulmarus glacialis

18½–19 in. (47–49 cm). A stiff-winged oceanic seabird; shearwater-like, but stockier with larger head, shorter, rounder wings; flies like shearwater but with quicker wingbeats, less gliding. Note rounded forehead; *stubby, yellowish, tubenose bill;* longish tail. Primaries may show a *pale flash or patch.* Comes in several color morphs. *Light morph:* Gull-like in plumage. *Dark morph* (scarce): Smoky gray, wingtips darker. **VOICE:** Hoarse, grunting *ag-ag-ag-arrr* or *ek-ek-ek-ek-ek.* **SIMILAR SPECIES:** Shape and flight style distinguish light morph from gulls and dark morph from Sooty Shearwater. **HABITAT:** Open ocean; breeds colonially on sea cliffs.

HERALD PETREL *Pterodroma arminjoniana*
Rare, local

15½–16 in. (40–41 cm). Dark, intermediate, and pale morphs. Most N. American records are dark, differing from Sooty Shearwater by *dark* wing linings, longer tail, and slower wingbeat. Light area at primary base suggests a jaeger. **RANGE:** Annual in Gulf Stream off NC coast from May to September. Nests in tropical S. Hemisphere.

BERMUDA PETREL (CAHOW) *Pterodroma cahow*
Casual

15 in. (38 cm). Endangered. One of the world's rarest seabirds. Differs from Black-capped Petrel by *smudgy gray* rump, absence of white collar, small bill. **RANGE:** Breeds only on certain small islets off ne. end of Bermuda. Sightings becoming more regular in Gulf Stream off NC coast during spring and summer as protection efforts in Bermuda enhance breeding success.

FEA'S PETREL *Pterodroma feae*
Very rare, local

14–15 in. (36–38 cm). Brownish gray above, with M pattern across wings. Distinguish from Black-capped Petrel by pale *gray rump and tail,* pale gray cowl on head, and *dark underwing.* **RANGE:** Breeds on islands off W. Africa. A rare but regular spring and summer visitor to Gulf Stream waters off NC; casual elsewhere.

BLACK-CAPPED PETREL
Uncommon, local M68

Pterodroma hasitata

16 in. (41 cm). Larger than Audubon's or Manx shearwater and looks quite similar to Greater Shearwater. Note white forehead, variable white collar, *white rump patch* extending to tail, thick bill. Rarely seen outside Gulf Stream. Nests on Hispanola and Cuba.

FULMAR AND PETRELS

tubed bill of Fulmar, also typical of petrels

light morph

dark morph

NORTHERN FULMAR

HERALD PETREL
dark morph

BERMUDA PETREL

FEA'S PETREL

BLACK-CAPPED PETREL

CORY'S SHEARWATER *Calonectris diomedea*   Fairly common M69
18–20 in. (46–51 cm). Large, pale seabird; large, gray-brown head *blends* into white of throat; bill dull *yellow.* Belly all white; rump usually dark with indistinct or no white. **SIMILAR SPECIES:** Greater Shearwater has white collar, dark cap, black bill, white rump, dark smudges on belly and underwing. Cory's has more pronounced bend to wing than Greater, and wingbeats are slower, more languid.

GREATER SHEARWATER *Puffinus gravis*   Fairly common M70
19 in. (48 cm). A shearwater dark above and white below, rising above waves on stiff wings, is likely to be this or Cory's Shearwater. Greater has dark cap separated by a whitish collar. Note also a narrow white rump patch and dark smudges on belly and underwing. Stiffer wingbeats than Cory's. **SIMILAR SPECIES:** Cory's Shearwater.

SOOTY SHEARWATER *Puffinus griseus*   Uncommon M71
17–18 in. (43–46 cm). Looks all dark at a distance; rises over and arcs above waves on narrow, rigid wings. In good light, note *whitish linings* on underwings. **SIMILAR SPECIES:** Dark jaegers (white in primaries), dark-morph Northern Fulmar.

MANX SHEARWATER *Puffinus puffinus*   Uncommon M72
13½ in. (34 cm). A small black-and-white shearwater; half the bulk of Greater Shearwater; no white rump patch. Note dark cap extends below eye; *white undertail.* **SIMILAR SPECIES:** See Audubon's Shearwater. Wingbeat quicker than in Greater or Cory's shearwater. **HABITAT:** Prefers colder water than Audubon's Shearwater.

AUDUBON'S SHEARWATER   Fairly common M73
Puffinus lherminieri
12 in. (30 cm). A very small shearwater, similar to Manx Shearwater but with slightly browner upperparts, *dark undertail.* Wings slightly shorter, *tail longer.* Often has *white markings* around eye. **HABITAT:** Prefers warmer water than Manx Shearwater.

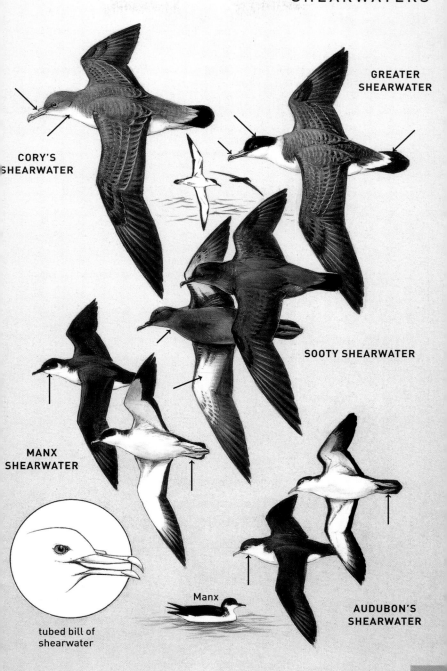

SHEARWATERS

GREATER
SHEARWATER

CORY'S
SHEARWATER

SOOTY SHEARWATER

MANX
SHEARWATER

Manx

tubed bill of
shearwater

AUDUBON'S
SHEARWATER

65

Storm-Petrels Family Hydrobatidae

Dark little birds that flutter or bound over open ocean; they nest colonially on islands, returning to burrows at night. Nostrils in a fused tube over top of bill. Usually silent at sea; most apt to call at feeding frenzies. FOOD: Plankton, crustaceans, small fish. RANGE: All oceans except Arctic.

WILSON'S STORM-PETREL *Oceanites oceanicus*   Common M74
7¼–7½ in. (18–19 cm). A small storm-petrel with somewhat triangular wings and *white rump patch that wraps around sides;* tail slightly rounded or square-cut, *not forked.* Feet yellow-webbed (hard to see), show *beyond tail* in flight. Direct flight, with short glides, pausing to flutter over water. SIMILAR SPECIES: Leach's and Band-rumped storm-petrels. HABITAT: Open ocean. Often follows ships (Leach's does not). Can be "chummed in" by tossing out ground fish, suet, puffed wheat in fish oil, etc. Regularly seen from shore.

LEACH'S STORM-PETREL   Uncommon M75
Oceanodroma leucorhoa
8 in. (20 cm). Note obscurely divided *white rump patch* and slightly forked tail. Pale bar on upperwing often reaches leading edge. In flight, bounds about erratically on fairly long angled wings, changing speed and direction — all suggesting a nighthawk. This is the breeding storm-petrel of N. Atlantic (but less often seen than Wilson's Storm-Petrel). *Does not follow ships.* VOICE: At night on breeding grounds, nasal chattering notes and long crooning trills. SIMILAR SPECIES: Wilson's and Band-rumped storm-petrels.

BAND-RUMPED STORM-PETREL *Oceanodroma castro*   Scarce M76
8½–9 in. (21–23 cm). A white-rumped storm-petrel, larger than Wilson's, similar to Leach's. Feet do not project beyond *squarish* tail. Pale bar on upperwing much less distinct than in Leach's or Wilson's; rump band more clean-cut than Leach's, less extensive under tail than Wilson's. A stiff-winged flier, with short glides, reminiscent of a shearwater.

WHITE-FACED STORM-PETREL *Pelagodroma marina*   Casual
7½ in. (19 cm). A storm-petrel with white head and underparts, two-toned underwing, dark crown and eye patch. Very long legs. When feeding, bounds "kangaroo style" over water on stiff flat wings. RANGE: Se. Atlantic, sw. Pacific, Indian Ocean. Casual but almost annual Aug.–Sept. off Atlantic Coast from MA to NC, usually far offshore.

EUROPEAN STORM-PETREL *Hydrobates pelagicus*   Vagrant
6 in. (15 cm). Smaller than Wilson's Storm-Petrel; shorter legs, which do not extend beyond square tail. Yellow on feet, not on webs. Shows whitish underwing patch. RANGE: Nests in ne. Atlantic and Mediterranean. Casual off NC in May and June, accidental off NS.

tubed bill of storm-petrel

WILSON'S STORM-PETREL

LEACH'S STORM-PETREL

BAND-RUMPED STORM-PETREL

WHITE-FACED STORM-PETREL

EUROPEAN STORM-PETREL

DARK STORM-PETRELS

Leach's

Wilson's

Band-rumped

European

ALBATROSSES Family Diomedeidae

Birds of open ocean, with rigid gliding and banking flight. Much larger than gulls; wings proportionately longer. "Tube-nosed" (nostrils in two tubes); bill large, hooked, covered with horny plates. Sexes alike. Largely silent at sea. **FOOD:** Cuttlefish, fish, squid, other small marine life; some feeding at night. **RANGE:** Mainly cold oceans of S. Hemisphere; two species are vagrants to w. North Atlantic.

BLACK-BROWED ALBATROSS *Thalassarche melanophris*   Vagrant
34–35 in. (86–88 cm); wingspan 7½ ft. (229 cm). Suggests a huge Great Black-backed Gull, but with short blackish tail and very large yellow bill (adult) with hooked tip. Dark eye streak gives it a frowning look. In stiff-winged gliding flight, shows white underwing *broadly outlined* with black. *Immature:* Bill dark. **RANGE:** Accidental off Atlantic Coast.

YELLOW-NOSED ALBATROSS *Thalassarche chlororhynchos*   Vagrant
31–32 in. (79–81 cm); wingspan 7–7½ ft. (213–229 cm). Similar to Black-browed Albatross, but bill *black with yellow ridge* on upper mandible. In flight, underwing whiter, with *narrower* black edging. **RANGE:** Accidental along Atlantic and Gulf coasts.

TROPICBIRDS Family Phaethontidae

These seabirds resemble (but are unrelated to) large terns with two greatly elongated central tail feathers (adults) and stouter, very slightly decurved bill. Fly with rapid, shallow wingbeats; dive headfirst; swim with tail held clear of water. Sexes alike. Largely silent at sea. **FOOD:** Squid, fish, crustaceans. **RANGE:** Tropical oceans.

WHITE-TAILED TROPICBIRD *Phaethon lepturus*   Rare M77
15 in. (38 cm), adults to 30 in. (76 cm) with tail-streamers. *Adult:* Distinguished from other tropicbirds by its *diagonal black bar* across each wing. Note two extremely long central tail feathers. Bill yellow to orange-red. *Immature:* Lacks tail-streamers; has *white*, not black, primary coverts, *coarsely* barred with black above; bill yellow. **VOICE:** Harsh ternlike scream. Also *tik-et, tik-et.* **SIMILAR SPECIES:** Red-billed Tropicbird.

RED-BILLED TROPICBIRD *Phaethon aethereus*   Casual M78
18 in. (45 cm), adults to 37 in. (94 cm) with tail-streamers. *Adult:* A slender white seabird with *two extremely long central tail feathers, heavy red bill,* black patch through cheek, black primaries, and *finely barred back. Immature:* Lacks long tail, has orange-yellow bill. **SIMILAR SPECIES:** White-tailed Tropicbird. Red-billed slightly larger and larger-billed; has more *finely barred* back than immature White-tailed, bright red to slight orange (not yellow) bill, more black on wing, including on *primary coverts,* black ear patch *extending to nape.*

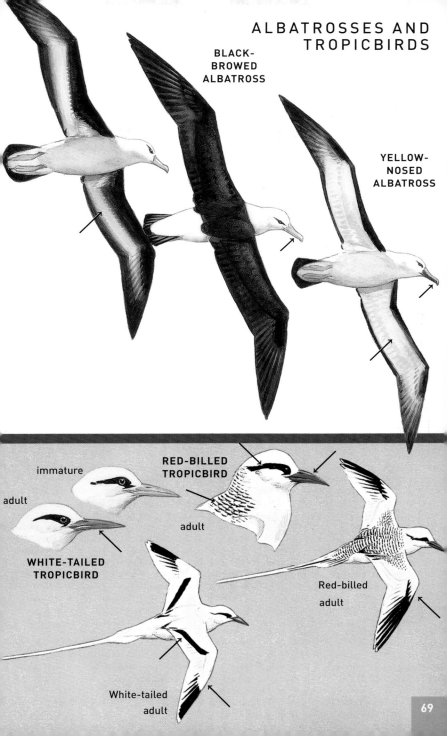

ALBATROSSES AND TROPICBIRDS

BLACK-BROWED ALBATROSS

YELLOW-NOSED ALBATROSS

immature

adult

RED-BILLED TROPICBIRD

adult

WHITE-TAILED TROPICBIRD

Red-billed
adult

White-tailed
adult

GANNETS AND BOOBIES Family Sulidae

Seabirds with large, pointed bill and pointed tail, making them appear tapered at both ends. Larger and longer necked than most gulls. Boobies sit on buoys, rocks; fish by plunging from air. Mostly silent at sea, except when at feeding frenzies. **FOOD:** Fish, squid. **RANGE:** Gannets live in cold seas (N. Atlantic, S. Africa, Australia); boobies in tropical seas. All nest colonially on islands.

NORTHERN GANNET *Morus bassanus* Common M81
37–38 in. (94–97 cm). A goose-sized seabird that scales over ocean and plunges headlong for fish. Migrates in long lines. Much larger than Herring Gull, with pointed bill, longer neck, larger bill (often pointed toward water). *Adult:* White with extensive black primaries. *Immature:* Dusky, but note "pointed-at-both-ends" shape. Young birds in transition may have a piebald look. **VOICE:** Commonly heard at sea in winter. In colony, a low barking *arrah.* **SIMILAR SPECIES:** Boobies. In windy conditions, gannets in flight may arc up and down, suggesting a large tubenose such as an albatross. **HABITAT:** Ocean, but seen regularly from shore. Breeds colonially on sea cliffs.

MASKED BOOBY *Sula dactylatra* Scarce, local M79
31–32 in. (79–81 cm). *Adult:* White; smaller than Northern Gannet, with *black tail,* black along entire *rear edge* of wing, and black in *face.* Greenish yellow bill. *Immature:* Variably mottled with dark on upperwing and head, but shows white collar. **VOICE:** Usually silent. In nesting colony, a variety of whistles, grunts, bill-rattling. **SIMILAR SPECIES:** Other boobies, immature Northern Gannet.

BROWN BOOBY *Sula leucogaster* Scarce, local M80
29–30 in. (74–76 cm). *Adult:* Sooty brown with *white belly in clean-cut contrast* to dark breast. White wing linings contrast with dark flight feathers. Bill and feet yellowish. *Immature:* Underparts mostly dark, with little contrast between breast and belly; bill grayish. **SIMILAR SPECIES:** Immature Northern Gannet lacks clean-cut breast contrast; shows some white patches or mottling above; feet dark (not yellowish). Immature Red-footed Booby (which has dark tail) more buffy overall with dark underwing; has lilac color at base of bill; feet orangey pink. Immature Masked Booby resembles adult Brown Booby, but brown of head not as sharply demarcated from paler underparts.

RED-FOOTED BOOBY *Sula sula* Vagrant
27–28 in. (69–71 cm). The smallest booby. *Adult:* Feet *bright red,* tail *white. White morph:* Gannetlike; white, with black trailing edge of wing (as in Masked Booby), tail white. *Brown morph:* Brown back and wings, paler head; white tail and belly; in flight, *underwing dark,* thin dark trailing edge on upperwing. *White-tailed brown morph:* Brown with white tail. *Immature:* Tan overall with *dark underwing,* pink and lilac base of bill, dull pink or orangey pink feet. **SIMILAR SPECIES:** Brown Booby. **RANGE:** Nests in tropics. Very rare, mostly young birds, at Dry Tortugas, FL; casual elsewhere in FL.

GANNET AND BOOBIES

adults

NORTHERN GANNET

juvenile

subadult

diving

adults

MASKED BOOBY

juvenile

♂

♀

♀

♂

subadult

BROWN BOOBY

RED-FOOTED BOOBY

brown morph

white-tailed brown morph

adults

white morph

PELICANS Family Pelecanidae

Huge waterbirds with long flat bill and great throat pouch (flat when deflated). Neck long, body robust. Sexes alike. Flocks fly in lines or Vs or kettles, alternating several flaps with a glide. In flight, head is hunched back on shoulders, the long bill resting on breast. Pelicans swim buoyantly. **FOOD:** Mainly fish, crustaceans. **RANGE:** N. and S. America, Africa, s. Eurasia, E. Indies, Australia.

AMERICAN WHITE PELICAN   Fairly common M82
Pelecanus erythrorhynchos
62 in. (157 cm). Huge; wingspan 8–9½ ft. (244–290 cm). White, with black primaries and a great orange-yellow bill. Adults in breeding condition have "centerboard" on ridge of bill; reduced or lacking at other seasons. *Immature:* Dusky wash on head, neck, and wings. Does not plunge from air like Brown Pelican but scoops up fish while swimming, often working in groups. Flocks may fly in lines and broken Vs and circle high in air on thermals. **VOICE:** In colony, a low groan. Young utter whining grunts. **SIMILAR SPECIES:** Swans, Wood Stork, Whooping Crane, Snow Goose. **HABITAT:** Lakes, marshes, salt bays, beaches.

BROWN PELICAN *Pelecanus occidentalis*   Common M83
48–50 in. (122–127 cm); wingspan 6½ ft. (198 cm). A ponderous dark waterbird. *Adult:* Much white and buff on head and front of neck. Dark chestnut brown on back of neck when breeding. *Immature:* Duskier brown overall, with dark head, paler underparts. Size, shape, and flight (a few flaps and a glide) indicate a pelican; dark color and habit of *plunging bill-first* proclaim it as this species. Lines of pelicans glide low over water, almost touching it with wingtips. **VOICE:** Adults silent (rarely a low croak). Nestlings squeal. **HABITAT:** Salt bays, beaches, ocean; more rarely inland lakes. Perches on posts, piers, rocks, buoys, beaches.

FRIGATEBIRDS Family Fregatidae

Dark tropical seabirds with extremely long wings (greater span in relation to body weight than that of any other bird). Bill long, hooked; tail deeply forked. Frigatebirds normally do not swim. **FOOD:** Fish, jellyfish, squid, young seabirds. Food snatched from water in flight, scavenged, or pirated from other seabirds. **RANGE:** Pantropical oceans.

MAGNIFICENT FRIGATEBIRD   Fairly common, local M88
Fregata magnificens
39–40 in. (100–102 cm); wingspan 7½ ft. (230–235 cm). A large, mostly black seabird with extremely long angled wings and *scissor-like* tail (often folded in a *point*). Soars with extreme ease. Bill long, hooked. *Male:* All black, with *red throat pouch* (inflated like a balloon in display). *Female:* White breast, dark head. *Immature:* Head and breast white. **VOICE:** Voiceless at sea. A gargling whinny during display. **SIMILAR SPECIES:** Lesser Frigatebird (*Fregata ariel*) is accidental in MI and ME. Adult male has white spur on axillars. Juvenile has russet head. **HABITAT:** Tropical oceans. May follow ships.

PELICANS AND FRIGATEBIRD

breeding adult

adults

immature

AMERICAN WHITE PELICAN

non-breeding adult

breeding adults

breeding adult

immature

BROWN PELICAN

♂ display

♀

♂

juveniles

MAGNIFICENT FRIGATEBIRD

73

CORMORANTS Family Phalacrocoracidae

Large blackish waterbirds that often stand erect on rocks, posts, or dead limbs with neck in an S; may rest with wings spread out to dry. Adults may have colorful facial skin, throat pouch, and eyes. Bill slender, hook-tipped. Sexes alike. Cormorants swim low like loons, but with bill tilted up at an angle. They often fly in lines or Vs, somewhat in manner of geese. Silent except for occasional low grunts at nesting colonies. **FOOD:** Fish, crustaceans. **RANGE:** Nearly worldwide.

DOUBLE-CRESTED CORMORANT　　　　　　Common M85
Phalacrocorax auritus
32–33 in. (81–84 cm). Almost any cormorant found inland can be called this species except for a few Great Cormorants and, in s.cen. states, Neotropic Cormorant. Told from others by its *orangey* throat pouch and *loral stripe* (adult). *Adult:* All black. Crest seldom evident. *Immature:* Brownish belly, pale throat and chest. **SIMILAR SPECIES:** Other cormorants, loons. **HABITAT:** Coasts, bays, lakes, rivers; nests colonially on rocky islands, sea cliffs, or in trees at lakes.

GREAT CORMORANT *Phalacrocorax carbo*　　Uncommon M86
36–37 in. (91–94 cm). *Adult:* Slightly larger than Double-crested Cormorant; note heavier bill and *yellow* throat pouch, bordered by *white throat* strap. In breeding plumage, has *white patch* on flanks. *Immature:* Dark breast and *pale belly*. Often shows suggestion of pale throat patch. **HABITAT:** Coasts and bays, locally inland on rivers, lakes. Nests on rocky islands and headlands.

NEOTROPIC CORMORANT　　　　　　　Uncommon M84
Phalacrocorax brasilianus
25–26 in. (64–66 cm). Similar to Double-crested Cormorant, but smaller, slimmer, and *longer tailed. Adult:* In breeding plumage, white filoplumes on neck. Note smaller and duller throat pouch and, in breeding plumage, *narrow white border* outlining it, forming a point at rear. Lacks orangey loral stripe of Double-crested. *Immature:* Paler below. **SIMILAR SPECIES:** Other cormorants. **HABITAT:** Freshwater wetlands, ponds, lakes; tidal waters, lakes near coasts.

DARTERS Family Anhingidae

This family is represented in N. America by one species. **FOOD:** Fish, small aquatic animals. **RANGE:** N. and S. America, Africa, India, se. Asia, Australia.

ANHINGA *Anhinga anhinga*　　　　　Fairly common M87
34–35 in. (86–89 cm). Similar to a cormorant, but neck snakier, bill more pointed, tail much longer. Note large silvery upperwing patch. Male black-bodied; female has buffy neck and breast. In flight, flaps and glides with neck extended, long tail spread. Often soars high, hawklike, with wings held flat (arched in cormorants). Perches like a cormorant, often with wings half-spread. May swim submerged, with only head emergent, appearing snakelike. **VOICE:** Occasional grunts and croaks. **SIMILAR SPECIES:** Soaring cormorants, sometimes with tail slightly splayed, regularly misidentified as Anhinga. **HABITAT:** Cypress swamps, rivers, wooded ponds.

CORMORANTS

DOUBLE-CRESTED CORMORANT

immature

adult

breeding adult

GREAT CORMORANT

immature

Double-crested

adult

immature

Great

immature

Double-crested

immature

Neotropic

GREAT CORMORANT

breeding

DOUBLE-CRESTED CORMORANT

breeding

NEOTROPIC CORMORANT

breeding

ANHINGA

♂

♀ swimming

♂

♀

Bitterns, Herons, and Allies
Family Ardeidae

Medium to large wading birds with long neck, spearlike bill. They stand with neck erect or head back on shoulders. In flight, neck is folded in an S; legs trail. Many herons have plumes when breeding. Sexes similar. **FOOD:** Fish, frogs, crawfish, other aquatic life; mice, gophers, small birds, insects. **RANGE:** Worldwide except colder regions.

GREAT BLUE HERON *Ardea herodias* Common M91
45–47 in. (115–120 cm). A lean gray bird, often miscalled a "crane"; may stand 4 ft. (122 cm) tall. Long legs, long neck, daggerlike bill, and, in flight, folded neck indicate a heron. Great size and blue-gray color mark it as this species. White subspecies, known as "Great White" Heron, is on p. 78. "Würdemann's" Heron is presumably an intergrade of Great Blue–"Great White" heron complex. **VOICE:** Deep harsh croaks: *frahnk, frahnk, frahnk.* **SIMILAR SPECIES:** Sandhill Crane, Reddish Egret. **HABITAT:** Marshes, swamps, shores, tidal flats, moist fields.

LITTLE BLUE HERON *Egretta caerulea* Fairly common M94
24 in. (61 cm). A small, slender heron. *Adult:* Bluish slate with deep maroon-brown neck; legs dark, bill pale blue with dark tip. *Immature:* All white with *grayish wingtips.* Legs *dull olive;* base of bill pale *blue-gray;* lores dull grayish or gray-green. Birds in transition are boldly pied white and dark. See p. 79. **VOICE:** Loud, nasal *scaaah.* **SIMILAR SPECIES:** Reddish Egret slightly larger overall and longer billed, with paler eye, medium gray color overall, and pinkish-based bill in breeding condition. Immature Little Blue like Snowy Egret except bill slightly thicker and grayer based, lores duller, and wingtips (usually) dusky. **HABITAT:** Marshes, ponds, mudflats, swamps, rice fields.

TRICOLORED HERON *Egretta tricolor* Uncommon M95
26 in. (66 cm). A very slender, dark heron with contrasting *white belly* and white rump. *Long* slender bill. *Adult:* Mostly bluish above and on neck. White crown plumes and pale rump plumes when breeding. *Immature:* Neck rusty brown. **VOICE:** Series of drawn-out nasal quacks. **SIMILAR SPECIES:** Great Blue and Little Blue herons. **HABITAT:** Marshes, swamps, shores.

REDDISH EGRET *Egretta rufescens* Uncommon M96
30–31 in. (76–79 cm). Note pinkish, black-tipped bill of adult in breeding condition. Loose-feathered; neck shaggy (adult). Pale eye. Two color morphs: (1) neutral gray, with rusty head and neck (immature duller, with all-dark bill); (2) white with blue-gray legs (see p. 78). When feeding, races about with spread wings. **VOICE:** Infrequently vocal; sometimes a harsh *kraaak!* **SIMILAR SPECIES:** Gray morph resembles adult Little Blue Heron, which is darker with bill pale bluish at base. White morph suggests Great or Snowy egret, but legs and feet blue-gray. **HABITAT:** Salt marshes, tidal flats, beaches.

DARK HERONS AND EGRET

juvenile

herons' necks may stretch or be looped in when they are standing

herons fly with neck pulled in

"WÜRDEMANN'S" HERON (intergrade)

adult

adult

GREAT BLUE HERON

juvenile

adult

LITTLE BLUE HERON

(juvenile on p. 79)

adult

TRICOLORED HERON

adult

REDDISH EGRET

dark morph

Reddish Egret "dancing" while feeding

(white morph on p. 79)

77

GREAT EGRET *Ardea alba*   Common M92

38–39 in. (97–100 cm). A tall, stately, slender white heron with largely *yellow bill.* Legs and feet *black.* When breeding, *straight plumes* on back extend beyond tail; bill may have dark ridge; lores greenish. When feeding, assumes an eager, forward-leaning pose, with neck extended. **VOICE:** Low, hoarse croak. Also *cuk, cuk, cuk.* **SIMILAR SPECIES:** Snowy Egret has all-black bill, yellow feet. Cattle Egret much smaller. **HABITAT:** Marshes, ponds, shores, mudflats, moist fields.

LITTLE EGRET *Egretta garzetta* (not shown)   Vagrant

25 in. (64 cm). A vagrant from Eurasia to East Coast, very similar to Snowy Egret, but slightly larger, larger billed, and with duller lores and feet. In breeding plumage, has two long head plumes. Young birds of both species very difficult to distinguish. **VOICE AND HABITAT:** Similar to Snowy Egret.

SNOWY EGRET *Egretta thula*   Common M93

24 in. (61 cm). Note the *"golden slippers."* A medium-sized heron, with *slender black bill,* black legs, and *yellow feet. Recurved plumes* on back during breeding season. Lores yellow (briefly red in high breeding condition). When feeding, rushes about, shuffling its feet to stir up food. Nonbreeding and young birds may show yellowish or greenish on much of rear side of legs, lores duller. **VOICE:** Low croak; in colony, a bubbling *wulla-wulla-wulla.* **SIMILAR SPECIES:** Great Egret larger, has largely yellow bill. Cattle Egret has yellow bill. White immature Little Blue Heron has blue-gray base to thicker bill, grayer lores, less active feeding style. **HABITAT:** Marshes, swamps, ponds, shores, tidal flats.

CATTLE EGRET *Bubulcus ibis*   Uncommon to common M97

19–20 in. (48–51 cm). Slightly smaller, stockier, and thicker necked than Snowy Egret. In breeding plumage shows *buff-orange* on crown, breast, and back (but may appear whitish at a distance); little or no buff at other times. Bill relatively short and yellow (orange-pink when nesting). Legs coral pink (nesting); immature may have yellow, greenish, or dusky legs. **VOICE:** Usually silent. Near breeding colony, a series of nasal grunts. **SIMILAR SPECIES:** Snowy Egret has black bill. Immature Little Blue Heron has blue-gray bill. Great Egret much larger. **HABITAT:** Farms, marshes, highway edges. Often associates with cattle.

REDDISH EGRET *Egretta rufescens* (dark morph on p. 76)

White morph: Note size, structure, feeding behavior, entirely blue-gray legs and feet. Adult has pink bill with black tip.

"GREAT WHITE" HERON *Ardea herodius* (in part) Uncommon, local

47 in. (120 cm). Our largest white heron, found regularly only in s. FL. Formerly believed to be (and may be) a distinct species *(A. occidentalis);* currently regarded as a subspecies of Great Blue Heron, p. 76. **HABITAT:** Mangrove keys, salt bays, marsh banks, open mudflats.

WHITE HERONS AND EGRETS

GREAT EGRET

SNOWY EGRET

changing

juvenile

LITTLE BLUE HERON

(adult on p. 77)

CATTLE EGRET

nonbreeding

breeding

REDDISH EGRET

(dark morph on p. 77)

white morph

"GREAT WHITE" HERON

(see also Great Blue Heron on p. 77)

79

BLACK-CROWNED NIGHT-HERON
Uncommon M99

Nycticorax nycticorax

25 in. (64 cm). This stocky, thick-billed, short-legged heron is usually hunched and inactive; flies to feed at dusk. *Adult: Black back and cap contrast with pale gray or whitish underparts.* Eyes red; legs yellowish or greenish (pinkish in high breeding condition). Breeding birds have two long white head plumes. *Immature:* Brown, streaked and spotted with buff and white. Bill with greenish base; eyes small, reddish. **VOICE:** Flat *quok!* or *quark!* Most often heard at dusk. **SIMILAR SPECIES:** Immature may be confused with American Bittern and immature Yellow-crowned Night-Heron. **HABITAT:** Marshes, shores; roosts in trees.

YELLOW-CROWNED NIGHT-HERON
Uncommon M100

Nyctanassa violacea

24 in. (61 cm). A chunky heron with longer neck and legs than Black-crowned. *Adult:* Gray overall; head black with buffy-white cheek patch and yellowish crown. *Immature:* Similar to young Black-crowned Night-Heron, but grayer, more finely streaked and spotted; wing coverts have pale edges. Bill thicker and lacks greenish yellow base. In flight, entire foot and some of lower leg extend beyond tail. **VOICE:** *Quark,* higher pitched than call of Black-crowned. **HABITAT:** Swamps, mangroves, bayous, marshes, streams.

GREEN HERON *Butorides virescens*
Fairly common M98

17–18 in. (43–46 cm). A small dark heron that looks crowlike in flight (but flies with bowed wingbeats). When alarmed, stretches neck, elevates shaggy crest, and jerks tail. *Adult:* Comparatively *short* legs are *greenish yellow* or *orange* (when breeding). Back with blue-green gloss; neck deep chestnut. *Immature:* Streaked neck and breast, browner above. **VOICE:** Loud *skyow* or *skewk;* series of *kuck* notes. **HABITAT:** Lakes, ponds, marshes, streams.

LEAST BITTERN *Ixobrychus exilis*
Uncommon, secretive M90

12–13 in. (31–33 cm). Very small, thin, furtive; straddles reeds. Note large *buff wing patch* (lacking in rails). Back black in adult male, rusty brown in female and immature. The dark "Cory's" form has not been recorded since the 1930s. **VOICE:** Song a low, muted *coo-coo-coo;* also gives a raspy, rail-like *khak-khak-khak* series. **SIMILAR SPECIES:** Green Heron. **HABITAT:** Freshwater marshes, reedy ponds.

AMERICAN BITTERN *Botaurus lentiginosus*
Uncommon M89

28 in. (71 cm). A stocky brown heron; size of a young night-heron but warmer brown with longer yellowish bill. In flight, *entire trailing edge of wing is black* and bill held horizontal. Wingbeats much more rapid than night-herons'. At rest or when approached, often stands rigid, bill pointing up. *Black stripe shows on neck.* **VOICE:** "Pumping" sound, a low, deep, resonant *oong-ka´ choonk,* etc. Flushing call *kok-kok-kok.* **SIMILAR SPECIES:** Immature night-herons, Green Heron, and (much smaller) Least Bittern. **HABITAT:** Marshes, reedy lakes. Unlike night-herons, seldom sits in trees.

HERONS AND BITTERNS

adult

BLACK-CROWNED NIGHT-HERON

juvenile

adult

YELLOW-CROWNED NIGHT-HERON

juvenile

"Cory's"

typical

LEAST BITTERN

juvenile

adult

GREEN HERON

AMERICAN BITTERN

LIMPKINS Family Aramidae

A monotypic family, represented by one species. **FOOD:** Mostly large freshwater snails (mainly apple snails); a few insects, frogs. **RANGE:** Se. U.S., W. Indies, s. Mex. to Argentina.

LIMPKIN *Aramus guarauna*　　　　Uncommon, local M146
26 in. (66 cm). A large, spotted swamp wader, a bit larger than an ibis. Long legs and drooping bill give it an ibislike aspect, but no ibis is brown with white streaks. Flight cranelike, with smart upward flaps. **VOICE:** Piercing, repeated wail, *kree-ow*, etc., especially at night and on cloudy days. **SIMILAR SPECIES:** Immature ibises, night-herons. **HABITAT:** Fresh swamps, marshes with large snails.

IBISES AND SPOONBILLS
Family Threskiornithidae

Ibises are long-legged, heronlike waders with slender, decurved bill. Spoonbills have spatulate bill. Both fly in Vs or lines and, unlike herons, fly with neck outstretched, alternately flapping and gliding. **FOOD:** Small crustaceans, small fish, insects, etc. **RANGE:** Tropical and temperate regions.

WHITE-FACED IBIS *Plegadis chihi*　　　Fairly common M103
23–24 in. (58–62 cm). Very similar to Glossy Ibis. *Breeding adult:* Note *white border* around face meets behind eye; variably red legs; pinkish to red lores; *red eye. Immature and nonbreeding adult:* Lacks white on face; pale streaks on head and neck. **VOICE:** Like Glossy. **SIMILAR SPECIES:** Glossy Ibis has thin cobalt blue borders on face, which do not meet behind dark eye; dark lores; less or no red on legs. Some immatures may be impossible to identify at least until the iris of young White-faced turns red (as early as midwinter). Hybrids with White-faced are known. **HABITAT:** Freshwater marshes, irrigated land.

GLOSSY IBIS *Plegadis falcinellus*　　　Fairly common M102
23–24 in. (58–62 cm). A medium-sized marsh wader with long decurved bill, thin pale blue lines edging dark face. At a distance, appears quite black, like a large dark curlew. Flies in lines with neck extended, flapping and gliding with wingbeats. *Adult:* Body a deep glossy bronzy chestnut. In nonbreeding season, duller with pale streaks on head and neck. *Immature:* Browner with no gloss. **VOICE:** Guttural *ka-onk*, repeated; low *kruk, kruk.* **SIMILAR SPECIES:** White-faced Ibis. **HABITAT:** Marshes, rice fields, swamps.

WHITE IBIS *Eudocimus albus*　　　　Common M101
24–25 in. (62–64 cm). *Adult:* White. Note *red face,* long *decurved red bill,* and *restricted black in wingtips.* Flies with neck outstretched; flocks fly in "roller-coasting" strings, flapping and gliding; may soar in circles. *Immature:* Dark brownish, with *white belly, white rump,* decurved *orangey pink bill.* **VOICE:** Low and nasal *uuhhnn!* or *quaahh!* **SIMILAR SPECIES:** Wood Stork, Glossy Ibis. **HABITAT:** Salt, brackish, and fresh marshes, rice fields, mangroves.

LIMPKIN AND IBISES

WHITE-FACED IBIS

Glossy Ibis

facial comparison in breeding season

LIMPKIN

adult

GLOSSY IBIS

immature

adult

WHITE IBIS

immature

83

ROSEATE SPOONBILL *Platalea ajaja* Uncommon M104

32 in. (81 cm). A *bright pink* wading bird with long, flat, spoonlike bill. When feeding, sweeps its bill from side to side. In flight, extends neck and often glides between series of wing strokes. *Adult: Shell pink,* with blood red "drip" on shoulders; tail orange. Head naked, greenish gray. *Immature:* Spatulate bill; whitish plumage tinged pale pink, brightest on underwing. **VOICE:** At nesting colony, a low grunting croak. **SIMILAR SPECIES:** American Flamingo. **HABITAT:** Coastal marshes, lagoons, mudflats, mangroves.

STORKS Family Ciconiidae

Large, long-legged, and heronlike, with straight, recurved, or decurved bill. Some have naked head. Sexes alike. Walk is sedate; flight deliberate, with neck and legs extended. **FOOD:** Frogs, crustaceans, lizards, rodents. **RANGE:** S. U.S. to S. America; Africa, Eurasia, E. Indies, Australia.

WOOD STORK *Mycteria americana* Uncommon M105

39–41 in. (100–105 cm). Very large; wingspan 5½ ft. (168 cm). White, with *dark naked head* and *much black in wing;* black tail. Bill long, thick, slightly decurved. *Immature:* Bill yellowish. When feeding, keeps head down and walks. In flight, alternately flaps and glides. Often soars very high on thermals. **VOICE:** Hoarse croak; usually silent. **SIMILAR SPECIES:** In flight, American White Pelican, Whooping Crane. **HABITAT:** Marshes, ponds, lagoons.

FLAMINGOS Family Phoenicopteridae

Pinkish white to vermilion wading birds with extremely long neck and legs. Thick bill is bent sharply down and lined with numerous lamellae for straining food. **FOOD:** Small mollusks, crustaceans, blue-green algae, diatoms. **RANGE:** W. Indies, Yucatán, Galápagos, S. America, Africa, s. Eurasia, India.

AMERICAN FLAMINGO *Phoenicopterus ruber* Rare, local

46–47 in. (115–118 cm). W. Indian subspecies of this widespread flamingo is an extremely slim, rose pink wading bird as tall as a Great Blue Heron but much more slender. Note thick, sharply bent bill. Feeds with bill or head immersed. In flight, shows much black in wings; extremely long neck is extended droopily in front, and long legs trail behind, giving impression the bird might as easily fly backward as forward. Pale, washed-out birds may be escapees from zoos, as color often fades under captive conditions. Immatures also much paler than normal adults. **VOICE:** Gooselike calls, gabbling: *ar-honk,* etc. **SIMILAR SPECIES:** Roseate Spoonbill. Escapees of all five other flamingo species have been recorded in N. America. **RANGE:** Closest colonies in Bahamas, Cuba, and Yucatán. Rare visitor to Florida Bay; accidental elsewhere. **HABITAT:** Salt flats, saline lagoons.

adult

juvenile

ROSEATE SPOONBILL

Wood Stork

adult

immature

White Ibis (p. 83)
for comparison

**WOOD
STORK**

adult

**AMERICAN
FLAMINGO**

CRANES Family Gruidae

Stately birds, more robust than herons, often with red facial skin. Note tufted appearance over rump. In flight, neck extended. Migrate in Vs or lines like geese. Large herons are sometimes wrongly referred to as cranes. **FOOD:** Omnivorous. **RANGE:** Nearly worldwide except Cen. and S. America and Oceania.

WHOOPING CRANE *Grus americana*　　Rare, very local M148
51–52 in. (130–132 cm); wingspan 7½ ft. (229 cm). The tallest N. American bird and one of the rarest. Large *white* crane with *red face*. Primaries *black*. Young birds washed with rust, especially on head. **VOICE:** Shrill, buglelike trumpeting, *ker-loo! ker-lee-oo!* **SIMILAR SPECIES:** Wood Stork has dark head, more black in wing. Egrets and swans lack black in wings. See also American White Pelican and Snow Goose. **HABITAT:** Prairies, fields and pastures, coastal marshes; in summer, muskeg. *Endangered* but slowly increasing.

COMMON CRANE *Grus grus*　　Vagrant
44–50 in. (112–127 cm). Eurasian. Note black neck, white cheek stripe. Feathers arching over rump are blacker than those of Sandhill Crane. This stray (probably from Asia) has been recorded in NE, KS, IN, and QC and should be looked for among flocks of Sandhill Cranes. Some escapees have also occurred (e.g., in NY, NJ).

SANDHILL CRANE *Grus canadensis*　　Uncommon M147
36–48 in. (90–122 cm); wingspan 6–7 ft. (183–213 cm). Note *bald red crown,* bustlelike rear. A long-legged, long-necked, gray bird, often stained with rust. Immature browner. In flight, neck extended and wings flap with an upward flick. **VOICE:** Rolling, bugled *garoo-a-a-a,* repeated. Young birds also give a very different, cricketlike call. **SIMILAR SPECIES:** Great Blue Heron is sometimes wrongly called a crane. **HABITAT:** Prairies, fields, marshes, tundra. Lesser (subspecies) nests in tundra, Greater (subspecies) in grasslands and bogs.

CRANES

storks, ibises, and cranes
fly with neck outstretched

WHOOPING CRANE

adult

juvenile

COMMON CRANE

adult

adult

SANDHILL CRANE

adult

juvenile

New World Vultures Family Cathartidae

Blackish; often seen soaring high in wide circles. Their naked heads are relatively smaller than those of hawks and eagles. Vultures are often locally called "buzzards." Silent away from nest site. FOOD: Carrion. RANGE: S. Canada to Cape Horn.

TURKEY VULTURE *Cathartes aura* (see also p. 114) Common M107
26–27 in. (66–69 cm); wingspan 6 ft. (183 cm). Nearly eagle-sized. Overhead, note dark color with *two-toned wings* (flight feathers paler). Soars with wings in dihedral (shallow V); rocks and tilts unsteadily. At close range, small, naked *red head* of adult is evident; immatures have dark head. SIMILAR SPECIES: Black Vulture; eagles have larger, feathered head, shorter tail, and soar in a steady flat plane. HABITAT: Usually seen soaring in sky or perched on dead trees, posts, or on ground feeding, or sunning with wings outstretched.

BLACK VULTURE *Coragyps atratus* (see also p. 114) Common M106
25 in. (64 cm); wingspan less than 5 ft. (152 cm). This dark scavenger is readily identified by short, square tail that barely projects beyond rear edge of wings and by *whitish patch* toward wingtip. Legs longer and whiter than Turkey Vulture's. Note *quick, shallow flapping*, alternating with short glides. SIMILAR SPECIES: Turkey Vulture has longer, rounded tail; flapping is slower, less frequent; soars with noticeable dihedral. *Caution:* Young Turkey Vulture has dark head. HABITAT: Similar to Turkey Vulture's but avoids higher mountains.

Caracaras Family Falconidae

Caracaras are large, long-legged birds of prey, some with naked face. Sexes alike. FOOD: Our one U.S. species feeds mostly on carrion. RANGE: S. U.S. to Tierra del Fuego, Falklands. See also falcons, p. 104.

CRESTED CARACARA   Uncommon, local M131
Caracara cheriway (see also p. 112)
23 in. (58 cm). A large, long-legged, big-headed, long-necked bird of prey, often seen feeding with vultures. *Adult: Black crest* and *red face* distinctive. In flight, underbody presents alternating areas of light and dark: white chest, black belly, and whitish, dark-tipped tail. Note combination of *pale wing patches, pale chest, and pale tail panel,* giving impression of "white at all four corners." *Immature:* Browner, streaked on breast. VOICE: Weird, guttural series of croaks and rattles, though seldom heard. HABITAT: Prairies, rangeland.

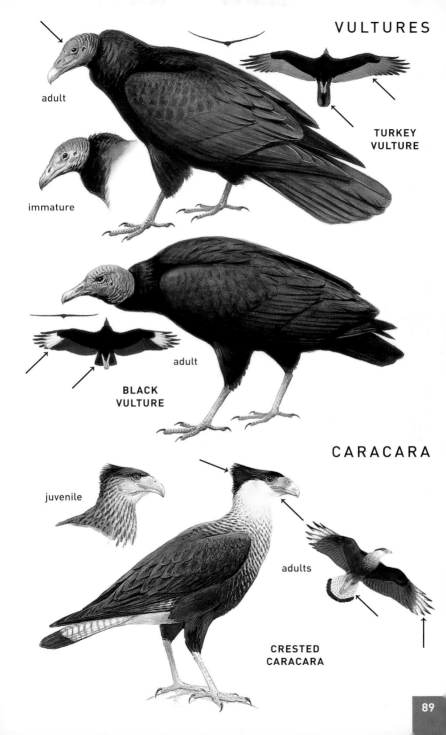

VULTURES

adult

immature

TURKEY VULTURE

adult

BLACK VULTURE

CARACARA

juvenile

adults

CRESTED CARACARA

89

BIRDS OF PREY

We tend to call all diurnal (day-flying) raptors with a hooked bill and hooked claws "birds of prey." Actually, they fall into two quite separate families:

1. The hawk group (Accipitridae) — kites, harriers, accipiters, buteos, and eagles
2. The falcon group (Falconidae) — falcons and caracaras

The illustrations on the following pages present the most obvious field marks. For a more in-depth treatment of variable plumages, see the various specialty guides that deal with raptors.

The many raptors can be sorted out by their basic shapes and flight styles. When not flapping, they may alternate between soaring, with wings fully extended and tail fanned, and gliding, with wings slightly pulled back and tail folded. These two pages show some basic silhouettes.

full soar

glide

BUTEOS are stocky, with broad wings and a wide, rounded tail. They soar and wheel high in the open sky.

full soar

glide

ACCIPITERS have a small head, short rounded wings, and a longish tail. They typically fly with several rapid beats and a short glide.

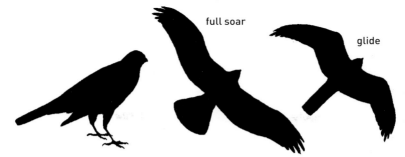

HARRIERS are slim, with long, slim, round-tipped wings and a long tail. They fly in open country and glide low, with a vulturelike dihedral.

KITES (except for Snail Kite and Hook-billed Kite) are falcon-shaped, but unlike falcons, they are buoyant gliders, not power fliers.

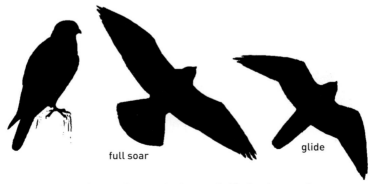

FALCONS have long pointed wings and a long tail. Their wing strokes are strong and rapid.

EAGLES, KITES, HAWKS, AND ALLIES
Family Accipitridae

Diurnal birds of prey, with hooked bill, hooked talons. Though persecuted and misunderstood by many, they are very important in the ecosystem. **RANGE:** Almost worldwide.

EAGLES

Distinguished from buteos, to which they are related, by their greater size, longer wings, larger bills. **FOOD:** Golden Eagle eats chiefly rabbits, large rodents, snakes, game birds; Bald Eagle, fish, injured waterfowl, carrion.

BALD EAGLE   Uncommon M114
Haliaeetus leucocephalus (see also p. 114)
31–37 in. (79–94 cm); wingspan 7–8 ft. (213–244 cm). National bird of U.S. *Adult:* With its *white head* and *white tail,* this bird is "all field mark." Bill yellow, massive. Wings held flat when soaring. *Immature:* Variable, depending on age; first year mostly dark with *whitish in wing linings.* Two- and three-year-olds mottled with white on belly and back; some show pale head with dark eye patch, reminiscent of Osprey. **VOICE:** Harsh, high-pitched cackle, *kleek-kik-ik-ik-ik,* or lower *kak-kak-kak.* **SIMILAR SPECIES:** Golden Eagle, Turkey Vulture. **HABITAT:** Coasts, rivers, large lakes; other open country in migration.

GOLDEN EAGLE *Aquila chrysaetos* (see also p. 114)   Scarce M130
30–40 in. (76–102 cm); wingspan 7 ft. (213 cm). This majestic eagle glides and soars flat-winged with occasional shallow wingbeats. *Adult:* Uniformly dark with *wash of buffy gold on nape. Immature:* In flight, shows *white flashes* at base of primaries and base of tail. **VOICE:** Seldom heard, a yelping bark, *kya;* also whistled notes. **SIMILAR SPECIES:** Immature Bald Eagle has larger head, usually has *extensive white in wing linings;* never shows clean-cut tail band. Dark-morph Rough-legged Hawk is smaller, has more white in wings. **HABITAT:** Open mountains, foothills, plains, marshes, open country.

OSPREYS

Formerly considered a monotypic family comprising a single large bird of prey that hovers above water and plunges feet-first for fish. Sexes alike. **FOOD:** Fish. **RANGE:** All continents except Antarctica.

OSPREY *Pandion haliaetus* (see also p. 114)   Fairly common M108
23–24½ in. (58–62 cm); wingspan to 6 ft. (183 cm). Hovers over water and plunges feet-first for fish (Bald Eagle picks up fish from surface). *Adult:* Blackish above, *white below;* head white with *broad black mask.* Flies with gull-like crook in wings, showing black "wrist" patch below. *Juvenile:* Has scaly pattern on back. **VOICE:** Series of sharp, annoyed whistles: *cheep, cheep* or *yewk, yewk,* etc. Near nest, a frenzied *cheereek!* **SIMILAR SPECIES:** Large gulls. Immature Bald Eagle may show dusky "mask." **HABITAT:** Rivers, lakes, marshes, coasts.

overhead flight patterns on p. 115

EAGLES AND OSPREY

BALD EAGLE

juvenile

adult

GOLDEN EAGLE

juvenile

Golden Eagle

adult

hovering

OSPREY

adult

93

KITES

Graceful birds of prey of southern distribution. U.S. species (except Snail Kite and Hook-billed Kite) are falcon-shaped with pointed wings. FOOD: Large insects, reptiles, rodents. Snail Kite and Hook-billed Kite specialize in snails.

SWALLOW-TAILED KITE *Elanoides forficatus*   Uncommon M110
22–23 in. (55–58 cm). A sleek, elegant, black-and-white hawk that flies with incomparable grace. Note blue-black upperparts, clean white head and underparts, and long, mobile, deeply forked tail. **VOICE:** Shrill, keen *ee-ee-ee* or *pee-pee-pee*. **HABITAT:** Wooded river swamps and pine lands, where it feeds mainly on snakes.

MISSISSIPPI KITE   Fairly common M113
Ictinia mississippiensis (see also p. 108)
14–14½ in. (36–37 cm). Falcon-shaped, graceful, and gray. Gregarious; spends much time soaring. *Adult:* Dark above, lighter below; head *pale gray;* tail and underwing blackish. No other falconlike bird has *black unbarred tail.* Broad *white patch* shows on rear edge of upperwing (not visible from below). *Immature:* Lacks pale patch on wing, has weak white bands on tail. *Juvenile:* Heavily streaked on rusty underparts. **VOICE:** Usually silent; near nest, a two-syllable *phee-phew.* **SIMILAR SPECIES:** Male Northern Harrier. **HABITAT:** Nests in riparian woodlands, residential areas, groves, shelterbelts.

WHITE-TAILED KITE   Uncommon M111
Elanus leucurus (see also p. 108)
15½–16 in. (39–41 cm). This whitish kite is falcon-shaped, with long pointed wings, long grayish white tail, and *black shoulders.* Overhead, shows oval black patch at carpal joint ("wrist") of underwing. Soars and glides like a small gull; *often hovers. Adult:* Pale gray above, with white head and underparts. *Juvenile:* Like adult, but has *rusty breast,* brown back, and narrow dark band near tip of pale grayish tail. **VOICE:** Whistled *kew kew kew,* abrupt or drawn out. **HABITAT:** Open groves, river valleys, marshes, grasslands, roadsides.

SNAIL KITE *Rostrhamus sociabilis*   Scarce, local M112
17 in. (43 cm). Suggests Northern Harrier at a distance, but with broader wings and without gliding, tilting flight; flies more floppily on cupped wings, head down, searching for snails. *Male:* All black except for broad white band across base of tail; legs, bill, and face red. *Female:* Heavily streaked on buffy body; white stripe over eye; white band across black tail. **VOICE:** Cackling *kor-ee-ee-a.* **HABITAT:** Freshwater marshes and canals with apple snails (*Pomacea* spp.).

HOOK-BILLED KITE *Chondrohierax uncinatus*   Rare, local M109
16½–17½ in. (42–45 cm). A scarce resident in s. TX. Bill has long, hooked tip. Legs yellow. Plumage varies from blackish or grayish in males to rufous brown in females to much paler below in juveniles. Adults have barred underparts. Note *paddle-shaped wings.* **HABITAT:** Subtropical woodlands. Spends most of its time in the woods, soaring only briefly as it travels to and from feeding areas.

additional overhead
flight patterns
on p. 109

SWALLOW-
TAILED KITE

adult

juvenile

MISSISSIPPI
KITE

adult

juvenile

adult

juvenile

adult

juvenile

WHITE-TAILED KITE

juvenile

♂

♀

SNAIL
KITE

black
morph

HOOK-
BILLED
KITE

♂

♀

ACCIPITERS (Bird Hawks)

Long-tailed woodland raptors with short, rounded wings, adapted for hunting among trees. Typical flight mixes quick beats and a glide. Sexes similar; females larger. Size helps distinguish species. **FOOD:** Chiefly birds, some small mammals. Sharp-shinned and Cooper's often seen hunting birds at backyard feeders.

SHARP-SHINNED HAWK
Fairly common M116

Accipiter striatus (see also p. 106)

10–14 in. (25–36 cm). A small, slim woodland hawk, with slim *square-tipped* tail and *short, rounded wings. Adult:* Dark back, *rusty-barred* breast. *Immature:* Dark brown above, *thickly streaked* with rusty brown on underparts. **VOICE:** A high *kik, kik, kik* given near nest. **SIMILAR SPECIES:** Female Cooper's obviously larger, with *larger head, rounded* tail, with thicker white tip, thicker legs; male Cooper's and female Sharp-shinned closer in size. Adult Cooper's has more defined cap. Immature Cooper's *tawnier* on head and has whiter, more *finely streaked* breast. **HABITAT:** Breeds in extensive forests; in migration and winter, open woodlands, edges, residential areas.

COOPER'S HAWK
Fairly common M117

Accipiter cooperii (see also p. 106)

14–20 in. (36–51 cm). Very similar to Sharp-shinned Hawk but larger, particularly female. See Sharp-shinned Hawk. **VOICE:** A rapid nasal *kek, kek, kek;* suggests a flicker. Also a sapsucker-like mewing. **SIMILAR SPECIES:** Sharp-shinned Hawk, Northern Goshawk. **HABITAT:** Like Sharp-shinned but prefers more open areas.

NORTHERN GOSHAWK
Scarce M118

Accipiter gentilis (see also p. 106)

21–26 in. (53–66 cm). Larger, broader-winged, broader-tailed, more buteo-like than Cooper's Hawk. *Adult: Broad white stripe over eye.* Underparts *pale gray. Immature:* Buffier than immature Cooper's with bolder eyebrow, more extensive streaking below, and wavy, irregular tail banding. **VOICE:** *Kak, kak, kak;* heavier, slower than Cooper's. **SIMILAR SPECIES:** Cooper's Hawk. **HABITAT:** Coniferous and mixed forests; forest edges. Periodic irruptions in fall and winter farther to south.

HARRIERS

Slim raptors with slim wings, long tail. Flight low, languid, gliding, with wings held in shallow V (dihedral). Sexes not alike. They hunt in open country.

NORTHERN HARRIER
Uncommon M115

Circus cyaneus (see also p. 106)

18–21 in. (46–54 cm). A slim, long-winged, long-tailed raptor of open country. Glides and flies buoyantly, unsteadily low over ground, with wings held above horizontal, suggesting Turkey Vulture. All plumages show *white rump patch. Adult male:* Pale gray and whitish, with black wing tips. *Adult female:* Brown, with heavy streaks. *Immature:* Russet below without streaks. **VOICE:** Weak, nasal whistle, *pee.* **SIMILAR SPECIES:** Short-eared Owl. **HABITAT:** Marshes, fields, prairies.

adult

juvenile

accipiters have small head, short rounded wings, long tail

SHARP-SHINNED HAWK

additional overhead flight patterns on pp. 107 and 109

juvenile

adult

COOPER'S HAWK

NORTHERN GOSHAWK

adult

juvenile

juvenile

NORTHERN HARRIER

♂

♀

Buteos and Buteo-like Hawks

Large, thickset hawks, with broad wings and wide, rounded tail. Many buteos habitually soar high in wide circles. Much variation; sexes similar, females slightly larger. Young birds usually streaked below. Dark morphs often occur. **FOOD:** Small mammals, sometimes small birds, reptiles, grasshoppers. **RANGE:** Widespread in New and Old Worlds.

GRAY HAWK *Buteo nitidus* (see also p. 108)   Scarce, local M122
17 in. (43 cm); wingspan 3 ft. (91 cm). A small buteo. *Adult:* Distinguished by its gray back, *thickly barred gray* breast, white rump band, and *banded* tail (similar to Broad-winged Hawk's). *Immature:* Narrowly barred tail, striped buffy breast, bold face pattern, *white U-shaped bar* across rump. **VOICE:** Drawn-out whistles, *ka-lee-oh* or *kleeeeoo.* **SIMILAR SPECIES:** Young Broad-winged Hawk has weaker face pattern, lacks white U on rump, has shorter tail, more pointed wings. **HABITAT:** Streamside and subtropical woodlands.

WHITE-TAILED HAWK   Uncommon, local M125
Buteo albicaudatus (see also p. 108)
21–23 in. (53–58 cm); wingspan 4 ft. (122 cm). Large, with long pointed wings. Flies with marked dihedral. *Adult:* White underparts contrasting with dark flight feathers; white tail with black band, shoulders rusty red. *Immature:* Narrower wings and longer tail than adult. Blackish below with white breast patch. Pale U across upper tail. May show Red-tailed Hawk–like dark belly patch. Tail pale gray with weak barring. **VOICE:** Nasal note followed by high-pitched series of doubled notes: *aaraahh kee-REEK, kee-REEK kee-REEK.* **SIMILAR SPECIES:** Adult Swainson's Hawk smaller, has dark chest. Juvenile White-tailed may be confused with other large buteos, particularly Red-tailed Hawk. **HABITAT:** Coastal prairies, brushlands.

HARRIS'S HAWK   Fairly common, local M119
Parabuteo unicinctus (see also p. 112)
20–21 in. (50–53 cm); wingspan 3½ ft. (107 cm). A blackish brown buteo-like hawk, with flashing *white rump* and *white band* at tip of tail. Often hunts cooperatively in small groups. *Adult:* Chestnut areas on thighs and shoulders. *Immature:* Light, streaked underparts, *rusty shoulders;* conspicuous *white* at base of tail. **VOICE:** Low-pitched, harsh *raaaah!* **SIMILAR SPECIES:** Dark-morph buteos. **HABITAT:** Mesquite, arid country.

ZONE-TAILED HAWK   Rare, local M126
Buteo albonotatus (see also p. 112)
20 in. (51 cm); wingspan 4 ft. (122 cm). Dull *black,* with more *slender* wings than most other buteos. Often mistaken for Turkey Vulture because of proportions, two-toned underwing, and up-tilted wings — but hawk has larger feathered head, square-tipped tail, barred underwing, yellow cere and legs. *Adult:* White tail bands (pale gray on topside). *Immature:* Narrower tail bands, *small white spots* on breast. **VOICE:** Nasal, drawn-out *keeeeah.* **SIMILAR SPECIES:** Turkey Vulture, dark-morph buteos. **HABITAT:** Riparian woodlands, canyons.

SOUTH-
WESTERN
BUTEOS

GRAY HAWK

WHITE-
TAILED
HAWK

juvenile

adult

juvenile

adult

adult

juvenile

HARRIS'S
HAWK

juvenile

adult

ZONE-TAILED
HAWK

99

ROUGH-LEGGED HAWK
Uncommon M129

Buteo lagopus (see also pp. 110 and 112)

21–22 in. (53–55 cm). This hawk of open country often *hovers on beating wings,* more so than other buteos. Longer, narrower wings and tail than other Buteos except Ferruginous Hawk. Many birds show *dark belly* and *black patch* at "wrist" (carpal joint) of underwing. Some adult males have dark bib but lack blackish belly band. Tail *white,* with *broad black band or bands* toward tip. White flash on upperwing. Legs feathered, feet small. Dark morph may lack extensive white on tail, but broad terminal band and extensive white on underwing are good field marks. **VOICE:** High-pitched squeal, mostly near nest site. **SIMILAR SPECIES:** Red-tailed Hawk, Northern Harrier, dark-morph Ferruginous Hawk. **HABITAT:** Nests on tundra escarpments, Arctic coasts; in winter, open fields, plains, marshes.

RED-SHOULDERED HAWK
Uncommon to fairly common M120

Buteo lineatus (see also p. 110)

16–20 in. (40–50 cm). In flight, note *translucent "window"* across primaries, longish tail. *Adult:* Black-and-white bands on wings and tail; *rufous shoulders,* wing linings, and underparts. *Immature:* Streaked below; recognized by proportions, and, in flight, wing "windows." Florida birds paler. **VOICE:** Two-syllable scream, *kee-yer* (dropping inflection), repeated in series. **SIMILAR SPECIES:** Broad-winged Hawk has paler wing linings, more pointed wing, broader bands on tail, lacks wing "windows." See also Cooper's and Red-tailed hawks. **HABITAT:** Damp woodlands, riparian areas, swamps.

BROAD-WINGED HAWK
Fairly common M121

Buteo platypterus (see also pp. 110 and 112)

15–16 in. (38–41 cm). A small, chunky, crow-sized buteo. Often seen migrating in "kettles." *Adult:* Note tail banding: high overhead shows one obvious white band (Red-shouldered shows multiple bands). Underwings whitish, trimmed with black. *Immature:* Streaked along sides of breast and belly; chest often unmarked. Tail has several narrow dark bands; terminal band wider. Rare dark morph (mostly in West) has dark body and wing linings but shows usual Broad-winged tail pattern. **VOICE:** Shrill *pwe-eeeeee.* **SIMILAR SPECIES:** Young Red-shouldered Hawk similar to immature Broad-winged but has streaking heaviest on breast, barred secondaries, blunter wingtips with bold pale "window." Missing flight feathers on molting Broad-wingeds in spring may appear like Red-shouldered's pale wing crescents. See also accipiters. **HABITAT:** Woods, groves.

SHORT-TAILED HAWK
Uncommon, local M123

Buteo brachyurus (see also p. 112)

15–16 in. (38–41 cm). A crow-sized buteo. Two morphs: (1) blackish brown body and black wing linings; (2) blackish above, white below, *two-toned* underwing. No other FL buteo is blackish or clear white below. **VOICE:** Descending, high-pitched scream: *kleeear!* **SIMILAR SPECIES:** Broad-winged Hawk in flight shows slimmer wings, whiter flight feathers below. Often perches in open, unlike Short-tailed. See Swainson's Hawk. **HABITAT:** Woodlands, cypress swamps, mangroves; often soars with vultures.

dark morph

light morph

ROUGH-LEGGED HAWK

juvenile

adult

pale FL form

Eastern

RED-SHOULDERED HAWK

adult

juvenile

adult

juvenile

BROAD-WINGED HAWK

light-morph juvenile

dark-morph adult

light-morph adult

light-morph adult

dark-morph adult

SHORT-TAILED HAWK

RED-TAILED HAWK
Common M127

Buteo jamaicensis (see also pp. 110 and 112)

19–22 in. (48–56 cm). The common hawk of roadsides and woodland edges. Soaring adults show *rufous* on topside of tail, pale pinkish below. Also note mottled *white patches* on scapulars. Overhead, a dependable mark on all but blackish birds is *dark patagial bar* on fore edge of wing. Immatures have brownish tail with narrow, dark banding. Underparts of typical Red-taileds are "zoned" (light breast, dark *belly band*). Some birds lack belly band. Dark and rufous morphs occur mostly in West and are scarce in our area. **VOICE:** Asthmatic squeal, *keeer-r-r* (slurring downward). **SIMILAR SPECIES:** Other buteos. **HABITAT:** Open country, woodlands, prairie groves, roadsides.

"HARLAN'S" RED-TAILED HAWK
Uncommon

Buteo jamaicensis harlani (see also p. 112)

A variable, usually blackish subspecies of Red-tailed. Note tail pattern: usually *dirty white with mottling and freckling* of gray, black, sometimes red, merging into dark subterminal band. Rare light morph has similar tail pattern, but body whitish below, dark above. **RANGE:** Breeds from cen. AK to nw. Canada. Winters primarily from Pacific Northwest diagonally to TX and lower Mississippi Valley.

"KRIDER'S" RED-TAILED HAWK
Uncommon

Buteo jamaicensis krideri

A pale prairie morph of Red-tailed, with whitish tail that may be tinged with pale rufous. **RANGE:** Prairies and plains of Canada and n. cen. U.S. Winters south through plains to TX, LA.

SWAINSON'S HAWK
Fairly common M124

Buteo swainsoni (see also pp. 110 and 112)

19–21 in. (48–53 cm). A buteo of the plains. Slimmer than Red-tailed Hawk, with narrower, more pointed wings. When gliding, holds wings slightly above horizontal. When perched, *wingtips extend to tail tip.* In light and intermediate morphs, overhead, *pale wing linings contrast with dark flight feathers.* *Adult:* Typical adults have dark breastband; dark and rufous morph birds best identified by shape and shaded flight feathers. *Immature:* Variably streaked below; best identified by shape and wing pattern. Many subadults are distinctly pale-headed. **VOICE:** Shrill, plaintive whistle, *kreeeeeeer.* **SIMILAR SPECIES:** Swainson's wing shape distinctive for a buteo. Lacks white scapular patches of bulkier Red-tailed. In TX, see White-tailed Hawk. **HABITAT:** Plains, grasslands, agricultural land, open hills, sparse trees.

FERRUGINOUS HAWK
Scarce M128

Buteo regalis (see also pp. 108 and 112)

23–24 in. (58–61 cm). A large buteo of plains. Note large bill, long gape line, *long tapered wings* with *pale panel* on upper side, *whitish tail.* *Adult:* Rufous above, whitish head and breast, rufous wash on tail, rufous thighs. Dark morphs rufous brown with whitish flight feathers, whitish tail. *Immatures:* Lack rufous tones. **SIMILAR SPECIES:** Red-tailed and Rough-legged hawks. **HABITAT:** Plains, grasslands, agricultural fields.

rufous adult

dark adult

Eastern juvenile

BUTEOS

RED-TAILED HAWK

Eastern adult

"KRIDER'S" juvenile

"Harlan's" adult

"HARLAN'S" adult

juvenile

light morph adult

dark morph

SWAINSON'S HAWK

adult light morph

light morph

adult light morph

dark morph

FERRUGINOUS HAWK

FALCONS Family Falconidae

Falcons are streamlined birds of prey with pointed wings, longish tail. **FOOD:** Birds, rodents, insects. **RANGE:** Almost worldwide. See also Caracaras, p. 88.

GYRFALCON *Falco rusticolus* (see also p. 106)   Scarce M134
20–25 in. (51–64 cm). A very large Arctic falcon, more robust than Peregrine. On perched birds, wingtips do not reach near tail tip. Thinner mustache. There are brown, gray, and white color morphs. **VOICE:** Harsh *kak-kak-kak* series. **SIMILAR SPECIES:** Peregrine and Prairie falcons. **HABITAT:** Arctic barrens, seacoasts, open mountains; in winter, open country.

PRAIRIE FALCON *Falco mexicanus* (see also p. 106)   Scarce M136
16–19 in. (41–50 cm). Like a sandy-colored Peregrine, with *white eyebrow, narrower mustache, blackish patches* in axillars ("wingpits"). **VOICE:** Harsh *kak-kak-kak* around nest. **HABITAT:** Open country, from alpine tundra to grasslands, agricultural land.

PEREGRINE FALCON   Uncommon M135
Falco peregrinus (see also p. 106)
16–20 in. (41–51 cm). Formerly endangered; reintroduced in many regions. Size and strong face pattern indicate this species. *Adult:* Slaty-backed, light-chested, barred and spotted below. *Immature:* Brown, heavily streaked below. **VOICE:** A rapid *kek kek kek kek*. **SIMILAR SPECIES:** Merlin, Gyrfalcon. **HABITAT:** Nests on cliffs and ledges; open country, from mountains to coasts. Established as a reintroduced breeder (on building ledges and bridges) in many major cities in East and Midwest.

APLOMADO FALCON *Falco femoralis* (see also p. 106)   Rare, local
15–16½ in. (38–42 cm). Slightly smaller than Peregrine. *Long wings and tail.* Note *dark underwing* and *belly,* contrasting with pale breast. **RANGE:** Formerly a very rare visitor from Mex., but population in U.S. growing because of reintroduction program. **HABITAT:** Arid brush and grasslands, yucca flats, coastal prairie.

AMERICAN KESTREL   Fairly common M132
Falco sparverius (see also p. 106)
9½–10½ in. (24–27 cm). A falcon the size of a large jay. No other *small* hawk has *rufous back or tail.* Note double mustache. *Hovers* for prey on rapidly beating wings. **VOICE:** Rapid, high *klee klee klee.* **SIMILAR SPECIES:** Merlin rarely perches on wires, does not hover. **HABITAT:** Open country, farmland, dead trees, wires, roadsides.

MERLIN *Falco columbarius* (see also p. 106)   Uncommon M133
11–12 in. (28–31 cm). Slightly larger than Kestrel. Note dark coloration, weak face pattern, banded tail. Faster and steadier in flight than Kestrel. Prairie subspecies *(richardsoni)* paler than widespread taiga form. **VOICE:** High, rapid *kee-kee-kee-kee.* **HABITAT:** Open woods, grasslands, tundra; in migration and winter, also open country, marshes, beaches, locally in neighborhoods.

FALCONS

gray morph

gray morph

brown morph

GYRFALCON

white morph

brown morph

PRAIRIE FALCON

juvenile

PEREGRINE FALCON

Tundra adult

adults

♂

adult

APLOMADO FALCON

♀

AMERICAN KESTREL

♂

♀

♂

♀

♂

♂

Prairie

Taiga

MERLIN

105

Accipiters (bird hawks) have short rounded wings and a long tail. They fly with several rapid beats and a short glide. They are better adapted to hunting in the woodlands than most other hawks. Females are larger than males. Immatures (not shown) have a streaked breast. Frequently soar.

COOPER'S HAWK *Accipiter cooperii*   p. 96
Underparts rusty (adult). Tail rounded and tipped with broad white terminal band. Note head and neck projecting noticeably beyond leading edge of wing.

NORTHERN GOSHAWK *Accipiter gentilis*   p. 96
Adult with bold facial pattern, underbody heavily barred with pale gray. Tail and wings broad.

SHARP-SHINNED HAWK *Accipiter striatus*   p. 96
Small. When folded, tail square or notched, with narrow pale tip. Fanned tail slightly rounded. Note small head and short neck barely projecting beyond wing.

Falcons have long, pointed wings and a relatively long tail. Wing strokes are typically rapid and continuous. Frequently soar.

PEREGRINE FALCON *Falco peregrinus*   p. 104
Falcon shape; large; bold face pattern; longer wings than Merlin or Kestrel.

AMERICAN KESTREL *Falco sparverius*   p. 104
Small; banded rufous tail. Paler underwing and less heavily marked underparts than Merlin.

MERLIN *Falco columbarius*   p. 104
Small; heavily marked underparts and dark underwing; heavily banded tail.

GYRFALCON *Falco rusticolus*   p. 104
Larger than Peregrine Falcon, without that bird's contrasting facial pattern, and with broader wings and tail. Varies in color from brown to gray to white.

APLOMADO FALCON *Falco femoralis*   p. 104
Black belly band or vest, light chest, orange undertail. Tail barred with black. Very long wings and tail.

PRAIRIE FALCON *Falco mexicanus*   p. 104
Size of Peregrine Falcon. *Dark axillars* ("wingpits") and inner coverts.

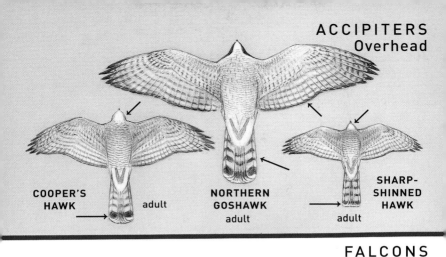

ACCIPITERS
Overhead

COOPER'S HAWK adult

NORTHERN GOSHAWK adult

SHARP-SHINNED HAWK adult

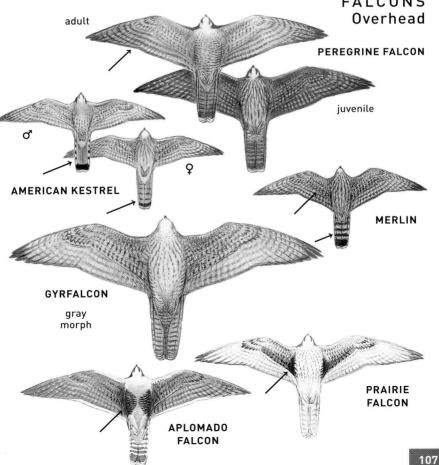

FALCONS
Overhead

adult

PEREGRINE FALCON

juvenile

♂

♀

AMERICAN KESTREL

MERLIN

GYRFALCON

gray morph

APLOMADO FALCON

PRAIRIE FALCON

107

FERRUGINOUS HAWK *Buteo regalis*   **p. 102**
Whitish underparts, with dark V formed by reddish thighs in adult. Wings and tail long for a buteo. A bird of western plains, barely enters western edge of our area.

GRAY HAWK *Buteo nitidus*   **p. 98**
Stocky. Broadly banded tail (suggestive of Broad-winged Hawk); adults have gray-barred underparts. Uncommon resident of Rio Grande Valley.

WHITE-TAILED HAWK *Buteo albicaudatus*   **p. 98**
Adult: Whitish underparts, gray head. White tail with black band near tip. Soars with marked dihedral. Resident of coastal prairie of TX.

NORTHERN HARRIER *Circus cyaneus*   **p. 96**
Male: Whitish wings with black tips and dark trailing edge. Gray hood.
Female: Brown, heavily streaked; note long, slim wings and tail.
Immature (not shown): Warm brown, unstreaked body, dark head. From above, all plumages have white rump.

WHITE-TAILED KITE *Elanus leucurus*   **p. 94**
Adult: Falcon-shaped. White body; whitish tail; dark underside to primaries.

MISSISSIPPI KITE *Ictinia mississippiensis*   **p. 94**
Falcon-shaped. *Adult:* Pale gray head, black tail, dark gray and blackish wings, gray body.
Immature: Streaked breast; banded square-tipped or notched tail.

Kites (except Snail Kite and Hook-billed Kite) are falcon-shaped but, unlike falcons, are buoyant gliders, not power fliers. All are southern.

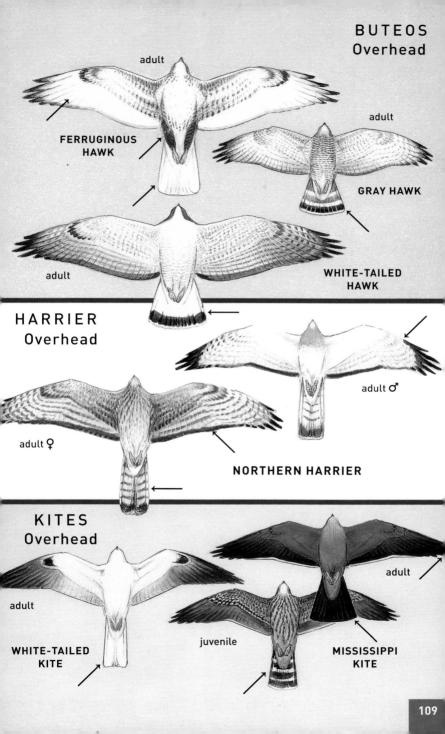

BUTEOS
Overhead

adult

FERRUGINOUS HAWK

adult

GRAY HAWK

adult

WHITE-TAILED HAWK

HARRIER
Overhead

adult ♂

adult ♀

NORTHERN HARRIER

KITES
Overhead

adult

adult

juvenile

WHITE-TAILED KITE

MISSISSIPPI KITE

RED-TAILED HAWK *Buteo jamaicensis*   p. 102
Dark patagial bar at fore edge of wing is best mark from below. *Adult:*
Light chest, streaked belly (often forming belly band); tail plain, with
hint of red and little or no banding.
Immature: Streaked below, has light tail banding.

SWAINSON'S HAWK *Buteo swainsoni*   p. 102
Adult: Dark breast-band. Long, pointed, two-toned wings.
Immature: Similar, but has streaks on underbody.

RED-SHOULDERED HAWK *Buteo lineatus*   p. 100
Adult: Tail strongly banded (white bands narrower than dark ones).
Strongly barred with rusty coloring on body and underwing coverts.
Immature: Chest and belly heavily streaked. Both immature and adult
show light crescent "window" on outer wings, longish tail.

BROAD-WINGED HAWK *Buteo platypterus*   p. 100
Smaller and chunkier than Red-shouldered with shorter tail, more
pointed wings. *Adult:* Widely banded tail (white bands wider); underwing pale with dark rear margin and tip.
Immature: Body usually streaked, tail narrowly banded. Pale underwings may show lighter "window" near wingtips when molting in first
spring.

ROUGH-LEGGED HAWK *Buteo lagopus*   p. 100
Note black carpal patch contrasting with white flight feathers. Broad,
blackish band ("cummerbund") across belly is distinctive in female
and immature. Tail light, with broad, dark subterminal band. Adult
male darker chested, has multiple bands on tail, less bold belly
patch.

Buteos are chunky, with broad wings and a broad, rounded tail.
They soar and wheel high in the air.

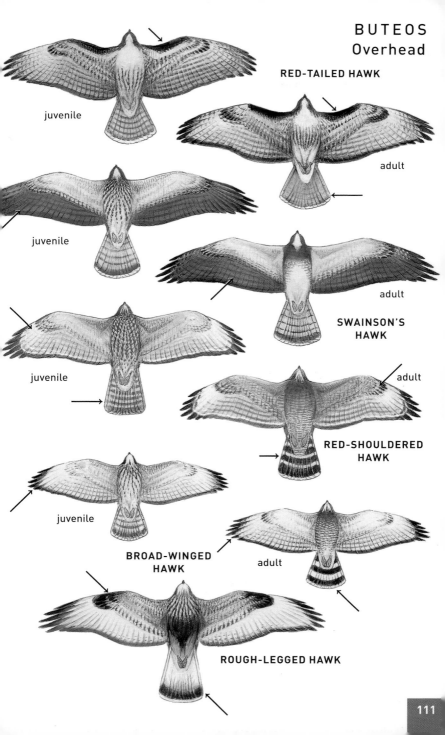

BUTEOS
Overhead

RED-TAILED HAWK

juvenile

adult

juvenile

adult

SWAINSON'S HAWK

juvenile

RED-SHOULDERED HAWK

adult

juvenile

BROAD-WINGED HAWK

adult

ROUGH-LEGGED HAWK

Dark Birds of Prey Overhead

CRESTED CARACARA *Caracara cheriway* **p. 88**
Whitish chest, black belly, large *pale patches* in primaries, white tail with black band. Elongated neck, stiff-winged flight. TX, FL only.

ROUGH-LEGGED HAWK *Buteo lagopus* (dark morph) **p. 100**
Dark body and wing linings; *whitish flight feathers;* tail light from below, with one broad, *black terminal band* in female; additional bands in male.

FERRUGINOUS HAWK *Buteo regalis* (dark morph) **p. 102**
Similar to dark-morph Rough-legged Hawk, but tail whitish, without dark banding. Note also white wrist marks, or "commas." A bird of the plains; barely enters western edge of our area.

SWAINSON'S HAWK *Buteo swainsoni* (dark morph) **p. 102**
In dark morph, fairly pointed wings are usually dark throughout, *including flight feathers;* tail narrowly banded, whitish undertail coverts. Rufous morph may be rustier, with lighter rufous wing linings.

RED-TAILED HAWK *Buteo jamaicensis* (dark morph) **p. 102**
Typical chunky shape of Red-tailed; tail reddish above, pale tinged with rusty below; variable. Dark patagial bar on leading edge of wing obscured.

"HARLAN'S" RED-TAILED HAWK **p. 102**
Buteo jamaicensis harlani (dark morph)
Similar to dark-morph Red-tailed Hawk. Breast mottled white; tail tends to be mottled with gray and whitish and with dusky subterminal band, lacks obvious red; primary tips barred dark and light. Western plains in winter.

BROAD-WINGED HAWK *Buteo platypterus* (dark morph) **p. 100**
Typical size and shape of Broad-winged. Tail pattern and flight feathers as in light morph, but body and wing linings dark. Note whiter flight feathers than Short-tailed.

ZONE-TAILED HAWK *Buteo albonotatus* (immature) **p. 98**
Slim and longish, *two-toned wings* (suggesting Turkey Vulture) with barred flight feathers. Several white bands on slim tail (only one visible on folded tail). Yellow legs. In our area, only seen in TX.

SHORT-TAILED HAWK *Buteo brachyurus* (dark morph) **p. 100**
Jet-black body and wing linings. Lightly banded tail; flight feathers more shaded than in dark Broad-wing. FL only.

HARRIS'S HAWK *Parabuteo unicinctus* **p. 98**
Chocolate brown body, chestnut wing linings. Very broad white band at base of black tail, narrow white terminal band. TX only.

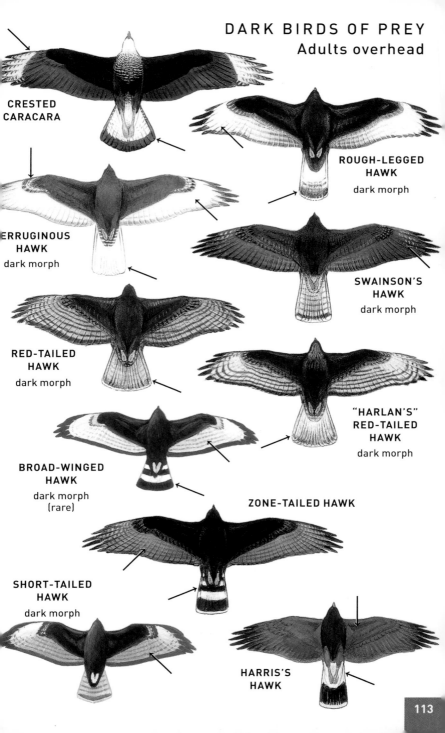

DARK BIRDS OF PREY
Adults overhead

CRESTED CARACARA

ROUGH-LEGGED HAWK
dark morph

FERRUGINOUS HAWK
dark morph

SWAINSON'S HAWK
dark morph

RED-TAILED HAWK
dark morph

"HARLAN'S" RED-TAILED HAWK
dark morph

BROAD-WINGED HAWK
dark morph
(rare)

ZONE-TAILED HAWK

SHORT-TAILED HAWK
dark morph

HARRIS'S HAWK

113

Eagles, Osprey, and Vultures Overhead

BALD EAGLE *Haliaeetus leucocephalus*   p. 92
Adult: White head and tail.
Immature: Some white in wing linings, often on body.

GOLDEN EAGLE *Aquila chrysaetos*   p. 92
Adult: Almost uniformly dark; wing linings dark.
Immature: White patch at base of primaries and tail; no white on body.

OSPREY *Pandion haliaetus*   p. 92
White body and coverts; black wrist patch; crooked wing.

TURKEY VULTURE *Cathartes aura*   p. 88
Mostly brownish black. Two-toned wings held in distinct dihedral. Small head, red in adult, gray in immature. Longish tail. Tips and teeters in flight.

BLACK VULTURE *Coragyps atratus*   p. 88
Blackish overall. Silver wing patch. Wings held flat or in very slight dihedral. Rapid, shallow wingbeats. Stubby tail. Gray head.

Where the Bald Eagle, Turkey Vulture, and Osprey all are found, they can be separated at a great distance by their manner of soaring: the Bald Eagle with flat wings; the Turkey Vulture with a dihedral; the Osprey often with a gull-like kink or crook in its wings.

Turkey Vulture (p. 88)

Black Vulture (p. 88)

EAGLES, OSPREY,
AND VULTURES
Overhead

BALD EAGLE
adult

Bald Eagle
juvenile

GOLDEN EAGLE
adult

Golden Eagle
juvenile

OSPREY
adult

115

Coots, Gallinules, and Rails
Family Rallidae

Rails are rather hen-shaped marsh birds, many of secretive habits and mysterious voices, more often heard than seen. Flight is brief and reluctant, with legs dangling. Gallinules and coots are much easier to see; they swim and might be confused with small ducks except for smaller head, forehead shield, and chickenlike bill. They spend most of their time swimming but may also feed on shores. Often vocal, giving loud squawks, grunts, and peeps. **FOOD:** Aquatic plants, seeds, insects, frogs, crustaceans, mollusks. **RANGE:** Nearly worldwide.

AMERICAN COOT *Fulica americana*   Uncommon to common M145
15–15½ in. (38–39 cm). A slaty, ducklike bird with blackish head and neck, slate gray body, *white bill*, and divided white patch under tail. No side striping. Its big feet are lobed ("scallops" on toes). Gregarious. When swimming, pumps head back and forth; dabbles but also dives from surface. Taking off, it skitters, flight labored, big feet trailing beyond short tail, narrow white border showing along rear of wings. Aberrant birds may show some additional white or yellowish on forehead above bill. *Immature:* Slightly paler, with duller bill. Downy young has hairy, *orange-red* head and shoulders. **VOICE:** Grating *kuk-kuk-kuk-kuk; kakakakakaka;* etc.; also a measured *ka-ha, ha-ha;* various cackles, croaks. **SIMILAR SPECIES:** Common Moorhen slightly smaller, browner above, has thin white band on flanks, different-colored bill. Coots flock more on open water and land. **HABITAT:** Ponds, lakes, marshes; in winter, also fields, park ponds, lawns, salt bays.

COMMON MOORHEN *Gallinula chloropus*   Uncommon M144
14 in. (36 cm). Note adult's rather chickenlike *red bill with yellow tip, red forehead shield,* and white band on flanks. When walking, flicks white undertail coverts; while swimming, pumps head like a coot. *Immature:* Duller bill. **VOICE:** Croaking *kr-r-ruk,* repeated; a froglike *kup;* also *kek, kek, kek* (higher than coot's call); loud, complaining, henlike notes. **SIMILAR SPECIES:** American Coot, immature Purple Gallinule. **HABITAT:** Freshwater marshes, reedy ponds.

PURPLE GALLINULE *Porphyrio martinica*   Uncommon M143
13 in. (33 cm). Very colorful; swims, wades, and climbs bushes. *Adult:* Head and underparts *deep violet-purple,* back bronzy green. Shield on forehead *pale blue;* bill red with yellow tip. Legs *yellow,* conspicuous in flight. *Immature:* Buffy brown below, dark above tinged greenish; bill dark; sides unstriped. **VOICE:** Henlike cackling, *kek, kek, kek;* also guttural notes, sharp reedy cries. **SIMILAR SPECIES:** Common Moorhen has *red* frontal shield, lacks greenish plumage, has duller legs and white side stripe; young moorhen also has whitish side stripe. Young American Coot much darker overall, has pale bill. Purple Swamphen (*Porphyrio porphyrio,* not illustrated), introduced from Eurasia and becoming established in s. FL, is much larger and has red legs and a huge all-red bill and frontal shield. **HABITAT:** Freshwater swamps, marshes, ponds.

COOTS AND GALLINULES

coots skitter on takeoff

lobed foot of coot

juvenile

adult

adult

coot chick

AMERICAN COOT

moorhen
chick

juvenile

adult

COMMON MOORHEN

juvenile

adult

**PURPLE
GALLINULE**

117

VIRGINIA RAIL *Rallus limicola*   Fairly common M141

9½ in. (24 cm). A small rusty rail with gray cheeks, black bars on flanks, and long, slightly decurved, reddish bill with dark tip. Only small rail with *long slender* bill. Juvenile in late summer shows much black. **VOICE:** Descending grunt, *wuk-wuk-wuk-wuk*, etc.; also *kidick, kidick,* etc.; various "kicking" and grunting sounds. **SIMILAR SPECIES:** Sora has small stubby bill, unbarred undertail coverts. Clapper and King rails much larger. **HABITAT:** Fresh and brackish marshes; in winter, also salt marshes.

KING RAIL *Rallus elegans*   Uncommon, secretive M140

15 in. (38 cm). A large rusty rail with long slender bill; twice the size of Virginia Rail, or about that of a small chicken. Similar to Clapper Rail, but note rusty/chestnut cheeks and black-and-white flanks, more rusty overall with *bolder back pattern* (blacker feathers with buffier edges); prefers fresh marshes. **VOICE:** Low, slow, grunting *bup-bup, bup-bup-bup,* etc., or evenly spaced *chuck-chuck-chuck* (deeper than Virginia Rail). **SIMILAR SPECIES:** Clapper Rail. Virginia Rail half the size, has slaty gray cheeks. *Note:* Hybrids between Clapper and King occur. **HABITAT:** Fresh and brackish marshes, rice fields, ditches, swamps. In winter, also salt marshes.

CLAPPER RAIL *Rallus longirostris*   Fairly common M139

14½ in. (37 cm). The large "marsh hen" of coastal marshes. Sometimes swims. Note henlike appearance; strong legs; long, slightly decurved bill; barred flanks; and white patch under short cocked tail, which it flicks nervously. Cheeks gray. Gulf Coast birds have rusty orange underparts. **VOICE:** Clattering *kek-kek-kek-kek,* etc., or *cha-cha-cha,* etc. **SIMILAR SPECIES:** King Rail prefers fresh (sometimes brackish) marshes, has bolder pattern on back and flanks, rusty brown on wings. Its breast is cinnamon, but Clappers along Gulf Coast show similar warm tawny tones. Clapper has grayer cheeks and wings, less boldly streaked upper back. Where these two rails occur in adjacent brackish marshes, they occasionally hybridize. **HABITAT:** Salt marshes, mangroves.

LONG-BILLED RAILS

juvenile

adult

VIRGINIA RAIL

KING RAIL

Atlantic
Coast

Gulf Coast

**CLAPPER
RAIL**

chick

Limpkin
(p. 82)
for comparison

SORA *Porzana carolina*   Fairly common M142
8½ in. (22 cm). Note *short yellow* bill. *Adult:* A small, plump, gray-brown rail with *black patch* on face and throat. Short, cocked tail reveals white or buff undertail coverts. *Immature:* Lacks dark throat patch and is browner. **VOICE:** Descending whinny, *whee-ee-ee-ee-ee-ee-e-e-e.* Also a plaintive whistled *keu-wee?* Clapping one's hands causes startled birds to utter a sharp *keek.* **SIMILAR SPECIES:** Immature may be confused with smaller and rarer Yellow Rail, which has large white wing patches and blacker-centered feathers above. Virginia Rail has slender bill. **HABITAT:** Freshwater marshes; in migration, also wet meadows; in winter, also salt marshes.

YELLOW RAIL *Coturnicops noveboracensis*   Scarce, secretive M137
7¼ in. (18 cm). Note *white wing patch* (in flight). A small buffy-and-black rail, suggesting a week-old chick. Bill very short, greenish or yellowish. Back dark, striped, barred, and checkered with buff, white, and black. *Mouselike; very difficult to see.* **VOICE:** Ticking notes, often in long series: *tic-tic, tic-tic-tic, tic-tic, tic-tic-tic,* etc., in alternating groups of two and three; compared to hitting two small stones together. Most vocal at night. **SIMILAR SPECIES:** Young Sora somewhat larger, buffier overall, lacks dark barring and checkering above, has thin pale trailing edge to wing. **HABITAT:** Grassy marshes, wet meadows; winters mostly in salt marshes and grain fields.

BLACK RAIL *Laterallus jamaicensis*   Scarce, local, secretive M138
6 in. (15 cm). A tiny blackish rail with small *black* bill; about the size of a young sparrow. Nape deep chestnut. *Very difficult to glimpse. Caution:* All young rails in downy plumage are black. **VOICE:** Male (mostly at night), *kiki-doo* or *kiki-krrr* (or *kitty go*). Also a growl. Most vocal at night. **HABITAT:** Salt marshes, freshwater marshes, grassy meadows.

JACANAS Family Jacanidae

Shorebird relatives that look like gallinules but walk like rails. Dark birds with very long toes perfect for walking over floating aquatic vegetation. Sexes alike. **FOOD:** Aquatic insects, seeds, and vegetation. **RANGE:** Pantropical.

NORTHERN JACANA *Jacana spinosa*   Vagrant
9½ in. (24 cm). This vagrant has spectacularly long toes for walking on lily pads. *Adult:* Chestnut body with dark head. Yellow bill and forehead frontal shield. Striking yellow primaries and secondaries in flight. Holds wings over head when it lands. *Immature:* Has white underparts, distinct line behind eye. **VOICE:** Rapid series of high, nasal notes: *jeek-jeek-jeek-jeek.* **RANGE:** Casual visitor from Mex. to TX. **HABITAT:** Frequents ponds with emergent vegetation, especially lily pads.

adult

immature

SORA

chick

immature

YELLOW RAIL

**NORTHERN
JACANA**

adult

BLACK RAIL

121

Shorebirds

Many shorebirds (or "waders," as they are called in the Old World) are real puzzlers to the novice, and to many experienced birders as well! There are 8 plovers in our area, and about 30 sandpipers and their allies. Most species have two or three different plumages: breeding adult, nonbreeding adult, and juvenal. Being able to properly age many species is an important part of correctly identifying them. Noting size, shape, and feeding style is also a critical part of the identification process.

Plovers are usually more compact and thicker necked than most sandpipers, with a pigeonlike bill and larger eyes. They run in short starts and stops.

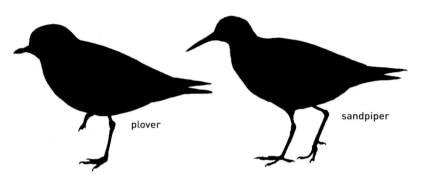

plover

sandpiper

Bill Shapes of Shorebirds

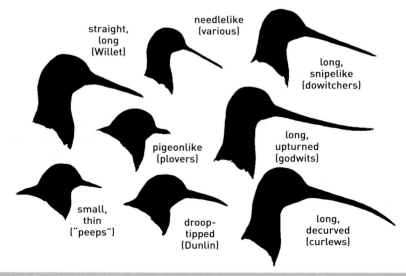

straight, long (Willet)

needlelike (various)

long, snipelike (dowitchers)

pigeonlike (plovers)

long, upturned (godwits)

small, thin ("peeps")

droop-tipped (Dunlin)

long, decurved (curlews)

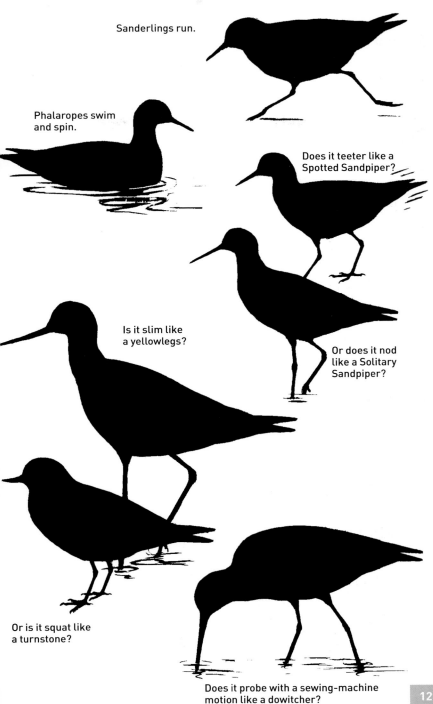

Sanderlings run.

Phalaropes swim and spin.

Does it teeter like a Spotted Sandpiper?

Is it slim like a yellowlegs?

Or does it nod like a Solitary Sandpiper?

Or is it squat like a turnstone?

Does it probe with a sewing-machine motion like a dowitcher?

123

PLOVERS Family Charadriidae

Wading birds, more compactly built and thicker necked than most sandpipers, with shorter, pigeonlike bill and larger eyes. Call notes assist identification. Unlike most sandpipers, plovers run in short starts and stops. Sexes alike or differ slightly. FOOD: Small marine life, insects, some vegetable matter. RANGE: Nearly worldwide.

BLACK-BELLIED PLOVER
Common M149

Pluvialis squatarola (see also p. 146)

11½ in. (29 cm). A large plover. *Breeding adult:* Have *black face and breast (slightly duller in female)* and pale speckled back. *Nonbreeding adult and immature:* Look tan-gray but can be recognized as plovers by stocky shape, hunched posture, and short, pigeonlike bill. In flight, in any plumage, note *black wingpits* and white rump and tail. VOICE: Plaintive slurred whistle, *tlee-oo-eee* or *whee-er-ee* (middle note lower). SIMILAR SPECIES: American Golden-Plover slightly smaller and slimmer, smaller billed, buffier or more golden on at least some feathering, has more distinct supercilium, and *lacks pattern of white in wings and tail.* Its wingpits are *gray,* not black. HABITAT: Mudflats, marshes, beaches, rocks, short-grass habitats; in summer, tundra.

AMERICAN GOLDEN-PLOVER
Uncommon M150

Pluvialis dominica (see also p. 146)

10¼–10½ in. (26–27 cm). Size of Killdeer. Shows distinct wingtip extension of three to five primary tips, well beyond tail tip. *Breeding adult:* Dark, spangled above with *whitish and pale yellow spots;* underparts black (slightly mottled in female). *Broad white stripe* runs over eye and down sides of neck and breast. *Nonbreeding adult and juvenile:* Gray-brown, darker above than below, with distinct pale supercilium, dark crown. VOICE: Whistled *queedle* or *que-e-a* (dropping at end). SIMILAR SPECIES: Black-bellied Plover. HABITAT: Prairies, mudflats, shores, short-grass pastures, sod farms; in summer, tundra.

MOUNTAIN PLOVER *Charadrius montanus*
Scarce, local M156

9 in. (23 cm). White forehead and line over eye, contrasting with dark crown. In nonbreeding plumage, may be told from nonbreeding American Golden-Plover by tan-brown back devoid of mottling and by tan, unmarked breast. Has drab legs, light wing stripe, and dark tail band. VOICE: Low whistle, variable. SIMILAR SPECIES: Killdeer, Black-bellied Plover, golden-plovers, Buff-breasted Sandpiper. HABITAT: Plowed fields, short-grass plains, dry sod farms.

PLOVERS

nonbreeding

onbreeding

breeding

juvenile

BLACK-BELLIED PLOVER

nonbreeding

breeding

nonbreeding

AMERICAN GOLDEN-PLOVER

MOUNTAIN PLOVER

nonbreeding

COMMON RINGED PLOVER *Charadrius hiaticula* — Rare, local

7½ in. (19 cm). Eurasian species, very similar to Semipalmated Plover; best distinguished by *voice.* Slightly longer bill, darker cheeks. Lacks obvious orbital ring. **VOICE:** Softer, more minor *poo-eep.* **RANGE:** Breeds in e. Canadian Arctic; winters in Old World. Casual or accidental migrant elsewhere in e. N. America.

SEMIPALMATED PLOVER — Common M153
Charadrius semipalmatus (see also p. 146)

7¼ in. (18 cm). A small, plump, brown-backed plover, half the size of Killdeer, with *single dark breast-band. Adult:* Bill orangey with black tip or (nonbreeding) nearly all dark. Orangey orbital ring. Legs bright orange or yellow. *Juvenile:* Slightly browner above, and breast-band may be incomplete. **VOICE:** Plaintive, upward-slurred *chi-we.* **SIMILAR SPECIES:** Piping and Snowy plovers. **HABITAT:** Shores, tidal flats, wet fields; in summer, tundra.

PIPING PLOVER — Uncommon M154
Charadrius melodus (see also p. 146)

7¼ in. (18 cm). As pallid as a beach flea or sand crab — color of dry sand. Complete or incomplete dark ring around neck. Legs orange. *Breeding adult:* Bill has yellow-orange base, black tip. *Nonbreeding adult and juvenile:* Black on collar lacking, bill all dark. Note tail pattern. Adults perform stiff-winged "bat-flight" on breeding territory. **VOICE:** Plaintive whistle: *peep-lo* (first note higher). **SIMILAR SPECIES:** Snowy and Semipalmated plovers. **HABITAT:** Sandy beaches, dry mudflats; in summer, also lakeshores and river islands.

SNOWY PLOVER — Uncommon M151
Charadrius alexandrinus (see also p. 146)

6¼–6½ in. (16–17 cm). A pale plover of beaches and alkaline flats. *Male:* Has *slim black bill, grayish legs,* and *dark ear patch. Female and juvenile:* May lack black in plumage. **VOICE:** Musical whistle, *pe-wee-ah* or *o-wee-ah;* also a low *prit.* **SIMILAR SPECIES:** Juvenile and nonbreeding Piping Plovers may also have dark (though thicker) bill, but they have *white on rump,* visible in flight, and orange legs. **HABITAT:** Beaches, sandy flats, alkaline lakeshores.

WILSON'S PLOVER — Uncommon M152
Charadrius wilsonia (see also p. 146)

7¾–8 in. (19–20 cm). A "ringed" plover, larger than Semipalmated Plover, with *wider breast-band* and longer, *heavier black bill.* Legs pinkish gray. **VOICE:** Emphatic whistled *whit!* or *wheet!* **HABITAT:** Open beaches, tidal flats, sandy islands.

KILLDEER *Charadrius vociferus* (see also p. 146) — Common M155

10½ in. (27 cm). The common, noisy plover of farm country and playing fields. Note *two black breast-bands* (chick has only one band and might be confused with Wilson's Plover). In flight or distraction display near nest, shows *rusty orange rump,* longish tail. **VOICE:** Noisy, and often heard at night. Loud, insistent *kill-deeah,* repeated; plaintive *dee-ee* (rising). **SIMILAR SPECIES:** Other banded plovers have single breast-band. **HABITAT:** Fields, airports, lawns, mudflats, shores.

BANDED PLOVERS

breeding

COMMON RINGED PLOVER

nonbreeding

breeding

SEMIPALMATED PLOVER

nonbreeding

♂

SNOWY PLOVER

breeding

non-breeding

PIPING PLOVER

♀

breeding

♂

WILSON'S PLOVER

KILLDEER

chick

Common Ringed

Piping

Snowy

Killdeer

Wilson's

Semipalmated

127

OYSTERCATCHERS Family Haematopodidae

Large waders with long, laterally flattened, chisel-tipped, red bill. Sexes alike. **FOOD:** Mollusks, crabs, marine worms. **RANGE:** Widespread on coasts of world; inland in some areas of Europe and Asia.

AMERICAN OYSTERCATCHER　　　　　Fairly common M157
Haematopus palliatus
17½–18½ in. (44–47 cm). A very noisy, thickset, black-headed shore-bird with dark back, white belly, and large white wing and tail patches. Outstanding feature is large straight red bill, flattened laterally. Legs pale pink. *Immature:* Bill dark-tipped. **VOICE:** Piercing *wheep!* or *kleep!;* a loud *pic, pic, pic.* **SIMILAR SPECIES:** Black Skimmer. **HABITAT:** Coastal beaches, tidal flats.

STILTS AND AVOCETS Family Recurvirostridae

Slim waders with very long legs and very slender bill (bent upward in avocets). Sexes fairly similar. **FOOD:** Insects, crustaceans, other aquatic life. **RANGE:** N., Cen., and S. America, Africa, s. Eurasia, Australia, Pacific region.

BLACK-NECKED STILT　　　　　Fairly common M158
Himantopus mexicanus
14 in. (36 cm). A large, extremely slim wader; black above (female and immature tinged brown), white below. Note *extremely long pinkish red legs,* needlelike bill. In flight, black *unpatterned* wings contrast strikingly with white rump, tail, and underparts. **VOICE:** Sharp yipping: *kyip, kyip, kyip.* **SIMILAR SPECIES:** Nonbreeding American Avocet. **HABITAT:** Marshes, mudflats, pools, shallow lakes (fresh and alkaline), flooded fields.

AMERICAN AVOCET *Recurvirostra americana* Fairly common M159
18 in. (46 cm). A large, slim shorebird with very slender, *upturned bill,* more upturned in female. This and striking white-and-black pattern make this bird unique. In breeding plumage, head and neck pinkish tan or orangey buff; in nonbreeding plumage, this color replaced by pale gray. Avocets feed with scythelike sweep of head and bill. **VOICE:** Sharp *wheek* or *kleet,* excitedly repeated. **HABITAT:** Mudflats, shallow lakes, marshes, prairie ponds.

OYSTERCATCHER, STILT, AND AVOCET

AMERICAN OYSTERCATCHER

BLACK-NECKED STILT

breeding

breeding

nonbreeding

AMERICAN AVOCET

Sandpipers, Phalaropes, and Allies
Family Scolopacidae

Small to large shorebirds. Bills more slender than those of plovers. Sexes mostly similar, except in phalaropes. **FOOD:** Insects, crustaceans, mollusks, worms, etc. **RANGE:** Cosmopolitan.

WILLET *Tringa semipalmata* (see also p. 148) **Fairly common M163**
15–16 in. (38–41 cm). Stockier than Greater Yellowlegs; has heavier bill, *blue-gray legs.* In flight, note *striking black-and-white wing pattern.* At rest, this large wader is rather nondescript. *Note:* Interior breeding population larger, has longer, thinner bill and is paler overall than coastal breeding population. **VOICE:** Musical, repetitious *pill-will-willet* (in breeding season); a loud *kree-ree-ree.* Also a rapidly repeated *kip-kip-kip,* etc. **SIMILAR SPECIES:** Greater Yellowlegs; see also dowitchers. **HABITAT:** Marshes, mudflats, beaches.

GREATER YELLOWLEGS **Common M162**
Tringa melanoleuca (see also p. 150)
14 in. (36 cm). Note *bright yellow legs,* long bill. Slim and gray, speckled above. Often teeters. In flight, appears *dark-winged* with *whitish rump and tail.* **VOICE:** Usually three-note whistle, *dear! dear! dear!* **SIMILAR SPECIES:** Lesser Yellowlegs, Willet. **HABITAT:** Marshes, mudflats, ponds, flooded fields; in summer, muskeg, spruce bogs.

LESSER YELLOWLEGS **Common M164**
Tringa flavipes (see also p. 150)
10½ in. (27 cm). Like Greater Yellowlegs, but smaller. Lesser's shorter, slimmer bill is *straight,* about *equal to length of head;* Greater's appears slightly uptilted, paler based, longer than bird's head. Readily separated by voice. **VOICE:** *Yew* or *yu-yu;* less forceful than Greater's call. **SIMILAR SPECIES:** Solitary and Stilt sandpipers, Wilson's Phalarope. **HABITAT:** Marshes, mudflats, ponds, flooded fields; in summer, open, moist boreal woods and taiga.

SOLITARY SANDPIPER **Uncommon M161**
Tringa solitaria (see also p. 150)
8½ in. (22 cm). Note *dark wings* and *white sides of tail.* A dark-backed sandpiper, whitish below, with *light eye-ring* and greenish legs. Nods like a yellowlegs. Usually alone. Seldom in groups. **VOICE:** *Peet!* or *peet-weet-weet!* (higher and more strident than Spotted Sandpiper's call). **SIMILAR SPECIES:** Lesser Yellowlegs has bright yellow legs, white rump, is paler overall. Spotted Sandpiper teeters tail (not head), has white wedge at breast-side, different wing and tail patterns. **HABITAT:** Streamsides, brushy ponds, rain pools.

STILT SANDPIPER *Calidris himantopus* **See p. 140**
Nonbreeding: Yellow-green legs, slightly drooped bill, white rump; bold eyebrow (supercilium).

WILSON'S PHALAROPE *Phalaropus tricolor* **See p. 144**
Nonbreeding: Straight needle bill, clear white underparts, pale gray back, dull yellow legs.

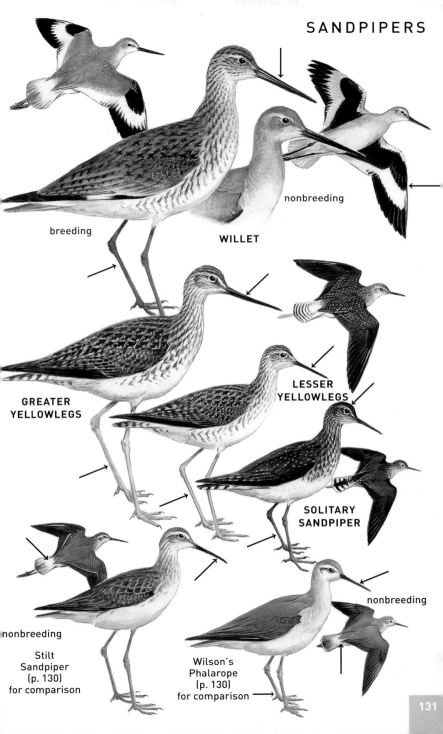

nonbreeding

breeding

WILLET

**GREATER
YELLOWLEGS**

**LESSER
YELLOWLEGS**

**SOLITARY
SANDPIPER**

nonbreeding

nonbreeding

Stilt
Sandpiper
(p. 130)
for comparison

Wilson's
Phalarope
(p. 130)
for comparison

HUDSONIAN GODWIT Scarce M168
Limosa haemastica (see also p. 148)
15–15½ in. (38–39 cm). Rather large size and long, *slightly upturned* bill mark this wader as a godwit; *blackish wing linings* proclaim it as this species. Black tail *ringed broadly with white. Breeding:* Male ruddy-breasted, female duller. *Nonbreeding:* Both sexes gray-backed, pale-breasted. **VOICE:** *Tawit!* (or *godwit!*); higher pitched than Marbled Godwit's call. **SIMILAR SPECIES:** Marbled Godwit. See also Bar-tailed and Black-tailed Godwits, vagrants from Eurasia. **HABITAT:** Mudflats, prairie pools; in summer, marshy taiga and tundra.

MARBLED GODWIT *Limosa fedoa* (see also p. 148) Uncommon M169
17½–18½ in. (44–46 cm). Rich, mottled *buff brown* color identifies this species. Underwing linings *cinnamon.* **VOICE:** Accented *kerwhit! (godwit!)*; also *raddica, raddica.* **SIMILAR SPECIES:** When head tucked in, may be difficult to tell from Long-billed Curlew except by leg color (blackish in godwit, blue-gray in curlew); Hudsonian Godwit has white on wings and tail, blackish wing linings. See also Bar-tailed Godwit, a vagrant from Eurasia. **HABITAT:** Prairies, pools, shores, mudflats, beaches.

LONG-BILLED CURLEW Uncommon to rare M167
Numenius americanus (see also p. 148)
22–24 in. (55–60 cm). Note *very long, sickle-shaped bill* (4–8½ in.; 10–21 cm). Larger than Whimbrel and more buffy overall; lacks distinct dark crown stripes. Overhead shows *cinnamon wing linings.* In young birds, bill may be scarcely longer than that of Whimbrel. **VOICE:** Loud *cur-lee* (rising inflection); rapid, whistled *kli-li-li-li.* "Song" a trilled, liquid *curleeeeeeeeuuu.* **SIMILAR SPECIES:** Whimbrel, Marbled Godwit. **HABITAT:** In summer, high plains, rangeland; in winter, cultivated land, mudflats, beaches, salt marshes.

WHIMBREL *Numenius phaeopus* (see also p. 148) Uncommon M166
17–18 in. (43–46 cm). A large gray-brown wader with long *decurved bill.* Much grayer brown than Long-billed Curlew; bill shorter (2¾–4 in.; 7–10 cm); crown *striped.* **VOICE:** Five to seven short, rapid whistles: *hee-hee-hee-hee-hee-hee.* **SIMILAR SPECIES:** Long-billed Curlew. **HABITAT:** Mudflats, beaches, marshes, pastures, short-grass habitats; in summer, tundra.

Basic Flight Patterns of Sandpipers

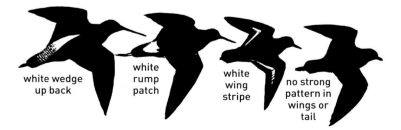

white wedge up back

white rump patch

white wing stripe

no strong pattern in wings or tail

LARGE SANDPIPERS

nonbreeding

breeding

nonbreeding

HUDSONIAN GODWIT

eeding ♂

MARBLED GODWIT

ONG-BILLED CURLEW

WHIMBREL

RUDDY TURNSTONE
Fairly common M170
Arenaria interpres (see also p. 146)
9½ in. (24 cm). A squat, robust, *orange-legged* shorebird, with *harlequin pattern. Breeding:* With russet back and curious face and breast pattern, bird is unique; in flight it is even more striking. *Nonbreeding and juvenile:* Duller, but retains enough of basic pattern to be recognized. **VOICE:** Staccato *tuk-a-tuk* or *kut-a-kut;* also *kewk.* **HABITAT:** Beaches, mudflats, rocky shores, jetties; in summer, tundra.

PURPLE SANDPIPER
Uncommon M179
Calidris maritima (see also p. 152)
9 in. (23 cm). Stocky, dark sandpipers on rocks, jetties, or breakwaters along our n. Atlantic Coast in winter are likely to be this hardy species. *Nonbreeding:* Slate gray with white belly, orange legs. At close range, note dull orangish base of bill, very faint purple sheen above. *Breeding:* Much browner, more heavily streaked above and below. **VOICE:** Low, scratchy *weet-wit* or *twit.* **SIMILAR SPECIES:** Nonbreeding Dunlin, also found roosting on jetties, is paler with black bill and legs. **HABITAT:** Wave-washed rocks, jetties, rarely sandy shoreline. Often quite tame. In summer, coastal tundra.

SANDERLING *Calidris alba* (see also p. 152)
Common M172
8 in. (20 cm). A plump, active sandpiper of outer beaches, where it chases retreating waves like a wind-up toy. Note bold *white wing stripe* in flight. *Breeding:* Bright rusty about head, back, and breast. *Nonbreeding:* The palest sandpiper; snowy white underparts, plain pale gray back, *black shoulders. Juvenile:* Differs from nonbreeding adults in having salt-and-pepper pattern on back and breast sides. **VOICE:** Short *kip* or *quit.* **SIMILAR SPECIES:** Western Sandpiper. **HABITAT:** Beaches, mudflats, lakeshores; when nesting, stony tundra.

DUNLIN *Calidris alpina* (see also p. 152)
Common M180
8½–8¾ in. (22–23 cm). Slightly larger than a peep or Sanderling, with *longish, droop-tipped bill.* Black legs. *Breeding: Rusty red above,* with *black patch on belly. Nonbreeding:* Unpatterned gray or gray-brown above, with *grayish wash across breast* (not clean white as in Sanderling or Western Sandpiper). *Juvenile* (this plumage rarely seen away from nesting areas): Rusty above, with buffy breast and suggestion of belly patch. **VOICE:** Nasal, rasping *cheezp* or *treezp.* **SIMILAR SPECIES:** Nonbreeding Sanderling and Western Sandpiper have clean white breast; Sanderling also paler above and has straighter bill; Western Sandpiper slightly smaller. **HABITAT:** Tidal flats, beaches, muddy pools; in summer, moist tundra.

RED KNOT *Calidris canutus* (see also p. 152)
Uncommon M171
10½ in. (27 cm). Larger than Sanderling. Stocky, with medium-length, straight bill and short legs. Plain rump. *Breeding:* Face and underparts *pale robin red;* back mottled with black, gray, and russet. *Nonbreeding:* A dumpy wader with washed-out gray look and mottled flanks; greenish legs. *Juvenile: Pale feather edgings* above. **VOICE:** Low *knut;* also a low, mellow *tooit-wit* or *wah-quoit.* **HABITAT:** Tidal flats, sandy beaches, shores; tundra when breeding.

SANDPIPERS

RUDDY TURNSTONE
nonbreeding
breeding

PURPLE SANDPIPER
breeding
nonbreeding

SANDERLING
juvenile
breeding
nonbreeding

DUNLIN
juvenile
nonbreeding
breeding

RED KNOT
nonbreeding
juvenile
nonbreeding
breeding

LEAST SANDPIPER
Common M175
Calidris minutilla (see also p. 152)

6 in. (15 cm). Distinguished from the other two common peep by its slightly smaller size, *browner* look, and *yellowish or greenish* — not blackish — legs (but which might appear dark if caked in mud). *Bill slighter, finer, and slightly drooped at tip.* Adult: Mostly brownish (breeding) or brownish gray (nonbreeding). *Juvenile:* Much brighter, with extensive rufous on upperparts and buff wash across breast. **VOICE:** Thin *krreet* or *kree-eet*. **SIMILAR SPECIES:** Western and Semipalmated sandpipers have blackish legs, thicker-based bill, paler upperparts, and different voice; whitish breast in nonbreeding plumage. **HABITAT:** Mudflats, marshes, rain pools, shores, flooded fields; in summer, taiga wetlands.

SEMIPALMATED SANDPIPER
Common M173
Calidris pusilla (see also p. 152)

6¼ in. (16 cm). Collectively, the three common small sandpipers resident in N. America are nicknamed "peep." The "Semi" is a small black-legged peep with a *straight,* somewhat *tubular bill* of variable length. *Breeding:* Gray-brown above, many birds with a tinge of russet to cheeks and back; dark streaks on breast. *Nonbreeding:* Rarely seen in our area. Uniformly plain gray across upperparts. *Juvenile:* Breast washed with buff and with fine streaks on sides; scaly upperpart pattern with pale edges, tinged buff when fresh. **VOICE:** Call *chit* or *chirt* (lacks *ee* sound of Least and Western sandpipers). **SIMILAR SPECIES:** Typical Western Sandpiper (especially female) has *longer bill, slightly drooped* at tip. Breeding Western more rufous above, more heavily streaked below, particularly on flanks. Juvenile has rusty scapulars and slightly paler face. Least Sandpiper smaller, browner, and thinner billed; has *yellowish or greenish* legs; in nonbreeding plumage, has darker breast. **HABITAT:** Mudflats, marshes, shores, beaches; in summer, tundra.

WESTERN SANDPIPER *Calidris mauri*
Fairly common M174

6½ in. (17 cm). Very similar to Semipalmated Sandpiper. Legs black. In typical female, bill thicker at base and *longer* than Semipalmated's and *droops near tip* (male's bill shorter and less drooped). *Breeding:* Heavily spotted on breast and flanks; *rusty scapulars, crown, and ear patch.* Nonbreeding: Gray or gray-brown above, perhaps the palest peep, unmarked whitish below. *Juvenile:* Buffy wash on breast; scaly upperparts, like juvenile Semipalmated but with distinct rusty scapulars. **VOICE:** Distinct high-pitched *jeet* or *cheet,* unlike lower, soft *chirt* of Semipalmated. **SIMILAR SPECIES:** Semipalmated and Least sandpipers, Dunlin. Because of their shorter bill, many male Westerns may be particularly difficult to separate from Semipalmated (especially longer-billed females); see also voice. Semipalmated does not winter in our area, but Western does. **HABITAT:** Shores, beaches, mudflats, marshes; in summer, tundra.

SMALL "PEEP" SANDPIPERS

nonbreeding

juvenile

breeding

LEAST SANDPIPER

nonbreeding

juvenile

breeding

SEMIPALMATED SANDPIPER

nonbreeding ♀

WESTERN SANDPIPER

juvenile

breeding ♀

Least

Semipalmated

Western

WHITE-RUMPED SANDPIPER
Uncommon M176

Calidris fuscicollis (see also p. 152)

7½ in. (19 cm). Larger than Semipalmated Sandpiper, smaller than Pectoral Sandpiper. The only peep with completely *white rump*. At rest, this long-winged bird has *tapered* look, with *wingtips extending well beyond tail*. Distinct pale supercilium. *Breeding:* Some rusty on back. *Dark streaks and chevrons on sides extend to flanks.* Bill reddish at base of lower mandible. *Nonbreeding:* Gray upperparts and *breast, gray smudging down flanks,* bold *white eyebrow. Juvenile:* Rusty edges on crown and back. **VOICE:** High, thin, mouselike *jeet,* like two flint pebbles scraping. **SIMILAR SPECIES:** Long wings and very attenuated look shared only by Baird's Sandpiper among other peep, but Baird's browner, has dark center to rump, lacks bold supercilium and dark streaks on flanks, and has much lower pitched call. **HABITAT:** Prairie pools, shores, mudflats, marshes; in summer, tundra.

BAIRD'S SANDPIPER
Uncommon M177

Calidris bairdii (see also p. 152)

7½ in. (19 cm). Larger than Semipalmated or Western sandpiper, with more *long-winged, tapered look* (wings extend ½ in., 1 cm, beyond tail tip). *Breeding and juvenile:* Brown or *buff* across breast (warmer buff in juvenile). Suggests large, long-winged Least Sandpiper with black legs. Back of juvenile has *scaled* look. **VOICE:** Call a low *kreep* or *kree;* a rolling trill. **SIMILAR SPECIES:** White-rumped and Pectoral sandpipers. Buff-breasted Sandpiper buffier below, without streaks, and has *yellowish* (not *blackish*) legs. **HABITAT:** Pond margins, grassy mudflats, shores, upper beaches; in summer, tundra.

PECTORAL SANDPIPER
Fairly common M178

Calidris melanotos (see also p. 150)

8¼–8¾ in. (21–23 cm). Medium sized (but variable); neck longer than in smaller peep. Note that heavy breast streaks end rather *abruptly,* like a bib. Dark back lined with white. Wing stripe faint or lacking; crown variably rusty. Legs usually dull yellowish. Bill may be pale yellow-brown at base. *Juvenile:* Brighter upperparts and crown, buffy wash on breast under streaking. **VOICE:** Low, reedy *churrt* or *trrip, trrip.* **SIMILAR SPECIES:** Sharp-tailed, Baird's, and Least sandpipers. **HABITAT:** In migration, prairie pools, sod farms, muddy shores, fresh and tidal marshes; in summer, tundra.

SANDPIPERS

nonbreeding

WHITE-RUMPED
SANDPIPER

breeding

juvenile

breeding

BAIRD'S SANDPIPER

breeding ♂

juvenile

PECTORAL
SANDPIPER

breeding

SPOTTED SANDPIPER
Fairly common M160

Actitis macularius (see also p. 152)

7½ in. (19 cm). The most widespread sandpiper along shores of small lakes and streams. Teeters rear body up and down nervously. Note *long tail. Breeding:* Note *round breast spots. Nonbreeding and juvenile:* No spots; brown above, with white line over eye. Dusky smudge enclosing white wedge near shoulder is a good aid. Flight distinctive: wings beat in a *shallow arc*, giving a stiff, bowed appearance. Underwing striped. **VOICE:** Clear *peet* or *peet-weet!* or *peet-weet-weet-weet-weet*. **SIMILAR SPECIES:** Solitary Sandpiper. **HABITAT:** Pebbly shores, ponds, streamsides, marshes; in winter, also seashores, rock jetties.

STILT SANDPIPER
Uncommon M181

Calidris himantopus (see also pp. 130 and 150)

8½ in. (22 cm). Slight *droop* to tip of bill. Legs long and greenish yellow. Feeds like a dowitcher (sewing-machine motion) but *tilts tail up* more than a dowitcher while feeding. *Breeding:* Heavily marked below with *transverse bars*. Note *rusty cheek patch. Nonbreeding:* Yellowlegs-like; gray above, white below; dark-winged and *white-rumped;* note more *greenish legs* and *white eyebrow. Juvenile:* Slight buffy wash to breast and pale edgings above. **VOICE:** Single *whu* (like Lesser Yellowlegs but lower, hoarser). **SIMILAR SPECIES:** Yellowlegs. Dowitchers pudgier, have longer, yellowish-based, less drooped bills, and in flight show white wedge up back. See also Curlew Sandpiper. **HABITAT:** Shallow pools, mudflats, marshes; in summer, tundra.

BUFF-BREASTED SANDPIPER
Scarce M182

Tryngites subruficollis (see also p. 150)

8¼ in. (21 cm). No other small shorebird is as *buffy* below (paling to whitish on undertail coverts). A tame, buffy bird, with erect stance, small head, short bill, and yellowish legs. Dark eye stands out on plain face. In flight or in "display," buff body contrasts with underwing (*white* with marbled tip). *Juvenile:* Scaly above, paler on belly (most fall birds along coasts are in this plumage). **VOICE:** Low, trilled *pr-r-r-reet*. Sharp *tik*. **SIMILAR SPECIES:** Juvenile Ruff. **HABITAT:** Dry dirt, sand, and short-grass habitats, including drying lakeshores, pastures, sod farms; in summer, drier tundra ridges.

UPLAND SANDPIPER
Uncommon to scarce M165

Bartramia longicauda (see also p. 150)

12 in. (30–31 cm). A "pigeon-headed" brown sandpiper; larger than Killdeer. Short bill, *small head,* shoe-button eye, thin neck, and *long tail* are helpful points. Often perches with erect posture on fenceposts and poles; on alighting, holds wings elevated. **VOICE:** Mellow, whistled *kip-ip-ip-ip,* often heard at night. Song a weird windy whistle: *whoooleeeeee, wheeloooooooooo*. **SIMILAR SPECIES:** Buff-breasted Sandpiper, yellowlegs. **HABITAT:** Grassy prairies, open meadows, fields, airports, sod farms.

SANDPIPERS

nonbreeding

SPOTTED SANDPIPER

nonbreeding

juvenile

nonbreeding

breeding

STILT SANDPIPER

UPLAND SANDPIPER

BUFF-BREASTED SANDPIPER

AMERICAN WOODCOCK

Fairly common but secretive M186

Scolopax minor (see also p. 150)

11 in. (28 cm). A woodland-loving shorebird. Near size of Northern Bobwhite, with extremely long bill and large bulging eyes placed high on head. Rotund, almost neckless, with leaflike brown camouflage pattern. When flushed, produces whistling sound with wings. **VOICE:** At dusk in spring, a nasal *beezp*. Aerial "song" a chipping trill made by wings as bird ascends, changing to a bubbling twittering on descent. **HABITAT:** Wet thickets, moist woods, brushy swamps. Spring courtship by male is a crepuscular display ("sky dance") high over semiopen fields, pastures.

WILSON'S SNIPE

Fairly common M185

Gallinago delicata (see also p. 150)

10¼–10½ in. (26–27 cm). A tight-sitting prober of grassy wetlands. On nesting grounds may be seen standing on posts. Note *extremely long bill, buff stripes on back* and *head*. When flushed, flies off in zigzag, uttering rasping note. **VOICE:** When flushed, a rasping *scaip*. Song a measured *chip-a, chip-a, chip-a*, etc. In high aerial display, a winnowing *huhuhuhuhuhuhu*. **SIMILAR SPECIES:** Dowitchers. **HABITAT:** Marshes, bogs, ditches, wet fields and meadows.

SHORT-BILLED DOWITCHER

Common M183

Limnodromus griseus (see also p. 152)

11–11¼ in. (27–28 cm). A snipelike bird of open mudflats. Note very long bill, sewing-machine feeding motion, and, in flight, *long white wedge up back. Breeding:* Breast rusty with some barring on flanks. Atlantic subspecies *(griseus)* shows extensive white belly. Great Plains subspecies *(hendersoni)* more extensively rusty below but color paler orange than Long-billed and fades toward belly. *Nonbreeding:* Gray. *Juvenile:* Distinguished from juvenile Long-billed by warm buffy tones and *patterned tertial feathers.* **VOICE:** Staccato *tu-tu-tu;* pitch of Lesser Yellowlegs. **SIMILAR SPECIES:** Long-billed Dowitcher, Stilt Sandpiper. **HABITAT:** Mudflats, tidal marshes, ponds. In summer, taiga and tundra.

LONG-BILLED DOWITCHER

Uncommon to common M184

Limnodromus scolopaceus (see also p. 152)

11½ in. (29 cm). When feeding, shows more round-bodied profile than Short-billed; dark tail bars average wider; bill averages longer — but bill lengths of the two dowitchers overlap, so only extreme birds are distinctive. *Breeding:* Underparts *evenly bright rusty to lower belly* (white or very pale lower belly in Short-billed Dowitcher), with dark spotting on neck and barring on sides. *Nonbreeding:* Averages darker than Short-billed with smoother gray breast and darker centers to scapulars. *Juvenile:* Much plainer than juvenile Short-billed with unpatterned tertials. **VOICE:** Single sharp, high *keek,* occasionally given in twos or threes. **SIMILAR SPECIES:** Short-billed Dowitcher. **HABITAT:** Shallow pools, marshes; when breeding, tundra. More partial to fresh water than Short-billed, but extensive overlap.

SNIPELIKE WADERS

AMERICAN WOODCOCK

winnowing display flight

WILSON'S SNIPE

snipe

SHORT-BILLED DOWITCHER

juvenile

nonbreeding

coastal breeding

central breeding

juvenile

non-breeding

breeding

LONG-BILLED DOWITCHER

probing

PHALAROPES

Sandpipers with lobed toes; equally at home wading or swimming. Placed by some taxonomists in a family of their own, Phalaropodidae. When feeding, phalaropes often spin like tops, rapidly dabbling at disturbed water for plankton, brine shrimp, and other marine invertebrates; mosquito larvae; and insects. Females slightly larger and more colorful than males. RANGE: Two of the three species are circumpolar, wintering at sea; the other species breeds in N. American interior, winters mostly in S. America.

WILSON'S PHALAROPE
Fairly common M187

Phalaropus tricolor (see also pp. 130 and 150)

9¼ in. (23½ cm). This trim phalarope is plain-winged, with white rump. In addition to spinning in water, may also feed by dashing about on shorelines. *Breeding:* Female unique, with *broad black face and neck stripe blending into cinnamon.* Male duller, with just a wash of cinnamon on sides of neck and white spot on hindneck. *Nonbreeding:* Suggests Lesser Yellowlegs, but whiter below, with no speckling; bill *needlelike;* legs greenish or straw colored. *Juvenile:* Shows buffy and brown pattern above, buffy wash on breast. VOICE: Low nasal *wurk;* also *check, check, check.* SIMILAR SPECIES: Other two phalaropes show white wing stripe, dark central tail, and bolder dark patch through eye. See also yellowlegs, which may swim for brief periods of time. HABITAT: Shallow lakes, freshwater marshes, pools, shores, mudflats; in migration, also salt marshes.

RED-NECKED PHALAROPE
Common offshore, scarce inland M188

Phalaropus lobatus (see also p. 152)

7¾ in. (20 cm). A shorebird far out to sea is most likely a phalarope. This is usually the more common of the two "sea snipes" and the one more likely to occur inland as well. Note dark patch through eye and needlelike black bill. *Breeding:* Female gray above, with *rufous chestnut on neck,* white throat and eyebrow. Male duller, but similar in pattern. *Nonbreeding:* Both sexes gray above with whitish streaks, white below. *Juvenile:* Has distinct buff stripes on back. VOICE: Sharp *kit* or *whit,* similar to call of Sanderling. SIMILAR SPECIES: Red Phalarope. HABITAT: Ocean, bays, lakes, ponds; in summer, tundra.

RED PHALAROPE
Uncommon offshore, very rare onshore M189

Phalaropus fulicarius (see also p. 152)

8¼–8½ in. (21–22 cm). Seagoing habits and buoyant swimming (like a tiny gull) distinguish this as a phalarope. *Breeding:* Female has deep *reddish underparts, white face,* and mostly yellow bill. Male duller. *Nonbreeding:* Both sexes plain gray above, white below; in flight suggest Sanderling, but with *dark patch* through eye. Bill mostly dark with small pale base. *Juvenile:* Has peach-buff wash on neck; acquires adult's pale gray back-feathering quickly. VOICE: *Whit* or *kit,* higher than Red-necked Phalarope's call. SIMILAR SPECIES: Red-necked Phalarope slightly smaller, has more needlelike bill; non-breeding birds darker gray above with thin pale back stripes. Slightly thicker bill of Red Phalarope may have small yellowish base. HABITAT: More strictly pelagic than Red-necked. In summer, tundra.

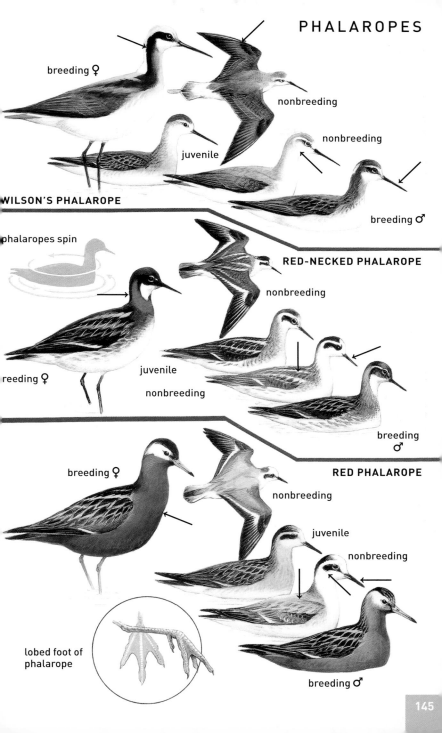

PHALAROPES

breeding ♀

nonbreeding

juvenile

nonbreeding

nonbreeding

WILSON'S PHALAROPE

breeding ♂

phalaropes spin

RED-NECKED PHALAROPE

nonbreeding

breeding ♀

juvenile

nonbreeding

breeding ♂

RED PHALAROPE

breeding ♀

nonbreeding

juvenile

nonbreeding

lobed foot of phalarope

breeding ♂

Plovers and Turnstone in Flight

Learn their distinctive flight calls.

PIPING PLOVER *Charadrius melodus*　　　　　　　　p. 126
Pale sand color above, wide black tail spot, whitish rump.
Call a plaintive whistle, *peep-lo* (first note higher).

SNOWY PLOVER *Charadrius alexandrinus*　　　　　　p. 126
Pale sand color above; tail with dark center, white sides; rump not white.
Call a musical whistle, *pe-wee-ah* or *o-wee-ah*.

SEMIPALMATED PLOVER *Charadrius semipalmatus*　　p. 126
Mud brown above; dark tail with white borders.
Call a plaintive upward-slurred *chi-we* or *too-li*.

WILSON'S PLOVER *Charadrius wilsonia*　　　　　　　p. 146
Similar in pattern to Semipalmated; larger with big bill.
Call an emphatic whistled *whit!* or *wheet!*

KILLDEER *Charadrius vociferus*　　　　　　　　　　p. 126
Tawny orange rump, longish tail.
Noisy; a loud *kill-deeah* or *killdeer*; also *dee-dee-dee,* etc.

BLACK-BELLIED PLOVER *Pluvialis squatarola*　　　p. 124
Breeding: Black below, white undertail coverts.
Year-round: Black wingpits, white in wing and tail.
Call a plaintive slurred whistle, *tlee-oo-eee* or *whee-er-ee*.

AMERICAN GOLDEN-PLOVER *Pluvialis dominica*　　p. 124
Breeding: Black below, black undertail coverts.
Nonbreeding: Speckled brown above, grayish below.
Year-round: Underwing grayer than Black-bellied Plover's; no black in wingpits.
Call a querulous whistled *queedle* or *que-e-a*.

RUDDY TURNSTONE *Arenaria interpres*　　　　　　p. 134
Harlequin pattern distinctive.
Call a low chuckling *tuk-a-tuk* or *kut-a-kut*.

PLOVERS AND TURNSTONE

PIPING PLOVER

SNOWY PLOVER

KILLDEER

SEMIPALMATED PLOVER

WILSON'S PLOVER

nonbreeding

BLACK-BELLIED PLOVER

breeding

nonbreeding

nonbreeding

nonbreeding

breeding

American Golden-Plover

AMERICAN GOLDEN-PLOVER

RUDDY TURNSTONE

breeding

Large Waders in Flight

Learn to know their flight calls, which are distinctive.

HUDSONIAN GODWIT *Limosa haemastica* p. 132
Upturned bill, white wing stripe, ringed tail. Blackish wing linings.
Flight call *tawit!,* higher pitched than Marbled Godwit's.

WILLET *Tringa semipalmata* p. 130
Contrasty black, gray, and white wing pattern. Overhead, wing pattern is even more striking.
Flight call a whistled *kay-ee* (second note lower) with Western's lower pitched and slower than Eastern's.

MARBLED GODWIT *Limosa fedoa* p. 132
Long upturned bill, tawny brown color. Cinnamon wing linings.
Flight call an accented *kerwhit!* (or *godwit!*).

WHIMBREL *Numenius phaeopus* p. 132
Decurved bill, gray-brown overall color, striped crown. Grayer than next species, lacks cinnamon wing linings.
Flight call five to seven short, rapid whistles: *hee-hee-hee-hee-hee-hee.*

LONG-BILLED CURLEW *Numenius americanus* p. 132
Very long, sicklelike bill; no head striping. Bright cinnamon wing linings. Juvenile's bill shorter but note head patterns.
Flight call a loud *cur-lee* (rising inflection).

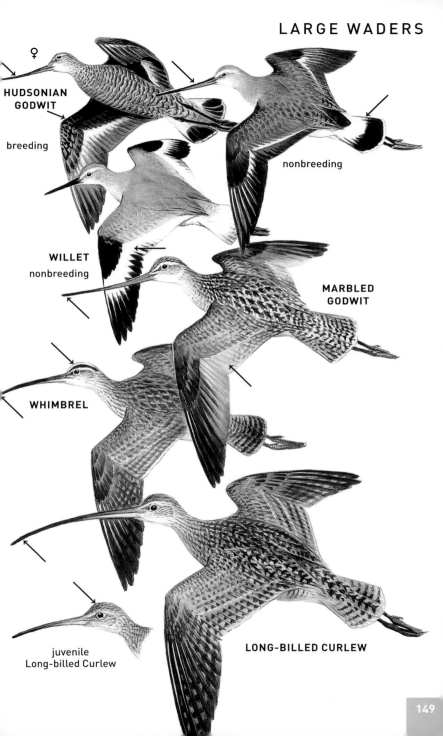

♀

**HUDSONIAN
GODWIT**

breeding

nonbreeding

WILLET
nonbreeding

**MARBLED
GODWIT**

WHIMBREL

LONG-BILLED CURLEW

juvenile
Long-billed Curlew

Snipelike Waders and Sandpipers in Flight

These species and those on the next plate show their basic flight patterns. Most of these have unpatterned wings, lacking a pale stripe. Learn their distinctive flight calls.

WILSON'S SNIPE *Gallinago delicata*　　　　p. 142
Long bill, pointed wings, rusty orange tail, zigzag flight.
Flight call, when flushed, a rasping *scaip.*

AMERICAN WOODCOCK *Scolopax minor*　　　　p. 142
Long bill, rounded wings, chunky shape. Wings whistle in flight.
At dusk, aerial flight "song."

SOLITARY SANDPIPER *Tringa solitaria*　　　　p. 130
Very dark unpatterned wings (underwing dark also — pale in yellowlegs), conspicuous bars on white sides of tail.
Flight call *peet!* or *peet-weet-weet!* (higher than Spotted Sandpiper's).

LESSER YELLOWLEGS *Tringa flavipes*　　　　p. 130
Similar to Greater Yellowlegs, but smaller, with smaller bill.
Flight call *yew* or *yu-yu* (rarely three), softer than Greater's call.

GREATER YELLOWLEGS *Tringa melanoleuca*　　　　p. 130
Plain unpatterned wings, whitish rump and tail, long bill.
Flight call a forceful three-note whistle, *dear! dear! dear!*

WILSON'S PHALAROPE *Phalaropus tricolor*　　　　p. 144
Nonbreeding: Suggests Lesser Yellowlegs; smaller, whiter, bill needlelike.
Flight call a low nasal *wurk.*

STILT SANDPIPER *Calidris himantopus*　　　　p. 140
Suggests Lesser Yellowlegs, but legs greenish yellow, bill longer and drooped.
Usually silent, but flight call a single *whu,* lower than Lesser Yellowlegs'.

UPLAND SANDPIPER *Bartramia longicauda*　　　　p. 140
Brown; small head, long tail.
Often flies "on tips of wings," like Spotted Sandpiper.
Flight call a mellow whistled *kip-ip-ip-ip.*

BUFF-BREASTED SANDPIPER *Tryngites subruficollis*　　　　p. 140
Buff below, contrasting with white wing linings; plain upperparts.
Flight call a low, trilled *pr-r-r-reet;* usually silent.

PECTORAL SANDPIPER *Calidris melanotos*　　　　p. 138
Like an oversized Least Sandpiper. Wing stripe faint or lacking.
Flight call a low, reedy *churrt* or *trrip, trrip.*

SNIPELIKE WADERS AND SANDPIPERS IN FLIGHT

WILSON'S SNIPE

SOLITARY SANDPIPER

AMERICAN WOODCOCK

GREATER YELLOWLEGS

LESSER YELLOWLEGS

WILSON'S PHALAROPE
nonbreeding

STILT SANDPIPER
nonbreeding

UPLAND SANDPIPER

BUFF-BREASTED SANDPIPER

PECTORAL SANDPIPER

151

SHORT-BILLED DOWITCHER *Limnodromus griseus*   p. 142
Long bill, long wedge of white up back. (Long-billed very similar.)
Flight call a staccato mellow *tu-tu-tu*.

DUNLIN *Calidris alpina*   p. 134
Nonbreeding: Slightly larger than peep, darker than Sanderling.
Flight call a nasal rasping *cheezp* or *treezp*.

RED KNOT *Calidris canutus*   p. 134
Nonbreeding: Washed-out gray look, pale rump.
Flight call a low *knut*.

PURPLE SANDPIPER *Calidris maritima*   p. 134
Slaty color.
Flight call a low, scratchy *weet-wit* or *twit*.

WHITE-RUMPED SANDPIPER *Calidris fuscicollis*   p. 138
White rump; other peeps have white rumps with dark divide.
Flight call a mouselike squeak, *jeet*.

CURLEW SANDPIPER *Calidris ferruginea*   p. 156
Nonbreeding: Suggests Dunlin, but rump white.

RUFF *Philomachus pugnax*   p. 156
If seen well, oval white patch on each side of dark tail distinctive.
Usually silent.

SPOTTED SANDPIPER *Actitis macularius*   p. 140
Shallow wing stroke gives stiff, bowed effect; longish tail.
Flight call a clear *peet* or *peet-weet*.

SANDERLING *Calidris alba*   p. 134
The most contrasting wing stripe of any small shorebird.
Flight call a sharp metallic *kip* or *quit*.

RED PHALAROPE *Phalaropus fulicarius*   p. 144
Nonbreeding: Paler above than Red-necked Phalarope;
bill slightly thicker.

RED-NECKED PHALAROPE *Phalaropus lobatus*   p. 144
Nonbreeding: Sanderling-like, but with dark eye patch.
Flight call (both pelagic phalaropes) a sharp *kit* or *whit*.

LEAST SANDPIPER *Calidris minutilla*   p. 136
Very small, brown with short wings and tail; faint wing stripe.
Flight call a thin single or double *krreet, krreet*.

SEMIPALMATED SANDPIPER *Calidris pusilla*   p. 136
Grayer than Least Sandpiper.
Flight call a soft *chit* or *chirt* (lacks *ee* sound of Least).

BAIRD'S SANDPIPER *Calidris bairdii*   p. 138
Larger and longer winged than above two. Buffy color.
Flight call a low, raspy *kreep* or *kree*.

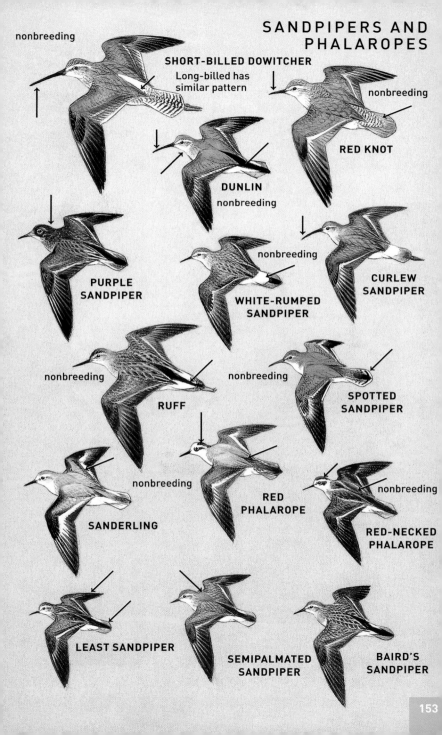

SANDPIPERS AND PHALAROPES

nonbreeding

SHORT-BILLED DOWITCHER
Long-billed has
similar pattern

nonbreeding

RED KNOT

DUNLIN
nonbreeding

PURPLE
SANDPIPER

WHITE-RUMPED
SANDPIPER

nonbreeding

CURLEW
SANDPIPER

nonbreeding

RUFF

nonbreeding

SPOTTED
SANDPIPER

SANDERLING

nonbreeding

RED
PHALAROPE

nonbreeding

RED-NECKED
PHALAROPE

LEAST SANDPIPER

SEMIPALMATED
SANDPIPER

BAIRD'S
SANDPIPER

153

PACIFIC GOLDEN-PLOVER *Pluvialis fulva*   Vagrant
10–10¼ in. (25–26 cm). Very similar to American Golden-Plover. Note *wingtips barely extend beyond tail tip. Breeding adult:* White neck stripe *extends down to flanks* and undertail coverts (but molting American may have this look). Golden spangles on back brighter. *Nonbreeding adult and juvenile: More golden* on upperparts, face, and breast. **VOICE:** Whistled *chu-wee* or *chu-wee-dle*. **RANGE:** Accidental visitor from Asia and Alaska.

NORTHERN LAPWING *Vanellus vanellus*   Vagrant
12–12½ in. (30–32 cm). A distinctive round-winged plover with unique long wispy crest. **RANGE:** Casual European vagrant to northeast, mostly in late fall and early winter. **HABITAT:** Farmland, marshes.

EUROPEAN GOLDEN-PLOVER *Pluvialis apricaria*   Vagrant
11 in. (28 cm). Very similar to American Golden-Plover but shows *white* underwings. **RANGE:** Very rare spring vagrant to NL, casual elsewhere in Maritimes. **HABITAT:** Farmland, marshes; in summer, tundra.

SPOTTED REDSHANK *Tringa erythropus*   Vagrant
12½ in. (32 cm). Similar to a yellowlegs but with *red legs,* long bill has *reddish base* and *slight droop at tip;* in flight shows *white wedge up back* and *white underwing. Breeding: Sooty black,* with small white speckles. *Nonbreeding and juvenile:* Gray and white. **RANGE:** Casual Eurasian visitor.

ESKIMO CURLEW *Numenius borealis*   Probably extinct
14 in. (36 cm). Last documented record in early 1960s. Much smaller, buffier than Whimbrel with weaker head pattern; shorter, thinner bill. Wing linings cinnamon-buff. **HABITAT:** Open grasslands, coastal areas; in summer, tundra.

"EURASIAN" WHIMBREL *Numenius phaeopus phaeopus*   Vagrant
European subspecies of Whimbrel, *N. p. phaeopus,* is a casual visitor along Atlantic Coast. Differs from N. American Whimbrel by showing mostly *white rump* and whiter underwing.

BAR-TAILED GODWIT *Limosa lapponica*   Vagrant
16–17 in. (41–44 cm). Note barred tail and *whitish rump. Breeding:* Male rich *reddish orange,* particularly on head and underparts. Female duller. *Nonbreeding and juvenile:* Grayish above, white below with bold supercilium. **RANGE:** Eurasian species; also breeds in AK. Casual vagrant on East Coast.

BLACK-TAILED GODWIT *Limosa limosa*   Vagrant
16½ in. (42 cm). This elegant Eurasian godwit resembles Hudsonian Godwit (white rump, white wing stripe, black tail), but bill straighter and has *white underwing.* In breeding plumage, has chestnut head and neck, black-and-white barred belly. **RANGE:** Casual visitor to East Coast and e. Great Lakes.

PACIFIC GOLDEN-PLOVER

RARE
SHOREBIRDS

NORTHERN
LAPWING

breeding

EUROPEAN
GOLDEN-
PLOVER

breeding

nonbreeding

ESKIMO
CURLEW

SPOTTED REDSHANK

breeding

WHIMBREL
"Eurasian"

underwing

BAR-TAILED
GODWIT

juvenile

nonbreeding

nonbreeding

breeding

BLACK-TAILED
GODWIT

Bar-tailed
nonbreeding

breeding

nonbreeding

SHARP-TAILED SANDPIPER *Calidris acuminata*   **Vagrant**
8½ in. (22 cm). Similar to Pectoral Sandpiper, but shows bolder whitish supercilium and brighter rusty crown. Most birds in N. America are juveniles, which have rich *orangey buff breast,* finely streaked on sides only. Breeding adults have heavy *dark chevrons* extending to flanks. Crissum streaked. In no plumage is there as sharp a demarcation between white belly and streaked breast as in Pectoral. **RANGE:** Casual, mostly fall visitor from Asia.

LITTLE STINT *Calidris minuta*   **Vagrant**
6 in. (15 cm). Size of Semipalmated Sandpiper, but bill slightly finer. *Breeding:* Rusty orange above and on breast. Similar to some Red-necked Stints, but *dark breast markings washed with orange.* **RANGE:** Casual visitor from Eurasia.

RED-NECKED STINT *Calidris ruficollis*   **Vagrant**
6¼ in. (17 cm). Size of Semipalmated Sandpiper, but bill finer. Recognized in breeding plumage by *bright rusty head and neck, bordered below by dark streaks.* **RANGE:** Casual visitor from Asia.

CURLEW SANDPIPER   **Very rare visitor**
Calidris ferruginea (see also p. 152)
8½–8¾ in. (21–22 cm). A Eurasian species with slim downcurved bill, blackish legs, and white rump in flight. *Breeding:* Variably rich rufous red (darker than Red Knot). *Nonbreeding and juvenile:* Resembles Dunlin, but slightly longer legged, bolder pale supercilium; bill curved slightly throughout; whitish rump. **RANGE:** Very rare but annual migrant along East Coast, casual inland.

RUFF *Philomachus pugnax* (see also p. 152)   **Very rare visitor**
Male (Ruff) 12–13 in. (30–32 cm); female (known informally as Reeve) 9 in. (23 cm). *Breeding male:* Unique, with erectile *ruffs* and *ear tufts* that may be black, brown, rufous, buff, white, or barred, in various combinations. Legs may be greenish, yellow, or orange. Bill color also variable. *Breeding female:* Smaller than male; lacks ruffs, breast *heavily blotched* with dark. *Nonbreeding:* Rather plain, with short bill, small head, thick neck, mottling of gray across breast. Note *erect stance* and (in flight) *oval white patch* on each side of dark tail. *Juvenile:* Buffy below, very scaly on back. **RANGE:** Breeds in Eurasia. Very rare but regular migrant along Atlantic Coast and in Great Lakes region; casual elsewhere inland. **HABITAT:** Mudflats, marshes, coastal pools, wet agricultural fields in migration. Marshes, tundra in summer.

RARE
SHOREBIRDS

juvenile

**SHARP-TAILED
SANDPIPER**

breeding

nonbreeding

breeding

**LITTLE
STINT**

nonbreeding

**CURLEW
SANDPIPER**

breeding

breeding

early spring
(breeding)

**RED-
NECKED
STINT**

breeding
dress of ♂
variable

nonbreeding ♀

juvenile ♂

♂

♂

RUFF

breeding ♀

157

GULLS Family Laridae

Long-winged swimming birds with superb flight. Most are more robust, wider winged, and longer legged than terns, and most have slightly hooked bills. Tails square or rounded (terns usually have forked tail). Gulls seldom dive (most terns hover, then plunge headfirst). FOOD: Omnivorous; marine life, plant and animal food, refuse, carrion. RANGE: Nearly worldwide.

AGING GULLS

It is often important to determine the age of a gull before identifying it. Knowing what a gull looks like in both its adult and first-year plumages is helpful in identifying the bird to species in its intermediate stages. Note that the molt of a gull from one plumage to the next is a gradual process. Therefore, a single "molt cycle" (which takes about a year in gulls) from, for example, fresh juvenal plumage in August to "first winter" plumage in January to "first summer" plumage in June will result in a range of appearances (particularly in larger species). Only one point in that range is pictured here.

SEQUENCE OF PLUMAGES IN A TWO-YEAR GULL

On the top of the opposite page, the Bonaparte's Gull illustrates the transition of plumages from first year to adult. Species in this category are mostly smaller gulls, including Bonaparte's, Black-headed, Little, Ross's, Sabine's, and Ivory gulls.

SEQUENCE OF PLUMAGES IN A THREE-YEAR GULL

In the middle of the opposite page, the Ring-billed Gull, widespread and abundant both coastally and inland, illustrates the transition of plumages from first year to adult. Species in this category are mostly medium-sized gulls, including Ring-billed, Laughing, Franklin's, and Mew gulls and Black-legged Kittiwake.

SEQUENCE OF PLUMAGES IN A FOUR-YEAR GULL

On the bottom of the opposite page, the Herring Gull, a widespread species, illustrates the transition of plumages from first year to adult. Species in this category are most of the larger gulls, including California, Herring, Lesser Black-backed, Great Black-backed, Slaty-backed, Glaucous, Iceland, and Thayer's gulls. These species attain full maturity in 3½ to 4½ years.

In this field guide, intended for identification on the species level, no other four-year gull receives similarly full treatment. That is the province of a larger text specifically on gulls. For in-depth analysis of other species, consult the *Peterson Reference Guide to Gulls of the Americas.*

Caution: There is extensive variation within species (particularly the immatures), resulting from several factors including dimorphism (males are larger than females), molt, variation in wear and bleaching, albinism, and other factors. In addition, hybridization is a regular phenomenon among most four-year species. Even expert birders leave some gulls unidentified.

BONAPARTE'S GULL

Plumage Transition of a Two-Year Gull

first year

adult

first year

second year

umage ansition of Three-Year Gull

adult

Plumage Transition of a Four-Year Gull

HERRING GULL

first year

second year

third year

adult

LAUGHING GULL *Leucophaeus atricilla*   Common **M197**
16–16½ in. (41–42 cm). A small coastal gull named for its call. *Dark mantle blends into black wingtips.* Head *black* in breeding plumage; pale in nonbreeding plumage, with dark gray smudge. Bill longish, often with slight droop; reddish when breeding, mostly dark when not breeding. *Immature:* See p. 166. **VOICE:** Nasal *ha-a* and strident laugh, *ha-ha-ha-ha-ha-haah-haah-haah*, etc. **SIMILAR SPECIES:** Franklin's Gull slightly smaller, shorter billed, has broader white eye-arcs, paler underwing, and *different wingtip pattern.* **HABITAT:** Salt marshes, coastlines, parks, farm fields.

FRANKLIN'S GULL *Leucophaeus pipixcan*   Fairly common **M198**
14½–15 in. (37–38 cm). Note *white band* near wingtip, separating black from gray. In breeding plumage, head black; breast has rosy bloom; bill red. In nonbreeding plumage, head paler but extensive *blackish "half-hood"*; bill mostly dark. *Immature:* See p. 166. **VOICE:** Shrill *kuk-kuk-kuk;* also mewing, laughing cries. **SIMILAR SPECIES:** Laughing and Bonaparte's gulls. **HABITAT:** Prairies, inland marshes, lakes; in winter, coasts, ocean.

SABINE'S GULL *Xema sabini*   Rare **M192**
13½–14 in. (34–36 cm). A small, *ternlike* gull with slightly *forked tail.* Note *bold upperwing pattern* of black outer primaries and *triangular white wing patch.* Bill black with *yellow tip. Immature:* See p. 166. **VOICE:** Various grating or buzzy ternlike calls. **HABITAT:** Ocean; nests on tundra pools.

BLACK-HEADED GULL *Chroicocephalus ridibundus*   Rare **M194**
15¾–16 in. (40–41 cm). This Eurasian species regularly visits the ne. coast of N. America, especially in Atlantic provinces. Similar to Bonaparte's Gull and often associates with it or with Ring-billed Gull. Slightly larger than Bonaparte's; mantle slightly paler; much *blackish on underside of primaries;* bill *dark red.* In nonbreeding plumage, loses dark brown hood and has black ear spot. *Immature:* See p. 166. **HABITAT:** Same as Bonaparte's Gull; also beaches, lawns.

BONAPARTE'S GULL *Chroicocephalus philadelphia* Common **M193**
13–13½ in. (33–34 cm). A petite, ternlike gull. Note *wedge of white* on *fore edge* of wing. Legs pinkish; bill small, black. In breeding plumage, head blackish. In nonbreeding plumage, head whitish with *black ear spot. Immature:* See p. 166. Also see Sequence of Plumages in a Two-Year Gull, p. 158. **VOICE:** Nasal, grating *cheeer* or *cherr.* **SIMILAR SPECIES:** Black-headed and Little gulls. **HABITAT:** Ocean, bays, lakes, sewage-treatment ponds; in summer, muskeg.

LITTLE GULL *Hydrocoloeus minutus*   Rare **M195**
11 in. (28 cm). This rare visitor is the smallest gull. Note *blackish undersurface* of *rather rounded wing* and absence of black above. In breeding plumage, head black. In nonbreeding plumage, head *dark-capped, black ear spot. Immature:* See p. 166. **VOICE:** Series of one- or two-syllable *key* notes. **SIMILAR SPECIES:** Bonaparte's Gull. **HABITAT:** Lakes, rivers, bays, coastal waters, sewage-treatment ponds; usually with Bonaparte's Gulls.

SMALL HOODED GULLS
Adults

nonbreeding

LAUGHING GULL

breeding

FRANKLIN'S GULL

nonbreeding

breeding

SABINE'S GULL

nonbreeding

breeding

BLACK-HEADED GULL

nonbreeding

breeding

BONAPARTE'S GULL

nonbreeding

breeding

LITTLE GULL

nonbreeding

breeding

HERRING GULL *Larus argentatus*   Common M201
24–25 in. (61–64 cm). A widespread large gull. *Pale gray* mantle, *pinkish* legs, *pale eye.* Outer primaries *black* with white spots or "mirrors." Bill yellow with red spot on lower mandible. In nonbreeding plumage, head and neck mottled with brownish. *Immature:* See p. 168. Also see Sequence of Plumages in a Four-Year Gull, p. 158. **VOICE:** A loud *hiyak . . . hiyak . . . hyiah-hyak* or *yuk-yuk-yuk-yuk-yuckle-yuckle.* Mewing squeals. Anxiety call *gah-gah-gah.* **SIMILAR SPECIES:** Thayer's and California gulls. **HABITAT:** Ocean, coasts, bays, beaches, lakes, dams, piers, farmland, dumps.

CALIFORNIA GULL *Larus californicus*   Scarce, local M200
21–21½ in. (53–55 cm). Resembles larger Herring Gull, but note darker mantle, *darker eye, yellowish legs.* Shows more white and black in wingtips than Herring. In nonbreeding plumage, head streaked or mottled brownish, dark spot on bill may extend to upper mandible, legs slightly duller. *Immature:* See p. 168. **HABITAT:** Lakes, farms, dumps; stray to Atlantic and Gulf coasts.

RING-BILLED GULL *Larus delawarensis*   Common M199
17–17½ in. (43–45 cm). A small gull, with *pale eye* and *light gray mantle* (similar to Herring's); *legs yellow or greenish yellow* (may be duller in nonbreeding plumage). Note complete *black ring* encircling bill. In nonbreeding plumage, shows some *fine dark streaking* on head. *Immature:* See p. 166. Also see Sequence of Plumages in a Three-Year Gull, p. 158. **VOICE:** Higher pitched than Herring Gull's. **SIMILAR SPECIES:** Mew Gull. **HABITAT:** Lakes, bays, coasts, piers, dumps, plowed fields, sewage outlets, shopping malls, fast-food restaurants.

MEW GULL *Larus canus*   Vagrant
16–17 in. (41–44 cm). Called "Common Gull" in Europe. Slightly smaller than Ring-billed Gull, with more greenish yellow legs and smaller, *unmarked greenish yellow bill. Darkish eye. Mantle noticeably darker than Ring-billed's.* Larger white "mirrors" in wingtips than Ring-billed. More extensive dark mottling on head and neck in winter. *Immature:* First year of European subspecies *(canus)* almost identical to first-year Ring-billed; best identified by smaller size, *slimmer, more grayish-based bill, darker gray back,* and cleaner white uppertail coverts and tail base (matched by some Ring-bills). **RANGE:** European subspecies *(canus)* annual in Atlantic provinces, casual in New England. American subspecies *(brachyrhynchus)* accidental in East.

BLACK-LEGGED KITTIWAKE *Rissa tridactyla*   Uncommon M190
16–17 in. (41–43 cm). A small, buoyant oceanic gull. Wingtips are *solid black,* as if dipped in ink. Bill small, pale yellow, and unmarked. Legs and feet *black. Eyes dark.* In nonbreeding plumage, rear head and nape dusky. *Immature:* See p. 166. **VOICE:** At nesting colony, a raucous *kaka-week* or *kitti-waak.* **SIMILAR SPECIES:** Ring-billed and Sabine's gulls. **HABITAT:** Chiefly oceanic; rarely on beaches, casual inland. Nests on sea cliffs.

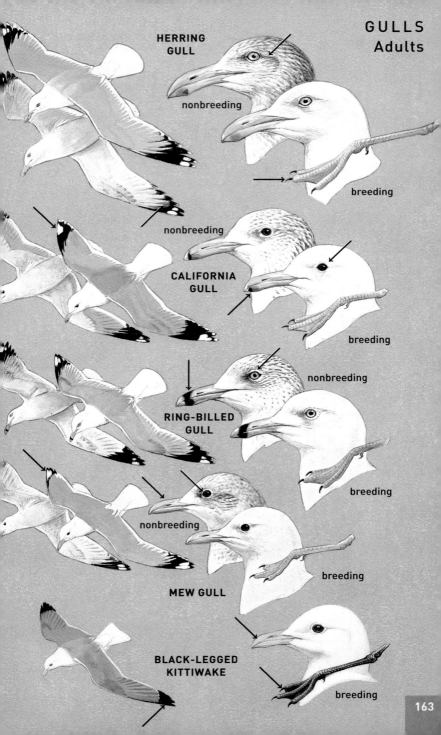

GULLS
Adults

HERRING GULL

nonbreeding

breeding

nonbreeding

CALIFORNIA GULL

breeding

nonbreeding

RING-BILLED GULL

breeding

nonbreeding

breeding

MEW GULL

BLACK-LEGGED KITTIWAKE

breeding

THAYER'S GULL *Larus thayeri*   Rare M202
23–24 in. (58–61 cm). Formerly thought to be a subspecies of Herring Gull. Now designated as a full species, but regarded by some as a subspecies of Iceland Gull. Very similar to Herring Gull. Typical adult has *pale to dark brown* eyes, *only a thin trailing edge of black* on *grayish* underside of primaries, slightly darker mantle, slightly deeper pink legs, and somewhat slighter bill, often with greenish-tinged base. In nonbreeding plumage, head and neck streaked or mottled with brownish. *Immature:* See p. 168. **VOICE:** Similar to Herring Gull. **SIMILAR SPECIES:** Iceland Gull. **HABITAT:** Similar to Herring Gull.

ICELAND GULL *Larus glaucoides*   Uncommon M203
22–23 in. (56–60 cm). A pale ghostly gull, slightly smaller than Herring Gull. Mantle pale gray; primaries whitish and extending *well beyond tail*. *Immature:* See p. 168. "Kumlien's" Gull *(Larus glaucoides kumlieni),* the subspecies that breeds in e. Arctic Canada, is the one seen in U.S.; has gray or dark markings, variable in extent, toward tips of whitish primaries (not black with white "mirrors" as in Herring Gull). **VOICE:** Similar to Herring Gull but higher pitched; rarely heard away from breeding grounds. **SIMILAR SPECIES:** Glaucous Gull larger, has larger bill, shorter primary extension. Adult Thayer's Gull has slightly darker mantle, blacker primaries, dark eye. **HABITAT:** Ocean, coastlines, dumps.

GLAUCOUS GULL *Larus hyperboreus*   Uncommon M205
27–28 in. (68–72 cm). A large, chalky white gull with pinkish legs. Note "frosty" wingtips. Has pale gray mantle and *unmarked white outer primaries. Light eye. Immature:* See p. 168. **VOICE:** Much like Herring Gull's. **SIMILAR SPECIES:** Iceland Gull, but that species is smaller than Herring Gull; also, Iceland's bill is smaller, head rounder, and wings proportionately longer and narrower. Breeding adult Iceland has narrow red eye-ring (Glaucous, yellow), but this is hard to see. **HABITAT:** Mainly coastal; a few inland at large lakes and dumps.

LESSER BLACK-BACKED GULL *Larus fuscus*   Scarce M204
21–22½ in. (53–57 cm). Similar to Great Black-backed Gull but slightly smaller (smaller than Herring Gull) and slimmer, with longer wings and smaller bill. Distinguished by yellowish (not pink) legs and slate gray (not black) mantle. Extensive head and neck streaking or mottling in nonbreeding plumage. Pale eye. Oblong red spot on bill. *Immature:* See p. 168. **VOICE:** Harsh *kyah.* **SIMILAR SPECIES:** Great Black-backed Gull. **HABITAT:** Same as Herring Gull.

GREAT BLACK-BACKED GULL *Larus marinus*   Common M206
29–30 in. (73–76 cm). Largest gull in the world, with broad wings and heavy body and bill. Black back and wings, snow-white underparts, no head streaking in winter. Legs and feet *pale* pinkish. *Immature:* See p. 168. **VOICE:** Harsh deep seal-like *kyow* or *owk.* **SIMILAR SPECIES:** Lesser Black-backed Gull. **HABITAT:** Mainly coastal waters, estuaries, dumps; a few well inland on large lakes and rivers.

GULLS
Adults

nonbreeding

THAYER'S
GULL

breeding

ICELAND GULL

"Kumlien's"
(typical)

pale
extreme

GLAUCOUS
GULL

nonbreeding

breeding

GREAT BLACK-
BACKED GULL

LESSER BLACK-
BACKED GULL

Great Black-backed Gull

IMMATURE SMALL GULLS

Immatures of many gull species are more difficult to identify than adults. They are usually darkest the first year and lighter the second, when some species start to show their adult eye and back color. Larger species do not develop their full adult plumage until the third or fourth year. (See pp. 158–159.) Identify mainly by pattern, size, and structure. The most typical plumages are shown here; intermediate and successive stages can be expected, but because of variables such as stage of molt, wear, age, individual variation, hybridization, and occasional albinism, some birds may remain a mystery even to the expert.

LAUGHING GULL *Leucophaeus atricilla*   Adult, p. 166
A three-year gull. *Juvenile:* Dark brown with black tail, white rump. *First year:* Neck and back become extensively smudged with gray. *Second year:* Similar to nonbreeding adult, but with trace of black in tail. SIMILAR SPECIES: Franklin's Gull.

FRANKLIN'S GULL *Leucophaeus pipixcan*   Adult, p. 160
A three-year gull. *First year:* Similar to first-year Laughing, but more petite with *smaller bill, blackish half-hood, white neck,* white outer tail feathers, whitish breast, paler underside to primaries. *Second year:* Close to second winter Laughing but with blackish half hood, pale underside to primaries.

BLACK-HEADED GULL *Chroicocephalus ridibundus*   Adult, p. 160
A two-year gull. *First year:* Similar to first-year Bonaparte's Gull but slightly larger; bill longer, *orange to red* at base, black at tip; *sooty underwing;* broad dusky trailing edge to upperwing.

BONAPARTE'S GULL *Chroicocephalus philadelphia*   Adult, p. 160
A two-year gull. Petite, ternlike. *First year:* Note dark ear spot, narrow black tail band, neat dark trailing edge to wings, and pattern of black and white in outer primaries. Pale underwing. See Sequence of Plumages in a Two-Year Gull, p. 158.

LITTLE GULL *Hydrocoloeus minutus*   Adult, p. 166
A two-year gull. *First year:* Slightly smaller than Bonaparte's Gull, with *blacker M pattern* across back and wings, *white trailing edge* to wings, *dusky cap.*

SABINE'S GULL *Xema sabini*   Adult, p. 160
A two-year gull. *Juvenile:* Dark grayish brown on back, but with adult's bold *triangular wing pattern.* Note also *forked* tail.

BLACK-LEGGED KITTIWAKE *Rissa tridactyla*   Adult, p. 162
A three-year gull. *First year:* Note *dark bar on nape* (held into early winter), *black M across back and wings;* tail may seem notched. White trailing edge to wings.

RING-BILLED GULL *Larus delawarensis*   Adult, p. 162
A three-year gull. *First year:* Usually *bicolored (pinkish-based) bill,* mostly whitish underneath and on rump and upper tail, *pale gray back.* Subterminal tail band narrow and usually well defined; contrasty wing pattern. SIMILAR SPECIES: Mew and California gulls.

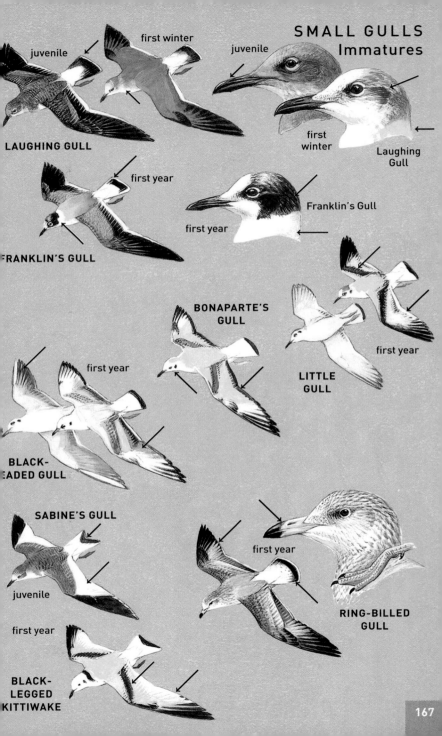

SMALL GULLS
Immatures

juvenile

first winter

juvenile

LAUGHING GULL

first winter

Laughing Gull

first year

Franklin's Gull

FRANKLIN'S GULL

first year

BONAPARTE'S GULL

LITTLE GULL

first year

BLACK-HEADED GULL

first year

SABINE'S GULL

first year

juvenile

first year

RING-BILLED GULL

BLACK-LEGGED KITTIWAKE

Immature Large Gulls

LESSER BLACK-BACKED GULL *Larus fuscus* Adult, p. 164
A four-year gull. Smaller, slimmer than Herring Gull. *First year:* Like miniature first-year Great Black-backed but with broader tail band, darker wings, more heavily streaked breast; colder brown than Herring with white tail base, paler head and underparts, darker wings.

HERRING GULL *Larus argentatus* Adult, p. 162
A four-year gull. *First year:* Brownish overall, with blackish tail and wingtips; only all-brown gull commonly seen in the East. Often shows much mottling or checkering on upperwing coverts and rump. *Pale area on inner primaries visible in flight.* Bill all dark at first, becoming paler at base later. *Second and third years:* Head and underparts whiter; eye pale; back pale gray; rump white; bill pale, dark-tipped. See Sequence of Plumages in a Four-Year Gull, p. 158.

GREAT BLACK-BACKED GULL *Larus marinus* Adult, p. 164
A four-year gull. *First year:* Larger than Herring with more *checkered look;* pale head and body contrast with dark back and underwing. *White tail* with dark band. *Second year:* Distinct "saddle-back" pattern.

CALIFORNIA GULL *Larus californicus* Adult, p. 162
A four-year gull. *First year:* Like Herring Gull, but slightly smaller, with smaller bicolored bill. In flight, shows double dark bar on wing and lacks pale area on inner primaries. *Second year:* Legs and bill base often dull gray-green-blue. Much like first-winter Ring-billed Gull, but somewhat larger, retains dark eye, darker gray on back, and tail mostly dark rather than with only a dark subterminal band.

GLAUCOUS GULL *Larus hyperboreus* Adult, p. 164
A four-year gull. *First year:* Recognized by its large size, pale tan or off-whitish (whiter by late winter) coloration, and unmarked *frosty primaries*, a shade lighter than rest of wing. Bill *pale pinkish* with dark tip *sharply demarcated. Second year:* Pale gray back and pale eye acquired.

THAYER'S GULL *Larus thayeri* Adult, p. 164
A four-year gull. *First year:* Tan-brown and checkered; similar to juvenile Herring Gull but lighter; primaries paler, usually *light tan-brown* (not brownish black) *with pale edges to tips; bill entirely or almost entirely blackish, more petite; underside of primaries pale.* Often shows dark smudge through eye. *Second year:* Paler and grayer; primaries gray-brown with darker outer webs.

ICELAND GULL *Larus glaucoides* Adult, p. 164
Similar to Glaucous Gull, but smaller (smaller than Herring) with smaller bill and proportionately longer wings (projecting beyond tail at rest). Bill of most first-year Iceland Gulls mostly dark, only very rarely as sharply demarcated as in Glaucous. Most birds show a hint of a tail band as well as some dark in outer primaries, both lacking in Glaucous; darkest birds approach Thayer's in appearance.

LARGE GULLS
Immatures

first year

HERRING
GULL

second year

LESSER BLACK-
BACKED GULL

first year

first year

GREAT BLACK-
BACKED GULL

first year

second
year

first
year

CALIFORNIA GULL

first year

THAYER'S
GULL

second year

GLAUCOUS
GULL

first
year

second
year

Glaucous Gull
first year

first year

Iceland Gull
first year

third year

ICELAND
GULL

BLACK-TAILED GULL *Larus carassirostris*   Vagrant
18–18½ in. (46–47 cm). Slightly larger than Ring-billed Gull, and with slightly longer wings and bill. Adult has red tip to black-banded bill, slate gray mantle, and wide black subterminal band on tail. **RANGE:** Casual visitor from e. Asia, with widely scattered records across much of N. America.

YELLOW-LEGGED GULL *Larus michahellis*   Vagrant
24–24½ in. (61–63 cm). This native of s. Europe was recently split from Herring Gull. Very similar to Herring Gull, but bill slightly stouter, adult's mantle slightly *darker gray,* and head flatter and only *finely streaked on crown* in nonbreeding plumage. Orbital ring red, and red spot on bill slightly larger. *Yellow legs* of adult usually distinctive, but beware some Herring Gulls that show yellowish tones to legs in late winter and early spring. **RANGE:** Casual visitor to Atlantic Seaboard, with most records to date from NL. **HABITAT:** Similar to Herring Gull.

SLATY-BACKED GULL *Larus schistisagus*   Vagrant
25–26 in. (64–67 cm). A dark-backed gull, chunkier and shorter winged than Lesser Black-backed, smaller and slimmer billed than Great Black-backed. Note deep pinkish legs and feet, *extensive head streaking, and dusky mark through eye in nonbreeding plumage.* Note how broad white trailing edge of wing invades outer wing, forming *thin white bar* crossing dark primaries (best seen across underwing). Primaries *gray* beneath. **SIMILAR SPECIES:** Lesser Black-backed Gull is slimmer and longer winged, has yellow legs. **RANGE:** Casual visitor from ne. Asia. **HABITAT:** Seacoasts, beaches, dumps.

ROSS'S GULL *Rhodostethia rosea*   Very rare M196
13–13½ in. (33–35 cm). A rare Arctic gull of drift ice. Note *wedge-shaped tail, medium gray wing linings,* and *small black bill.* A two-year gull. *Breeding:* Rosy blush on underparts, *fine black collar. Nonbreeding:* Rosy blush duller or lacking, lacks black collar, may be washed with gray. *First winter:* Similar in pattern to immature Black-legged Kittiwake or Little Gull, but intermediate in size and note *wedge-shaped tail* (not square or notched) and *gray* linings of underwing; lacks dark nape of young kittiwake. **HABITAT:** Arctic waters, tundra in summer.

IVORY GULL *Pagophila eburnea*   Very rare, threatened M191
17 in. (43 cm). A declining species of Arctic pack ice. Most individuals that wander south of normal range are immatures. A two-year gull. *Adult:* The only all-white gull with black legs. Pigeon sized with dove-like head; wings long, flight ternlike. Bill greenish with yellow tip. *Immature:* White, with dark *smudge on face,* a *sprinkling of black spots* above, black spots on primary tips, and narrow black tip to tail. Legs and feet black, a distinction from all other white gulls. **HABITAT:** Open Arctic waters near pack ice.

BLACK-
TAILED
GULL

nonbreeding

YELLOW-
LEGGED GULL

nonbreeding

SLATY-BACKED
GULL

breeding

ROSS'S
GULL

nonbreeding

breeding

first year

breeding

adult

first year

IVORY GULL

171

TERNS Subfamily Sterninae

Graceful waterbirds, more streamlined than gulls; wings more pointed, tail usually forked. Bill sharp-pointed, often tilted toward water when bird is flying. Most terns are whitish with black cap; in nonbreeding plumage, black of forehead replaced by white. Sexes alike. Terns often hover and plunge headfirst for fish. **FOOD:** Small fish, marine life, large insects. **RANGE:** Almost worldwide.

FORSTER'S TERN *Sterna forsteri*   Common M217
14½ in. (37 cm). Very similar to Common Tern, but paler; all adults have frosty wingtips (lighter than rest of wing). White below, lacking gray wash of breeding Common. Bill slightly thicker and more orange than red. Nonbreeding adult and immature have isolated *black mask* and lack dark carpal ("shoulder") bar of Common in similar plumages. **VOICE:** Harsh, nasal *kyarr.* **HABITAT:** Fresh and salt marshes, lakes, bays, beaches, nearshore ocean.

COMMON TERN *Sterna hirundo*   Uncommon to common M215
14 in. (36 cm). A graceful, small, black-capped, slim bird with deeply forked tail. *Breeding adult:* Similar to Forster's Tern, but darker gray above with darker primaries, *grayer below, bill slightly smaller and redder. Nonbreeding adult and immature:* Cap, nape, and bill blackish. *Show dark shoulder (carpal) bar.* **VOICE:** Drawling *kee-arr* (two-parted); also *kik-kik-kik.* **HABITAT:** Lakes, ocean, bays, marshes, beaches; nests colonially on sandy beaches and small islands.

ARCTIC TERN *Sterna paradisaea*   Uncommon M216
15 in. (38 cm). A pelagic (seagoing) tern. Similar to Common Tern. Bill and neck shorter, head rounder. *Legs shorter.* Overhead, note *translucent* effect of primaries and *narrow* black trailing edge. *Breeding adult:* Bill usually *blood red* to tip; uniform pale gray upperwing; breast slightly darker gray than Common. *Nonbreeding and juvenile:* Like Common, but black on head slightly more extensive, shoulder bar somewhat *weaker, secondaries whitish.* **VOICE:** *Kee-yak,* similar to Common Tern's but higher. A high *keer-keer* is characteristic. **HABITAT:** Open ocean, coasts; in summer, also taiga lakes, tundra.

ROSEATE TERN *Sterna dougallii*   Uncommon, local M214
15½ in. (39 cm). Similar to Common Tern, but *much paler* with *quicker wingbeats. At rest, tail extends well beyond wingtips.* In spring and summer, note *thin, long black bill* (some red at base in late summer), pale rosy blush to breast. *Immature:* Back of juvenile shows pattern of coarse crescents. Secondaries pale (darker in Common). **VOICE:** Rasping *ka-a-ak;* a soft two-syllable *chu-ick* or *chiv-ick.* **HABITAT:** Salt bays, estuaries, ocean.

LEAST TERN   Uncommon to fairly common M210
Sternula antillarum
9 in. (23 cm). A *very small,* pale tern, with rapid wingbeats (quicker than other terns). *Breeding adult:* Dark-tipped *yellow bill* (in fall, may have dark bill) and *white forehead. Immature:* Dark bill, dark cheek and nape, dusky crown, dark shoulder bar. **VOICE:** A harsh, squealing *zree-k-zeek.* **HABITAT:** Beaches, bays, ponds, large rivers, sandbars.

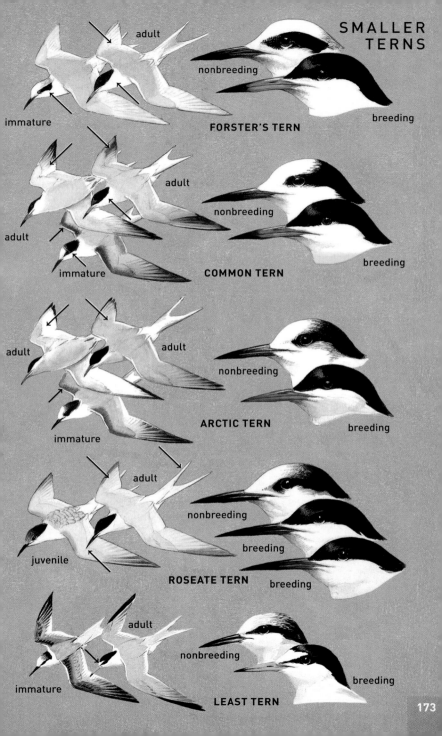

SMALLER TERNS

FORSTER'S TERN

adult

immature

nonbreeding

breeding

COMMON TERN

adult

adult

immature

nonbreeding

breeding

ARCTIC TERN

adult

adult

immature

nonbreeding

breeding

ROSEATE TERN

adult

juvenile

nonbreeding

breeding

breeding

LEAST TERN

adult

immature

nonbreeding

breeding

173

GULL-BILLED TERN *Gelochelidon nilotica*   Uncommon M211
14 in. (36 cm). Note *stout black* bill. Stockier and paler than Common Tern; tail much less forked; feet *black*. In nonbreeding plumage, head white with smudgy dark ear patch, pale dusky on nape; suggests a small gull with notched tail. *Immature:* Similar to nonbreeding adult. This tern plucks food from water's surface and often hawks for insects over marshes and fields, swooping (rarely diving) after prey. **VOICE:** *Kay-weck, kay-weck;* also a throaty, rasping *za-za-za.* **SIMILAR SPECIES:** Sandwich Tern, midsized gulls. **HABITAT:** Marshes, fields, coastal bays.

SANDWICH TERN *Thalasseus sandvicensis*   Fairly common M219
15–15½ in. (38–40 cm). Larger than Common Tern. Note *long black bill with yellow tip* "as though dipped in mustard." Bill of young can be mostly black or mostly yellow. Dark outer primaries. *Adult:* All-black cap in breeding plumage, white forehead in nonbreeding plumage; feathers on back of crown elongated, forming crest. Legs black. **VOICE:** Grating *kirr-ick* (higher than Gull-billed Tern's *kay-weck*). **SIMILAR SPECIES:** Gull-billed Tern has stout black bill. **HABITAT:** Coastal waters, jetties, beaches. Often seen with Royal Tern.

ROYAL TERN *Thalasseus maximus*   Common M218
20 in. (51 cm). A large tern, slimmer than Caspian, with large *orange* bill (Caspian's bill heavier, redder, and has dark mark near tip). Tail forked. Although some Royal Terns in spring show solid black crown, for most of year they have *much white on forehead,* black crown feathers forming a crest. Dusky upperside and *pale underside to primaries,* opposite of Caspian. **VOICE:** Sonorous *karr-rik,* mellower (slower and lower-pitched) than Sandwich; also *kaak* or *kak.* **SIMILAR SPECIES:** Caspian Tern. **HABITAT:** Ocean, coasts, beaches, salt bays. More closely tied to coastal waters than Caspian, which is common inland.

CASPIAN TERN *Hydroprogne caspia*   Uncommon M212
21 in. (53 cm). Large size and *stout reddish bill with small dark mark near tip* set Caspian apart from all other terns. Tail of Caspian *shorter;* head and bill larger, crest shorter. Royal's forehead is usually *clear white* (in adult nonbreeding plumage, Caspian has *streaked* forehead). Caspian shows obvious *grayish black on undersurface of primaries, but pale upper surface.* Caspian ranges inland, Royal does not. **VOICE:** Raspy, low *kraa-uh* or *karr,* also repeated *kak;* juveniles give whistled *wheee-oo.* **SIMILAR SPECIES:** Royal Tern. **HABITAT:** Large lakes, rivers, coastal waters, beaches, bays.

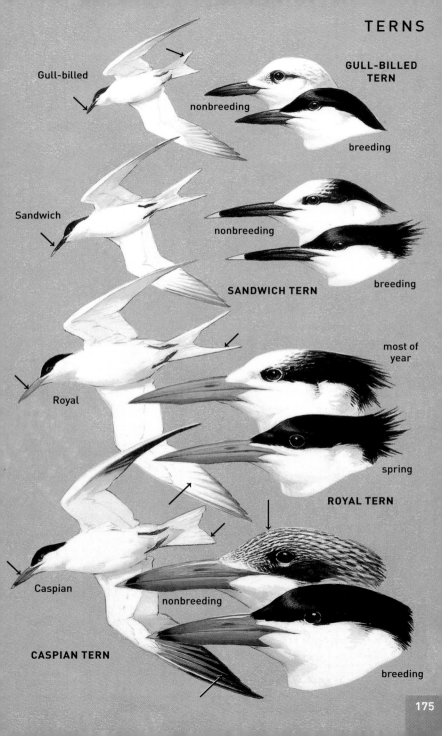

TERNS

Gull-billed

GULL-BILLED TERN

nonbreeding

breeding

Sandwich

nonbreeding

SANDWICH TERN

breeding

most of year

Royal

spring

ROYAL TERN

Caspian

nonbreeding

CASPIAN TERN

breeding

175

BLACK TERN *Chlidonias niger*   Uncommon M213
9½–9¾ in. (24–25 cm). A small dark tern. Short tail only slightly forked. *Breeding adult:* Head and underparts *black; back, wings, and tail dark gray;* wing linings whitish. *Nonbreeding adult and immature:* Note pied head, with dark smudge from crown to ear coverts and on sides of breast. **VOICE:** Sharp *kik, keek,* or *klea.* **HABITAT:** Marshes, lakes; in migration, also coastal waters, including open ocean.

WHITE-WINGED TERN *Chlidonias leucopterus*   Vagrant
9¼–9½ in. (23–24 cm). *Breeding: Underwing lining black, upperwing* and tail *mostly white. Nonbreeding:* Paler than Black Tern; lacks dark shoulder spot. **RANGE:** Vagrant from Eurasia.

BROWN NODDY *Anous stolidus*   Uncommon, local M207
15–15½ in. (38–40 cm). A sooty brown tern with *whitish cap.* Wedge-shaped tail. Immature has duller cap. **VOICE:** Ripping *karrrrk* or *arrr-rowk;* a harsh *eye-ak.* **SIMILAR SPECIES:** Black Noddy. **HABITAT:** Warm ocean waters.

BLACK NODDY *Anous minutus*   Very rare
13½ in. (34 cm). A rare spring visitor to Dry Tortugas, FL; casual visitor to TX. Slightly smaller and slimmer than Brown Noddy, with thinner, *longer bill,* darker body, more *sharply defined white cap.*

SOOTY TERN *Onychoprion fuscatus*   Uncommon, local M208
16 in. (41 cm). *Adult:* A cleanly patterned tern, black above and white below. Cheeks and patch on forehead white; bill and feet black. *Immature:* Dark brown; back spotted with white; note forked tail. **VOICE:** Nasal *wide-a-wake* or *wacky-wack.* **SIMILAR SPECIES:** Bridled Tern. **HABITAT:** Warm ocean waters.

BRIDLED TERN *Onychoprion anaethetus*   Uncommon, local M209
15 in. (38 cm). A tern of warm oceans and, after hurricanes, farther north. Immature has more white on crown. **VOICE:** Mostly silent; sometimes gives a soft, nasal *wheeep.* **SIMILAR SPECIES:** Resembles Sooty Tern, but back brownish, not blackish; *note whitish collar separating black cap from back;* white forehead patch extends behind eye (in Sooty, to above eye). Sooty also has *darker underside of primaries.* **HABITAT:** Warm ocean waters, usually well offshore.

SKIMMERS Subfamily Rynchopinae

Slim, short-legged relatives of gulls and terns. Scissorlike red bill; *lower mandible longer than upper.* **FOOD:** Small fish, crustaceans. **RANGE:** Coasts, ponds, marshes, beaches, rivers of warmer parts of world.

BLACK SKIMMER *Rhynchops niger*   Fairly common M220
18–18½ in. (46–47 cm). Slender, with very long wings. Skims low, dipping lower mandible in water, snapping shut when it comes in contact with a food item. (Forages mostly at night.) *Adult:* Black above; white face and underparts. Bright red bill is long and flat vertically; *lower mandible juts a third beyond upper. Immature:* Brownish and speckled above, bill smaller, duller. **VOICE:** Soft, short, barking notes. **HABITAT:** Bays, marshes, beaches, protected ocean waters.

DARK TERNS AND SKIMMER

BLACK TERN

nonbreeding

WHITE-WINGED TERN

BROWN NODDY

BLACK NODDY

juvenile

Sooty Tern adult

adult

SOOTY TERN

juvenile

adult

BRIDLED TERN

juvenile

adult

BLACK SKIMMER

adult

177

SKUAS AND JAEGERS Family Stercorariidae

Falconlike seabirds that harass gulls and terns, forcing them to disgorge or drop their food. Light, intermediate, and dark morphs exist in at least two species; all have flash of white in primaries. Adult jaegers have two projecting central tail feathers, which are sometimes broken or missing. Young birds lack these feathers. Separating jaegers in most plumages can be very difficult. Skuas are larger, lack tail points, and are broader winged. Sexes alike. **FOOD:** In Arctic and Antarctic, lemmings, eggs, young birds. At sea, food taken from other birds or from water. **RANGE:** Seas of world, breeding in subpolar regions.

GREAT SKUA *Stercorarius skua*   Scarce M221
22–23 in. (56–58 cm). Note conspicuous white wing patch visible on both upper- and underwing. Near size of Herring Gull, but stockier. Dark brown, with rusty and streaked upperparts and short, slightly wedge-shaped tail. Flight strong and swift; harasses other seabirds. **SIMILAR SPECIES:** Dark jaegers may lack distinctive tail-feather extensions. However, skuas' wings wider, less falconlike, white wing patches more striking both above and below, and flight more powerful. Very much like South Polar Skua but averages larger and heavier-billed. Note *warmer brown color, dark cap, less distinct pale nape,* and more *streaked appearance* to upperparts.

SOUTH POLAR SKUA *Stercorarius maccormicki*   Scarce M222
21 in. (53 cm). Near size of Herring Gull, but stockier, with deep-chested, hunch-backed look. Dark, with short, slightly wedge-shaped tail and *conspicuous white wing patch at base of primaries visible on both upper- and underwing.* "Blond" morph has *pale head and underparts* contrasting with darker wings; dark morph uniform gray-brown with *paler nape.* **SIMILAR SPECIES:** Great Skua; dark jaegers (particularly Pomarine Jaeger) may lack tail points, but skuas larger, their wings wider, and they have more striking white wing patches.

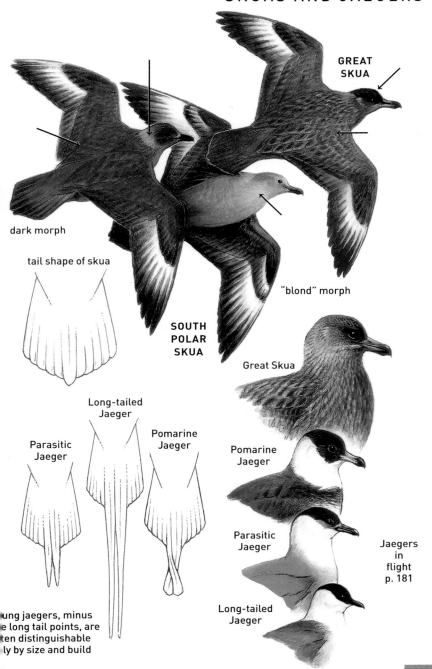

GREAT SKUA

dark morph

tail shape of skua

"blond" morph

SOUTH POLAR SKUA

Great Skua

Long-tailed Jaeger

Parasitic Jaeger

Pomarine Jaeger

Pomarine Jaeger

Parasitic Jaeger

Jaegers in flight p. 181

Long-tailed Jaeger

...ung jaegers, minus ...e long tail points, are ...en distinguishable ...ly by size and build

PARASITIC JAEGER *Stercorarius parasiticus*   Uncommon M224
17–19 in. (44–49 cm). This is the jaeger most frequently seen from shore. Flies with strong, falconlike wing strokes. Like other jaegers, it shows white wing-flash. *Adult:* Dark crown, pale underparts. Sharp tail points project up to 3½ in. (9 cm). Shows small *pale spot* above base of bill. Varies from light to dark morphs. *Juvenile:* Juvenile jaegers show heavy barring, especially on underwing. Juvenile Parasitic is usually *warmer brown* than other juvenile jaegers, often with *more distinct white patch on upperwing.* Up close, look for *streaked head* and *pale-edged primary tips.* **HABITAT:** Primarily ocean, regularly seen from shore; in summer, tundra.

POMARINE JAEGER *Stercorarius pomarinus*   Uncommon M223
19–21 in. (48–53 cm). Like Parasitic Jaeger, but slightly heavier with more gull-like flight style. *Adult: Broad and twisted* central tail feathers project 2–7 in. (5–18 cm). Dark cap extends *farther down* through face to "jowls." Bill heavy and *pink-based;* breast band *darker* and more barred than in Parasitic. *Juvenile:* Plumage variable, but compared with juvenile Parasitic it lacks warm tones, and very short central tail feathers are blunt-tipped. Look for white-based primary coverts creating *double white flash* on underwing. **HABITAT:** Open ocean, seen from shore in small numbers; in summer, tundra.

LONG-TAILED JAEGER *Stercorarius longicaudus*   Scarce M225
17–22 in. (44–56 cm). The smallest, slimmest jaeger with buoyant, ternlike flight style. *Adults:* Paler and grayer above than other jaegers with distinctly *two-toned upperwing* in flight; *long tail streamers* project 3–6 in. (8–15 cm); black cap neat and *sharply defined; no breast band;* almost *no white in wings. Juvenile:* Varies from light to dark morph. All show very *limited white on upperwing* (two or three primary shafts), *stubby bill,* and longer, blunter-tipped central tail feathers than other juvenile jaegers. Light morph has distinctively *pale grayish head and breast* and extensively *white belly.* Dark morph cold gray-brown and often with pale nape and *pale lower breast patch.* **HABITAT:** Open ocean; tundra in summer. Most pelagic of the jaegers.

JAEGERS

light morph

Parasitic

PARASITIC
JAEGER

Pomarine

dark morph

Long-tailed

intermediate
morph

dark-
morph
juvenile
Parasitic

juvenile

POMARINE
JAEGER

dark morph

Pomarine

LONG-TAILED
JAEGER

light-morph
juvenile
Long-tailed

light morph

juvenile
Long-
tailed

dark
morph

Auks, Murres, and Puffins Family Alcidae

The northern counterparts of penguins, but alcids can fly, beating their small narrow wings in a whir, often veering. They have short neck and pointed, stubby, or deep and laterally compressed bill. Alcids swim and dive expertly. Most species nest on sea cliffs or in burrows, often in crowded colonies, and most winter on open ocean. Mostly silent away from breeding grounds. Sexes alike. **FOOD:** Fish, squid, zooplankton. **RANGE:** N. Atlantic, N. Pacific, and Arctic oceans.

RAZORBILL *Alca torda*   Uncommon M229

17 in. (43 cm). Size of a small duck. Black above and white below; characterized by rather heavy head, thick neck, and flat bill crossed midway by a white mark. On water, cocked-up pointed tail is often characteristic. **VOICE:** Weak whirring whistle; a deep growling *hey Al.* **SIMILAR SPECIES:** Nonbreeding face pattern suggests Common Murre. Bill of immature Razorbill is smaller than adult's and lacks white mark (hence resembling a murre's), but it is stubby and rounded enough to suggest bird's identity as an auk. See also Long-tailed Duck. **HABITAT:** Nests on rocky offshore islands. Forages in coastal waters.

THICK-BILLED MURRE *Uria lomvia*   Scarce M228

18 in. (46 cm). Similar to Common Murre, but a bit *blacker above.* Bill slightly shorter, thicker, with *whitish line along gape.* Overall a bit stockier. White of foreneck forms inverted V. In nonbreeding plumage, dark on head extends *well below eye;* no dark line through white ear coverts. White bill mark less evident. **VOICE:** Guttural calls and moans, hence the name "murre." **SIMILAR SPECIES:** Common Murre, Razorbill. **HABITAT:** Nests on coastal cliff ledges. Spends nonbreeding season on offshore ocean waters.

COMMON MURRE *Uria aalge*   Uncommon M227

17–17½ in. (43–45 cm). Size of a small duck, with slender pointed bill. *Breeding:* Head, neck, back, and wings dark, *tinged brownish;* underparts, wing linings, and line on rear edge of wing white. *Dusky markings on flanks* on some birds. *Nonbreeding:* Similar, but throat and cheeks white. *Black mark extends from eye to cheek* (see also Razorbill). Murres often raft on water, fly in lines, stand erect on sea cliffs. Bridled morph occurs within regular plumage. **SIMILAR SPECIES:** Thick-billed Murre, Razorbill, Long-tailed Duck. **HABITAT:** Same as Thick-billed Murre.

ALCIDS (AUKS)

immature

breeding

RAZORBILL

nonbreeding

nonbreeding

THICK-BILLED MURRE

Common

breeding

nonbreeding

COMMON MURRE

breeding

Common

breeding

Thick-billed breeding

bridled morph

Razorbill

breeding

Great Auk extinct 1844

183

DOVEKIE *Alle alle* Scarce M226

8–8¼ in. (20–21 cm). A very small alcid, about the size of European Starling. Chubby and seemingly neckless, with very stubby bill. In flight, flocks bunch tightly, starlinglike. Contrasting pattern — black above, white below. Black-hooded in breeding plumage, white-chested in nonbreeding plumage. **VOICE:** Shrill chatter. Noisy on nesting grounds. **SIMILAR SPECIES:** Much smaller and shorter billed than murres or Razorbill. **HABITAT:** Nests in high Arctic on coastal cliffs. Winters at sea in N. Atlantic.

ANCIENT MURRELET *Synthliboramphus antiquus* Vagrant

10 in. (25 cm). In all plumages, *gray back contrasts with black cap.* Bill yellow. **RANGE AND HABITAT:** Casual visitor from AK and BC to lakes, reservoirs, and rivers far inland all the way to Atlantic Coast.

LONG-BILLED MURRELET *Brachyramphus perdix* Vagrant

10–11 in. (25–28 cm). A small alcid with a slim bill. *Breeding:* Mottled brown with whitish throat and pale eye-arcs. *Nonbreeding:* Blackish above and white below with mottled whitish bar on scapulars. **SIMILAR SPECIES:** Nonbreeding Dovekie has white hind neck, stubbier bill. **RANGE AND HABITAT:** Casual visitor (mostly between late summer and early winter) from Asia to lakes, reservoirs, and rivers far inland all the way to Atlantic Coast.

BLACK GUILLEMOT *Cepphus grylle* Fairly common M230

13 in. (33 cm). *Breeding:* Midsized black bird with large white wing patch, bright red feet, and pointed bill. Inside of mouth red. *Nonbreeding:* Pale with whitish underparts and barred back. Wings black with white patch as in summer. *Immature:* Darker above than non-breeding adult, with dingier, mottled wing patch. **VOICE:** Wheezy or hissing *peeee;* very high pitched. **SIMILAR SPECIES:** No other Atlantic alcid has white wing patch (although others show a narrow line of white on trailing edge of wing). In winter, much larger White-winged Scoter (with white wing patch) is black, whereas Black Guillemot is usually whitish. Wing patch of White-winged Scoter is positioned at rear of wing. **HABITAT:** Inshore ocean waters; breeds in small groups or singly in holes in ground or under rocks on rocky shores, islands. Less pelagic than most other alcids.

ATLANTIC PUFFIN *Fratercula arctica* Uncommon M231

12½ in. (32 cm). Colorful triangular bill is most striking feature of chunky little "Sea Parrot." On the wing, it is a stubby, short-necked, thick-headed bird with buzzy flight. No white border on wing. *Breeding:* Upperparts black, underbody white, cheeks pale gray; triangular bill broadly tipped with red. Feet bright orange. *Nonbreeding:* Cheeks grayer; bill smaller, duller, but obviously a puffin. *Immature:* Bill much smaller, mostly dark, but both mandibles well curved. Chunky shape and gray cheeks are unmistakably those of a puffin. **VOICE:** Usually silent. When nesting, a low, growling *ow* or *arr.* **SIMILAR SPECIES:** Immature may be mistaken for young Razorbill, but note gray cheeks, all-dark underwing. **HABITAT:** Very rarely seen from shore except near breeding colonies.

ATLANTIC ALCIDS (AUKS) AND MURRELETS

nonbreeding

breeding

DOVEKIE

nonbreeding

breeding

nonbreeding

ANCIENT MURRELET

nonbreeding

LONG-BILLED MURRELET

breeding

nonbreeding

BLACK GUILLEMOT

breeding

breeding

immature

breeding

ATLANTIC PUFFIN

nonbreeding

breeding adults

Black Guillemot breeding

Dovekie breeding

185

PIGEONS AND DOVES Family Columbidae

Plump, fast-flying birds with small head and low, cooing voice; nod their head as they walk. Two types: (1) birds with fanlike tails (e.g., Rock Pigeon) and (2) smaller birds with rounded or pointed tail (e.g., Mourning Dove). Sexes mostly similar. **FOOD:** Seeds, waste grain, fruit, insects. **RANGE:** Nearly worldwide in tropical and temperate regions.

BAND-TAILED PIGEON *Patagioenas fasciata*   Vagrant

14½–15 in. (37–38 cm). Heavily built; might be mistaken for Rock Pigeon except for its woodland habitat and tendency to alight in trees. Note *broad pale band* across end of tail; *white band* on nape. Feet yellow. Bill *yellow* with *dark tip.* **VOICE:** Hollow owl-like *oo-whoo* or *whoo-oo-whoo*, repeated. **SIMILAR SPECIES:** Rock Pigeon. **RANGE:** Casual visitor from the west to Great Plains; accidental farther east.

RED-BILLED PIGEON *Patagioenas flavirostris*   Scarce, local M234

14–14½ in. (36–37 cm). A large all-dark pigeon (in good light deep maroon). Bill red with yellowish tip. Shy, mostly arboreal. Recent decline in numbers. **VOICE:** *Whoo, whoo, whooooooo.* **SIMILAR SPECIES:** Rock Pigeon. **HABITAT:** Riparian woodlands with tall trees and brush.

WHITE-CROWNED PIGEON   Uncommon, local M233
Patagioenas leucocephala

13½ in. (34 cm). A stocky, shy pigeon completely dark except for immaculate white crown. **VOICE:** Low owl-like *wof, wof, wo, co-woo.* **SIMILAR SPECIES:** Rock Pigeon. **HABITAT:** Mangrove keys, thickets, hardwood hammocks. Perches on power lines, treetops.

AFRICAN COLLARED-DOVE *Streptopelia roseogrisea*   Exotic

12 in. (30 cm). Escaped cage bird. Smaller and much paler than Eurasian Collared-Dove with whiter undertail coverts, different call. Hybrids with Eurasian occur. **VOICE:** Soft series of two-syllable cooing notes.

EURASIAN COLLARED-DOVE   Locally common, exotic M235
Streptopelia decaocto

12½–13 in. (32–33 cm). Recent colonizer of N. America from Caribbean but native to Eurasia; rapidly increasing and spreading. Slightly chunkier than Mourning Dove, *paler beige,* and with *square-cut tail.* Note *narrow black ring on hindneck. Grayish undertail coverts.* Three-toned wing pattern in flight. **VOICE:** *Three*-noted *coo-COOO-cup.* **SIMILAR SPECIES:** African Collared-Dove. **HABITAT:** Towns, field edges, cultivated land.

ROCK PIGEON (ROCK DOVE, DOMESTIC PIGEON)   Common M232
Columba livia

12½ in. (32 cm). Introduced from Eurasia. Typical birds are gray with *whitish rump, two black wing bars,* and broad, dark tail band. Domestic stock or feral birds may have many color variants. **VOICE:** Soft, gurgling *coo-roo-coo.* **SIMILAR SPECIES:** Band-tailed Pigeon. **HABITAT:** Cities, farms, cliffs, bridges.

PIGEONS AND DOVES

BAND-TAILED PIGEON

RED-BILLED PIGEON

WHITE-CROWNED PIGEON

AFRICAN COLLARED-DOVE

EURASIAN COLLARED-DOVE

plumages variable

ROCK PIGEON

typical form

187

WHITE-WINGED DOVE *Zenaida asiatica*   Common M236
11½–12 in. (29–30 cm). Readily known by *white wing patches, large when bird is in flight, narrow when at rest.* Otherwise similar to Mourning Dove, but tail *rounded* and tipped with broad white corners, bill slightly longer, eye orangey red. **VOICE:** Harsh cooing, *who cooks for you?*; also, *ooo-uh-CUCK oo.* Sounds vaguely like crowing of a young rooster. **SIMILAR SPECIES:** Mourning and White-tipped doves. **HABITAT:** River woods, mesquite, groves, towns, feeders.

MOURNING DOVE *Zenaida macroura*   Common M237
12 in. (30–31 cm). The common widespread wild dove. Brown; smaller and slimmer than Rock Pigeon. Note *pointed tail* with large white spots. **VOICE:** Hollow, mournful *coah, cooo, coo, cooo.* At a distance, only the three *coo*s are audible. **SIMILAR SPECIES:** White-winged Dove. **HABITAT:** Farms, towns, open woods, fields, scrub, roadsides, grasslands, feeders.

WHITE-TIPPED DOVE *Leptotila verreauxi*   Uncommon, local M240
11½ in. (29 cm). Large stocky dove with broad, dark wings. Short tail has *white corners.* Body pale, underwings cinnamon. Flies fast through woods. **VOICE:** Long, drawn-out, hollow *who — whooooooooo.* **SIMILAR SPECIES:** White-winged and Mourning doves. **HABITAT:** Often seen walking in shadows of brushy tangles or dense woods.

RUDDY GROUND-DOVE *Columbina talpacoti*   Vagrant
6½–6¾ in. (16–17 cm). This rare stray from Mex. to TX is similar to Common Ground-Dove but is slightly larger, longer tailed, and longer billed; has *dark, grayish base* to bill; *lacks all scaliness.* Has *blackish* spots and streaks on wing coverts and *scapulars. Male:* Washed rufous. *Female and immature:* Plain brown and gray. *Caution:* A bright male Common Ground-Dove may be misidentified as a Ruddy. **VOICE:** Cooing similar to Common Ground-Dove's, but faster and more repetitive: *pity-you pity-you pity you.* **SIMILAR SPECIES:** Inca Dove, Common Ground-Dove. **HABITAT:** Farms, livestock pens, fields, brushy areas. Often found with Inca Dove and Common Ground-Dove.

COMMON GROUND-DOVE *Columbina passerina*   Uncommon M239
6¼–6½ in. (15–16 cm). A very small dove. Note *stubby black tail,* scaly breast, pinkish or orangey base of bill, and rounded wings that flash *rufous* in flight, *bronzy* spots and streaks on wing coverts. Feet yellow or pink. Adult male's body washed pinkish. **VOICE:** Soft, monotonously repeated *woo-oo, woo-oo,* etc. May sound monosyllabic — *wooo,* with rising inflection. **SIMILAR SPECIES:** Inca Dove, Ruddy Ground-Dove, juvenile Mourning Dove. **HABITAT:** Farms, orchards, brushy areas, roadsides.

INCA DOVE *Columbina inca*   Fairly common M238
8¼–8½ in. (21–22 cm). A very small, slim dove with *scaly* look. *Rufous* in primaries (as in ground-doves), but has *longer tail* with *white sides.* **VOICE:** Monotonous *coo-hoo* or *no-hope.* **SIMILAR SPECIES:** Common Ground-Dove has short tail without obvious white, lacks scaling on back. **HABITAT:** Towns, parks, farms.

DOVES

PASSENGER
PIGEON
extinct
1914

WHITE-
WINGED
DOVE

MOURNING
DOVE

WHITE-TIPPED DOVE

INCA DOVE

RUDDY
GROUND-DOVE
adult ♂

COMMON
GROUND-DOVE

PARAKEETS AND PARROTS Family Psittacidae

Noisy and gaudily colored. Compact, short-necked birds with stout, hooked bill. Parakeets smaller, with long, pointed tail. Feet zygodactyl (two toes fore, two aft). **RANGE:** Worldwide in Tropics and subtropics. Several exotic species have been released or have escaped, especially around Miami.

MONK PARAKEET *Myiopsitta monachus*　　Locally fairly common
(Argentina) 11 in. (28 cm). Pale gray face and chest, buff band across belly. Established in spots from CT to FL and west to IL and TX. Massive nest of sticks (only parrot to build a stick nest), with several compartments. Raucous calls. Comes to feeders.

GREEN PARAKEET *Aratinga holochlora*　　Locally established
10–12 in. (25–30 cm). *Aratinga* parakeets have long pointed tails, so are readily separable from chunkier square-tailed parrots. This, the largest (size of Mourning Dove), is green above, yellow-green below. **VOICE:** Sharp, squeaky notes, shrill noisy chatter. **RANGE AND HABITAT:** Tropical Mex. to s. Nicaragua. Resident populations established in some residential areas of s. Rio Grande Valley in TX.

RED-CROWNED PARROT *Amazona viridigenalis* Locally established
12 in. (30 cm). Large, with red crown (reduced in first year), blue nape, red wing panels. Established in s. TX, possibly from Mexican population.

BLACK-HOODED PARAKEET *Nandayus nenday*
(S. America) 12 in. (30 cm). Locally established in FL.

MITRED PARAKEET *Aratinga mitrata*
(S. America) 15 in. (38 cm). Found in s. FL.

WHITE-WINGED PARAKEET *Brotogeris versicolurus*　　　Local
(S. America) 9 in. (23 cm). Locally established in Miami area. Now outnumbered by Yellow-chevroned Parakeet.

YELLOW-CHEVRONED PARAKEET *Brotogeris chiriri*
(S. America) 9 in. (23 cm). Found in s. FL.

BUDGERIGAR *Melopsittacus undulatus*　　　Local
(Australia) 7 in. (18 cm). Formerly established in FL; declining; escapees seen in many areas.

LILAC-CROWNED PARROT *Amazona finschi*
(Mex.) 12½–13½ in. (30–34 cm). Like first-year Red-crowned but darker. Red forehead, *lilac* crown, longer tail. A few live in s. TX.

YELLOW-HEADED PARROT *Amazona oratrix*
(Mex. and Belize) 14–15 in. (36–38 cm). Escapees found in several areas; established locally in s. FL and s. TX.

RED-LORED PARROT *Amazona autumnalis*
(Cen. and S. America) 12–13 in. (30–33 cm). Small numbers in TX, FL.

WHITE-FRONTED PARROT *Amazona albifrons*
(Cen. America) 9–10 in. (23–25 cm). Found in small numbers in FL.

PARAKEETS AND PARROTS

CAROLINA PARAKEET
extinct 1920s

MONK PARAKEET

GREEN PARAKEET

RED-CROWNED PARROT

UNESTABLISHED EXOTICS

LACK-HOODED PARAKEET

BUDGERIGAR

WHITE-WINGED PARAKEET

YELLOW-CHEVRONED PARAKEET

some individuals may be blue or yellow

MITRED PARAKEET

ILAC-CROWNED PARROT

YELLOW-HEADED PARROT

RED-LORED PARROT

WHITE-FRONTED PARROT

Cuckoos, Roadrunners, and Anis
Family Cuculidae

Slender, long-tailed birds; feet zygodactyl (two toes forward, two backward). Sexes alike. **FOOD:** Cuckoos eat caterpillars, other insects; roadrunners eat reptiles, rodents, large insects, small birds; anis eat seeds, fruit. **RANGE:** Warm and temperate regions of world. N. American cuckoos are not parasitic.

YELLOW-BILLED CUCKOO Fairly common M241
Coccyzus americanus
12 in. (30–31 cm). Note *rufous* in wings, *large white* spots on black undertail, and *yellow* lower mandible. **VOICE:** Song a rapid throaty *ka-ka-ka-ka-ka-ka-ka-kow-kow-kowlp-kowlp, kowlp, kowlp* (slowing toward end). **HABITAT:** Deciduous woodlands.

MANGROVE CUCKOO *Coccyzus minor* Uncommon, local M242
12 in. (30–31 cm). Similar to Yellow-billed Cuckoo (both found in s. FL), but belly creamy buff; no rufous in wing. Note black ear patch. **VOICE:** Accelerating series of guttural notes: *unh unh unh unh unh unh aanngg aanngg.* **HABITAT:** Mangroves, hardwood forests.

BLACK-BILLED CUCKOO Uncommon M243
Coccyzus erythropthalmus
11½–12 in. (29–30 cm). *Adult:* Similar to Yellow-billed Cuckoo, but *bill dark gray to blackish;* narrow *red orbital ring. No rufous in wing;* undertail spots small. *Immature:* Has yellow orbital ring and may have small amount of rufous in wing. **VOICE:** Fast, rhythmic *cucucu, cucucu, cucucu,* etc. The grouped rhythm (three or four) is typical, but often employs irregular cadences. May sing at night. **HABITAT:** Wood edges, groves, thickets.

GROOVE-BILLED ANI Uncommon, local M246
Crotophaga sulcirostris
13–13½ in. (33–34 cm). Very similar to Smooth-billed but bill has fine grooves (lacking in juvenile) and less arched ridge. **VOICE:** Repeated *whee-o* or *tee-ho,* first note slurring up. **HABITAT:** Thickets, open woodlands.

SMOOTH-BILLED ANI *Crotophaga ani* Rare, local M245
14–14½ in. (35–37 cm). A coal black, grackle-sized bird with long loose-jointed tail, short wings, and *huge bill with high curved ridge* (giving it puffinlike profile). Flight weak; alternately flaps and sails. Often in groups. **VOICE:** Whining whistle. Querulous *que-lick.* **SIMILAR SPECIES:** Groove-billed Ani, grackles. **HABITAT:** Brushy edges, thickets. Recent major population declines in FL.

GREATER ROADRUNNER *Geococcyx californianus* Uncommon M244
22–23 in. (56–58 cm). The familiar cuckoo that runs on ground. A large, slender, streaked bird, with long, white-edged tail; shaggy crest; long legs. **VOICE:** Six to eight low, dovelike *coos,* descending in pitch. **SIMILAR SPECIES:** Thrashers are much smaller. **HABITAT:** Open country with scattered cover, brush, regenerating clearcuts.

CUCKOOS, ETC.

YELLOW-BILLED
CUCKOO

adults

BLACK-
BILLED
CUCKOO

MANGROVE
CUCKOO

immature

adult

GROOVE-
BILLED
ANI

SMOOTH-
BILLED
ANI

GREATER
ROADRUNNER

Owls Families Tytonidae (Barn Owls) and Strigidae (Typical Owls)

Chiefly nocturnal birds of prey, with large heads and flattened faces forming facial disk; large, forward-facing eyes; hooked bill and claws; usually feathered feet (outer toe reversible). Flight noiseless, mothlike. Some species have "horns," or ear tufts. Sexes similar; female larger. **FOOD**: Rodents, birds, reptiles, fish, large insects. **RANGE**: Nearly worldwide.

SHORT-EARED OWL *Asio flammeus* Uncommon M258

15 in. (38 cm). An owl of open country; often abroad by day, particularly at dawn and dusk or when cloudy. Often tussles with Northern Harrier. Streaked, tawny brown color and irregular flopping flight identify it. Large buffy wing patches show in flight, along with black carpal ("wrist") patch. *Dark facial disk* emphasizes yellow eyes. **VOICE**: Emphatic, sneezy bark: *kee-yow!, wow!,* or *waow!* **SIMILAR SPECIES**: Long-eared Owl somewhat similar in flight, but with jerkier wing action. **HABITAT**: Grasslands, fresh and salt marshes, dunes, tundra. Roosts on ground, rarely in and under trees. Winter range and numbers vary from year to year.

EASTERN SCREECH-OWL *Megascops asio* Common M248

8½ in. (22 cm). The only small eastern owl with ear tufts. Two color morphs: red and gray. No other owl is bright foxy red. Young birds may lack conspicuous ear tufts. **VOICE**: Mournful whinny or wail; tremulous, *descending* in pitch. Sometimes a series of notes on one pitch. **HABITAT**: Deciduous woodlands, shade trees, residential areas.

LONG-EARED OWL *Asio otus* Uncommon M257

15 in. (38 cm). A slender, crow-sized owl with long ear tufts. Usually seen "frozen" close to trunk of a tree. Much smaller than Great Horned Owl; underparts streaked *lengthwise,* not barred crosswise. Ears *closer together, erectile;* much black around eyes. **VOICE**: One or two long *hooo*s; usually silent. Also a catlike whine and doglike bark. **SIMILAR SPECIES**: In flight, similar to Short-eared Owl, which has more mothlike, meandering flight. See Great Horned Owl. **HABITAT**: Coniferous and deciduous woodlands, shelterbelts. Often roosts in groups in nonbreeding season. Hunts over open country.

GREAT HORNED OWL *Bubo virginianus* Common M249

21–22 in. (54–56 cm). A *very large* owl with ear tufts, or "horns." Heavily *barred* beneath; conspicuous *white throat bib.* In flight, as large as our larger hawks; looks neckless, large-headed. Varies regionally from very dark to rather pale. Often active just before dark. **VOICE**: Male usually utters five or six resonant hoots: *hu-hu-hu-hu, hoo! hoo!* Female's hoots slightly higher pitched, in shorter sequence. Young make catlike screams, especially when begging or when separated from adults in late summer and fall. **SIMILAR SPECIES**: Long-eared Owl smaller (crow-sized in flight), with lengthwise streaking rather than crosswise barring beneath; ears closer together; lacks white bib. **HABITAT**: Forests, woodlots, open country.

OWLS

SHORT-EARED
OWL

red morph

gray morph

EASTERN
SCREECH-OWL

LONG-EARED
OWL

subarctic

GREAT
HORNED
OWL

typical

NORTHERN HAWK OWL *Surnia ulula*   Scarce M251

16 in. (41 cm). A medium-sized day-flying owl, with *long, rounded tail* and *barred underparts*. Often *perches at tip of tree* and jerks tail like a kestrel. Shrikelike, it flies low, rising abuptly to perch. **VOICE:** Falcon-like chattering *kikikiki,* and kestrel-like *illy-illy-illy-illy.* Also a harsh scream. **HABITAT:** Open coniferous forests, birch scrub, tamarack bogs, muskeg, field edges. Sporadically appears south of normal range.

BARRED OWL *Strix varia*   Fairly common M255

20–21 in. (51–53 cm). A large, brown, puffy-headed woodland owl with large, moist *brown* eyes. Barred *across* chest and streaked *lengthwise* on belly. **VOICE:** Usually eight accented hoots, in two groups of four: *hoohoo-hoohoo, hoohoohooHOOaaw.* The *aaw* at end is characteristic. Sometimes rendered as *who cooks for you, who cooks for you-all.* Also simply a *hoo-aww.* **SIMILAR SPECIES:** Other large owls, except Barn, have yellow eyes. **HABITAT:** Woodlands, wooded river bottoms, wooded swamps.

BARN OWL *Tyto alba*   Uncommon M247

16 in. (41 cm). A long-legged, knock-kneed, pale, monkey-faced owl. *White heart-shaped face and dark eyes;* no ear tufts. Distinguished in flight as an owl by large head and mothlike flight; as this species by unstreaked whitish, buff, or pale cinnamon underparts (ghostly at night) and warm brown back. **VOICE:** Shrill, rasping hiss or snore: *kschh* or *shiiish.* **SIMILAR SPECIES:** Short-eared Owl streaked, has darker face and underparts, *yellow* eyes. **HABITAT:** Open country, groves, farms, barns, towns, cliffs.

GREAT GRAY OWL *Strix nebulosa*   Scarce M256

26–28 in. (67–73 cm). Our largest N. American owl; very tame. Dusky gray, heavily striped *lengthwise* on underparts. Round-headed, with-out ear tufts; large, *strongly lined facial disk* dwarfs *yellow* eyes. Note *black chin spot* bordered by two broad white patches like *white mus-taches.* Tail long for an owl. An irruptive species. Invades to the south one year, then may be rare for several years. **VOICE:** Deep *whoo-hoo-hoo.* Also deep single *whoo*s. **SIMILAR SPECIES:** Barred Owl much smaller. **HABITAT:** Coniferous forests, adjacent meadows, bogs. Often hunts by day, particularly in winter.

SNOWY OWL *Bubo scandiacus*   Scarce M250

22–24 in. (56–61 cm). An irruptive, large, mostly *white,* Arctic, day-flying owl; variably flecked or barred with dusky. Round head, *yellow eyes.* Females and young birds more heavily flecked than adult males. **VOICE:** Usually silent. Flight call when breeding a loud, re-peated *krow-ow;* also a repeated *rick.* **SIMILAR SPECIES:** Barn Owl whitish on underparts only; much smaller and has dark eyes. Many young owls are whitish when in down. See Gyrfalcon (white morph). **HABITAT:** Prairies, fields, marshes, beaches; in summer, Arctic tun-dra. Perches on dunes, posts, haystacks, ground in open country, sometimes buildings. Cyclic winter irruptions southward into U.S.

LARGE OWLS
Without ear tufts

NORTHERN HAWK OWL

BARN OWL
female
(male is whiter below)

BARRED OWL

SNOWY OWL
adult male

GREAT GRAY OWL

197

BURROWING OWL *Athene cunicularia* Uncommon M254
9½ in. (24 cm). A small owl of open country, often seen by day standing erect on ground or low perches. Note *long legs*. Barred and spotted, with white chin stripe, round head. Bobs and bows when agitated. **VOICE:** Rapid, chattering *quick-quick-quick*. At night, a mellow *co-hoo*, higher than Mourning Dove's *coo*. Young in burrow rattle like rattlesnake to deter predators. **HABITAT:** Open grasslands, unplowed prairies, farmland, airfields, golf courses. Nests in burrows in ground or in pipes.

NORTHERN SAW-WHET OWL *Aegolius acadicus* Uncommon M260
8 in. (20 cm). A very tame little owl; smaller than a screech-owl, without ear tufts. Underparts have blotchy, reddish brown streaks. Bill black. Forehead streaked white. *Juvenile:* Chocolate brown in summer, with conspicuous white eyebrows; belly *tawny ocher*. **VOICE:** Song a mellow, whistled note repeated in endless succession, often 100 to 130 times per minute: *too, too, too, too,* etc. Also raspy, squirrel-like yelps. **SIMILAR SPECIES:** Boreal Owl. **HABITAT:** Coniferous and mixed woods, swamps.

BOREAL OWL *Aegolius funereus* Scarce M259
10 in. (25 cm). A small, flat-headed, earless owl of northern coniferous forests. Tame. Similar to Northern Saw-whet Owl, but a bit larger; facial disk pale grayish white, *framed with black;* bill pale horn color or *yellowish;* forehead *thickly spotted* with white. *Juvenile:* Similar to young Northern Saw-whet, but duskier; eyebrows grayish; belly obscurely blotched. **VOICE:** "Song" an accelerating series of hoots, similar to a winnowing snipe; call includes a raspy *skew*. **SIMILAR SPECIES:** Northern Saw-whet Owl. **HABITAT:** Forests primarily of spruce and fir; muskeg. Sporadically appears south of normal range.

FERRUGINOUS PYGMY-OWL *Glaucidium brasilianum* Scarce M252
6½–6¾ in. (16–17 cm). Hunts by day, particularly early and late. Often mobbed by birds. Streaking on breast *brownish* rather than black; crown has fine pale streaks. Tail *rusty, barred with black*. **VOICE:** *Chook* or *took;* sometimes repeated monotonously two or three times per second. Calls both in day and at night. **HABITAT:** Mesquite and subtropical woods.

ELF OWL *Micrathene whitneyi* Uncommon M253
5¾ in. (15 cm). A tiny, small-headed, short-tailed, earless owl. Underparts softly striped with rusty; eyebrows white. Hides by day in woodpecker holes in saguaros, telephone poles, or trees. Found at night by call. **VOICE:** Rapid, high-pitched *whi-whi-whi-whi-whi-whi* or *chewk-chewk-chewk-chewk,* etc., often becoming higher and more yipping or puppylike, and chattering in middle of series. **SIMILAR SPECIES:** Eastern Screech-Owl. **HABITAT:** Saguaro and mesquite woodlands and deserts, wooded canyons.

SMALL OWLS

BURROWING OWL

juvenile

adult

NORTHERN SAW-WHET OWL

note "eye pattern" on nape

FERRUGINOUS PYGMY-OWL

adult

BOREAL OWL

ELF OWL

Goatsuckers (Nightjars)
Family Caprimulgidae

Nocturnal birds with ample tail, large eyes, tiny bill, large bristled gape, and very short legs. By day, they rest on limbs or on ground, camouflaged by their "dead-leaf" pattern. Best identified at night by voice. **FOOD:** Nocturnal insects. **RANGE:** Nearly worldwide in temperate and tropical land regions.

COMMON NIGHTHAWK *Chordeiles minor*　　　　Uncommon M262
9½ in. (24 cm). A slim-winged, gray-brown bird, often seen high in air; flies with easy strokes, changing gear to quicker erratic strokes. Prefers dusk, but may be abroad at midday. Note *broad white bar* across pointed wing. Barred white-and-gray undertail coverts. Male has white bar across notched tail and white throat. At rest, *tertial feathers extend well past white wing patch;* wingtips extend to or beyond tail tip. **VOICE:** Nasal *peer* or *pee-ik*. In aerial display, male dives, then zooms up sharply with sudden deep whir of wings. **SIMILAR SPECIES:** Antillean Nighthawk regular in FL Keys; best distinguished by voice. Lesser Nighthawk's white on wing closer to tip, wings more bluntly tipped; most are browner than Common. **HABITAT:** Open country from mountains to lowlands; open pine woods; often seen in air over cities, towns. Also over ponds. Sits on ground, posts, rails, roofs, limbs.

LESSER NIGHTHAWK　　　　Uncommon, local M261
Chordeiles acutipennis
8½–9 in. (21–23 cm). Slightly smaller than Common Nighthawk; white bar (*buffy* in female) *closer to tip of wing* (at rest, this bar even with or slightly beyond tips of tertial feathers). More extensive brown spotting on inner primaries. Undertail coverts browner, less sharply barred. Readily identified by odd calls. Does not power-dive. **VOICE:** Low *chuck chuck* and soft purring or whinnying sound, much like trilling of a toad. **SIMILAR SPECIES:** Common Nighthawk. **RANGE:** Primarily southwestern. A few may wander east along Gulf Coast as far as FL in fall and winter. **HABITAT:** Lowlands; arid scrub, dry grasslands, farm fields, dirt roads. Also seen in air over ponds. Sits on branches and ground.

ANTILLEAN NIGHTHAWK *Chordeiles gundlachii*　　　Scarce, local
8–8½ in. (20–22 cm). This W. Indian species is a regular late-spring and summer visitor to FL Keys and Dry Tortugas. Somewhat tawnier and smaller than Common Nighthawk, but readily distinguished from it only by call. **VOICE:** Katydid-like *killy-kadick* or *pity-pit-pit*. **SIMILAR SPECIES:** Common and Lesser nighthawks. **HABITAT:** Open fields, suburban areas.

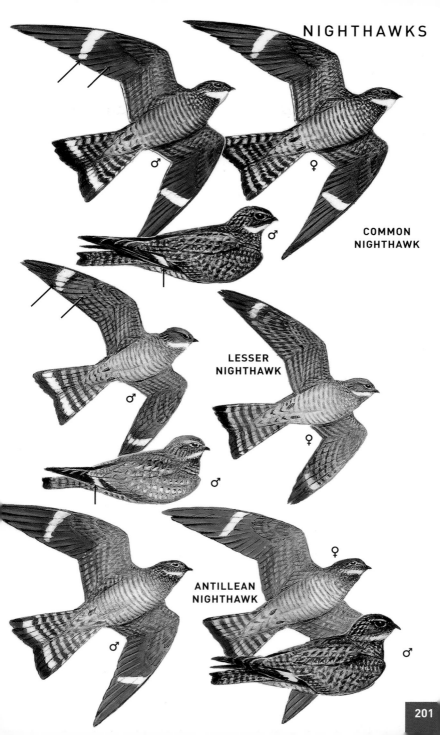

NIGHTHAWKS

COMMON
NIGHTHAWK

LESSER
NIGHTHAWK

ANTILLEAN
NIGHTHAWK

WHIP-POOR-WILL *Caprimulgus vociferus*   Uncommon M266

9½–9¾ in. (24–25 cm). A voice in the night woods, this species is more often heard than seen. When flushed by day, flits away on rounded wings, like a large brown moth. Male shows large *white tail patches;* in female these are buffy. At rest, tail extends beyond wings, unlike nighthawk's. Note *black throat* and *broad black crown stripe.* **VOICE:** At night, a rolling, tiresomely repeated *WHIP poor-WEEL,* or *purple-rib,* etc. **SIMILAR SPECIES:** Common Poorwill, Chuck-will's-widow. **HABITAT:** Drier second-growth woodlands, especially oak and pine.

CHUCK-WILL'S-WIDOW   Uncommon M265
Caprimulgus carolinensis

12 in. (30 cm). Similar to Whip-poor-will; larger, much browner, with *brown* (not blackish) throat and *streaked crown.* Identify by size (flat, bull-headed appearance), brownish look; more restricted white areas in tail of male; also by voice, range. **VOICE:** Call four-syllable *chuck-will-widow* (less vigorous than effort of Whip-poor-will); *chuck* often very low and difficult to hear. **SIMILAR SPECIES:** Whip-poor-will, Common Poorwill. **HABITAT:** Pine and mixed forests, river woodlands, groves.

COMMON POORWILL *Phalaenoptilus nuttallii*   Uncommon M264

7½–7¾ in. (19–20 cm). Best known by its night cry in arid hills. Appears smaller than a nighthawk, has shorter, more rounded wings *(no white bar)*, and short, rounded tail has *white corners.* Short wings and tail give it a *compact look* at rest. **VOICE:** At night, a loud, repeated *poor-will* or *poor-jill.* **SIMILAR SPECIES:** Whip-poor-will. **HABITAT:** Dry or rocky hills, juniper; roadsides.

COMMON PAURAQUE   Uncommon, local M263
Nyctidromus albicollis

11 in. (28 cm). Larger than Whip-poor-will. Dark brown, with long, round wings and tail. Flight floppy with deep wingbeats. Note *broad white band* across pointed wing of male (female's wing bars buffy). *White in tail* feathers is obvious. At rest, note *pale-edged scapulars.* Recognized by its call. **VOICE:** A hoarse slurred whistle: *purr-WEE-eeerrr.* **SIMILAR SPECIES:** Other nightjars. **HABITAT:** Dense brushy woodlands.

GOATSUCKERS

WHIP-POOR-WILL

CHUCK-WILL'S-
WIDOW

COMMON
POORWILL

COMMON
PAURAQUE

203

HUMMINGBIRDS Family Trochilidae

The smallest birds. Iridescent, with needlelike bill for sipping nectar. Jewel-like gorget (throat feathers) adorns most adult males; in poor light, however, iridescence may not show and throat will appear dark. Hummingbirds hover when feeding; their wing motion is so rapid that wings appear as a blur. They can fly backward. Pugnacious. **FOOD:** Nectar (red flowers favored), small insects, spiders. **RANGE:** W. Hemisphere; majority in Tropics.

RUBY-THROATED HUMMINGBIRD
Fairly common M269

Archilochus colubris

3¾ in. (10 cm). *Male: Fiery red throat,* green back, forked tail. *Female:* White throat; tail blunt, with white spots. *The only widespread species in East;* several other hummers may turn up as strays, especially in Southeast states in fall and winter. **VOICE:** Male's wings hum in courtship display. Chase calls high, squeaky. Other call a soft *chew.* **SIMILAR SPECIES:** Female and immature similar to Black-chinned but have *crown brighter green,* bill slightly shorter, throat whiter, pump tail less. *Outermost primary narrower at tip* (more club-shaped in Black-chinned). Adult male Black-chinned has shallower tail fork than male Ruby-throated (both look black-throated in poor light). See also Anna's and Broad-tailed hummingbirds. Some day-flying sphinx moths (Sphingidae) might be mistaken for hummers. **HABITAT:** Flowers, gardens, feeders, wood edges.

BUFF-BELLIED HUMMINGBIRD
Uncommon, local M268

Amazilia yucatanensis

4¼ in. (11 cm). Note buff underparts, rufous tail, and green throat. Bill orange-red with dark tip. Sexes similar. **VOICE:** Call a surprisingly loud *smak smak smak.* Aggressive flight call an unmusical buzz: *chr chr chr chr chr.* **HABITAT:** Open woodlands, gardens, feeders.

BLACK-CHINNED HUMMINGBIRD
Uncommon to rare M270

Archilochus alexandri

3¾ in. (10 cm). *Male:* Note *black throat* and conspicuous white collar. Blue-violet of lower throat shows only in certain lights. *Caution:* Throat of other hummers may look black until it catches the light. *Female:* See Ruby-throated Hummingbird. **VOICE:** Like Ruby-throated. **SIMILAR SPECIES:** Ruby-throated and Anna's hummingbirds. **HABITAT:** Riparian woodlands, wooded canyons, semiarid country, suburbs, feeders.

RUFOUS HUMMINGBIRD *Selasphorus rufus*
Scarce to rare M273

3¾ in. (9–10 cm). *Male:* No other N. American hummingbird has *rufous back.* Throat flaming orange-red. *Female and immature:* Green-backed; dull *rufous on sides and at base of outer tail feathers* (visible when tail fully spread). Adult females often have a few patchy orange-red feathers on throat. **VOICE:** Produces a variety of vocal and nonvocal sounds. Aggressive flight call a buzzy *zap* followed by sputtering notes, or *zeee chippity chippity.* Male's wings make high trill in flight. **SIMILAR SPECIES:** Allen's, Calliope, and Broad-tailed hummingbirds. **HABITAT:** Wooded or brushy areas, parks, gardens, feeders.

HUMMINGBIRDS

RUBY-THROATED HUMMINGBIRD

♂

♀

♂

sphinx moths resemble hummingbirds

BUFF-BELLIED HUMMINGBIRD

♂

♀

BLACK-CHINNED HUMMINGBIRD

♂

♀

RUFOUS HUMMINGBIRD

BROAD-BILLED HUMMINGBIRD *Cynanthus latirostris*   Vagrant
4 in. (10 cm). *Male: All dark* with blue throat, black tail, *red bill. Female: Orange-red on bill, dark tail, pearly gray* throat; white line behind eye. **VOICE:** Husky *ji-dit,* similar to Ruby-crowned Kinglet. **RANGE AND HABITAT:** Casual visitor from Southwest, mostly at feeders.

GREEN-BREASTED MANGO *Anthracothorax prevostii*   Vagrant
4¾ in. (12 cm). Large, with long downcurved bill. *Adult male:* Dark emerald green. Tail purple. *Female and immature male:* Light underparts with irregular dark stripe. **VOICE:** Call a high-pitched *tzat.* **RANGE AND HABITAT:** Accidental stray from Mex., primarily to s. TX, and almost always at feeders.

ALLEN'S HUMMINGBIRD *Selasphorus sasin*   Vagrant
3¾ in. (9–10 cm). *Male:* Like Rufous but back *green.* (*Note:* Some male Rufous have some green on back.) *Female and immature:* Not safely told from female Rufous (when measured in the hand, Allen's has narrower outer tail feathers). **RANGE AND HABITAT:** Accidental visitor from w. U.S., mostly at feeders.

GREEN VIOLETEAR *Colibri thalassinus*   Vagrant
4¾ in. (12 cm). Large and dark green with violet ear patch. Sexes similar. **VOICE:** Call a series of dry *chip*s. **RANGE AND HABITAT:** Casual, widespread, mostly summer stray from Mex., most records from TX. In U.S. almost always seen at feeders.

BROAD-TAILED HUMMINGBIRD   Vagrant M272
Selasphorus platycercus
4 in. (10 cm). *Male:* Slightly larger than Ruby-throated with longer, squarish tail, white markings on chin. *Female:* Slightly larger and larger-tailed than female Rufous with less rufous in tail, lacks distinct pale semi-collar, paler buff flanks. **VOICE:** Male's wings produce distinctive high trill. Call a sharp *chit!* **RANGE AND HABITAT:** Casual visitor to Gulf Coast from w. U.S., mostly at feeders.

CALLIOPE HUMMINGBIRD *Stellula calliope*   Vagrant M271
3¼ in. (8 cm). Our smallest hummer. *Adult male: Throat with purple-red rays. Female and immature:* Similar to female Broad-tailed and Rufous hummingbirds but slightly smaller, shorter-billed, *shorter tailed (wingtips extend beyond tail at rest);* rust on sides paler, weak *pale line* over base of bill. **VOICE:** High-pitched *chip*s. **RANGE AND HABITAT:** Casual visitor from w. U.S., mostly at feeders.

ANNA'S HUMMINGBIRD *Calypte anna*   Vagrant
4 in. (10 cm). *Male:* Note rose *red crown* and throat. *Female:* Slightly larger and "messier" than female Ruby-throated or Black-chinned hummingbirds, with more spotted throat and more mottled flanks and undertail coverts; often with red throat patch. **VOICE:** Feeding call *chick.* Chase call a raspy chatter. **SIMILAR SPECIES:** Black-chinned and Ruby-throated hummingbirds. Voice important. **RANGE AND HABITAT:** Accidental visitor from w. U.S., mostly at feeders.

RARE HUMMINGBIRDS

GREEN-BREASTED MANGO

BROAD-BILLED HUMMINGBIRD

GREEN VIOLETEAR

BROAD-TAILED HUMMINGBIRD

ALLEN'S HUMMINGBIRD

ANNA'S HUMMINGBIRD

CALLIOPE HUMMINGBIRD

SWIFTS Family Apodidae

Swallowlike, but structurally distinct, with flat skull and all four toes pointing forward. Flight very rapid, "twinkling," sailing between spurts; narrow wings often stiffly bowed. **FOOD:** Flying insects. **RANGE:** Nearly worldwide.

CHIMNEY SWIFT *Chaetura pelagica*   Fairly common M267
5¼ in. (13 cm). Like a cigar with wings. A blackish swallowlike bird with long, slightly curved, stiff wings and stubby tail. Rapid, twinkling wingbeats interspersed with bowed-winged glides. **VOICE:** Loud, rapid ticking or twittering notes. **SIMILAR SPECIES:** Has longer, slimmer wings than swallows. **HABITAT:** Open sky, especially over cities, towns; nests and roosts in chimneys (originally in large hollow trees and cliff crevices).

KINGFISHERS Family Alcedinidae

Solitary birds with large head, long pointed bill, and small syndactyl feet (two toes partially joined). Most are fish eaters, perching above water or hovering and plunging headfirst. **FOOD:** Mainly fish; some species eat insects, lizards. **RANGE:** Almost worldwide.

GREEN KINGFISHER   Uncommon, local M276
Chloroceryle americana
8½–8¾ in. (22 cm). Kingfisher shape, small size; flight buzzy, direct. Upperparts deep green with white spots; collar and underparts white, sides spotted. *Male:* Has *rusty* breast-band. *Female:* Has one or two greenish bands. (The reverse is true in Belted Kingfisher: female has rusty band.) **VOICE:** Sharp clicking, *tick tick tick*; also a sharp squeak. **SIMILAR SPECIES:** Belted Kingfisher. **HABITAT:** Ponds with overhanging low branches, small rivers and streams with clear water.

RINGED KINGFISHER *Ceryle torquatus*   Uncommon, local M274
16 in. (41 cm). Larger than Belted Kingfisher; bill very large. *Male:* Has entirely chestnut breast and belly. *Female:* Has broad blue-gray band across breast, separated from chestnut belly by narrow white line. **VOICE:** Rusty *cla-ack* or *wa-ak* or rolling rattle after a loud *chack*. **SIMILAR SPECIES:** Belted Kingfisher. **HABITAT:** Slow rivers, ponds, marshes.

BELTED KINGFISHER *Ceryle alcyon*   Fairly common M275
13 in. (33 cm). Hovering on rapidly beating wings in readiness for the plunge, or flying with uneven wingbeats (as if changing gear), rattling as it goes, Belted Kingfisher is easily recognized. Perched, it is big-headed and big-billed, larger than a robin. *Male:* Blue-gray above, with ragged bushy crest and broad gray breast-band. *Female:* Has an additional rusty breast-band. **VOICE:** Loud dry rattle. **SIMILAR SPECIES:** Ringed Kingfisher in TX. **HABITAT:** Streams, lakes, bays, coasts; nests in banks, perches on wires.

SWIFT AND KINGFISHERS

CHIMNEY SWIFT

roosting swifts

GREEN KINGFISHER

♀

♂

RINGED KINGFISHER

♀

hovering

♀

♂

plunging

BELTED KINGFISHER

WOODPECKERS AND ALLIES Family Picidae

Chisel-billed, wood-boring birds with strong zygodactyl feet (usually two toes front, two rear), remarkably long tongue, and stiff spiny tail that acts as prop for climbing. Flight usually undulating. **FOOD:** Tree-boring insects; some species eat ants, flying insects, berries, acorns, sap. **RANGE:** Most wooded parts of world; absent in Australian region, Madagascar, most oceanic islands.

RED-HEADED WOODPECKER   Uncommon M277
Melanerpes erythrocephalus
9¼ in. (24 cm). *Adult:* A black-backed woodpecker with *entirely red* head (other woodpeckers may have patch of red). Back *solid black,* rump white. Large, square *white patches* conspicuous on wing (making lower back look white when bird is on a tree). Sexes similar. *Immature:* Dusky-headed; wing patches mottled with dark. **VOICE:** Loud *queer* or *queeah.* **SIMILAR SPECIES:** Red-bellied Woodpecker has partially red head. **HABITAT:** Groves, farm country, shade trees in towns, large scattered trees.

GOLDEN-FRONTED WOODPECKER   Common M278
Melanerpes aurifrons
9½ in. (25 cm). *Male:* Note *multicolored head* (yellow near bill, poppy red on crown, orange nape). A zebra-backed woodpecker with light underparts and white rump. Shows white wing patch in flight. *Female:* Lacks red crown patch. *Immature:* Lacks color patches on head. **VOICE:** Tremulous *churrrr;* flickerlike *kek-kek-kek-kek.* **SIMILAR SPECIES:** Red-bellied Woodpecker. **HABITAT:** Mesquite, woodlands, groves.

RED-BELLIED WOODPECKER *Melanerpes carolinus* Common M279
9¼ in. (24 cm). *Adult:* A *zebra-backed* woodpecker with *red cap, white rump.* Red covers both crown and nape in male, *only nape in female.* *Juvenile:* Also zebra-backed, but has brown head, devoid of red. **VOICE:** Call *kwirr, churr,* or *chaw;* also *chiv, chiv.* Also a muffled flickerlike series. **SIMILAR SPECIES:** Golden-fronted and Red-headed woodpeckers. **HABITAT:** Woodlands, groves, orchards, towns, feeders.

YELLOW-BELLIED SAPSUCKER   Fairly common M280
Sphyrapicus varius
8½ in. (22 cm). Sapsuckers drill orderly rows of small holes in trees for sap and the insects it attracts. Note *longish sapsucker wing patch* and *striped head.* *Adult:* Red forehead. Male has all-red throat, female white. **VOICE:** Nasal mewing note, *cheerrrr;* drum is several rapid thumps followed by several slow, rhythmic thumps. **HABITAT:** Coniferous, mixed, and deciduous woods, shade trees.

RED-NAPED SAPSUCKER *Sphyrapicus nuchalis*   Vagrant
8½ in. (22 cm). Very similar to Yellow-bellied but note *red nape.* (A few Yellow-bellied Sapsuckers show tinge of *red on nape.*) Black frame around throat *broken* toward rear. Female shows both red and white on throat. **RANGE AND HABITAT:** Casual winter visitor to s. TX from w. U.S. Coniferous, mixed, and deciduous woodlands.

WOODPECKERS

juvenile

RED-HEADED WOODPECKER

GOLDEN-
FRONTED
WOODPECKER

RED-BELLIED
WOODPECKER

YELLOW-
BELLIED
SAPSUCKER

RED-NAPED
SAPSUCKER

211

LADDER-BACKED WOODPECKER
Fairly common M281
Picoides scalaris
7¼ in. (18 cm). A black-and-white zebra-backed woodpecker with *black-and-white-striped face.* Male has red crown. **VOICE:** Rattling series, *chikikikikikikikikik,* diminishing. Call a sharp *pick* or *chik* (like Downy Woodpecker). **SIMILAR SPECIES:** In Southeastern pine forests, see Red-cockaded Woodpecker. **HABITAT:** Canyons, riparian woodlands, brushlands.

DOWNY WOODPECKER *Picoides pubescens*
Common M282
6½–6¾ in. (17 cm). Note *white back* and *small bill.* This industrious bird is like a small edition of Hairy Woodpecker. Outer tail feathers spotted, red nape patch of male in unbroken square. *Juvenile male:* Briefly shows red crown patch. **VOICE:** Rapid whinny of notes, descending in pitch. Call a flat *pick,* not as sharp as Hairy's *peek!* **SIMILAR SPECIES:** Hairy Woodpecker is larger, has larger bill, and has clean white outer tail feathers. Ladder-backed Woodpecker has similar call. **HABITAT:** Forests, woods, residential areas, suet feeders, even corn and cattail stems.

HAIRY WOODPECKER *Picoides villosus*
Fairly common M283
9–9¼ in. (23–24 cm). Note *white back* and *large bill.* Downy and Hairy woodpeckers are almost identical in pattern, checkered and spotted with black and white; males with small red patch on back of head, females without. Hairy is like an exaggerated Downy, especially its bill. *Juvenile male:* Briefly shows red crown patch. **VOICE:** Kingfisher-like rattle, run together more than that of Downy. Call a sharp *peek!* (Downy says *pick.*) **SIMILAR SPECIES:** Downy Woodpecker. American Three-toed Woodpecker has some barring on back and barred sides. **HABITAT:** Forests, woodlands, shade trees, suet feeders.

AMERICAN THREE-TOED WOODPECKER
Scarce M285
Picoides dorsalis
8½–8¾ in. (22 cm). Males of this and the next species are our only woodpeckers that normally have *yellow cap.* Both have *barred sides.* This species is distinguished by irregular whitish bars on back. Female lacks yellow cap and suggests Downy or Hairy woodpecker, but note *barred sides.* **VOICE:** A level-pitched whinny and a flat *pyik.* **SIMILAR SPECIES:** Black-backed Woodpecker, Hairy Woodpecker (especially juvenile). **HABITAT:** Coniferous forests, particularly where deadwood is present.

BLACK-BACKED WOODPECKER *Picoides arcticus*
Scarce M286
9½ in. (24 cm). Note combination of *solid black back* and *barred sides.* Male has *yellow cap.* This and preceding species (both have three toes) inhabit boreal and montane forests; their presence can be detected by patches of bark scaled from dead conifers. **VOICE:** Low flat *kuk* or *puk* and a short buzzy call. **SIMILAR SPECIES:** American Three-toed and Hairy woodpeckers. **HABITAT:** Coniferous forests, particularly where deadwood is present.

WOODPECKERS

LADDER-BACKED WOODPECKER

♀

DOWNY WOODPECKER

♀
♂

♀
♂
♂

southern form

HAIRY WOODPECKER

AMERICAN THREE-TOED WOODPECKER

♀
♂

BLACK-BACKED WOODPECKER

♀
♂

NORTHERN FLICKER *Colaptes auratus* Common M287

12–12½ in. (30–32 cm). In flight, note conspicuous *white rump.* This and barred *brown back* mark bird as a flicker. Close up, it shows *black patch* across chest. Flight undulating. Often hops awkwardly on ground, feeding on ants. Two basic subspecies groups are recognized: "Yellow-shafted" Flicker, the Northern and eastern form, has *golden yellow* underwings and tail. *Red crescent* on nape; *gray crown; tan-brown cheeks;* male has *black* mustache. "Red-shafted" Flicker, the widespread western form (rare in Plains), has underwing and undertail *salmon red.* Both sexes lack red crescent on nape; have *brownish crown* and *gray cheeks;* male has *red* mustache. Intergrades occur. **VOICE:** Loud *wick wick wick wick wick,* etc. Also a loud *klee-yer* and a squeaky *flick-a, flick-a,* etc. (see also Pileated Woodpecker). **HABITAT:** Open forests, woodlots, towns.

RED-COCKADED WOODPECKER *Picoides borealis* Rare, local M284

8½ in. (22 cm). Zebra-backed, with black cap. White cheek is obvious field mark. Male's tiny red cockade hard to see. Endangered. **VOICE:** Rough rasping *sripp* or *zhilp* (suggests flock note of young European Starling). Sometimes a higher *tsick.* Forms colonial "clans." **SIMILAR SPECIES:** Downy and Hairy woodpeckers. On Southern plains, see Ladder-backed Woodpecker. **HABITAT:** Open pine woodlands that have trees with heartwood disease.

PILEATED WOODPECKER *Dryocopus pileatus* Uncommon M288

16½–17 in. (42–44 cm). A spectacular black, *crow-sized* woodpecker, with flaming red *crest.* Female has blackish forehead, lacks red on mustache. Great size, sweeping wingbeats, and flashing white underwing coverts identify Pileated in flight. Large foraging pits in dead or dying trees — large *oval* or *oblong* holes — indicate its presence. **VOICE:** Call resembles a flicker, but louder, irregular: *kik-kik-kikkik-kik-kik,* etc. Also a more ringing, hurried call that may rise or fall slightly in pitch and volume. **SIMILAR SPECIES:** Ivory-billed Woodpecker (possibly extinct). **HABITAT:** Coniferous, mixed, and hardwood forests; woodlots.

IVORY-BILLED WOODPECKER Possibly extinct
Campephilus principalis

19–19½ in. (40–50 cm). Separated from Pileated Woodpecker by its slightly larger size, ivory white bill, large white wing patch visible at rest, and all-white underwing pattern with black line through it. Female has black crest. **VOICE:** Call unlike that of Pileated: a single loud tooting note constantly uttered as bird forages — a sharp nasal *kent* suggesting to some a big nuthatch. Audubon wrote it as *pait,* resembling high false note of a clarinet. Drum is a quick double knock, unique among N. American woodpeckers. **SIMILAR SPECIES:** Pileated Woodpecker. **RANGE:** Formerly throughout the Southeast. Reports persist, but the last universally accepted sightings were in the 1940s. **HABITAT:** Bottomland hardwood forests, wooded bayous and swamps.

WOODPECKERS

"Yellow-shafted"

"Red-shafted"

"Red-shafted"

♂

"Yellow-shafted"

♂

"Yellow-shafted"

♀

NORTHERN FLICKER

PILEATED WOODPECKER

♀

♂

RED-COCKADED WOODPECKER

♂

IVORY-BILLED WOODPECKER

♂

below

above

Pileated below

TYRANT FLYCATCHERS Family Tyrannidae

New World Flycatchers, or Tyrant Flycatchers, make up the largest family of birds in the world, with approximately 425 known species. They are found chiefly in the Neotropics. A large number are very similar and require attention to fine points to separate them. Most species perch quietly, sitting upright on exposed branches, and sally forth to snap up insects. Bill flattened, with bristles at base. **FOOD:** Mainly flying insects. Some species also eat fruit in winter. **RANGE:** New World; majority in Tropics.

OLIVE-SIDED FLYCATCHER *Contopus cooperi*   Uncommon M290
7½ in. (19 cm). A stout, large-headed flycatcher; often perches on dead snags at tops of trees. Note large bill and *dark chest patches* separated by narrow strip of white (like unbuttoned vest). A *cottony tuft* may poke from behind wing (often not visible). **VOICE:** Call a two- or three-note *pip-pip-pip*. Song a spirited whistle, *I SAY there* or *Quick three beers!*, middle note highest, last one sliding. **SIMILAR SPECIES:** Wood-pewees. **HABITAT:** Coniferous forests, bogs, burns. In migration, usually seen on dead branches at tips of trees.

WESTERN WOOD-PEWEE *Contopus sordidulus*   Vagrant M291
6¼ in. (16 cm). Very similar to Eastern Wood-Pewee and best distinguished by voice. Slightly darker and browner than Eastern, often with weaker upper wing bar and darker "vest" below (with "top button buttoned; vest "not buttoned" on Eastern). Often shows darker lower mandible. **VOICE:** Nasal *peeyee* or *peeeer* with buzzy quality. **RANGE AND HABITAT:** Casual migrant from w. U.S. Woodlands, groves.

EASTERN WOOD-PEWEE *Contopus virens*   Fairly common M292
6¼ in. (16 cm). About the size of Eastern Phoebe, but with *two narrow wing bars, no eye-ring,* and variably pale orangish lower mandible. *Slightly larger* than *Empidonax* flycatchers, but with no eye-ring; wings extend farther down tail; *does not flick tail.* Olive wash on flanks gives weakly vested appearance. **VOICE:** Sweet plaintive whistle, *pee-a-wee,* slurring down, then up. Also *pee-ur,* slurring down, and a *chip.* **SIMILAR SPECIES:** See Western Wood-Pewee. Eastern Phoebe lacks wing bars; bobs tail downward. Olive-sided Flycatcher larger, more strongly "vested," different voice. Lack of any tail flicking, and calls, distinguish wood-pewees from *Empidonax* flycatchers, most of which have eye-ring. **HABITAT:** Woodlands, groves.

NORTHERN BEARDLESS-TYRANNULET   Scarce, local M289
Camptostoma imberbe
4¼ in. (11 cm). A very small, nondescript flycatcher that may suggest a kinglet, Bell's Vireo, or immature Verdin. Grayish olive, with *slight crested* look. *Dull wing bars* and indistinct pale supercilium. Distinguished from *Empidonax* flycatchers by its smaller size, smaller head, stubby bill, and voice. **VOICE:** Thin *peeee-yuk.* A gentle, descending *ee, ee, ee, ee, ee.* **HABITAT:** Lowland woods, mesquite, stream thickets, lower canyons.

OLIVE-SIDED
FLYCATCHER

WESTERN
WOOD-PEWEE

EASTERN
WOOD-PEWEE

NORTHERN
BEARDLESS-
TYRANNULET

Empidonax Flycatchers

Several small, drab flycatchers share the characters of light eye-ring and two pale wing bars. When breeding, some of these birds may be separated by habitat and manner of nesting. Voice is *always* the best means of identification. Silent individuals are very tough to identify, so many may have to be let go simply as "empids." Distinguishing characters to emphasize are subtle and include size and shape of bill and color of lower mandible; shape and boldness of eye-ring; pattern of underparts; primary (wingtip) projection; tail length; direction of tail wag; habitat; and calls.

ACADIAN FLYCATCHER *Empidonax virescens* **Fairly common M294**
5¾ in. (15 cm). A *greenish Empidonax* with *pale* underparts, thin eye-ring, and *long* bill. **VOICE:** "Song" a sharp explosive *pit-see!* or *wee-see!* (sharp upward inflection); also a sharp *peet.* **SIMILAR SPECIES:** Other eastern empids. **HABITAT:** Shady deciduous and mixed forests, ravines, swampy woods, beech and hemlock groves.

YELLOW-BELLIED FLYCATCHER   **Uncommon M293**
Empidonax flaviventris
5½ in. (14 cm). Yellowish *throat* separates this from all other eastern empids. (*Caution:* Other empids may show yellow *belly* but *not throat.*) **VOICE:** Song a simple *chi-lek;* also a rising *chu-wee,* whistled *chew.* **SIMILAR SPECIES:** Among other eastern empids, only Acadian is so green above but Acadian has *white* throat and *paler,* less olive washed underparts. **HABITAT:** In summer, boreal forests, muskeg, bogs.

LEAST FLYCATCHER *Empidonax minimus*   **Fairly common M297**
5¼ in. (13 cm). A small empid, *grayish* above and *pale* below with *bold white eye-ring,* short wingtip projection, and short, wide-based bill. Whitish wing bars on mostly blackish wing. Actively flicks tail. **VOICE:** Emphatic, sharply snapped *che-bek!* Call a sharp, dry *whit.* **SIMILAR SPECIES:** Alder and Willow flycatchers are browner above with longer wingtips and weaker eye-rings; Willow often looks longer billed. **HABITAT:** Deciduous and mixed woodlands, poplars, aspens.

WILLOW FLYCATCHER *Empidonax traillii*   **Fairly common M296**
5¾ in. (15 cm). Alder and Willow flycatchers (formerly lumped as one species) are almost identical in appearance, a bit larger, longer billed, and browner than Least Flycatcher. They may be separated from each other mainly by voice and breeding habitat. Willow averages paler and browner (less olive) than Alder and shows little or no eye-ring (weak to moderately bold in Alder). **VOICE:** Song a sneezy *fitz-bew,* unlike *fee-BE-o* of Alder. Call a soft *whit.* **HABITAT:** Bushes, willow thickets, etc.; often in drier situations (brushy fields, upland copses, etc.) than Alder, but found side by side in some areas.

ALDER FLYCATCHER *Empidonax alnorum*   **Fairly common M295**
5¾ in. (15 cm). The northern counterpart of Willow Flycatcher, with which it was formerly lumped as Traill's Flycatcher. Safely separated only by voice. (See Willow Flycatcher.) **VOICE:** Song an accented *fee-BE-o* or *rree-BE-o.* Call *kep* or *pit.* **HABITAT:** Willows, alders, brushy swamps, swales. Usually in moister areas than Willow.

EMPIDONAX FLYCATCHERS

Empidonax flycatchers are best identified by voice. Breeding habitat is also a helpful clue.

pit-see!

chi-lek

ciduous woods, esp.
eech trees; wooded
vamps; s. and cen. U.S.

coniferous woods, bogs;
Canada, northern edge of U.S.

ACADIAN FLYCATCHER

LEAST FLYCATCHER

YELLOW-BELLIED FLYCATCHER

greener than
Least, Alder, or
Willow

che-BEK or
chebek

throat and
breast washed
with yellow

farms, orchards, groves,
open woods; n. U.S. and
Canada

grayest of the group

fitz-bew

fee-bee´-o

wet and dry thickets,
brushy pastures, old
orchards, willows; n.
and cen. U.S.

alder swamps, wet
thickets, usually near
water; n. U.S., Canada

WILLOW FLYCATCHER

ALDER FLYCATCHER

219

MISCELLANEOUS FLYCATCHERS

VERMILION FLYCATCHER *Pyrocephalus rubinus*   Uncommon M301
6 in. (15 cm). *Adult male:* Crown (often raised in slight bushy crest) and underparts *flaming vermilion;* upperparts brown and tail blackish. *Immature male:* Breast whitish, with some streaks; crown, belly, and undertail coverts washed with vermilion. *Female:* Breast whitish, narrowly streaked; belly washed with pinkish or yellowish. **VOICE:** *P-p-pit-zee* or *pit-a-zee.* **SIMILAR SPECIES:** Female told from Say's Phoebe by shorter tail, pale supercilium, and dusky streaks on breast. See also male Scarlet Tanager (which has scarlet back and black wings). **HABITAT:** Moist areas in arid country, such as streams, ponds, pastures, golf courses, ranches.

BLACK PHOEBE *Sayornis nigricans*   Uncommon, local M298
6¾–7 in. (17–18 cm). Our only *black-breasted* flycatcher; belly white. Has typical phoebe tail-bobbing habit. *Immature:* Wing bars cinnamon-buff. **VOICE:** Thin, strident *fi-bee, fi-bee,* rising then dropping; also a sharp slurred *chip.* **SIMILAR SPECIES:** Eastern Phoebe, juncos (which are ground-loving birds). **HABITAT:** Streams, dams, walled canyons, farmyards, towns, parks; usually near water.

EASTERN PHOEBE *Sayornis phoebe*   Fairly common M299
7 in. (18 cm). Note *downward tail-bobbing.* A grayish, sparrow-sized flycatcher *without eye-ring or strong wing bars* (thin buff wing bars on immature); small, *all-dark bill* and dark head; yellowish belly in fall. **VOICE:** Song a well-enunciated *phoe-be* or *fi-bree* (second note alternately higher or lower). Call a sharp *chip.* **SIMILAR SPECIES:** Eastern Wood-Pewee and smaller *Empidonax* flycatchers have conspicuous wing bars; bills partly yellowish or horn colored on lower mandible. All eastern *Empidonax* flick tail *upward.* **HABITAT:** Streamsides, bridges, farms, field edges, roadsides, towns.

SAY'S PHOEBE *Sayornis saya*   Uncommon M300
7½ in. (19 cm). A midsized, brownish flycatcher with contrasty black tail and pale *orange-buff belly.* **VOICE:** Plaintive, down-slurred *pweer* or *pee-ee.* **SIMILAR SPECIES:** Ash-throated Flycatcher, Eastern Phoebe. **HABITAT:** Open country, scrub, canyons, ranches, parks.

GREAT KISKADEE *Pitangus sulphuratus* Fairly common, local M305
9¾ in. (25 cm). A large, *big-headed* flycatcher, like Belted Kingfisher in actions, even catching small fish. Note *striking head pattern,* rufous wings and tail, *yellow underparts and crown.* **VOICE:** Loud *kiss-ka-dee;* also a loud *reea.* Often heard before it is seen. **SIMILAR SPECIES:** Tropical and Couch's kingbirds, which share this kiskadee's limited range. **HABITAT:** Woodlands and brushy edges, usually near water.

adult
♂

immature
♂

adult
♀

immature
♀

VERMILION FLYCATCHER

BLACK PHOEBE

EASTERN PHOEBE

SAY'S PHOEBE

GREAT KISKADEE

MYIARCHUS FLYCATCHERS

BROWN-CRESTED FLYCATCHER
Uncommon M304

Myiarchus tyrannulus

8¾ in. (22 cm). Similar to Ash-throated Flycatcher, but larger, with noticeably larger bill. Underparts brighter yellow. Tail rusty, a bit less so than in Ash-throated. Voice important. **VOICE:** Sharp *whit* and rolling, throaty *purreeer.* Voice much more vigorous and raucous than Ash-throated's. **SIMILAR SPECIES:** Great Crested Flycatcher. **HABITAT:** Woodlands and well-vegetated residential areas.

GREAT CRESTED FLYCATCHER
Fairly common M303

Myiarchus crinitus

8½–8¾ in. (21–22 cm). A kingbird-sized flycatcher with cinnamon wings and tail, dark olive back, *mouse gray breast,* and bright yellow belly. Often erects bushy crest. Note *strongly contrasting tertial pattern* and pink-based bill. **VOICE:** Loud whistled *wheeep!* Also a rolling *prrrrrreet!* **SIMILAR SPECIES:** Brown-crested Flycatcher equal in size but has all-dark bill, paler gray breast, paler yellow belly, less contrasting tertials. Ash-throated Flycatcher has grayer back, much paler below. Vocal differences important. **HABITAT:** Deciduous and mixed woodlands, groves.

ASH-THROATED FLYCATCHER
Fairly common M302

Myiarchus cinerascens

8–8¼ in. (20–21 cm). A medium-sized flycatcher, smaller than a kingbird, with two wing bars, *whitish* throat, *pale* gray breast, *pale yellowish belly,* and *rufous tail.* Head slightly bushy. **VOICE:** *Prrt;* also a rolling *chi-queer* or *prit-wheer.* **SIMILAR SPECIES:** Great Crested and Brown-crested flycatchers; Say's Phoebe. **HABITAT:** Semiarid country, brush, mesquite, open woods.

LA SAGRA'S FLYCATCHER *Myiarchus sagrae*
Vagrant

7¼–7½ in. (19 cm). Very rare visitor to FL from W. Indies. Similar to Ash-throated Flycatcher, but has only a *hint of yellow on belly.* Tail *brownish, not rufous.* Short primaries. Often "droopy" posture. **VOICE:** High, rapid double *wick-wick.* **SIMILAR SPECIES:** Great Crested and Ash-throated flycatchers. **HABITAT:** Shrubby coastal woods.

MYIARCHUS FLYCATCHERS

Most have extensively rusty tails

BROWN-CRESTED FLYCATCHER

GREAT CRESTED FLYCATCHER

ASH-THROATED FLYCATCHER

LA SAGRA'S FLYCATCHER

Kingbirds, Becard, and Flycatchers

WESTERN KINGBIRD   Uncommon to fairly common M308
Tyrannus verticalis
8¾ in. (22 cm). Note *pale gray head and breast,* white throat, *yellowish belly.* Western's *black tail* has *narrow white edges.* **VOICE:** Shrill, bickering calls; a sharp *kip* or *whit-ker-whit;* dawn song *pit-PEE-tu-whee.* **SIMILAR SPECIES:** Eastern, Couch's, and Tropical kingbirds. **HABITAT:** Farms, shelterbelts, semiopen country, fences, wires.

EASTERN KINGBIRD *Tyrannus tyrannus*   Common M309
8½ in. (22 cm). The *white band* across tail tip marks Eastern Kingbird. Red crown mark is concealed and rarely seen. Often seems to fly quiveringly on tips of wings. Harasses crows, hawks. **VOICE:** Rapid sputter of high, bickering electric-shock notes: *dzee-dzee-dzee,* etc., and *kit-kit-kitter-kitter,* etc. Also a nasal *dzeep.* **SIMILAR SPECIES:** Gray Kingbird, Eastern Phoebe. **HABITAT:** Wood edges, river groves, farms, shelterbelts, roadsides, fences, wires.

GRAY KINGBIRD   Fairly common, local M310
Tyrannus dominicensis
9 in. (23 cm). Resembles Eastern Kingbird, but larger and much paler. Conspicuously *notched tail* has no white band. *Very large bill* gives large-headed look. Dark ear patch. **VOICE:** Rolling *pi-teer-rrry* or *pe-cheer-ry.* **SIMILAR SPECIES:** Eastern Kingbird. **HABITAT:** Roadsides, wires, mangroves, edges.

TROPICAL KINGBIRD   Uncommon, local M306
Tyrannus melancholicus
9¼ in. (23 cm). Nearly identical to Couch's Kingbird. Both species similar to Western Kingbird, but *bill larger and longer,* tail *notched* and *brownish;* bright yellow on underparts *includes breast.* **VOICE:** Insectlike twittering. **SIMILAR SPECIES:** See Couch's Kingbird. **HABITAT:** Groves along streams and ponds, open areas with scattered trees and short cut grass (golf courses, ball fields, etc.).

COUCH'S KINGBIRD *Tyrannus couchii*   Fairly common, local M307
9¼ in. (23 cm). Very similar to Tropical Kingbird and best distinguished by voice. Couch's has slightly shorter, thicker bill and brighter green back. **VOICE:** Nasal *queer* or *beeer* (suggests Common Pauraque). Also a sharp *kip.* **HABITAT:** Open wooded and brushy areas with large trees; most common in native habitat.

ROSE-THROATED BECARD   Rare, local M312
Pachyramphus aglaiae
7¼ in. (18 cm). Big-headed and thick-billed. *Male:* Dark gray above, pale to dusky below, with *blackish cap and cheeks* and lovely *rose-colored throat* (lacking in some males). *Female:* Brown above, with *dark cap* and *light buffy collar* around nape. Underparts strong buff. **VOICE:** Thin, slurred whistle, *seeoo.* **SIMILAR SPECIES:** Kingbirds, Say's Phoebe. **HABITAT:** Woodlands.

KINGBIRDS AND BECARD

WESTERN KINGBIRD

EASTERN KINGBIRD

GRAY KINGBIRD

ROSE-THROATED BECARD

TROPICAL KINGBIRD

COUCH'S KINGBIRD

Tropical

225

FORK-TAILED FLYCATCHER *Tyrannus savana*   Vagrant

14½–16 in. (37–41 cm). Vagrant from Tropics. Told from Scissor-tailed Flytcatcher by *black cap,* white flanks and underwing. Black tail not rigid in flight. *Immature:* Much shorter tail; might be confused with Eastern Kingbird. **VOICE:** Mechanical-sounding *tik-tik-tik.* **SIMILAR SPECIES:** Scissor-tailed Flycatcher. **RANGE:** Normal range from Mex. to S. America. Widespread vagrant to U.S. and Canada; records predominantly in fall. **HABITAT:** Open fields, pastures with scattered trees, wires.

SCISSOR-TAILED FLYCATCHER   Common M311
Tyrannus forficatus

13–15 in. (33–38 cm). A beautiful bird, pale pearly gray, with *extremely long, scissorlike tail* that is usually folded. Flanks orange-buff, wing linings salmon pink. *Immature:* Shorter tail and duller sides may suggest Western Kingbird. Hybrids are known. **VOICE:** Harsh *keck* or *kew;* a repeated *ka-leep;* also shrill, kingbirdlike bickerings and stutterings. **SIMILAR SPECIES:** Western Kingbird, Fork-tailed Flycatcher. **HABITAT:** Semiopen country, ranches, farms, roadsides, fences, wires.

SHRIKES Family Laniidae

Songbirds with hook-tipped bill. Shrikes perch watchfully on bush tops, tree-tops, wires; often impale prey on thorns, barbed wire. **FOOD:** Insects, lizards, small rodents, small birds. **RANGE:** Widespread in Old World; two species in our area.

NORTHERN SHRIKE *Lanius excubitor*   Scarce M314

10–10¼ in. (25–26 cm). This denizen of North is an irregular winter visitor south of Canadian border. Similar to Loggerhead Shrike, but paler; note *narrower dark mask with more white around eye, faintly barred* breast, and longer, more hooked bill with *pale base. Juvenile:* Plumage held throughout first winter; *brown,* with weak mask and extensive *fine barring* below. **VOICE:** Song a disjointed, thrasherlike succession of harsh notes and musical notes. Call *shek-shek;* a grating *jaaeg.* **SIMILAR SPECIES:** Loggerhead Shrike, Northern Mockingbird. **HABITAT:** Semiopen country with lookout posts; in summer, taiga, muskeg, tundra.

LOGGERHEAD SHRIKE   Uncommon to rare M313
Lanius ludovicianus

9 in. (23 cm). Big head, slim tail; gray, black, and white, with *black mask, short hooked bill.* Sits quietly on wires or bush tops; flies low with flickering flight showing white patches in wings, then swoops up to perch. *Juvenile:* Shows faint barring below *briefly in late summer.* **VOICE:** Song consists of harsh, deliberate notes and phrases, repeated 3 to 20 times, suggesting mockingbird's song; *queedle, quee-dle,* over and over, or *tsurp-see, tsurp-see.* Call *shack shack* or *jeeer jeeer.* **SIMILAR SPECIES:** Northern Shrike. Northern Mockingbird lacks dark mask and hooked bill. **HABITAT:** Semiopen country with lookout posts: wires, fences, trees, shrubs.

FLYCATCHERS

FORK-TAILED FLYCATCHER

adult

SCISSOR-TAILED FLYCATCHER ♂

immature

SHRIKES

adult

juvenile

NORTHERN SHRIKE

LOGGERHEAD SHRIKE

VIREOS Family Vireonidae

Small olive- or gray-backed birds, much like wood-warblers, usually less active. Bill slightly thicker, with more curved ridge and small hook to tip. May be divided into those with wing bars (and "spectacles") and those without (these have eye stripes). **FOOD:** Mostly insects, also fruit in winter. **RANGE:** Canada to Argentina.

WHITE-EYED VIREO *Vireo griseus*　　　　Fairly common M315

5 in. (13 cm). Distinctive combination of *yellow spectacles, whitish throat.* Also note wing bars, yellowish sides, white eye (dark in immature). Somewhat skulking. **VOICE:** Song a sharply enunciated *CHICK-a-per-weeoo-CHICK.* Variable; usually starts and ends with *chick.* **SIMILAR SPECIES:** Bell's Vireo. **HABITAT:** Wood edges, brush, brambles, dense undergrowth.

BELL'S VIREO *Vireo bellii*　　　　　　　　Scarce M316

4¾ in. (12 cm). Small, nondescript. Usually stays concealed in dense cover. Greenish back and yellowish flanks; thin, pale, broken eye-ring and loral stripe; one or two weak wing bars. Pumps tail. **VOICE:** Sings as if through clenched teeth; husky phrases at short intervals: *cheedle cheedle chee? cheedle cheedle chew!* **SIMILAR SPECIES:** Warbling Vireo has plain wings, bold eyebrow. Immature White-eyed Vireo has bolder wing bars, yellow spectacles. **HABITAT:** Willows, streamsides, hedgerows, mesquite.

BLACK-CAPPED VIREO *Vireo atricapilla*　　Scarce, local M317

4½ in. (11 cm). Endangered. Small and sprightly; cap *glossy black* in male, slate gray in female. Note wing bars, white spectacles, *red* eyes. **VOICE:** Song hurried, harsh; phrases remarkable for restless, almost angry quality. Call a harsh *chit-ah.* **SIMILAR SPECIES:** Blue-headed Vireo larger with dark eyes. **HABITAT:** Oak scrub, brushy hills, rocky canyons. Often hard to see.

YELLOW-THROATED VIREO　　Uncommon to fairly common M318
Vireo flavifrons

5½ in. (14 cm). Bright yellow throat, yellow spectacles, and white wing bars. Olive back contrasts with gray rump. **VOICE:** Song similar to Blue-headed Vireo's, but lower pitched with *burry quality;* swings back and forth with phrases that sound like *ee-yay, three-eight.* **SIMILAR SPECIES:** Pine Warbler has some dusky streaks below, white tail spots, smaller bill. **HABITAT:** Deciduous woodlands, shade trees, particularly oaks.

BLUE-HEADED VIREO *Vireo solitarius*　　Fairly common M319

5¼ in. (14 cm). Note *sharply demarcated* blue-gray cap, *bright white* spectacles and throat, *bright green* back, yellowish wash to side. **VOICE:** Song of burry phrases with deliberate pauses between; sweet and high pitched: *wee-ay, chweeo, chuweep* (slower than Red-eyed Vireo with fewer notes per phrase). Also gives a whiny chatter. **HABITAT:** Coniferous, mixed, and deciduous woods.

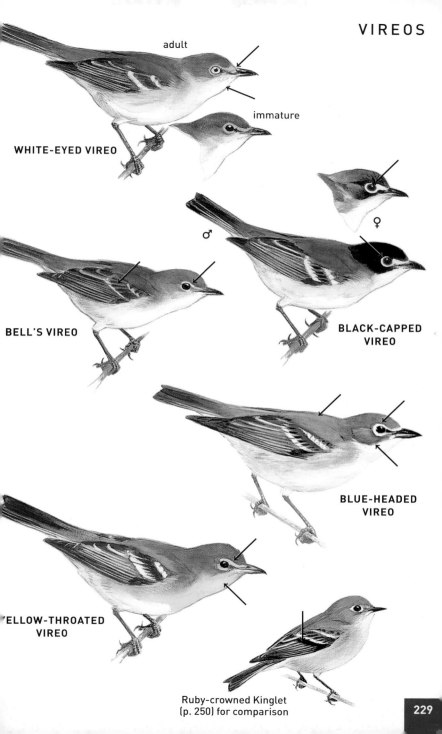

adult

immature

WHITE-EYED VIREO

♀

♂

BELL'S VIREO

**BLACK-CAPPED
VIREO**

**BLUE-HEADED
VIREO**

**YELLOW-THROATED
VIREO**

Ruby-crowned Kinglet
(p. 250) for comparison

RED-EYED VIREO *Vireo olivaceus*   Common M322

6 in. (15 cm). Note *gray cap* contrasting with olive back, and strong, *black-bordered white eyebrow stripe (supercilium)*. Red iris may not be obvious at a distance. Iris is brown in immature birds in fall. **VOICE:** Song is abrupt, robinlike phrases, monotonous. Call a nasal, whining *chway*. **SIMILAR SPECIES:** Warbling Vireo slightly smaller, duller and less contrasty above, with pale lores and arching supercilium. See Yellow-green and Black-whiskered vireos, both scarce and local. **HABITAT:** Deciduous woodlands, shade trees, groves.

YELLOW-GREEN VIREO *Vireo flavoviridis*   Very rare, local

6–6¼ in. (15–16 cm). This tropical species is very similar to Red-eyed Vireo, but has *strong yellow tones* on sides, flanks, and undertail coverts; back *yellower* green; head stripes *less distinct;* bill slightly *longer* and paler. (Immature Red-eyed Vireos may have yellow on flanks and undertail coverts.) **VOICE:** Song slower than Red-eyed's, suggestive of House Sparrow. **RANGE:** Rare summer resident in lower Rio Grande Valley, TX. Casual farther north in TX and in FL. **HABITAT:** Woodlands and well-vegetated residential areas.

BLACK-WHISKERED VIREO   Uncommon, local M323
Vireo altiloquus

6¼ in. (16 cm). Narrow dark whisker on each side of throat. Otherwise similar to Red-eyed Vireo, but duller overall, particularly head pattern, and more brownish olive above, with slightly longer bill. **VOICE:** Song slightly slower than Red-eyed's. **HABITAT:** Mangroves, subtropical hardwoods.

WARBLING VIREO *Vireo gilvus*   Uncommon to fairly common M320

5½ in. (14 cm). One of the widespread vireos that lack wing bars. In this *very plain* species, note *whitish breast, pale lores,* and *lack of black borders* on eyebrow stripe that arches slightly above dark eye. Back tinged dull greenish. Immatures have more yellow on sides. **VOICE:** Song distinctive: a languid warble, unlike broken phrases of other vireos; suggests Purple Finch's song, but less spirited, with burry undertone. Call a wheezy querulous *twee* and short *vit.* **SIMILAR SPECIES:** See Philadelphia Vireo. Red-eyed Vireo larger, greener above, and has bolder eyebrow stripe. See also Tennessee Warbler. **HABITAT:** Deciduous woods, cottonwoods, riparian woodlands.

PHILADELPHIA VIREO *Vireo philadelphicus*   Uncommon M321

5¼ in. (13 cm). This smallish vireo is similar to Warbling, but with more distinct dark eye line (including lores), slightly greener back, and a *wash of yellow on breast* (bright in immatures, dull in adults). **VOICE:** Song very similar to Red-eyed Vireo's; higher, slower. Call, a quick, husky *niff-niff-niff-niff.* **SIMILAR SPECIES:** Bright Warbling Vireos in fall tinged green above and have yellow on sides, but that yellow is *dull or lacking in center of breast and throat;* lores paler than Philadelphia's. Different song. Tennessee Warbler slightly smaller, has finer bill, clear white (not yellow) undertail coverts, blackish rather than blue-gray legs. **HABITAT:** Second-growth woodlands, poplars, willows, alders.

RED-EYED
VIREO

immature

YELLOW-
GREEN
VIREO

BLACK-WHISKERED
VIREO

WARBLING VIREO

adult

Tennessee Warbler
(p. 266)
for comparison

nonbreeding

breeding

showing
variation

PHILADELPHIA VIREO

Jays, Crows, and Allies Family Corvidae

Large perching birds with strong, longish bill, nostrils covered by forward-pointing bristles. Crows and ravens are very large and black. Jays are often colorful (usually blue). Magpies are black and white, with long tail. Sexes alike. Most immatures resemble adults. **FOOD:** Almost anything edible. **RANGE:** Worldwide except s. S. America, some islands, Antarctica.

FLORIDA SCRUB-JAY
Uncommon, local M328

Aphelocoma coerulescens

11–11¼ in. (29 cm). Look for this *crestless* jay in FL in stretches of oak scrub. Note *whitish forehead, pale* gray-brown back, solid blue wings and tail (no white markings). **VOICE:** Rough, rasping *kwesh . . . kwesh*. Also a low, rasping *zhreek* or *zhrink*. **SIMILAR SPECIES:** Blue Jay. **HABITAT:** Mainly scrub, low oaks.

WESTERN SCRUB-JAY
Fairly common, local M329

Aphelocoma californica

11–11¼ in. (29 cm). *Crestless* with blue head, wings, and tail, *brownish* back, white throat with *necklace*. **VOICE:** Rough, rasping *kwesh . . . kwesh*. Also a harsh *shreck-shreck-shreck-shreck* and a rasping *zhreek, zhreek*. **SIMILAR SPECIES:** Blue Jay. **HABITAT:** Oaks, riparian woodlands, juniper woodland, residential areas, parks.

BLUE JAY *Cyanocitta cristata*
Common M325

11 in. (28 cm). A showy, noisy, *crested jay*. Bold *white spots on wings and tail;* whitish or dull gray underparts; *black necklace*. **VOICE:** Harsh slurring *jeeah* or *jay;* a musical *queedle, queedle;* also many other notes. Mimics calls of Red-shouldered and Red-tailed hawks. **SIMILAR SPECIES:** Scrub-Jays. **HABITAT:** Oak and pine woods, suburban gardens, groves, towns, feeders.

GRAY JAY *Perisoreus canadensis*
Uncommon M324

11¼–11½ in. (28–29 cm). A fluffy, gray bird of cool northern forests. Called "Whiskey Jack" by woodsmen. *Adult: Black* partial cap and *white forehead;* suggests an overgrown chickadee. *Juvenile: Dark sooty*, with *whitish whisker.* **VOICE:** Soft *whee-ah;* also many other notes, some harsh. **HABITAT:** Spruce and fir forests.

GREEN JAY *Cyanocorax yncas*
Fairly common, local M326

10½ in. (27 cm). The *only green-colored jay*. Black throat, violet crown, yellow outer tail feathers. Often seen in noisy flocks. **VOICE:** Four or more harsh notes given rapidly: *cheek, cheek, cheek, cheek*. Also a variety of jaylike croaks and squeaks. **HABITAT:** Dense cover in scrubby woods. Visits feeders for fruit and seeds.

BROWN JAY *Cyanocorax morio*
Very rare, local M327

16½–17 in. (42–43 cm). A very large jay with *brown upperparts and pale belly*. Adult has dark bill; juvenile has yellow bill. In flight, pale belly stands out. **VOICE:** Very loud *chaa-chaa-chaa* repeated over and over. Flocks can make a loud noise. **HABITAT:** Dense scrub and brushy woods, feeders.

JAYS

FLORIDA
SCRUB-JAY

WESTERN
SCRUB-JAY

BLUE JAY

adult

GRAY
JAY

GREEN JAY

Gray Jay
juvenile

BROWN JAY

CHIHUAHUAN RAVEN *Corvus cryptoleucus*   **Fairly common M333**
19–19½ in. (48–50 cm). Slightly larger than American Crow; a small raven of plains. Flies with typical flat-winged glide of a raven; has somewhat wedge-shaped tail. White feather bases on neck and breast sometimes show when feathers are ruffled by the wind, hence former name White-necked Raven. **VOICE:** Hoarse *kraak,* flatter and higher than Common Raven's. **SIMILAR SPECIES:** Difficult to tell from Common Raven, particularly when separate, but slightly smaller and tail slightly less wedge-shaped, calls higher pitched, and bristles extend farther down upper mandible. **HABITAT:** Arid and semiarid scrub and grasslands, yucca, mesquite, towns, dumps.

COMMON RAVEN *Corvus corax*   **Common M334**
23½–24 in. (59–61 cm). Note *wedge-shaped tail.* Much larger than American Crow; has heavier voice and is not inclined to be as gregarious, often solitary or in family groups. More hawklike in flight, it alternates flapping and sailing, gliding on flat, somewhat sweptback wings (crow glides much less and with slight upward dihedral). When bird is perched and not too distant, note "goiter" look created by shaggy throat feathers and heavier "Roman-nose" bill. **VOICE:** Croaking *cr-r-ruck* or *prruk;* also a metallic *tok.* **SIMILAR SPECIES:** American Crow. **HABITAT:** Boreal and mountain forests, cliffs, tundra, dumps.

BLACK-BILLED MAGPIE *Pica hudsonia*   **Fairly common, local M330**
18½–19½ in. (47–49 cm); tail 9½–12 in. (24–30 cm). A large, slender, *black-and-white bird,* with *long, graduated tail.* In flight, iridescent greenish black tail streams behind and large *white patches flash in wings.* **VOICE:** Harsh, rapid *queg queg queg queg* or *wah-wah-wah.* Also a querulous, nasal *maag?* or *aag-aag?* **HABITAT:** Rangeland, brushy country, streamsides, forest edges, farms. Often in flocks.

...y show white on
...pe when
...thers are
...fled

**CHIHUAHUAN
RAVEN**

**COMMON
RAVEN**

ravens have
wedge-
shaped tails

American
Crow
(p. 236)

BLACK-BILLED MAGPIE

TAMAULIPAS CROW *Corvus imparatus* Very rare, local

14¼–14½ in. (36–37 cm). A small crow with small bill, long tail, and slim wings. Glossier colored than other crows. **VOICE:** A "stressed" voice (a harsh, froglike *awwwk*). **SIMILAR SPECIES:** In its range this is the only small crow — next larger all-black corvid is Chihuahuan Raven. **RANGE:** Found irregularly near Brownsville, TX. **HABITAT:** Scrub, mesquite thickets; also residential areas, dumps.

FISH CROW *Corvus ossifragus* Fairly common M332

15¼–15½ in. (38–39 cm). Slightly smaller and more delicately proportioned than American Crow. Tail slightly longer and wings slightly more tapered. *Best identified by voice,* as measurements of the two species broadly overlap. **VOICE:** Short nasal *car* or *ca.* Most distinctive is *two*-syllable *ca-ha.* (American Crow utters *caw.*) Some calls of young American Crows may sound like those of Fish Crows. **SIMILAR SPECIES:** American Crow larger, has different call. **HABITAT:** Near tidewater, river valleys, lakes. Also farm fields, wood edges, towns and cities, dumps.

AMERICAN CROW *Corvus brachyrhynchos* Common M331

17–17½ in. (43–45 cm). A large, chunky, ebony bird. Completely black; glossed with purplish in strong sunlight. Bill and feet strong and black. Often gregarious. **VOICE:** Loud *caw, caw, caw* or *cah* or *kahr.* **SIMILAR SPECIES:** Fish Crow is smaller with longer, slimmer tail, more tapered wings; most readily distinguished by voice. Common and Chihuahuan Ravens larger, have wedge-shaped tails, more sweptback wings, different calls. **HABITAT:** Woodlands, farms, fields, river groves, shores, towns, dumps.

CROWS

TAMAULIPAS
CROW

FISH CROW

AMERICAN
CROW

American Crow

Fish Crow

Tamaulipas
Crow

Swallows Family Hirundinidae

Slim, streamlined form and graceful flight characterize these sparrow-sized birds. Pointed wings; short bill with very wide gape; tiny feet. FOOD: Mostly flying insects. RANGE: Worldwide except for polar regions, some islands.

TREE SWALLOW *Tachycineta bicolor*   Common M337

5¾ in. (15 cm). *Adult:* Male *steely blue,* tinged green, above; *white below.* Female slightly duller than male. *Juvenile:* Dusky gray-brown back and dusky smudge across breast. Tree Swallows have distinctly notched tail; glide in circles, ending glide with quick flaps and a short climb. **VOICE:** Rich *cheet* or *chi-veet;* a liquid twitter, *weet, trit, weet,* etc. **SIMILAR SPECIES:** May be confused with Northern Rough-winged Swallow (dingy throat, different flight style) or Bank Swallow (bolder dark breast-band than juvenile Tree, smaller overall, browner above). See Violet-Green Swallow. All species also have different calls. **HABITAT:** Open country near water, marshes, meadows, streams, lakes, wires. Fall premigratory flocks roost in reeds. Nests in holes in trees, birdhouses.

BANK SWALLOW *Riparia riparia*   Fairly common M339

5 in. (12 cm). Our smallest swallow. Brown-backed with slightly darker wings and paler rump. Note distinct dark breast-band. White of throat curls up behind ear. Wingbeats rapid and shallow. **VOICE:** Dry, trilled chitter or rattle, *brrt* or *trr-tri-tri.* **SIMILAR SPECIES:** Northern Rough-winged Swallow and juvenile Tree Swallow. When perched in mixed-species flocks, Bank's smaller size stands out. **HABITAT:** Near water; fields, marshes, lakes. Nests colonially in dirt and sand banks.

NORTHERN ROUGH-WINGED SWALLOW   Fairly common M338
Stelgidopteryx serripennis

5¼ in. (12 cm). *Adult:* Brown-backed; does not show contrast above that Bank Swallow does; *throat and upper breast dusky;* no breast-band. Flight more languid; wings pulled back at end of stroke. *Juvenile:* Has cinnamon-rusty wing bars. **VOICE:** Call a low, liquid *trrit,* lower and less grating than Bank Swallow's. **SIMILAR SPECIES:** Bank Swallow and juvenile Tree Swallow. **HABITAT:** Near streams, lakes, rivers. Nests in banks, pipes, and crevices, but not colonially as Bank Swallow does.

VIOLET-GREEN SWALLOW *Tachycineta thalassina*   Vagrant

5¼ in. (13 cm). Note *white patches that almost meet* over base of tail. *Male:* Dark and shiny above; adults glossed with beautiful *green on back and purple on rump and uppertail;* clear white below. *White of face partially encircles eye. Female and immature:* Somewhat duller above, and white above eye tinged grayish or brownish. **VOICE:** A twitter; a thin *ch-lip* or *chew-chit;* rapid *chit-chit-chit wheet, wheet.* **SIMILAR SPECIES:** Separated from Tree Swallow by pale feathering above eye, greener back, white patches on sides of rump, slightly smaller size, and shorter wings. **RANGE AND HABITAT:** Casual visitor from w. U.S.

SWALLOWS

ests in
e holes
r nest
boxes

adult

TREE SWALLOW

juvenile

Bank Swallow colony

BANK SWALLOW

NORTHERN ROUGH-WINGED SWALLOW

VIOLET-GREEN SWALLOW

adult

Violet-green

Cliff (p. 240)

Barn (p. 240)

Purple Martin (p. 240)

Bank

Northern Rough-winged

Tree

Swallows on a wire

PURPLE MARTIN *Progne subis*   Fairly common M336

8 in. (20 cm). The largest N. American swallow. *Male:* Uniformly blue-black *above and below;* no other swallow is dark-bellied. *Female and juvenile:* Light-bellied; throat and breast grayish, often with faint gray collar. Glides in circles, alternating quick flaps and glides; often spreads tail. **VOICE:** Throaty and rich *tchew-wew*, etc., or *pew, pew.* Song gurgling, ending in a succession of rich, low guttural notes. **SIMILAR SPECIES:** Tree and Violet-green swallows, much smaller than female Purple Martin, are cleaner white below. In flight, male martin might be confused with European Starling. **HABITAT:** Towns, farms, open or semiopen country, often near water. Nests almost exclusively in human-supplied martin houses.

CAVE SWALLOW *Petrochelidon fulva*   Uncommon, local M341

5½ in. (14 cm). Similar to Cliff Swallow (rusty rump, square-cut tail), but face colors reversed: *throat and cheeks buffy* (not dark), forehead *dark chestnut* (not pale, although Cliff Swallows in Southwest have chestnut forehead). *Buff color sets off dark mask and cap.* **VOICE:** Clear, sweet *weet* or *cheweet;* a loud, accented *chu, chu.* **SIMILAR SPECIES:** Cliff Swallow; Cave has buffier throat and face, more deeply colored rump, different call. **HABITAT:** Open country. Cuplike nest placed in caves, culverts, and under bridges; nests colonially.

CLIFF SWALLOW *Petrochelidon pyrrhonota*   Uncommon M340

5½ in. (14 cm). Note *rusty* or *buffy rump.* Overhead, appears square-tailed, with dark throat patch. Glides in a long ellipse, ending each glide with a roller coaster–like climb. **VOICE:** *Zayrp;* a low *chur.* Alarm call *keer!* Song consists of creaking notes and guttural gratings; harsher than Barn and Cave swallows' songs. **SIMILAR SPECIES:** Barn and Cave swallows. **HABITAT:** Open to semiopen land, farms, cliffs, lakes. Nests colonially on cliffs, barn sides, under eaves and bridges; rarely on trees. Builds mud jug, or gourdlike, nest. Barn and Cave swallows build cuplike open nest; and Barn Swallows often but not always nest *inside* the barn.

BARN SWALLOW *Hirundo rustica*   Common M342

6¾ in. (17 cm). Our only swallow that is truly *swallow-tailed;* also the only one with *white tail spots.* *Adult:* Blue-black above; cinnamon-buff below, with darker throat. *Immature:* More whitish below. Flight direct, close to ground; wingtips pulled back at end of stroke; not much gliding. **VOICE:** Soft *vit* or *kvik-kvik, vit-vit.* Also *szee-szah* or *szee.* Anxiety call a harsh, irritated *ee-tee* or *keet.* Song a long, musical twitter interspersed with guttural notes. **SIMILAR SPECIES:** Most other N. American swallows have notched (not deeply forked) tail. Cliff Swallow is colonial, building mud jugs under eaves or cliffs. See Cave Swallow. **HABITAT:** Open or semiopen land; farms, fields, marshes, lakes; often perches on wires; usually near habitation. Builds *cuplike nest inside* barns or under eaves, not in tight colonies like Cliff Swallow.

SWALLOWS

martin house

PURPLE MARTIN

♂

♀

CAVE SWALLOW

CLIFF SWALLOW

juglike nests under eaves or on cliffs; colonial

Southwest

nests on beams inside barns

juvenile

BARN SWALLOW

259

Chickadees, Titmice, Bushtits, and Verdin Families Paridae, Aegithalidae, and Remizidae

Chickadees, titmice, and bushtits form mixed flocks; verdins are more solitary. **RANGE:** Chickadees and titmice are widespread in North America, Eurasia, and Africa; bushtits from B.C. to s. Guatemala; verdin in sw. North America.

CAROLINA CHICKADEE *Poecile carolinensis*   Common M343
4¾ in. (12 cm). Distinguish from Black-capped by range and voice. **VOICE:** Call higher pitched and more rapid than Black-capped's. Whistled *fee-bee, fee-bay.* **SIMILAR SPECIES:** Black-capped larger, cleaner rear edge of cheek patch, more prominent wing edging. **HABITAT:** Mixed and deciduous woods; residential areas, feeders.

BLACK-CAPPED CHICKADEE *Poecile atricapillus*   Common M344
5–5¼ in. (12–13 cm). A familiar visitor to feeders. Note *black cap, gray back,* buffy flanks. Very similar to Carolina Chickadee. **VOICE:** Clearly enunciated *chick-a-dee-dee-dee.* Song a clear whistle, *fee-bee-ee* or *fee-bee,* first note higher. **HABITAT:** Mixed and deciduous woods; willows, residential areas, feeders.

BOREAL CHICKADEE *Poecile hudsonicus*   Uncommon M345
5½ in. (14 cm). Note *dull brown cap,* pinkish brown flanks, extensively *grayish cheeks.* **VOICE:** Wheezy *chick-che-day-day;* slower, more raspy and drawling than lively call of Black-capped Chickadee. **HABITAT:** Coniferous forests, evergreen plantations.

BLACK-CRESTED TITMOUSE   Fairly common M347
Baeolophus atricristatus
6¼ in. (16 cm). Like Tufted Titmouse but with *black crest,* white forehead. Juveniles have mostly gray crest briefly in summer. **VOICE:** Chickadee-like calls. Song a whistled *peter peter peter peter* or *here here here here.* **HABITAT:** Woodlands, canyons, towns, feeders.

TUFTED TITMOUSE *Baeolophus bicolor*   Common M346
6¼ in. (16 cm). A *mouse-colored bird with tufted crest,* large black eyes. Very inquisitive and loudly vocal. **VOICE:** Clear whistled chant similar to those of chickadees, but more nasal, wheezy, and complaining. **HABITAT:** Woodlands, shade trees, groves, residential areas, feeders.

BUSHTIT *Psaltriparus minimus*   Common, local M349
4½ in. (11 cm). A very small, plain bird with longish tail and stubby bill. Except briefly during nesting season, travels in straggling talkative flocks, often joined by warblers and other species. **VOICE:** Insistent light *tsits, pits,* and *clenks.* **SIMILAR SPECIES:** Verdin. **HABITAT:** Oak scrub, mixed woods, pinyon-juniper.

VERDIN *Auriparus flaviceps*   Uncommon, local M348
4½ in. (11 cm). Tiny. *Adult:* Gray, with *yellowish head, rufous bend of wing* (often hidden). *Juvenile:* Just plain gray. **VOICE:** Insistent *see-lip.* Rapid chipping. Song a three-note whistle, *tsee see-see.* **SIMILAR SPECIES:** Juvenile might be confused with Northern Beardless-Tyrannulet. **HABITAT:** Semiarid lowlands, mesquite.

CHICKADEES
AND TITMICE,
BUSHTIT,
VERDIN

CAROLINA
CHICKADEE

BLACK-CAPPED
CHICKADEE

BLACK-
CRESTED
TITMOUSE

BOREAL
CHICKADEE

TUFTED
TITMOUSE

adult

VERDIN

BUSHTIT

females have
yellow eyes

juvenile

243

NUTHATCHES Family Sittidae

Small, stubby tree climbers with strong, woodpecker-like bill and strong feet. Short, square-cut tail is not braced like a woodpecker's tail during climbing. Nuthatches habitually go down trees headfirst. Sexes similar, or mostly so. **FOOD:** Bark insects, seeds, nuts; attracted to feeders by suet, sunflower seeds. **RANGE:** Most of N. Hemisphere.

WHITE-BREASTED NUTHATCH *Sitta carolinensis* **Common M351**
5¾ in. (15 cm). This, the most widespread nuthatch, is known by its *black cap* (gray in female) and beady black eye on white face. Undertail coverts chestnut. **VOICE:** Song a rapid series of low, nasal, whistled notes on one pitch: *whi, whi, whi, whi, whi, whi* or *who, who, who,* etc. Call a distinctive nasal *yank, yank, yank;* also a nasal *tootoo.* **SIMILAR SPECIES:** Red-breasted Nuthatch. **HABITAT:** Forests, woodlots, groves, river woods, shade trees, feeders.

RED-BREASTED NUTHATCH *Sitta canadensis* **Common M350**
4½ in. (11 cm). A small nuthatch with *broad black line* through eye and white line above it. Underparts washed with rusty (deeper in male). **VOICE:** Call higher, more nasal than White-breasted Nuthatch, *ank* or *enk,* sounding like a baby nuthatch or tiny tin horn. **SIMILAR SPECIES:** Brown-headed Nuthatch has brown crown, lacks white supercilium, has very different call. **HABITAT:** Coniferous forests; in winter, also other trees, feeders.

BROWN-HEADED NUTHATCH *Sitta pusilla* **Uncommon M352**
4½ in. (11 cm). A small nuthatch of southern pinelands. Smaller than White-breasted Nuthatch, with brown cap coming down to eye and a usually pale or whitish spot on nape. Travels in groups. **VOICE:** Sounds like a toy rubber mouse: a high, rapid *kit-kit-kit;* also a squeaky piping *ki-day* or *ki-dee-dee,* constantly repeated, sometimes becoming an excited twitter or chatter. **SIMILAR SPECIES:** Other nuthatches, Brown Creeper. **HABITAT:** Open pine woods.

CREEPERS Family Certhiidae

Small, slim, stiff-tailed birds, with slender, slightly curved bill used to probe bark of trees. **FOOD:** Bark insects. **RANGE:** Cooler parts of N. Hemisphere.

BROWN CREEPER *Certhia americana* **Uncommon M353**
5¼ in. (13 cm). A very small, slim, camouflaged tree climber. Brown above, whitish below, with *slender decurved bill* and *stiff tail,* which is used as a brace during climbing. Ascends trees spirally from base, hugging bark closely. **VOICE:** Call a single high, thin, *seee,* similar to quick three-note call *(see-see-see)* of Golden-crowned Kinglet. Song a high, thin, sibilant *see-ti-wee-tu-wee* or *trees, trees, trees, see the trees.* **SIMILAR SPECIES:** Brown-headed Nuthatch. **HABITAT:** Nests in variety of coniferous and mixed woodlands; in nonbreeding season, also in deciduous woods, groves, shade trees.

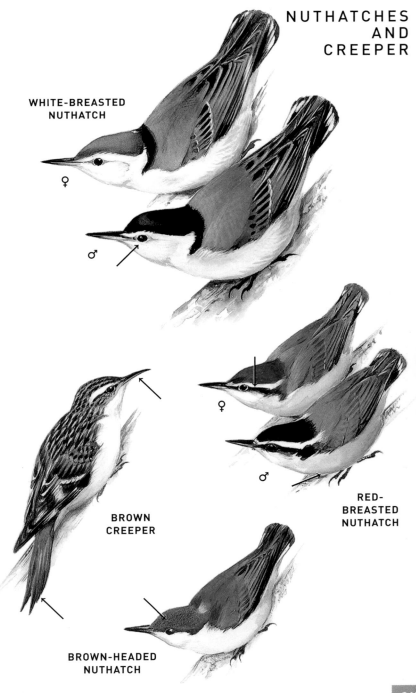

WHITE-BREASTED
NUTHATCH

♀

♂

BROWN
CREEPER

♀

♂

RED-
BREASTED
NUTHATCH

BROWN-HEADED
NUTHATCH

WRENS Family Troglodytidae

Mostly small, energetic brown birds; stumpy, with slim, slightly curved bill; tail often cocked. **FOOD:** Insects, spiders. **RANGE:** N., Cen., and S. America; also in Eurasia.

HOUSE WREN *Troglodytes aedon*   Common M359
4½–4¾ in. (11–12 cm). A small, energetic, gray-brown wren with light eye-ring and no strong eyebrow stripe. **VOICE:** Stuttering, gurgling song rises in a musical burst, then falls at end; calls a rolled *prrrrr* and harsh *cheh, cheh.* **SIMILAR SPECIES:** Winter Wren. **HABITAT:** Open woods, thickets, towns, gardens; often nests in bird boxes.

WINTER WREN *Troglodytes troglodytes*   Uncommon M360
4 in. (10 cm). A very small, round, dark wren, told from House Wren by its smaller size, *much stubbier tail,* stronger eyebrow, and *dark, heavily barred belly.* Often bobs body and flicks wings. Mouselike and secretive; stays near ground. **VOICE:** Song a rapid succession of high tinkling warbles, trills. Call a hard, two-syllable *kimp-kimp* (suggests Song Sparrow). **SIMILAR SPECIES:** House Wren and other small wrens. **HABITAT:** Dense, shaded woodland underbrush, ferns, fallen trees; in summer, also coniferous forests.

BEWICK'S WREN *Thryomanes bewickii*   Scarce, declining M358
5¼ in. (13 cm). Note longish tail with *white corners* and bold *white eyebrow stripe.* Brown above with grayish tail. **VOICE:** Song suggests Song Sparrow's, but thinner, with "inhale-exhale" quality; starts on two or three high notes, drops lower, ends on a thin trill; calls sharp *vit, vit* and buzzy *dzzzzzt.* **SIMILAR SPECIES:** Some Carolina Wrens have limited buff below. **HABITAT:** Thickets, underbrush, gardens; often nests in bird boxes.

CAROLINA WREN *Thryothorus ludovicianus*   Common M357
5½ in. (14 cm). A large wren, near size of a sparrow. *Warm rusty brown* above, variably buff below; conspicuous *white eyebrow stripe.* **VOICE:** Two- or three-syllable chant. Variable; *tea-kettle, tea-kettle, tea kettle,* or *chirpity, chirpity, chirpity, chirp.* Variety of *chip*s and *churr*s. **SIMILAR SPECIES:** Bewick's and Marsh wrens. **HABITAT:** Tangles, undergrowth, gardens; often nests in bird boxes.

SEDGE WREN *Cistothorus platensis*   Uncommon, secretive M361
4½ in. (11 cm). Stubbier than Marsh Wren; buffier, with *buffy* undertail coverts, *barred wings,* and *finely streaked* crown. **VOICE:** Song a dry staccato chattering: *chap chap chap chap chap chap chap chapper-rrrrr.* Call a single or double *chap,* like first note of song. **SIMILAR SPECIES:** House Wren. **HABITAT:** Grassy and sedgy marshes and meadows.

MARSH WREN *Cistothorus palustris*   Fairly common M362
5 in. (13 cm). *White stripes on back* and white eyebrow stripe identify this marsh dweller. **VOICE:** Song reedy, gurgling, often ending in a guttural rattle: *cut-cut-turrrrrrrrr-ur;* often heard at night. Call a low *tsuck-tsuck.* **SIMILAR SPECIES:** Sedge Wren. **HABITAT:** Fresh and brackish marshes (cattail, tule, bulrush); in winter, also salt marshes.

HOUSE
WREN

WINTER
WREN

BEWICK'S
WREN

CAROLINA
WREN

SEDGE
WREN

MARSH
WREN

CANYON WREN *Catherpes mexicanus*   Uncommon, local M356
5¾–6 in. (15 cm). Mostly rufous-brown with contrasting *white bib.*
VOICE: Gushing cadence of clear, curved notes tripping down scale;
te-you, te-you, tew tew. Or *tee tee tee tee tew tew tew tew.* Call a shrill
beet. **HABITAT:** Cliffs, canyons, rockslides, stone buildings.

ROCK WREN *Salpinctes obsoletus*   Uncommon M355
6 in. (15 cm). A gray-brown western wren with *finely streaked breast,*
rusty rump, and *buffy terminal tail band.* Frequently bobs. **VOICE:** Song
a harsh chant. Call a loud dry trill; also *ti-keer.* **SIMILAR SPECIES:**
Canyon Wren. **HABITAT:** Rocky slopes, canyons, rubble.

CACTUS WREN   Uncommon, local M354
Campylorhynchus brunneicapillus
8½ in. (22 cm). A very large wren of arid country. Note *size, spotted
breast, white supercilium.* **VOICE:** Monotonous *chu-chu-chu-chu* or
chug-chug-chug-chug, on one pitch, gaining speed. **SIMILAR SPECIES:**
Sage Thrasher. **HABITAT:** Arid areas of cactus, mesquite, yucca.

Pɪᴘɪᴛꜱ Family Motacillidae

Streaked birds with white outer tail feathers, long hind claws, thin bill. They
walk briskly; flight undulating. **FOOD:** Insects, seeds. **RANGE:** Nearly worldwide.

AMERICAN PIPIT   Uncommon to fairly common M384
Anthus rubescens
6½ in. (17 cm). A *slim-billed, sparrowlike* bird of open country. *Bobs
tail* almost constantly as it *walks. Outer tail feathers white.* **VOICE:** Call
a thin *jee-eet.* In flight, *chwee chwee chwee,* etc. **SIMILAR SPECIES:**
Sprague's Pipit. Sparrows have thicker bills, do not wag tails. **HABI-
TAT:** In summer, tundra; in migration and winter, fields, shores.

SPRAGUE'S PIPIT *Anthus spragueii*   Uncommon, secretive M385
6½ in. (17 cm). A furtive solitary grassland species; towers high in
the sky when flushed. Distinguished from American by *plain buffy
face with beady dark eye, striped back, pinkish legs.* Does *not* wag
tail. **VOICE:** Sings high in air; a thin jingling series, descending in
pitch. Call a distinctive *squeet* or *squeet-squeet.* **HABITAT:** Short- to
medium-grass prairies and fields.

Lᴀʀᴋꜱ Family Alaudidae

Brown terrestrial birds with long hind claws. Gregarious in nonbreeding season,
when they may be joined by longspurs and Snow Buntings. Larks often sing in
high display flights. **FOOD:** Seeds, insects. **RANGE:** Mainly Old World.

HORNED LARK *Eremophila alpestris*   Uncommon to common M335
7–7¼ in. (18–19 cm). A pale bird of open ground; *walks,* does not hop.
Adult: Distinctive face pattern with tiny "horns." *Juvenile:* Streaked
breast, scaly above, no black; compare Sprague's Pipit. **VOICE:** Song
tinkling and high-pitched, given from ground or air. Call a clear *tsee-
titi.* **HABITAT:** Prairies, short-grass and dirt fields, shores, tundra.

WRENS

CANYON WREN

ROCK WREN

juvenile

CACTUS WREN

adult

PIPITS AND LARK

Sprague's overhead

towering flight

American Pipit wags its tail

SPRAGUE'S PIPIT

nonbreeding

breeding

AMERICAN PIPIT

prairie

immature

HORNED LARK

overhead

northern

249

KINGLETS Family Regulidae

Tiny active birds with small slender bill, short tail, bright crown. In nonbreeding season, often found in mixed-species flocks with chickadees and warblers. **FOOD:** Insects, larvae. **RANGE:** N. America, Eurasia.

RUBY-CROWNED KINGLET *Regulus calendula*   Common M364
4¼ in. (11 cm). A tiny, stub-tailed, olive-gray birdlet, smaller than most warblers, *flicks wings constantly*. Note bold wing bars bordered behind by *black "highlight bar,"* broken white eye-ring. Male has *scarlet crown patch* (usually concealed; erect when excited). **VOICE:** Husky *ji-dit.* Song is three or four high notes, several lower notes, and a chant, *tee tee tee-tew tew — ti-didee, ti-didee, ti-didee.* **SIMILAR SPECIES:** Golden-crowned Kinglet, Orange-crowned Warbler. **HABITAT:** In summer, coniferous forests; in migration and winter, variety of other woodlands, parks, gardens.

GOLDEN-CROWNED KINGLET   Fairly common M363
Regulus satrapa
4 in. (10 cm). Tiny olive-gray bird, smaller than warblers. Note *boldly striped face,* wing bars. Flicks wings, though less emphatically than Ruby-crowned Kinglet. **VOICE:** High, wiry *see-see-see.* Song a series of high thin notes, ascending, then dropping into a little chatter. **SIMILAR SPECIES:** Ruby-crowned Kinglet. **HABITAT:** Conifers; in migration and winter, also other trees.

GNATCATCHERS Family Sylviidae

Active birds with slender bill. Gnatcatchers have long, mobile tail. **FOOD:** Insects, larvae. **RANGE:** Worldwide.

BLUE-GRAY GNATCATCHER   Fairly common M365
Polioptila caerulea
4½ in. (11 cm). A tiny, slim mite, blue-gray above, whitish below, with narrow *white eye-ring. Long tail* is *mostly white underneath* and often flipped about and cocked. **VOICE:** Call a thin, peevish *zpee;* often doubled, *zpee-zee.* Song a thin, squeaky, wheezy, bubbly series of notes, easily overlooked. **SIMILAR SPECIES:** Black-tailed Gnatcatcher. **HABITAT:** Swampy woods, riparian areas; also brushy habitats in winter.

BLACK-TAILED GNATCATCHER   Uncommon, local M366
Polioptila melanura
4½ in. (11 cm). Similar to Blue-gray Gnatcatcher, but breeding male has *black cap,* both sexes have darker underparts, underside of tail *largely black.* **VOICE:** Call a thin harsh *chee,* repeated two or three times; soft *chip-chip-chip* series. **SIMILAR SPECIES:** Blue-gray Gnatcatcher. **HABITAT:** Arid brush, ravines, dry washes, mesquite.

KINGLETS AND GNATCATCHERS

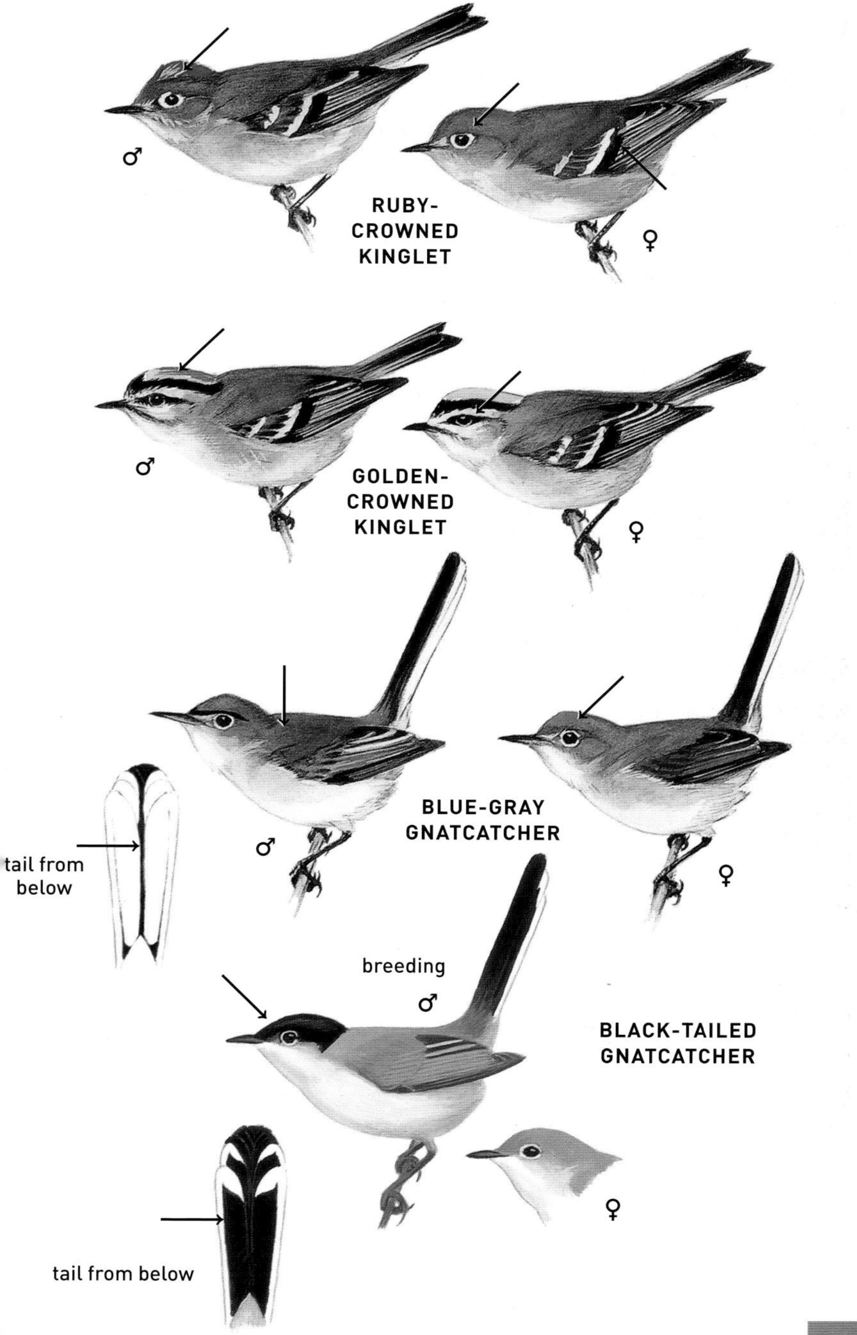

RUBY-
CROWNED
KINGLET

GOLDEN-
CROWNED
KINGLET

tail from
below

BLUE-GRAY
GNATCATCHER

breeding

BLACK-TAILED
GNATCATCHER

tail from below

THRUSHES Family Turdidae

Large-eyed, slender-billed songbirds. Most species that bear the name "thrush" are brown-backed with spotted breasts. Robins and bluebirds, etc., suggest their relationship through their speckle-breasted young. Often fine singers. **FOOD:** Insects, worms, snails, berries, fruit. **RANGE:** Nearly worldwide.

NORTHERN WHEATEAR
Oenanthe oenanthe   Uncommon, local **M367**

5¾ in. (15 cm). A small, dapper bird of Arctic barrens. Note *white rump and sides of tail. Breeding male:* Pale gray back, black wings, and *black ear patch. Female and nonbreeding:* Buffier, with brown back, reduced black. **VOICE:** Call a hard *chak-chak* and a soft *heet.* **RANGE AND HABITAT:** Casual visitor to e. U.S. and se. Canada, mostly in fall. Open, stony areas; in summer, rocky tundra.

EASTERN BLUEBIRD *Sialia sialis*   Fairly common **M368**

7 in. (18 cm). A blue bird with *rusty red breast;* appears round-shoul-dered when perched. Female duller than male; has rusty throat and breast, *white belly. Juvenile:* Speckle-breasted. **VOICE:** Call a musical *chur-wi.* Song three or four gurgling notes. **SIMILAR SPECIES:** Fresh female and immature Mountain Bluebirds may have warm buff wash on throat and breast, but flanks not as bright, and they are longer winged and slightly longer billed. **HABITAT:** Open country with scat-tered trees; farms, roadsides. Often nests in bluebird boxes.

MOUNTAIN BLUEBIRD *Sialia currucoides*   Uncommon **M369**

7¼–7½ in. (18–19 cm). *Male:* Turquoise blue, paler below; belly whit-ish. No rusty. *Female and immature:* Dull brownish gray, with touch of pale blue on rump, tail, and wings. **VOICE:** Low *chur* or *vhew.* Song a short, subdued warble. **SIMILAR SPECIES:** Has straighter posture than female Eastern Bluebird, with slightly longer bill and tail. Warm-colored birds in fresh plumage lack rusty-colored flanks. Often hov-ers over fields in search of prey. **HABITAT:** Open country with some trees; in winter, also treeless terrain. Often nests in bluebird boxes.

TOWNSEND'S SOLITAIRE *Myadestes townsendi*   Rare **M370**

8½ in. (22 cm). A slim gray bird with *white eye-ring, white sides on tail,* and *buffy wing patches.* Pattern in wing and tail gives it a not-too-remote resemblance to Northern Mockingbird, but note eye-ring, darker breast, and especially buff wing patches. *Juvenile:* Dark over-all with light spots and scaly belly. **VOICE:** Song a rich warbling. Call a high-pitched *eek,* like a squeaky bicycle wheel. **SIMILAR SPECIES:** Northern Mockingbird, shrikes. **RANGE:** Rare winter visitor from w. U.S. to e. Great Plains, casual farther east. **HABITAT:** Variety of conif-erous forests, rocky cliffs; in winter, particularly fond of junipers, also open woods.

THRUSHES

NORTHERN WHEATEAR

breeding ♂

non-breeding

EASTERN BLUEBIRD

juvenile

♂

MOUNTAIN BLUEBIRD

♂

♀

TOWNSEND'S SOLITAIRE

juvenile

VEERY *Catharus fuscescens*　　　　　Fairly common **M371**
7 in. (18 cm). Note *uniform rusty brown* cast above and grayish flanks. No strong eye-ring (may have dull ring) on grayish face. Of all our brown thrushes, this is the least spotted (spots often indistinct). **VOICE:** Song liquid, breezy, ethereal, wheeling downward: *vee-ur, vee-ur, veer, veer.* Call a down-slurred *phew* or *view.* **SIMILAR SPECIES:** Warmer brown than Gray-cheeked or Bicknell's thrushes, with weaker breast spots. **HABITAT:** Moist deciduous woods, willow and alder thickets along streams.

SWAINSON'S THRUSH *Catharus ustulatus*　　　Fairly common **M374**
7 in. (18 cm). This spotted thrush is marked by its conspicuous *buffy eye-ring* or *spectacles,* buff on cheeks and upper breast. Dull *olivey brown* above. **VOICE:** Song is breezy, flutelike phrases, each phrase sliding *upward.* Call a liquid *whit* or *foot.* Migrants at night (in sky) give a short whistled *quee.* **SIMILAR SPECIES:** Gray-cheeked Thrush has thin, often *incomplete* grayish eye-ring on *grayish face.* Young Hermit Thrush may have buff-tinged eye-ring, but all Hermits show *contrasty rufous tail, no buffy* on breast, regularly *flick wings and raise tail,* and *vocalizations differ.* See Veery. **HABITAT:** Moist spruce and fir forests, riparian woodlands; in migration, other woods.

BICKNELL'S THRUSH *Catharus bicknelli*　　　Scarce, local **M373**
6½–6¾ in. (17 cm). Very similar to Gray-cheeked Thrush but slightly smaller, upperparts *warmer brown, tail dull chestnut,* breast *washed with buffy,* lower mandible more than half yellow (less than half in Gray-cheeked). Legs more dusky than toes (uniform pale in Gray-cheeked). **VOICE:** Song similar to Gray-cheeked but thinner and rising at close (falling in Gray-cheeked). **SIMILAR SPECIES:** Gray-cheeked and Hermit thrushes. **HABITAT:** Breeds in stunted mountain fir forests of Northeast to shoreline in Maritimes. In migration, forests.

GRAY-CHEEKED THRUSH *Catharus minimus*　　　Uncommon **M372**
7–7¼ in. (17–18 cm). A dull, "cold-colored," *gray-brown,* furtive thrush, distinguished from Swainson's by its *grayish* cheeks, *grayish,* less conspicuous, often broken eye-ring. *Little or no buffy on breast.* See Bicknell's Thrush. **VOICE:** Song thin and nasal, downward, suggesting Veery's: *whee-wheeoo-titi-wheew.* Call a downward *pheu,* much higher than Veery's call. **HABITAT:** Boreal forests, tundra willow and alder scrub; in migration, other woodlands.

HERMIT THRUSH *Catharus guttatus*　　　Fairly common **M375**
6¾ in. (17 cm). A spot-breasted brown thrush with *rufous* tail. When perched, it has habit of *flicking wings* and of *cocking tail and dropping it slowly.* Some birds wintering in the western part of our area are grayer. **VOICE:** Call a low *chuck;* also a scolding *tuk-tuk-tuk* and a rising, whiny *pay.* Song clear, ethereal, flutelike; three or four phrases at *different pitches,* each with a *long introductory note.* **SIMILAR SPECIES:** Swainson's and Gray-cheeked thrushes. **HABITAT:** Coniferous or mixed woods; in winter, woods, thickets, parks, gardens.

SPOTTED
THRUSHES

VEERY

SWAINSON'S
THRUSH

BICKNELL'S
THRUSH

GRAY-CHEEKED
THRUSH

tail-lifting

interior
West

HERMIT
THRUSH

East

AMERICAN ROBIN *Turdus migratorius*   Common **M377**
10 in. (25 cm). A very familiar bird; often seen on lawns, with an erect stance, giving short runs then pauses. Recognized by dark gray back and brick red breast. Dark stripes on white throat. On male, head and tail blackish, underparts solid, deep reddish; those colors duller on female. *Juvenile:* Has speckled breast, but rusty wash identifies it. **VOICE:** Song a clear caroling; short phrases, rising and falling, often prolonged. Calls *tyeep* and *tut-tut-tut.* **SIMILAR SPECIES:** Varied Thrush (vagrant from West), Clay-colored Thrush. **HABITAT:** Wide variety of habitats, including towns, parks, lawns, farmland, shade trees, many types of forests and woodlands; in winter, also berry-producing trees.

VARIED THRUSH *Ixoreus naevius*   Vagrant
9½ in. (24 cm). Similar to American Robin, but with orangish eye stripe, orange wing bars, and orange bar on underwing visible in flight. *Male:* Blue-gray above, with wide black breast-band. *Female:* Duller gray above, with gray breast-band. *Juvenile:* Breast-band imperfect or speckled. **VOICE:** Song a long, eerie, quavering, whistled note, followed, after a pause, by one on a lower or higher pitch. Call a liquid *chup.* **SIMILAR SPECIES:** Orangey wing bars and eye stripe, and a breast-band, distinguish it from a robin, with which it only rarely mingles. **RANGE:** Casual winter visitor from West. **HABITAT:** Thick, wet coniferous and mixed forests; in winter, also other moist, dense woods, ravines, thickets, gardens, feeders.

WOOD THRUSH *Hylocichla mustelina*   Fairly common **M376**
7¾ in. (20 cm). *Rusty-headed.* Smaller than a robin; plumper than other brown thrushes, distinguished by deepening rufous about head, *streaked gray cheeks,* white eye-ring, and *rounder, bolder,* more numerous *breast spots.* **VOICE:** Song with rounder phrases than other thrushes. Listen for flutelike *ee-o-lay.* Occasional guttural notes are distinctive. Call a rapid *pip-pip-pip-pip.* **SIMILAR SPECIES:** Other brown thrushes, juvenile American Robin. **HABITAT:** Mainly deciduous woodlands, moist glades.

♂ ♀ juvenile

AMERICAN ROBIN

♂ ♀

VARIED THRUSH

juvenile

WOOD THRUSH

FIELDFARE *Turdus pilaris* — Vagrant

10 in. (25 cm). Robinlike, with heavily marked tawny breast. *Back rusty, contrasting with gray head and rump, dark tail.* **VOICE:** Harsh, chattering *tchak-tchak-tchak* and a quiet *see*. Song a rapid mix of feeble squeaking, chuckling notes, often given in flight. **SIMILAR SPECIES:** Juvenile American Robin, Redwing (vagrant), other spot-breasted thrushes. **RANGE:** Eurasian species; most N. American records from Northeast in winter. **HABITAT:** Open country, woodland edge, hedgerows, residential areas.

REDWING *Turdus iliacus* — Vagrant

8¼ in. (21 cm). Named for its rust-colored wing linings (most visible in flight). Broad *pale eyebrow, heavily streaked below.* Bill two-toned, black at tip, yellow at base. **VOICE:** Flight call a thin, high, reedy *seeeh*. **SIMILAR SPECIES:** Fieldfare (vagrant), juvenile American Robin. **RANGE:** Eurasian species; most N. American records from Northeast in winter. **HABITAT:** Semiopen country and young woodlands.

RUFOUS-BACKED ROBIN *Turdus rufopalliatus* — Vagrant

9¼ in. (24 cm). This very rare Mexican winter visitor is like a pale American Robin (extensive cinnamon underparts; grayish head, wings, and tail), but with orangier tinge below, *rufous back,* and *no white around eye.* More heavily streaked throat. *Orangier bill.* A timid skulker. **VOICE:** Call a soft whistled *teeww*. Song a mellow series of warbles, each repeated two or more times. **SIMILAR SPECIES:** American Robin. **RANGE:** Casual visitor to s. TX. **HABITAT:** Woods and thickets, often near water.

CLAY-COLORED THRUSH *Turdus grayi* — Scarce, local

9 in. (23 cm). Scarce resident of southernmost TX. Warm brown above, dull tan on chest, paling to light tawny buff on belly. Throat streaked with light brown, not black. **VOICE:** Lower-pitched, simpler version of American Robin's song. **SIMILAR SPECIES:** Brown thrushes (which are smaller and less like American Robin). **HABITAT:** Subtropical woodlands and well-vegetated residential areas.

MOCKINGBIRDS AND THRASHERS
Family Mimidae

Often called "mimic thrushes." Excellent songsters; some mimic other birds. Strong-legged; usually longer tailed than true thrushes, bill usually longer and more decurved. **FOOD:** Insects, fruit. **RANGE:** New World.

CURVE-BILLED THRASHER — Fairly common M382
Toxostoma curvirostre

11 in. (28 cm). This thrasher can be told by its *well-curved* bill and *mottled breast.* Some individuals have narrow white wing bars. Eyes pale orange. *Juvenile:* Yellow eyes, somewhat straighter bill. **VOICE:** Call a sharp, liquid *whit-wheet!* (like a whistle to attract attention). Song a musical series of notes and phrases, almost grosbeaklike in quality but faster. Not much repetition. **HABITAT:** Arid brush, lower canyons, ranch yards.

RARE THRUSHES

REDWING

FIELDFARE

♂

RUFOUS-BACKED
ROBIN

CLAY-COLORED
THRUSH

HRASHER

CURVE-BILLED
THRASHER

259

LONG-BILLED THRASHER   Uncommon, local M381
Toxostoma longirostre
11½ in. (29 cm). *Duller brown* above than Brown Thrasher, breast stripes *blacker, cheeks grayer;* bill longer and all dark. **VOICE:** Song similar to Brown Thrasher's, but more jumbled. Call a harsh *tchuk.* **SIMILAR SPECIES:** Brown Thrasher. **HABITAT:** Brush, mesquite.

BROWN THRASHER   Uncommon to fairly common M380
Toxostoma rufum
11½ in. (29 cm). Slimmer but longer than a robin; *bright rufous* above, *heavily streaked* below. Note *wing bars,* curved bill, long tail, yellow eyes. **VOICE:** Song a succession of deliberate notes and phrases resembling Gray Catbird's song, but each phrase usually *in pairs.* Call a harsh *chack!* **SIMILAR SPECIES:** Brown thrushes have shorter tails and have brown (not yellow) eyes. In s. TX see Long-billed Thrasher. **HABITAT:** Thickets, brush, gardens.

SAGE THRASHER *Oreoscoptes montanus*   Vagrant
8½ in. (22 cm). A bit smaller than a robin. Gray-backed, with streaked breast, wing bars, and *white tail corners.* Eyes pale yellow, duller in immature. **VOICE:** Song is clear, ecstatic warbled phrases, sometimes repeated but more often continuous, suggestive of Rose-breasted Grosbeak. Call a blackbirdlike *chuck.* **SIMILAR SPECIES:** Cactus Wren, juvenile Northern Mockingbird. **RANGE:** Wintering birds barely enter our area in arid areas of s. TX. Casual visitor elsewhere. **HABITAT:** Sagebrush, mesas; in winter, also arid open country.

GRAY CATBIRD *Dumetella carolinensis*   Common M378
8¾ in. (23 cm). Slate gray; slim. Note *black cap. Chestnut undertail coverts.* Flips tail jauntily. **VOICE:** *Catlike mewing;* distinctive. Also a grating *tcheck-tcheck.* Song is disjointed notes and phrases; not repetitious, compared with other mimids. **SIMILAR SPECIES:** Northern Mockingbird. **HABITAT:** Riparian undergrowth, brush.

NORTHERN MOCKINGBIRD *Mimus polyglottos*   Common M379
10 in. (25 cm). A familiar and conspicuous species. Slimmer, longer tailed than a robin. Note *large white patches* on wings and tail. **VOICE:** Song a varied, prolonged succession of notes and phrases, may be repeated a half-dozen times or more before changing. Often heard at night. Mockingbirds are excellent mimics. Call a loud *tchack;* also *chair.* **SIMILAR SPECIES:** Shrikes have dark facial masks. See Bahama Mockingbird (vagrant). **HABITAT:** Towns, parks, gardens, farms, roadsides, thickets.

BAHAMA MOCKINGBIRD *Mimus gundlachii*   Vagrant
11 in. (28 cm). Chunkier than Northern Mockingbird and overall browner with *less white in tail* and *no white in wings.* Dark streaks on flanks, belly, and neck give this species a thrasherlike appearance. **VOICE:** Song simpler than Northern's, with two-syllable phrases. Call a sharp *tchak,* like Northern's but harsher. **RANGE:** Straggler to s. FL from Caribbean. **HABITAT:** A skulker in deep brushy cover.

THRASHERS
AND
MOCKINGBIRDS

LONG-
BILLED
THRASHER

BROWN
THRASHER

SAGE
THRASHER

BAHAMA
MOCKINGBIRD

GRAY
CATBIRD

NORTHERN
MOCKINGBIRD

wing-flashing

juvenile

shrike (p. 226)
for comparison

WAXWINGS Family Bombycillidae

Pointed crest may be raised or lowered. Waxy red tips on secondaries in most individuals. Gregarious. FOOD: Berries, insects. RANGE: N. Hemisphere.

BOHEMIAN WAXWING   Uncommon, irregular M386
Bombycilla garrulus
8¼ in. (21 cm). Similar to Cedar Waxwing but larger and grayer, with *no yellow on belly;* wings with strong white markings, *rusty* undertail coverts (white in Cedar). VOICE: Rougher than Cedar. HABITAT: In summer, boreal forests, muskeg; in winter, widespread in search of berries, especially in towns where fruiting trees attract them.

CEDAR WAXWING *Bombycilla cedrorum*   Common M387
7¼ in. (18 cm). Note *yellow band* at tip of tail, *black mask.* A sleek, crested, brown bird, larger than House Sparrow. *Juvenile:* Grayer, with blurry streaks. Gregarious in nonbreeding season, roaming in compact flocks. VOICE: High, thin lisp or *zeee,* slightly trilled. HABITAT: Open woodlands, orchards; in winter, anywhere with fruiting trees and bushes.

BULBULS Family Pycnonotidae

Native to Old World. One species introduced in FL. FOOD: Insects, fruit.

RED-WHISKERED BULBUL *Pycnonotus jocosus*   Uncommon, local
7 in. (18 cm). Note black crest, red cheek and undertail coverts. VOICE: Noisy chattering. RANGE: Native of se. Asia; established locally in s. Miami, FL. HABITAT: Heavy vegetation in suburban neighborhoods.

STARLINGS Family Sturnidae

A varied family; some blackbirdlike. Sharp-billed. Gregarious. FOOD: Insects, seeds, berries. RANGE: Widespread in Old World. Introduced in New World.

EUROPEAN STARLING *Sturnus vulgaris*   Common M383
8½ in. (22 cm). Introduced from Europe in 1890. A gregarious, garrulous "blackbird"; note *short tail, sharply pointed bill.* In flight, has *triangular wings.* VOICE: Harsh *tseeeer;* a whistled *whooee.* Also clear whistles, clicks, chuckles; often mimics other birds. HABITAT: Cities, suburbs, farms. Has had substantial negative impact on several native cavity-nesting species.

HILL MYNA *Gracula religiosa*   Uncommon, local
10½ in. (27 cm). *Glossy black* with orange bill. *White wing patches.* VOICE: Squawks, buzzes, whistles; excellent mimic. RANGE: Exotic from Asia, found in s. FL. HABITAT: Lush suburban neighborhoods.

COMMON MYNA *Acridotheres tristis*   Common, local
10 in. (25 cm). A *brown-bodied* relative of European Starling, with black head and *white undertail.* VOICE: Starlinglike gurgles, squeaks, and cackles. RANGE: Introduced from s. Asia. Widespread and increasing in s. and cen. FL. HABITAT: Urban and suburban habitats.

WAXWINGS, BULBUL, AND STARLINGS

BOHEMIAN
WAXWING

juvenile

CEDAR
WAXWING

breeding

RED-WHISKERED
BULBUL

adult

juvenile

EUROPEAN
STARLING

nonbreeding

HILL MYNA

COMMON
MYNA

WOOD-WARBLERS Family Parulidae

Active, brightly colored birds, usually smaller than sparrows, with thin, needle-pointed bill. Most have some yellow in plumage. **FOOD:** Mainly insects but many species also eat fruit in fall and winter. **RANGE:** AK and Canada to n. Argentina.

BACHMAN'S WARBLER *Vermivora bachmanii*   Probably extinct
4¾ in. (12 cm). *Male: Face and underparts yellow;* bib and crown black (suggests a small Hooded Warbler with incomplete hood). *Female:* Lacks black bib; forehead yellow; crown and cheek grayish; eye-ring yellow. Bill thin and *downcurved.* **VOICE:** Song a rapid series of flat mechanical buzzes rendered on one pitch: *bzz-bzz-bzz-bzz-bzz-bzz-bzz-bzz,* also given in flight. **SIMILAR SPECIES:** Female may resemble female Yellow Warbler but note more decurved bill and lack of yellow edging in wings and tail; female Wilson's lacks gray head and white undertail. **RANGE:** Former resident of Southeast; last definite record in 1962. **HABITAT:** Swampy areas, canebrakes.

"LAWRENCE'S" WARBLER   Rare
Recessive hybrid of Blue-winged × Golden-winged warbler combination. Yellow below like Blue-winged, but with black head pattern of Golden-winged. Note black ear patch. **VOICE:** Like Golden-winged or Blue-winged. **HABITAT:** Same as Blue-winged and Golden-winged.

GOLDEN-WINGED WARBLER   Uncommon M389
Vermivora chrysoptera
4¾ in. (12 cm). *Male:* The only warbler with combination of *yellow wing patch* and *black throat.* Note yellow forecrown, black *ear patch,* whitish underparts. *Female:* Ear and throat patches grayer. **VOICE:** Song a buzzy note followed by one to three on a lower pitch: *bee-bz-bz-bz.* (Blue-winged Warbler sings a lazier *beee-bzzz.*) Call like Blue-winged's. **SIMILAR SPECIES:** "Brewster's," "Lawrence's," and Blue-winged warblers. **HABITAT:** Open woodlands, swampy edges, brushy clearings. Declining in many northeastern and southern areas.

"BREWSTER'S" WARBLER   Scarce
Golden-winged and Blue-winged warblers hybridize where their ranges overlap, producing two basic types, "Lawrence's" and "Brewster's" warblers ("Brewster's" is more frequent and more variable). Typical "Brewster's" is like Blue-winged with whitish underparts. Some have white wing bars, others yellow; some are tinged with yellow below. Black eye mark and white or largely white (not solid yellow) underparts are diagnostic. **VOICE:** May sing like either parent. **HABITAT:** Same as Blue-winged and Golden-winged warblers.

BLUE-WINGED WARBLER *Vermivora pinus*   Fairly common M388
4¾ in. (12 cm). Note *narrow black line through eye.* Face and underparts yellow; undertail coverts white; wings *with two white bars.* Female averages duller than male. **VOICE:** Song a buzzy *beeee-bzzz,* as if inhaled and exhaled. Call a sharp *tsik.* **SIMILAR SPECIES:** "Brewster's," "Lawrence's," Prothonotary, Golden-winged, and Yellow warblers. **HABITAT:** Field edges, undergrowth, bushy edges, woodland openings.

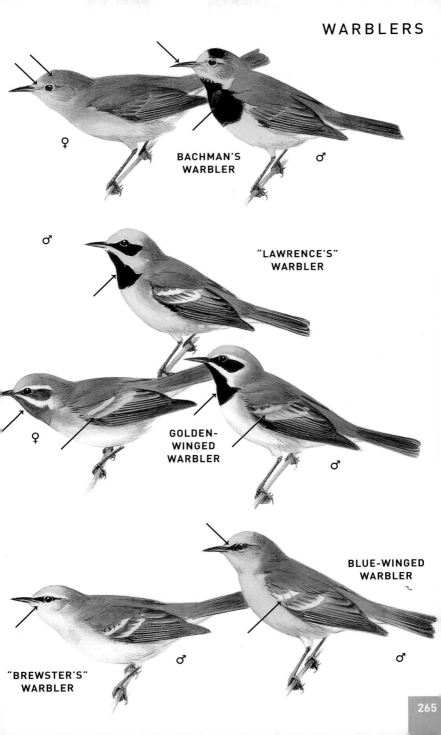

WARBLERS

♀

♂

BACHMAN'S WARBLER

♂

"LAWRENCE'S" WARBLER

♀

GOLDEN-WINGED WARBLER

♂

BLUE-WINGED WARBLER

♂

"BREWSTER'S" WARBLER

♂

TENNESSEE WARBLER
Uncommon to fairly common M390

Vermivora peregrina

4¾ in. (12 cm). Note short tail, *bold eyebrow, white undertail coverts.* *Breeding male: Pale gray head contrasting with greenish back. Female and immature:* Washed with greenish on head, yellow on breast; often showing a trace of a single wing bar. **VOICE:** Song staccato, three-part: *ticka ticka ticka ticka, swit swit, chew-chew-chew-chew-chew.* Call a sweet *chip.* **SIMILAR SPECIES:** Orange-crowned Warbler. War-bling and Philadelphia vireos slightly larger and thicker billed, duller on back. **HABITAT:** Deciduous and mixed forests; in migration, variety of woodlands.

ORANGE-CROWNED WARBLER
Uncommon to fairly common M391

Vermivora celata

5 in. (13 cm). Usually drab *olive green* with *yellow undertail coverts* and *blurry breast streaking.* Some (especially immatures) quite drab and gray-headed, others brighter yellow-green. "Orange" of crown seldom visible. **VOICE:** Song a colorless trill, becoming weaker to-ward end. Often changes pitch, rising or dropping slightly. Call a sharp *stik.* **SIMILAR SPECIES:** Nonbreeding Tennessee Warbler has white undertail coverts, shorter tail, brighter green above, lacks dusky breast streaks. See Yellow Warbler. **HABITAT:** Open woodlands, brushy clearings, willows, parks, gardens.

NASHVILLE WARBLER *Vermivora ruficapilla*
Uncommon M392

4¾ in. (12 cm). Note *white eye-ring* in combination with *yellow* throat. *Head gray,* contrasting with olive green back. No wing bars. Under-parts bright yellow with white vent. Regularly bobs tail. **VOICE:** Song two-part: *seebit, seebit, seebit, seebit, titititi* (ends like Chipping Sparrow's song). Call a sharp *pink.* **SIMILAR SPECIES:** Connecticut Warbler is larger, behaves very differently (*walks* on limbs and ground, does *not* flutter about actively), and has grayish or brownish throat. Some dull Nashvilles in fall can look almost as dull as Or-ange-crowned, but always have clear *yellow on breast.* **HABITAT:** Open mixed woods with undergrowth, forest edges, bogs; in migration, also brushy areas.

immature

breeding
♂

**TENNESSEE
WARBLER**

♀

immature

**ORANGE-
CROWNED
WARBLER**

♀

♂

**NASHVILLE
WARBLER**

267

NORTHERN PARULA *Parula americana*　　　Fairly common M393

4½ in. (11 cm). A small, short-tailed warbler, *pale bluish above,* with yellow throat and breast and two white wing bars. Suffused *greenish patch* on back. Distinct *broken white eye-ring.* Adult male has *dark breast-band;* immature lacks breast-band, has greenish wash on head. **VOICE:** Song a buzzy trill that climbs scale and trips over the top: *zeeeeeeeee-up.* Also *zh-zh-zh-zheeeeeee.* **SIMILAR SPECIES:** Tropical Parula. **HABITAT:** Breeds mainly in humid woods where either *Usnea* lichen or Spanish moss hangs from trees (occasionally in some woods where neither is found).

TROPICAL PARULA *Parula pitiayumi*　　　Rare, local M394

4½ in. (11 cm). Similar to Northern Parula, but limited in range to s. TX. Note *more extensive yellow on breast* and *lack of white eye-ring.* Male has black mask and lacks distinct bands across chest. **VOICE:** Like Northern Parula's. **HABITAT:** Breeds mainly in humid woods near water, usually where Spanish moss hangs from trees.

YELLOW WARBLER *Dendroica petechia*　　　Common M395

5 in. (13 cm). No other warbler is so extensively yellow. Male has *rusty breast streaks* (faint or lacking in female). *Immature:* Lacks breast streaks; some individuals may be quite dull, with bright yellow restricted to lower vent and undertail coverts. All show *yellow edgings to wing and tail,* yellow underside of tail, and dark beady eye. **VOICE:** Song a bright cheerful *tsee-tsee-tsee-tsee-titi-wee* or *weet weet weet weet tsee-tsee wew.* Variable. Call a soft, slurred, rich *chip.* **SIMILAR SPECIES:** Shorter tailed than Wilson's or Orange-crowned warbler, with yellow edging in wings and tail. Note vocal differences. **HABITAT:** Riparian woodlands and understory, swamp edges, particularly alders and willows; also parks, gardens.

CHESTNUT-SIDED WARBLER　　　Fairly common M396
Dendroica pensylvanica

5 in. (13 cm). Usually holds tail cocked up at an angle. *Breeding:* Note *yellow crown, chestnut sides. Nonbreeding:* Lime greenish above, whitish below; white eye-ring, *pale yellow* wing bars. Adults retain some chestnut; immatures do not. **VOICE:** Song similar to Yellow Warbler's: *see see see see Miss BEECHer* or *please please pleased to MEETcha,* last note dropping. Call a rich, slurred *chip,* like Yellow Warbler's. **HABITAT:** Overgrown field edges, small trees.

MAGNOLIA WARBLER *Dendroica magnolia*　　　Fairly common M397

5 in. (13 cm). The "black-and-yellow warbler." *Breeding male:* Upperparts blackish, with large white patches on wings and tail; underparts yellow, with heavy black stripes. Note black tail crossed by *broad white band* (from beneath, tail is white with broad black tip). *Female and nonbreeding male:* Duller. *Immature:* Has weak stripes on sides, but tail pattern distinctive; often shows weak grayish band across breast. **VOICE:** Song suggests Yellow Warbler's but is shorter: *weeta weeta weetsee* (last note rising); or a Hooded Warbler–like *weeta weeta wit-chew.* Call an odd nasal note. **HABITAT:** Low conifers; in migration, a variety of woodlands.

WARBLERS

♀

NORTHERN
PARULA

♂

TROPICAL
PARULA

♂

♀

YELLOW
WARBLER

♂

breeding
♀

CHESTNUT-SIDED
WARBLER

breeding
♂

breeding
♀

MAGNOLIA
WARBLER

breeding
♂

269

CAPE MAY WARBLER *Dendroica tigrina*   Uncommon M398

5 in. (13 cm). *Breeding male:* Note *chestnut* cheeks. Yellow below, striped with black; rump yellow, crown black. *Female and nonbreeding:* Lack chestnut cheeks; duller, breast often whitish, streaked. Note dull *patch of yellow behind ear, yellowish rump,* and *one wing bar bolder than the other.* Immature female distinctly *gray.* **VOICE:** Song a very high, thin *seet seet seet seet.* May be confused with song of Bay-breasted or Black-and-white warbler. **SIMILAR SPECIES:** Dull birds in nonbreeding plumage may be confused with Yellow-rumped Warbler. **HABITAT:** Spruce forests; often searches out isolated spruce and fir trees in migration, also broadleaf trees.

BLACK-THROATED BLUE WARBLER   Fairly common M399
Dendroica caerulescens

5¼ in. (13 cm). *Male:* Clean-cut; upperparts *deep blue;* throat and sides *black,* belly white. *Female:* Olive-brown back, with light line over eye and small *white wing spot.* Immature female may lack this white "pocket handkerchief," but note *dark cheek.* **VOICE:** Song a husky, lazy *zur, zur, zur, zreee* or *beer, beer, bree* (ending higher). Call a hard *thip,* similar to call of Dark-eyed Junco. **SIMILAR SPECIES:** Orange-crowned Warbler may show pale crescent along leading edge of wing. **HABITAT:** Understory of deciduous and mixed woodlands.

YELLOW-RUMPED WARBLER *Dendroica coronata*   Common M400

5½ in. (14 cm). Includes two subspecies groups, formerly considered separate species: "Myrtle" Warbler (widespread in East) and "Audubon's" Warbler (primarily western, enters our area in winter in s. TX; casually elsewhere). Note bright *yellow rump* and call. *Breeding male:* Blue-gray above; heavy black breast patch (like an inverted U); crown and side patches yellow. "Audubon's" differs from "Myrtle" in having *yellow throat* (which does not extend back below cheek, as white does in "Myrtle"), large white wing patches, no white supercilium. *Breeding female:* Duller. *Nonbreeding:* More brownish above; whitish below, streaked; throat yellowish (sometimes dim) in "Audubon's"; *rump yellow.* **VOICE:** Variable song, juncolike but two-part, rising or dropping in pitch, *seet-seet-seet-seet-seet, trrrrrrrr.* Call a loud *check* ("Myrtle") or higher *tchip* ("Audubon's"). **SIMILAR SPECIES:** Cape May and Magnolia warblers. **HABITAT:** Coniferous forests. In migration and winter, varied; open woods, brush, dune scrub.

BLACK-THROATED GRAY WARBLER   Rare M401
Dendroica nigrescens

5 in. (13 cm). *Male:* Gray above, with black throat, cheek, and crown separated by *white. Small yellow spot in lores. Female:* Slaty crown and cheek; dusky or light throat; loral spot duller yellow. *Immature:* May be tinged brownish above; loral spot pale. **VOICE:** Song a buzzy chant, "full of Zs," *zeedle zeedle zeedle ZEETche* (next-to-last or last note higher). Call a dull *tup.* **SIMILAR SPECIES:** Suggests Black-and-white Warbler, but lacks white stripes on back and crown, does not crawl around on branches and limbs. **RANGE AND HABITAT:** Rare winter visitor to s. TX from West, casual elsewhere in East. Nests in pinyon-juniper, mixed woods; in migration and winter, open woods.

WARBLERS

breeding
♀

breeding
♂

**CAPE MAY
WARBLER**

♀

**BLACK-
THROATED
BLUE WARBLER**

♂

mature

**YELLOW-
RUMPED
WARBLER**

breeding
♂

♀

breeding

"Myrtle"
Warbler

breeding
♂

♀

"Audubon's"
Warbler

breeding

**BLACK-THROATED
GRAY WARBLER**

♂

♂

immature

♀

GOLDEN-CHEEKED WARBLER
Scarce, local M402

Dendroica chrysoparia

5¼ in. (14 cm). Breeds in Ashe Juniper hills of Edwards Plateau, TX. *Male:* Similar to Black-throated Green Warbler, but with *black back* and blacker line through eye. *Female:* Similar to female Black-throated Green, but back darker olive with dusky streaks, belly snowy white (lacking tinge of yellow on flanks). **VOICE:** Song a hurried *tweeah, tweeah, tweesy* or *bzzzz, laysee, daysee.* Call like Black-throated Green's. **SIMILAR SPECIES:** Black-throated Green Warbler. **HABITAT:** Junipers, oaks; also streamside trees.

TOWNSEND'S WARBLER *Dendroica townsendi*
Vagrant

5 in. (13 cm). *Male:* Easily distinguished by *black-and-yellow pattern of head*, with *blackish cheek patch; underparts yellow*, with heavily striped sides. *Female and immature:* Throat largely yellow, not black; may be known by well-defined dark cheek patch, bordered by yellow as in male. **VOICE:** Song a wheezy *dzeer dzeer dzeer tseetsee* or *weazy, weazy, seesee.* Call a soft, flat *tip.* **SIMILAR SPECIES:** Black-throated Green Warbler. **RANGE:** Casual visitor from West. **HABITAT:** Tall conifers, cool fir forests; in migration and winter, variety of woodlands.

BLACK-THROATED GREEN WARBLER
Fairly common M403

Dendroica virens

5 in. (13 cm). *Male:* Bright *yellow face* is framed by black throat and olive green crown. *Female and immature:* Recognized by yellow face; much less black on throat; unmarked olive green back. All birds show small yellow spot on rear flank. **VOICE:** Lisping, weezy or buzzy *zoo zee zoo zoo zee* or *zee zee zee zee zoo zee; zee* notes on same pitch, *zoo* notes lower. Call a flat *tip* or *tup.* **SIMILAR SPECIES:** Townsend's Warbler (a stray from West) has darker cheek, darker above, yellow on lower breast. Golden-cheeked Warbler (rare and very local in TX) has black line through eye, darker back. **HABITAT:** Mainly coniferous or mixed woods; in migration, variety of woodlands.

BLACKBURNIAN WARBLER *Dendroica fusca*
Fairly common M404

5 in. (13 cm). The "fire throat." *Breeding male:* Black and white, with *flame orange* on head and throat. *Female and nonbreeding:* Paler orange (adult female and immature male) or yellowish (immature female) on throat; dark cheek patch. Note head stripes, *pale back stripes.* **VOICE:** Song *zip zip zip titi tseeeeee,* ending on a very high, upslurred note (inaudible to some ears). Also a two-part *teetsa teetsa teetsa teetsa zizizizizi,* more like Nashville Warbler. Call a rich *chip.* **SIMILAR SPECIES:** Yellow-rumped ("Audubon's"), Yellow-throated, and Cerulean warblers. **HABITAT:** Woodlands; in summer, conifers.

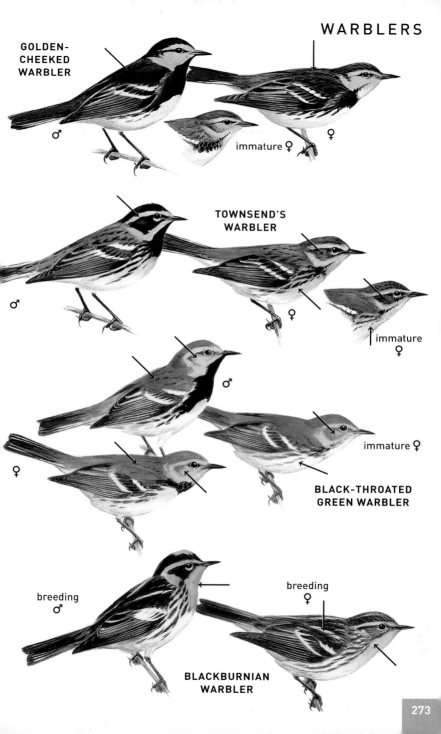

WARBLERS

GOLDEN-CHEEKED WARBLER

♂

immature ♀

♀

TOWNSEND'S WARBLER

♂

♀

immature ♀

♂

♀

immature ♀

BLACK-THROATED GREEN WARBLER

breeding ♂

breeding ♀

BLACKBURNIAN WARBLER

PINE WARBLER *Dendroica pinus*   Common M406

5½ in. (14 cm). All plumages show dark cheeks, blurry streaking at breast-sides, unstreaked back, and white tail spots. *Male:* Yellow-breasted, with olive green back, *white wing bars. Female:* Duller; brownish olive above; immature females often obscure. **VOICE:** Song a trill on one pitch like Chipping Sparrow's song, but more musical, slower. Call a sweet *chip.* **SIMILAR SPECIES:** Nonbreeding Blackpoll and Bay-breasted warblers. **HABITAT:** Pine woods. In winter sometimes in fields with bluebirds.

PRAIRIE WARBLER *Dendroica discolor*   Fairly common M408

4¾ in. (12 cm). This warbler *bobs its tail* (like Palm Warbler); underparts yellow, paling on undertail coverts; black stripes *confined to sides; two black face marks,* one through eye, one below. At close range, chestnut marks may be seen on back of male (reduced in female). **VOICE:** Song a thin *zee zee zee zee zee zee zee zee,* ascending the chromatic scale. Call a sharp *tschip.* **SIMILAR SPECIES:** Pine and Palm warblers. **HABITAT:** Brushy fields, low pines, mangroves.

PALM WARBLER *Dendroica palmarum*   Common M409

5¼ in. (14 cm). A ground-loving warbler. Note constant tail *bobbing.* Brownish or olive above; yellowish or dirty white below, narrowly streaked; *bright yellow* undertail coverts, white spots in tail corners. In breeding plumage has *chestnut cap.* Two subspecies: Eastern breeders show more yellow below and on eyebrow; western breeders duller, may have yellow restricted to undertail coverts in fall. **VOICE:** Song weak, repetitious notes: *zhe-zhe-zhe-zhe-zhe-zhe.* Call a sharp *tsup.* **SIMILAR SPECIES:** Prairie Warbler. **HABITAT:** In summer, muskeg, bogs. In migration and winter, bushes, weedy fields.

YELLOW-THROATED WARBLER   Fairly common M405
Dendroica dominica

5½ in. (14 cm). A gray-backed warbler with *yellow throat. Black eye mask,* white wing bars, black stripes on sides. Sexes similar. Creeps about branches of trees. "Sutton's" Warbler is a very rare hybrid of Yellow-throated Warbler and Northern Parula. **VOICE:** Song a series of clear slurred notes dropping slightly in pitch: *tee-ew, tew, tew, tew, tew, tew wi* (last note rising). Call a rich *chip.* **SIMILAR SPECIES:** Female Blackburnian Warbler. **HABITAT:** Open woodlands, especially sycamores, live oaks, pines. In winter, often in palms.

KIRTLAND'S WARBLER *Dendroica kirtlandii*   Rare, local M407

5¾ in. (15 cm). Bluish gray above, *streaked with black;* yellow below, with black spots or streaks confined to sides. *Male:* Has *blackish mask. Female:* Duller, lacks mask; immature female browner. Persistently wags tail (like Prairie Warbler). **VOICE:** Song, loud and low-pitched, resembles Northern Waterthrush's song. Typical song starts with three or four low staccato notes, continues with rapid ringing notes on higher pitch, and ends abruptly. **SIMILAR SPECIES:** Prairie, Yellow-rumped, and Magnolia warblers. **HABITAT:** Groves of young jack pines 5 to 18 ft. high with ground cover of blueberries, bearberry, or sweet fern. Habitat succession and Brown-headed Cowbird are having an impact on endangered Kirtland's population.

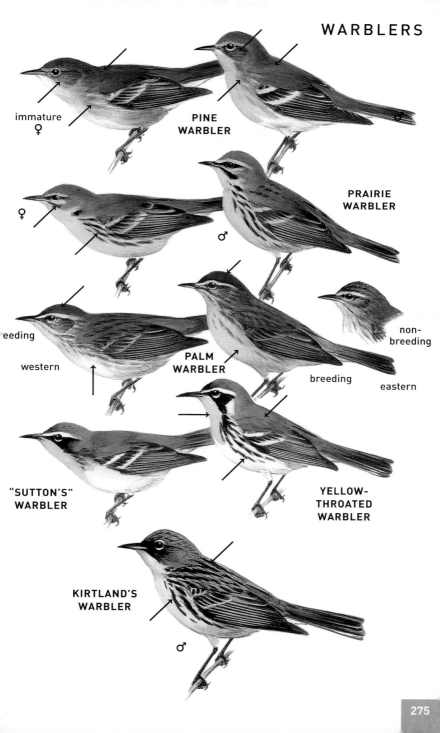

WARBLERS

immature ♀

PINE WARBLER

♂

♀

PRAIRIE WARBLER

♂

breeding

western

PALM WARBLER

non-breeding

breeding

eastern

"SUTTON'S" WARBLER

YELLOW-THROATED WARBLER

KIRTLAND'S WARBLER

♂

BAY-BREASTED WARBLER *Dendroica castanea*   Uncommon M410
5½ in. (14 cm). *Breeding male:* Note *chestnut breast* and *buff neck patch. Breeding female:* Paler, with whitish throat. *Nonbreeding:* Olive green above; two white wing bars; pale *buff below, dark feet; no streaks on back or breast.* **VOICE:** High, sibilant *tees teesi teesi;* resembles song of Black-and-white Warbler, but thinner, shorter, more on one pitch. **SIMILAR SPECIES:** See nonbreeding Blackpoll and Pine warblers. **HABITAT:** Woodlands; in summer, conifers and mixed woods.

BLACK-AND-WHITE WARBLER *Mniotilta varia*   Common M413
5¼ in. (13 cm). *Creeping along trunks* and branches of trees, this warbler is *striped lengthwise with black and white. Male:* Black throat partly or mostly lost in winter. *Female and immature:* Paler cheek, fainter streaks below, and buffy wash on flanks. **VOICE:** Song a high thin *weesee weesee weesee weesee;* some songs drop in pitch midway through. Call a sharp *chip.* **SIMILAR SPECIES:** Blackpoll and Black-throated Gray (rare) warblers. **HABITAT:** Woods.

BLACKPOLL WARBLER *Dendroica striata*   Fairly common M411
5½ in. (14 cm). *Breeding male:* A striped gray warbler with *black cap, white cheeks. Breeding female:* Greenish gray above, whitish below, streaked. *Nonbreeding:* Olive above, greenish yellow below, *faintly streaked* on back and breast; *white undertail coverts;* usually *pale legs* (or at least *feet*). **VOICE:** Song a thin, deliberate, mechanical *zi-zi-zi-zi-zi-zi-zi-zi* on one pitch, becoming stronger, then diminishing. Call a sharp *chip.* **SIMILAR SPECIES:** Black-and-white Warbler. Nonbreeding Bay-breasted Warbler lacks streaking on breast and flanks, has buff wash on flanks and undertail coverts, and dark feet. See Pine Warbler. **HABITAT:** Conifers; in migration, broadleaf trees.

AMERICAN REDSTART *Setophaga ruticilla*   Common M414
5¼ in. (13 cm). Butterfly-like; actively flitting, with drooping wings and spread tail. *Adult male: Black and orange. Female:* Gray-olive; *yellow patches* on wings and tail. *Immature male:* Like female, but tinged with orange on chest, sometimes with black splotches on face. **VOICE:** Songs (often alternated) *zee zee zee zee zwee* (last note higher), *tsee tsee tsee tsee tsee-o* (last syllable dropping), and *teetsa teetsa teetsa teetsa teet* (notes paired). Call a slurred, rich *chip.* **HABITAT:** Second-growth woods, riparian woodlands.

CERULEAN WARBLER   Scarce to uncommon M412
Dendroica cerulea
4¾ in. (12 cm). A small, short-tailed warbler, often high up in large trees. *Male:* Blue above, white below. Note *narrow black band* across chest. *Female:* Olive-gray above with dull *blue crown, bold supercilium,* creamy white underparts, bold wing bars. *Immature:* Like female; washed with pale yellow on breast. **VOICE:** Buzzy notes on same pitch, followed by longer note on a higher pitch: *zray zray z-z-z zeeeee.* Call a rich, slurred *chip.* **SIMILAR SPECIES:** Dull female Blackburnian Warbler has streaked back pattern. **HABITAT:** High in deciduous forests, especially in river valleys and ridges.

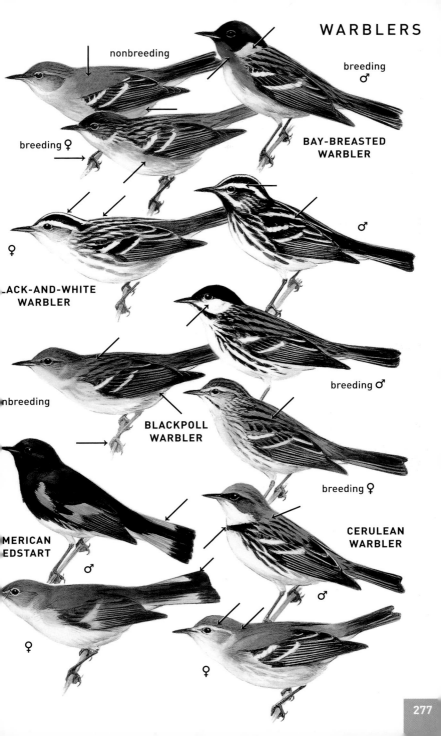

WARBLERS

nonbreeding

breeding ♂

breeding ♀

BAY-BREASTED WARBLER

♀

♂

_ACK-AND-WHITE WARBLER

nbreeding

breeding ♂

BLACKPOLL WARBLER

breeding ♀

MERICAN EDSTART

♂

♀

CERULEAN WARBLER

♂

♀

SWAINSON'S WARBLER *Limnothlypis swainsonii*   Scarce M417

5½ in. (14 cm). A skulker, difficult to see. Long bill. Olive-brown above and plain buffy white below, with *brown crown* and *light eyebrow stripe*. Sexes alike. **VOICE:** Song suggests Louisiana Waterthrush's, but shorter (five notes: two slurred notes, two lower notes, and a higher note): *wee-wee-chip-poor-will*. Call a sharp, loud *chip*. **SIMILAR SPECIES:** Ovenbird, Worm-eating Warbler, waterthrushes. **HABITAT:** Cane thickets, swamps, stream bottoms, thick woodland brush; locally in rhododendron-hemlock tangles in Appalachians.

WORM-EATING WARBLER   Uncommon M416
Helmitheros vermivorum

5¼ in. (13 cm). An unobtrusive forager of wooded slopes and thick understory. Often probes hanging dead-leaf clusters. *Dull olive,* with *black stripes on buffy head*. Breast *rich buff*. Sexes alike. **VOICE:** Song a series of thin dry notes; resembles trill of Chipping Sparrow, but thinner, more insectlike. Call a flat *chip*. **SIMILAR SPECIES:** Ovenbird, Swainson's Warbler, waterthrushes. **HABITAT:** Wooded hillsides, undergrowth, ravines.

OVENBIRD *Seiurus aurocapilla*   Common M418

6 in. (15 cm). Usually seen walking on leafy floor of woods. Suggests a small thrush, but *striped* rather than spotted beneath. *Orangish patch on crown bordered by blackish stripes. White eye-ring.* **VOICE:** Song an emphatic *TEACHer, TEACHer, TEACHer*, etc., in crescendo. Or a monosyllabic *TEACH, TEACH, TEACH*, etc. Call a loud, sharp *tshuk*. **SIMILAR SPECIES:** Waterthrushes. See also spotted thrushes (p. 254). **HABITAT:** Near or on ground in leafy and pine-oak woods; in migration, also thickets.

NORTHERN WATERTHRUSH   Common M419
Seiurus noveboracensis

5¾ in. (15 cm). Suggests a small thrush. *Walks* along water's edge and *teeters* like a Spotted Sandpiper. Brown-backed, with *striped* underparts, strong eyebrow stripe; both eyebrow and underparts vary from whitish to pale yellow. *Throat striped.* **VOICE:** Call a sharp *chink*. Song a vigorous, rapid *twit twit twit sweet sweet sweet chew chew chew* (*chew*s drop in pitch). **SIMILAR SPECIES:** Louisiana Waterthrush, Ovenbird. **HABITAT:** Swamps, bogs, woods with standing water, pond shores; in migration, also marsh edges, puddles, mangroves.

LOUISIANA WATERTHRUSH *Seiurus motacilla*   Uncommon M420

6 in. (15 cm). Similar to Northern Waterthrush, but underparts *white on breast, pinkish buff on flanks and undertail coverts*. Bill slightly larger. *Eyebrow stripe pure white and flares behind eye*. Throat usually *lacks stripes*. Legs pinkish. **VOICE:** Song musical and ringing; three clear slurred whistles, followed by a jumble of twittering notes dropping in pitch. **SIMILAR SPECIES:** Northern Waterthrush has *smaller bill*, usually *buffy eyebrow, streaked throat*, and *even-toned* ground color to underparts (yellow to off white), not bicolored like Louisiana. Song of Swainson's Warbler somewhat similar. **HABITAT:** Streams, brooks, ravines, wooded swamps.

SWAINSON'S WARBLER

WORM-EATING WARBLER

OVENBIRD

typical

NORTHERN WATERTHRUSH

whitish variant

LOUISIANA ATERTHRUSH

PROTHONOTARY WARBLER   Fairly common M415
Protonotaria citrea
5½ in. (14 cm). A golden bird of wooded swamps. *Male:* Entire head
and breast deep *yellow to orangey.* Wings blue-gray *with no bars. Female:* Duller. **VOICE:** Song *zweet zweet zweet zweet zweet zweet,* on
one pitch. Call a loud *seep.* **SIMILAR SPECIES:** Yellow and Blue-winged
warblers. **HABITAT:** Wooded swamps, backwaters, river edges.

KENTUCKY WARBLER *Oporornis formosus*   Uncommon M421
5¼ in. (13 cm). Note *broad black sideburns* extending down from eye
and *yellow spectacles.* Sexes similar, though female and immature
slightly duller. Learn song; 10 Kentuckies are heard for every 1 seen.
VOICE: Song a rapid rolling chant, *tory-tory-tory-tory* or *churry-churry-
churry-churry,* suggestive of Carolina Wren, but less musical (two-
syllable rather than three-syllable). Call a rich, low *tup.* **SIMILAR SPE-
CIES:** Common Yellowthroat lacks spectacles. See also Hooded
Warbler. **HABITAT:** Woodland undergrowth.

CONNECTICUT WARBLER *Oporornis agilis*   Uncommon M422
5¾–6 in. (15 cm). Shy and skulking. Similar to Mourning Warbler, but
slightly larger; note *walking behavior* — on limbs and ground — and
complete white eye-ring, long undertail coverts reaching almost to tail
tip. *Breeding:* Hood gray in male, gray-brown in female. *Nonbreeding
female and immature:* Duller, with brownish hood, paler throat. **VOICE:**
Repetitious *chip-chup-ee, chip-chup-ee, chip-chup-ee, chip* or *sugar-
tweet, sugar-tweet, sugar-tweet.* **SIMILAR SPECIES:** Breeding Mourning Warbler lacks eye-ring (but immature has slightly broken one).
Male has black throat. Also, Connecticut walks, Mourning hops.
Nashville Warbler also has eye-ring, but is smaller, has yellow
throat, and is a more active feeder. **HABITAT:** Poplar bluffs, muskeg,
mixed woods; in migration, undergrowth. Feeds mostly on ground.

MOURNING WARBLER *Oporornis philadelphia*   Uncommon M423
5¼ in. (13 cm). Shy and skulking. Olive above, yellow below, with slate
gray hood encircling head and neck. *Male:* Has irregular black bib.
Female and immature: May have thin, light eye-ring that is barely broken (compare to Connecticut's complete eye-ring). Some breeding
females and most nonbreeding birds show *yellow wash* on throat,
sometimes extending through middle breast and resulting in bird *not*
appearing "hooded." Yellow undertail coverts shorter than Connecticut's. **VOICE:** Song *chirry, chirry, chorry, chorry* (*chorry* lower). Considerable variation. Call a hard, buzzy, wrenlike *chack.* **SIMILAR SPECIES:**
Connecticut Warbler. **HABITAT:** Thickets, undergrowth.

WARBLERS

♀ ♂

PROTHONOTARY
WARBLER

♂

Nashville Warbler
(p. 266)
for comparison

immature

CONNECTICUT
WARBLER

KENTUCKY
WARBLER

♀

immature
♀

♀

MOURNING
WARBLER

281

COMMON YELLOWTHROAT *Geothlypis trichas*   Common M424
5 in. (13 cm). Wrenlike. *Male: Black (Lone Ranger) mask,* yellow throat
and upper breast. *Female and immature:* Olive-brown, with rich
yellow throat, duller below, but brighter yellow undertail coverts;
lack or have only a suggestion of black mask. **VOICE:** Bright rapid
chant, *witchity-witchity-witchity-witch;* sometimes *witchy-witchy-
witchy-witch.* Call a husky *tchep.* **SIMILAR SPECIES:** Female and immature distinguished from immature *Oporornis* warblers by whitish
belly, smaller size. **HABITAT:** Swamps, marshes, wet thickets, woodland edges.

GRAY-CROWNED YELLOWTHROAT   Vagrant
Geothlypis poliocephala
5½ in. (14 cm). Male has partial mask *not extending to forehead or
cheeks; gray crown.* Both sexes have *thick bill* with *pale lower mandible;* broken white eye-ring. **VOICE:** Burbling warble. Call *chlee-dee.*
SIMILAR SPECIES: Common Yellowthroat slightly smaller, and slightly
smaller billed. **RANGE:** Very rare visitor from Mex. to s. TX, where formerly bred. **HABITAT:** Reeds and weedy vegetation near water.

RUFOUS-CAPPED WARBLER *Basileuterus rufifrons*   Vagrant
5 in. (13 cm). *Rufous cap and cheek* separated by white eyebrow stripe.
Throat and upper breast bright yellow, upperparts olive. Long, spin-
dly tail often held cocked up at angle. **VOICE:** Accelerating series of
whistled, musical *chip*s and warbles. Call *tick.* **SIMILAR SPECIES:**
Common Yellowthroat. **RANGE:** Casual visitor from Mex. to s. TX. **HAB-
ITAT:** Thick brush, oak woodlands near water.

GOLDEN-CROWNED WARBLER *Basileuterus culicivorus*   Vagrant
5 in. (13 cm). Yellow crown and gray eyebrow stripe bordered by
black. Broken eye-ring. Dusky yellow below. Drab olive above. **VOICE:**
Song a series of slurred whistles. Call a short, sharp *tuk.* **SIMILAR
SPECIES:** Common Yellowthroat, Orange-crowned Warbler. **RANGE:**
Casual stray from Mex. to s. TX. **HABITAT:** Dense woodland understory.

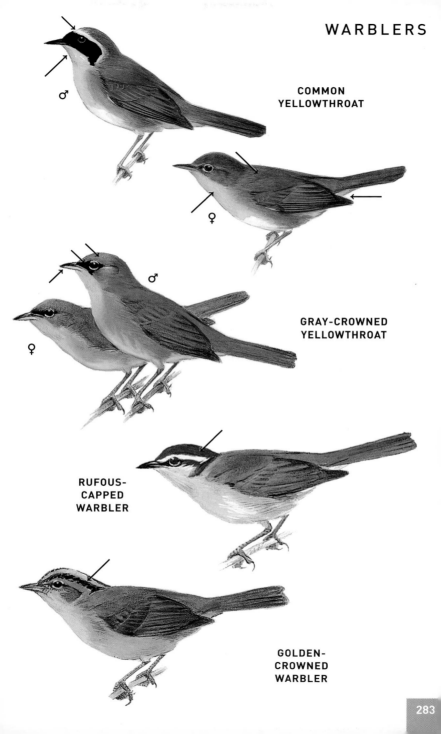

WARBLERS

COMMON YELLOWTHROAT

♂

♀

GRAY-CROWNED YELLOWTHROAT

♂

♀

RUFOUS-CAPPED WARBLER

GOLDEN-CROWNED WARBLER

WILSON'S WARBLER *Wilsonia pusilla*   Uncommon M426
4¾ in. (12 cm). Note longish tail, dark beady eye. *Male:* Golden yellow
with *round black cap. Female:* May show trace of cap (on forecrown).
Immature: Some lack even suggestion of dark cap; they are golden-
looking birds with yellow stripe above *beady eye* and *yellow lores.*
Constantly moving and flitting about. **VOICE:** Song a thin, rapid little
chatter, dropping in pitch at end: *chi chi chi chi chi chet chet.* Call a
flat *timp.* **SIMILAR SPECIES:** Female Hooded Warbler has white spots
on tail, dark lores. Yellow Warbler has yellow spots on shorter tail,
yellow edging in wings. See also Orange-crowned Warbler. Vocal differences important. **HABITAT:** Thickets and trees along streams,
moist tangles, low shrubs, willows, alders.

HOODED WARBLER *Wilsonia citrina*   Fairly common M425
5¼ in. (13 cm). *Male: Black hood* or cowl encircles yellow face and
forehead. *Female:* Lacks hood, although yellow face may be sharply
outlined (adults); aside from *white tail spots,* may lack other distinctive marks. **VOICE:** Song a loud whistled *weeta wee-tee-o.* Also other
arrangements; slurred *tee-o* is a clue. Call a sharp *chink,* like waterthrushes. **SIMILAR SPECIES:** Female and immature Wilson's Warbler
lack tail spots and any suggestion of Hooded's face pattern. **HABITAT:**
Wooded undergrowth, laurels, wooded swamps.

CANADA WARBLER *Wilsonia canadensis*   Uncommon M427
5¼ in. (13 cm). The "necklaced warbler." *Male: Solid gray above;* bright
yellow below, with *necklace of short black stripes;* white vent. *Female
and immature:* Similar; necklace fainter, upperparts may be washed
with brownish. All have *spectacles of white eye-ring and yellow loral
stripe.* No white in wings or tail. **VOICE:** Song a staccato burst, irregularly arranged. *Chip, chupety swee-ditchety.* Call *tchip.* **HABITAT:** Forest undergrowth, shady thickets.

YELLOW-BREASTED CHAT *Icteria virens*   Uncommon M428
7½ in. (19 cm). Our largest warbler with *heavy bill* and *long tail.* Note
white spectacles, *bright yellow* throat and breast. No wing bars. Habitat and voice suggest a thrasher or mockingbird. **VOICE:** Repeated
whistles, alternating with harsh notes and soft *caws.* Suggests
Northern Mockingbird, but repertoire more limited; much longer
pauses between phrases. Single notes: *whoit, kook, zhairr,* etc. Often
sings in short, awkward courtship display flight. **SIMILAR SPECIES:**
Common Yellowthroat (much smaller). **HABITAT:** Brushy tangles, bri-
ars, stream thickets.

WARBLERS

WILSON'S WARBLER

♀

♂

HOODED WARBLER

♀

♂

CANADA WARBLER

♀

♂

YELLOW-BREASTED CHAT

♂

Common Yellowthroat
(p. 282)
for comparison

Fall Warblers

Most of these have streaks or wing bars.

RUBY-CROWNED KINGLET *Regulus calendula*   p. 250
(Not a warbler.) Broken eye-ring, pale wing bars with black "highlight," wing-flicking behavior, skinny legs.

CHESTNUT-SIDED WARBLER *Dendroica pensylvanica*   p. 268
Immature: Green above, grayish-white below; eye-ring; tail cocked at angle.

PINE WARBLER *Dendroica pinus*   p. 274
Immatures differ from Blackpoll and Bay-breasted warblers in heavier bill, less contrasting wing patterns, darker cheeks.

BAY-BREASTED WARBLER *Dendroica castanea*   p. 276
Note dark legs and feet, buff undertail coverts, unstreaked breast and back. Adult shows "bay" on flanks. See Blackpoll Warbler.

BLACKPOLL WARBLER *Dendroica striata*   p. 276
Very similar to Bay-breasted Warbler, but slimmer. Note streaked back and breast, white (not buff) undertail coverts, yellow wash to breast; pale yellowish legs and especially feet.

NORTHERN PARULA *Parula americana*   p. 268
Immature: Small and short-tailed. Combination of bluish head, broken eye-ring, and yellow throat; wing bars.

MAGNOLIA WARBLER *Dendroica magnolia*   p. 268
Immature: Broad white band at midtail. Note yellow rump. Faint dusky band across yellow breast. Side streaking.

PRAIRIE WARBLER *Dendroica discolor*   p. 274
Immature: Jaw stripe, side streaks. Bobs long tail.

YELLOW WARBLER *Dendroica petechia*   p. 268
Yellow edging to wings and tail. Beady dark eye. Some females and immatures are so dusky that they may resemble Orange-crowned Warbler.

BLACKBURNIAN WARBLER *Dendroica fusca*   p. 272
Immature: Yellow or yellow-orange throat, dark cheek; broad supercilium, pale back stripes. Obvious wing bars.

BLACK-THROATED GREEN WARBLER *Dendroica virens*   p. 272
Immature: Dusky outline frames yellow cheek. Plain greenish back.

PALM WARBLER *Dendroica palmarum*   p. 274
Brownish back, yellowish undertail coverts. Bobs long tail.

YELLOW-RUMPED WARBLER *Dendroica coronata*   p. 270
Immature: Bright yellow rump, streaked back; brownish above.

CAPE MAY WARBLER *Dendroica tigrina*   p. 270
Immature: Streaked breast, greenish yellow rump. Immature female very gray (not brownish like Yellow-rumped).

RUBY-CROWNED KINGLET

♀

not a warbler

CHESTNUT-SIDED WARBLER

immature

SELECTED FALL WARBLERS with streaks or wing bars

♂

PINE WARBLER

immature

BLACKPOLL WARBLER

PINE WARBLER

immature ♀

BAY-BREASTED WARBLER

immature

MAGNOLIA WARBLER

immature ♀

PRAIRIE WARBLER

NORTHERN PARULA

mature

YELLOW WARBLER

immature

mature

BLACKBURNIAN WARBLER

immature ♀

BLACK-THROATED GREEN WARBLER

PALM WARBLER western

immature ♀

YELLOW-RUMPED WARBLER

immature ♀

CAPE MAY WARBLER

287

ORANGE-CROWNED WARBLER *Vermivora celata*   **p. 266**
Dingy breast with faint dusky streaks, yellow undertail coverts, faint eye line. Immature greenish drab overall, barely paler below. Some birds often quite gray.

TENNESSEE WARBLER *Vermivora peregrina*   **p. 266**
Similar to Orange-crowned Warbler but has white undertail coverts; more conspicuous eyebrow stripe; greener look above; paler underparts, with no hint of streaks; trace of a light wing bar; shorter tail. Note also needle-thin bill.

PHILADELPHIA VIREO *Vireo philadelphicus*   **p. 230**
(Not a warbler.) "Vireo" song and actions. Note also thicker vireo bill. Compare with female Tennessee Warbler.

HOODED WARBLER *Wilsonia citrina*   **p. 284**
Immature female: Yellow eyebrow stripe, mostly yellow cheeks, dark lores, bold white tail spots. (Immature male resembles adult male.)

WILSON'S WARBLER *Wilsonia pusilla*   **p. 284**
Immature: Beady dark eye. Smaller and slimmer than Hooded Warbler with yellow lores, mostly olive cheeks, slimmer tail with no white.

BLACK-THROATED BLUE WARBLER *Dendroica caerulescens*   **p. 270**
Female: Dark cheek, white wing spot ("handkerchief"). Some immature females lack this white spot and may suggest Tennessee Warbler, but note dark cheek and duller (browner olive) back. (Immature male resembles adult male.)

CONNECTICUT WARBLER *Oporornis agilis*   **p. 280**
Immature: Large size. Brownish hood; complete, bold eye-ring. Walks.

MOURNING WARBLER *Oporornis philadelphia*   **p. 280**
Immature and fall female: Suggestion of hood; broken eye-ring. Brighter yellow below than Connecticut Warbler, including often on throat (unlike Connecticut).

NASHVILLE WARBLER *Vermivora ruficapilla*   **p. 266**
Yellow throat (may be dull) and undertail coverts, white eye-ring, grayish crown and nape. Short tail, which it bobs.

COMMON YELLOWTHROAT *Geothlypis trichas*   **p. 282**
Female: Yellow throat, breast, and undertail coverts; brownish sides; white belly.

PROTHONOTARY WARBLER *Protonotaria citrea*   **p. 280**
Female: Dull golden head tinged greenish on crown in some immatures; dark eye stands out on plain face. Gray wings, white undertail, long bill.

CANADA WARBLER *Wilsonia canadensis*   **p. 284**
Immature: Lores yellow, eye-ring white. Solid gray above, yellow below, trace of necklace.

SELECTED FALL WARBLERS
without streaks or wing bars

ORANGE-CROWNED WARBLER

mature

PHILADELPHIA VIREO
not a warbler

TENNESSEE WARBLER

WILSON'S WARBLER

♀

immature ♀

HOODED WARBLER ♀

adult ♀

BLACK-THROATED BLUE WARBLER

immature

CONNECTICUT WARBLER

immature

MOURNING WARBLER

immature

NASHVILLE WARBLER

♀

♀

PROTHONOTARY WARBLER

immature

CANADA WARBLER

COMMON YELLOWTHROAT

289

CARDINALS, BUNTINGS, AND ALLIES
Family Cardinalidae (see p. 310)

SUMMER TANAGER *Piranga rubra*   Fairly common M467
7¾ in. (20 cm). *Male: Rose red,* with *pale* bill. *Female: Mustard yellow* below, sometimes flushed with orange; pale bill. Young males patched with red. **VOICE:** Call a staccato *pi-tuk* or *pik-i-tuk-i-tuk.* Song robinlike phrases; richer, less nasal than Scarlet Tanager's. **SIMILAR SPECIES:** Northern Cardinal. Female Scarlet Tanager is yellow-green and has smaller, duskier bill. **HABITAT:** Riparian woodlands, oaks.

SCARLET TANAGER *Piranga olivacea*   Fairly common M468
7 in. (18 cm). *Breeding male: Flaming scarlet,* with *black* wings and tail. *Female and nonbreeding male: Greenish* above, *yellowish* below; male has black wings. Young has single faint wing bar. **VOICE:** Song four or five short phrases, robinlike but hoarse (suggesting a robin with a sore throat): *hurry-worry-flurry-blurry.* Call *chip-burr.* **SIMILAR SPECIES:** Summer and Western tanagers. **HABITAT:** Deciduous and mixed forests, especially oaks. Often stays in canopy.

WESTERN TANAGER *Piranga ludoviciana*   Vagrant M469
7¼ in. (18 cm). Our only tanager with *strong wing bars.* **VOICE:** Song similar to Scarlet's. Call a dry *pri-ti-tic.* **SIMILAR SPECIES:** Orioles have longer tails, pointier bills; Scarlet Tanager may have single weak wing bar. **RANGE:** Casual visitor from West, mostly in fall and winter. **HABITAT:** Forested areas, often at feeders (in winter).

TANAGERS Family Thraupidae

Male tanagers are brightly colored; females usually duller; stout bills. Songs mostly weak and simple. **FOOD:** Insects, fruit. **RANGE:** New World Tropics.

WESTERN SPINDALIS *Spindalis zena*   Vagrant
6¾ in. (17 cm). *Male:* Bold head stripes and burnt orange breast distinctive. *Female:* Plain gray-brown with pale wing spot; note thick bill. **VOICE:** Series of thin high notes, *tzee-tzee-tzee,* often with buzzy phrase toward end. **RANGE:** Very rare visitor to s. FL from W. Indies. **HABITAT:** Brushy woodlands, fruit trees.

BANANAQUIT Family Coerebidae

The Bananaquit is currently "homeless" taxonomically, although the species is likely most closely related to several tropical Emberizids. **FOOD:** Nectar, insects. **RANGE:** New World tropical areas centered on Caribbean.

BANANAQUIT *Coereba flaveola*   Vagrant
4½ in. (11 cm). A small, short-tailed bird with decurved bill, bold supercilium, black back, and yellow wash on belly. Juvenile paler than adult. **VOICE:** Explosive series of buzzy notes and squeaks. **RANGE:** Very rare visitor to s. FL from W. Indies. **HABITAT:** Open brushy areas, nectar- and fruit-bearing trees.

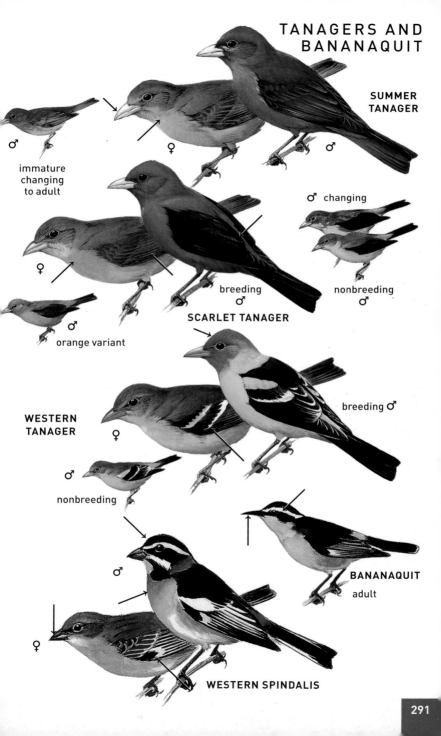

TANAGERS AND BANANAQUIT

SUMMER TANAGER

♂

immature
changing
to adult

♀

♂

♂ changing

nonbreeding
♂

♀

orange variant

breeding
♂

SCARLET TANAGER

WESTERN TANAGER

♀

breeding ♂

♂

nonbreeding

BANANAQUIT

adult

♂

♀

WESTERN SPINDALIS

Emberizids: Sparrows, Old World Buntings, and Relatives
Family Emberizidae

This large family of songbirds, whose taxonomic relationships are incompletely understood, comprises species with short conical bills, such as seedeaters, towhees, sparrows, longspurs, and Old World buntings. **FOOD:** Seeds, insects, fruit, varying seasonally. **RANGE:** Worldwide.

GREEN-TAILED TOWHEE *Pipilo chlorurus*   Scarce, local M431
7¼ in. (18 cm). A slender finchlike bird, known by its *rufous cap*, conspicuous *white throat*, black mustache, gray chest, and plain *olive green upperparts*, brightest on wings and tail. **VOICE:** Call a catlike mewing note. Song variable; opening with sweet notes, followed by burry notes: *weet-churr-cheeeeee-churr.* **HABITAT:** Brushy areas.

OLIVE SPARROW *Arremonops rufivirgatus*   Uncommon, local M430
6¼ in. (16 cm). Olive above, gray below with two dull brown stripes on crown. **VOICE:** Song composed of dry notes on one pitch going into Chipping Sparrow–like rattle. Call a sharp *chip* like Orange-crowned Warbler; also a hissing trill. **HABITAT:** Bushy thickets.

WHITE-COLLARED SEEDEATER   Scarce, local M429
Sporophila torqueola
4½ in. (11 cm). Tiny, with stubby bill. *Male:* Dark cap, incomplete light collar, white wing spot. Variable. *Female:* Buffy with eye-ring, wing bars. **VOICE:** High, then low *sweet, sweet, sweet, cheer, cheer, cheer.* Call a high *wink*. **HABITAT:** Tall, thick stands of grass.

EASTERN TOWHEE *Pipilo erythrophthalmus*   Fairly common M433
8 in. (20–21 cm). Smaller and more slender than a robin; rummages among leaf litter. Readily recognized by rufous sides and flash of white in tail. Eye usually red (but white in birds of s. Atlantic Coast and FL). *Juvenile:* Streaked below, but with diagnostic towhee tail pattern. **VOICE:** Song *drink-your-tea,* last syllable higher, wavering. Call a loud *chewink!* Southern white-eyed race gives a more slurred *shrink* or *zree;* song *cheet cheet cheeeeee.* **SIMILAR SPECIES:** Spotted Towhee. **HABITAT:** Open woods, undergrowth, brushy edges, hedgerows, feeders.

SPOTTED TOWHEE *Pipilo maculatus*   Uncommon to rare M432
8 in. (20–21 cm). Formerly lumped with Eastern Towhee. Distinguished by *white spots* on back and *white wing bars*. **VOICE:** Song *chup chup chup zeeeeeeee;* variable. Call a catlike *gu-eeee?* **HABITAT:** Open woods, undergrowth, brushy edges.

CANYON TOWHEE *Pipilo fuscus*   Uncommon, local M434
8¾ in. (22 cm). Drab brown with rufous crown, faint dusky necklace, and dark spot on breast. **VOICE:** Call an odd *shed-lp* or *kedlp.* Song an accelerating string of call notes. **HABITAT:** Brushy areas, residential areas, feeders.

EMBERIZIDS

GREEN-TAILED
TOWHEE

OLIVE
SPARROW

WHITE-
COLLARED
SEEDEATER

♀

♂

♂
white-eyed
form

♀
EASTERN
TOWHEE

juvenile

CANYON
TOWHEE

♂

♂

juvenile

SPOTTED TOWHEE

♀

293

BLACK-THROATED SPARROW Uncommon, local
Amphispiza bilineata

5½ in. (14 cm). *Adult:* Note face pattern. A pretty, gray sparrow, with *white face stripes* and *jet-black throat and chest*. White corners to *distinct black tail*. *Juvenile:* Seen into fall; *lacks* black throat but has similar cheek pattern and broad white supercilium; breast weakly streaked. **VOICE:** Song a sweet *cheet cheet cheeeeeeee* (two short, clear opening notes and a fine trill on lower or higher pitch); calls are light tinkling notes. **HABITAT:** Arid brush, cactus, juniper hillsides.

RUFOUS-CROWNED SPARROW Uncommon, local M438
Aimophila ruficeps

6 in. (15 cm). A dark sparrow with plain dusky breast, rufous cap and line behind eye, and rounded tail. Note *black whiskers* bordering throat and *distinct circular whitish eye-ring*. Seen singly or in pairs. **VOICE:** Song stuttering, gurgling, suggesting a thin, weak House Wren song. Call *dear, dear, dear.* **SIMILAR SPECIES:** Chipping Sparrow. **HABITAT:** Grassy or rocky slopes with sparse low bushes.

BOTTERI'S SPARROW *Aimophila botterii* Uncommon, local M437
6 in. (15 cm). Nondescript. Has buffy breast, plain brown tail lacking white corners. *Best told by voice.* Bill slightly curved on upper edge. **VOICE:** Song a constant tinkling and "pitting," sometimes running into a dry trill on same pitch. Very unlike song of Cassin's Sparrow. **SIMILAR SPECIES:** Cassin's Sparrow, breeding in same habitat, is almost identical, but grayer, has faint dusky streaks on flanks, small white corners to tail, straighter upper edge to bill; upperparts often look spotted (streaked in Botteri's). **HABITAT:** Coastal prairie.

CASSIN'S SPARROW *Aimophila cassinii* Fairly common M435
6 in. (15 cm). A large, drab sparrow of open arid country; underparts dingy without markings, or with faint streaking on flanks. Upperparts often appear more spotted than streaked. *Pale or whitish corners* on *rounded*, gray-brown tail. *Best clue is song.* **VOICE:** Song one or two short notes, a high sweet trill, and two lower notes: *ti ti tseeeeeee tay tay.* Often "skylarks" in air, giving trill at climax; Botteri's Sparrow does not skylark. **SIMILAR SPECIES:** Botteri's Sparrow. Savannah Sparrow also has yellow lore spots but is streakier overall, and shorter tailed, than Cassin's. **HABITAT:** Semiarid and coastal prairies, bushes.

BACHMAN'S SPARROW *Aimophila aestivalis* Scarce M436
6 in. (15 cm). In dry open pine woods with grass and palmetto scrub of South, this shy sparrow flushes reluctantly, then drops back into cover. A large sparrow, with long, rounded tail. Striped with reddish brown above, washed with dingy buff across plain breast, with gray bill. **VOICE:** Song variable; usually a clear liquid whistle followed by loose trill or warble on a different pitch, e.g., *seeeee, slip slip slip slip slip.* **SIMILAR SPECIES:** Field Sparrow smaller, with pink bill. Grasshopper Sparrow lives in meadows, has light crown stripe and short tail. Juvenile Bachman's suggests Lincoln's Sparrow, which would not be in South in summer and has eye-ring and streaked buffy breast. **HABITAT:** Open pine or oak woods, palmetto scrub.

SPARROWS

juvenile

adult

BLACK-THROATED SPARROW

RUFOUS-CROWNED SPARROW

BOTTERI'S SPARROW

CASSIN'S SPARROW

BACHMAN'S SPARROW

AMERICAN TREE SPARROW
Spizella arborea
Fairly common M439

6¼ in. (16 cm). Note *dark "stickpin,"* on breast, and *red-brown cap. Bill dark above, yellow below;* white wing bars; rufous wash on flanks. **VOICE:** Song sweet, variable, opening on one or two high, clear notes. Call *tseet;* feeding call a musical *teelwit.* **SIMILAR SPECIES:** Field and Chipping sparrows. **HABITAT:** Arctic and taiga scrub, willow thickets; in winter, brushy roadsides, weedy edges, freshwater marshes (particularly with cattails), feeders.

CHIPPING SPARROW *Spizella passerina*
Common M440

5½ in. (14 cm). *Breeding:* A small, slim, long-tailed, plain-breasted sparrow with bright *rufous cap, black eye line, white eyebrow. Nonbreeding:* Duller; note *dark eye line, dirty grayish breast, gray rump. Juvenile:* Shows fine streaks on breast, rump not as gray. **VOICE:** Song a dry chipping rattle on one pitch. Call a thin *tseet.* **SIMILAR SPECIES:** Clay-colored Sparrow. Also Swamp Sparrow. **HABITAT:** Open woods, especially pine, oak; orchards, farms, towns, lawns, feeders. Often forms flocks in fall and winter.

CLAY-COLORED SPARROW *Spizella pallida*
Fairly common M441

5½ in. (14 cm). Like a pale, nonbreeding Chipping Sparrow, but buffier, with *pale lores, sharply outlined ear patch,* more contrasting gray nape, bolder white mustache, *browner rump,* whiter underparts. **VOICE:** Unbirdlike; three or four low, flat buzzes: *bzzz, bzzz, bzzz.* Call a thin *tseet,* like Chipping's but higher. **HABITAT:** Scrub, brushy prairies, jack pines, weedy areas.

FIELD SPARROW *Spizella pusilla*
Fairly common M442

5¾ in. (15 cm). A small, slim, rusty-capped sparrow. Note *pink bill,* white eye-ring, plain buffy breast; rusty upperparts, and weak face striping. *Juvenile:* Has finely streaked breast, but this plumage not held long. **VOICE:** Song opens on deliberate, sweet, slurring notes, speeding into a trill (which ascends, descends, or stays on same pitch). Call *tseew.* **SIMILAR SPECIES:** American Tree and Chipping sparrows. **HABITAT:** Overgrown fields, pastures, brush, feeders.

SWAMP SPARROW *Melospiza georgiana*
Fairly common M457

5¾ in. (15 cm). A rather plump, dark, *rusty-winged* sparrow with tawny flanks and *broad black back striping. Adult:* White throat, rusty cap, *blue-gray neck and breast. Immature:* Blackish or dark rust crown, *olive-gray neck and breast;* dim flank streaking. **VOICE:** Song a loose trill, similar to Chipping Sparrow's but slower, sweeter, and stronger. Call a hard *cheep,* similar to Black or Eastern phoebe. **SIMILAR SPECIES:** Song Sparrow slightly larger, has *heavier breast streaks,* lacks tawny flanks. Lincoln's Sparrow has buff breast with fine sharp streaks. Chipping, Field, and American Tree sparrows are longer tailed and have wing bars. **HABITAT:** Nests in freshwater marshes with bushes, cattails, sedges, willows; winters in marshes, pond edges, moist brushy areas, weedy ditches.

SPARROWS

AMERICAN
TREE
SPARROW

breeding

nonbreeding

juvenile

CHIPPING SPARROW

breeding

nonbreeding

CLAY-COLORED SPARROW

FIELD
SPARROW

juvenile

adult

SWAMP
SPARROW

immature

adult

SAVANNAH SPARROW *Passerculus sandwichensis* Common M446

5½–5¾ in. (14–15 cm). This streaked, open-country sparrow suggests a small Song Sparrow, but it usually has *yellowish on front of eyebrow* (may be lacking or difficult to see in some birds); *whitish stripe through crown;* short, notched tail; pinker legs. "Ipswich" subspecies (*P. s. princeps;* breeding on Sable I., NS, and wintering along Atlantic Coast) are paler overall, slightly larger, and usually *walk* rather than hop. **VOICE:** Song a lisping, buzzy *tsit-tsit-tsit, tseeee-tsaaay* (last note lower). Call a light *tsu.* **SIMILAR SPECIES:** Song Sparrow's tail longer, rounded. See also Vesper Sparrow. Song similar to Grasshopper Sparrow's except for Savannah's lower last note. **HABITAT:** Open fields, farms, meadows, salt marshes, prairies, dunes.

GRASSHOPPER SPARROW Uncommon M447
Ammodramus savannarum

5 in. (13 cm). A small-bodied, large- and flat-headed, short- and sharp-tailed sparrow of taller grasslands. Crown with pale median stripe; *yellow lores; whitish eye-ring;* note relatively *unstriped buffy breast.* Yellow bend in wing hard to see. *Juvenile:* Has dusky streaks on breast. **VOICE:** Very thin, dry, insectlike *pi-tup zeeeeeeeeeeeee.* **SIMILAR SPECIES:** Le Conte's Sparrow has bolder, orangier eyebrow; bold side streaking. Grasshopper's song fairly similar to Savannah Sparrow's. **HABITAT:** Grasslands, hayfields, pastures, prairies.

BAIRD'S SPARROW Scarce, local, secretive M448
Ammodramus bairdii

5½ in. (14 cm). An elusive, skulking prairie sparrow. Light breast crossed by *narrow band* of fine black streaks. Head ocher-buff, streaked. Key mark is broad *ocher* median crown stripe. *Double mustache stripes.* Flat head. Hard to see well except when singing. *Juvenile:* Pale edges form scaly pattern above. **VOICE:** Song begins with two or three high musical *zips,* ends with trill on lower pitch; more musical than Savannah Sparrow. **SIMILAR SPECIES:** Savannah Sparrow has more extensive streaking below, narrow white median crown stripe, and lacks dark marks at rear of auriculars and double mustache stripes. See Henslow's Sparrow. **HABITAT:** Native prairies, scattered bushes used as song perches.

HENSLOW'S SPARROW Scarce, secretive M449
Ammodramus henslowii

5 in. (13 cm). A secretive sparrow of fields, easily overlooked were it not for its odd song. Short-tailed and flat-headed, with large pale bill; finely striped across breast. Olive-colored head and reddish wings help identify it. Also note double mustache stripes. **VOICE:** Song a poor vocal effort: a hiccuping *tsi-lick.* May sing on quiet, windless nights. **SIMILAR SPECIES:** Grasshopper Sparrow. Young Henslow's Sparrow (summer) is practically without breast streaks, thus resembles adult Grasshopper. Conversely, young Grasshopper has breast streaks, but lacks adult Henslow's olive and russet tones. **HABITAT:** Very specific. Partially overgrown fields with certain plant development of exacting components. Disappearing from many former haunts. Winters in dense cover in southern pine forests.

STREAK-BREASTED GRASS SPARROWS

typical

adult

juvenile

GRASSHOPPER SPARROW

"Ipswich"

SAVANNAH SPARROW

BAIRD'S SPARROW

juvenile

HENSLOW'S SPARROW

adult

SALTMARSH SPARROW
Uncommon M452
Ammodramus caudacutus
5¼ in. (13 cm). A short-tailed, often shy sparrow of coastal marshes. Note deep ocher yellow or orange of face, which completely surrounds gray ear patch. Distinct streaks on mostly whitish or light buff breast, flat-headed appearance. **VOICE:** Song a weak varied jumble of buzzy hisses and clicks; not distinctly two-part like Nelson's. **SIMILAR SPECIES:** Nelson's and Le Conte's sparrows. Juvenile Seaside Sparrow in late summer has streaked buffy breast but lacks the bold orange supercilium. Savannah Sparrow has yellow in lores only, has notched tail. **HABITAT:** Salt marshes.

NELSON'S SPARROW
Uncommon M451
Ammodramus nelsoni
5 in. (13 cm). A shy marshland skulker with three widely separated breeding populations. Note bright *orange on face,* completely surrounding gray ear patch. *Breast warm buff with faint blurry streaks,* stronger streaks on flanks. Gray central crown and *unmarked gray nape.* Back sharply striped with white. Breeders in New England and Maritimes grayer with less distinct stripes. **VOICE:** Song a buzzy, two-part *shleeee-tup.* **SIMILAR SPECIES:** Saltmarsh Sparrow has heavier breast streaking and any orange on breast is *paler* than orange on face (breast and face equally bright in Nelson's). Le Conte's Sparrow has white median crown stripe, purplish chestnut streaks on nape. **HABITAT:** In summer, prairie and coastal marshes, muskeg; in winter, coastal marshes.

LE CONTE'S SPARROW *Ammodramus leconteii* Uncommon M450
5 in. (13 cm). A skulking sparrow of prairie marshes, boggy fields. Note *bright orange eyebrow* and buffy breast (with streaks *confined to sides*). Other points are *purplish chestnut streaks on nape,* white median crown stripe, strong stripes on back. **VOICE:** Song two extremely thin, grasshopper-like hisses. **SIMILAR SPECIES:** Nelson's Sparrow. Grasshopper Sparrow has yellow in front of eye only and faint side streaks, if any. **HABITAT:** Grassy marshes, tallgrass fields, weedy hayfields.

SEASIDE SPARROW
Fairly common M453
Ammodramus maritimus
6 in. (15 cm). A dark, *gray* sparrow of salt marshes, with short *yellow area above lores. Whitish throat* and *white malar.* Shares marshes with Saltmarsh and Nelson's sparrows. "Cape Sable" Seaside Sparrow is an endangered subspecies confined to s. FL (the only Seaside that breeds there); more greenish than typical birds with *much heavier streaking.* Seasides of the Gulf Coast show buffy breast with blurry gray streaks but with face pattern similar to Atlantic Coast birds. **VOICE:** Song *cutcut ZHE-eeeeeeee;* much stronger than Saltmarsh Sparrow. Call *chack.* **HABITAT:** Salt marshes.

MARSH SPARROWS

SALTMARSH SPARROW

NELSON'S SPARROW

coastal

interior

LE CONTE'S SPARROW

juvenile

adult

SEASIDE SPARROW

"Cape Sable"

LARK SPARROW *Chondestes grammacus*　　Uncommon, local M444

6½ in. (17 cm). *Adult:* Note *black tail with much white at corners;* also single dark *central breast spot* on clean grayish white underparts, and *quail-like head pattern,* with *chestnut ear patch* and striped crown. *Immature:* Head pattern duller, but still clearly of this species; a few dusky streaks on breast sides. **VOICE:** A broken song; clear notes and trills with pauses between, characterized by buzzing and churring passages. Call a sharp *tsip.* **SIMILAR SPECIES:** Vesper Sparrow. **HABITAT:** Open country with bushes, trees; pastures, farms, roadsides.

VESPER SPARROW *Pooecetes gramineus*　　Uncommon M443

6¼ in. (16 cm). *White outer tail feathers* are conspicuous when bird flies. Otherwise suggests slightly largish Savannah Sparrow, but has *whitish eye-ring.* Bend of wing *chestnut (often difficult to see).* Note white malar stripe and lack of central crown stripe. **VOICE:** Song throatier than Song Sparrow's; usually begins with two clear minor notes, followed by two higher ones. **SIMILAR SPECIES:** Savannah Sparrow. Other sparrowlike field birds with white tail-sides or corners include pipits, longspurs, juncos, and Lark Sparrow. **HABITAT:** Meadows and prairies with scattered trees or bushes, roadsides, farm fields.

SONG SPARROW *Melospiza melodia*　　Common M455

5¾–6½ in. (15–17 cm). This common midsized sparrow has a *long rounded tail* and *heavy breast streaks* that merge into a *large central spot.* Broad grayish eyebrow. *Juvenile:* More finely streaked, often lacks central spot. Many different subspecies are recognized by taxonomists. **VOICE:** Song a variable series of notes, some musical, some buzzy; usually starts with three or four bright repetitious notes, *sweet sweet sweet,* etc. Call a low, nasal *tchep.* **SIMILAR SPECIES:** Savannah Sparrow more of a field bird; often shows yellowish over eye, has shorter notched tail, pinker legs. See Lincoln's and Swamp sparrows. **HABITAT:** Thickets, brush, marshes, roadsides, feeders.

LINCOLN'S SPARROW *Melospiza lincolnii*　　Uncommon M456

5¾ in. (15 cm). A skulking species, prefers to be near cover. Similar to Song Sparrow, but smaller and trimmer, breast streaks *much finer* and overlay band of *creamy buff* that contrasts with white belly and throat; also has narrow eye-ring and buffy mustache. **VOICE:** Song sweet and gurgling; suggests House Wren; starts with low passages, rises abruptly, drops. Calls a flat *tup* and buzzy *zzzeeet.* **SIMILAR SPECIES:** Immature Swamp Sparrow has duller breast, with blurry streaks and rustier wing. **HABITAT:** Willow and alder thickets, muskeg, brushy bogs; in winter, thickets, bushes.

FOX SPARROW *Passerella iliaca*　　Uncommon M454

7 in. (18 cm). A large, plump sparrow with a *rusty rump and tail.* Action towhee-like, kicking among dead leaves and other ground litter. *Breast heavily streaked* with triangular rusty spots; these often cluster in large blotch on upper breast. **VOICE:** Song brilliant and musical; a varied arrangement of short clear notes and sliding whistles. Call a strong, flat *chup.* **HABITAT:** Wooded undergrowth, brush, feeders; in summer, taiga scrub.

SPARROWS

adult

immature

LARK SPARROW

VESPER SPARROW

SONG SPARROW

FOX SPARROW

LINCOLN'S SPARROW

303

WHITE-THROATED SPARROW
Zonotrichia albicollis

Common M458

6¾ in. (17 cm). *Breeding:* A gray-breasted sparrow with white throat and yellow above the lores. Bill grayish. Polymorphic; some adults have black and white head stripes, others brown and tan. *Nonbreeding:* Somewhat duller; darker head stripes varying shades of black, brown, tan. *Immature:* May be somewhat streaked on breast; throat duller. **VOICE:** Song several clear pensive whistles, easily imitated; one or two clear notes, followed by three quavering notes on a different pitch. Call a thin, slurred *tseet;* also a hard *chink.* **SIMILAR SPECIES:** White-crowned Sparrow. **HABITAT:** Thickets, brush, undergrowth of coniferous and mixed woodlands. Visits feeders, preferring to stay on ground.

WHITE-CROWNED SPARROW
Zonotrichia leucophrys

Uncommon M460

7 in. (18 cm). This species comprises multiple subspecies, which exhibit variation in color of lores (whitish or black) and bill (orangey or pinkish). *Adult:* Clear grayish breast, puffy crown *striped with black and white. Immature:* Head stripes dark red-brown and light buff. **VOICE:** Song one or more clear, plaintive whistles (similar to White-throated Sparrow), followed by husky trilled whistles. Variable. Call a sharp *pink.* **SIMILAR SPECIES:** White-throated Sparrow browner, has well-defined white throat, yellow spot before eye, grayish bill. "Gambel's" subspecies nests on western tundra and is a scarce to rare migrant and winter visitor east of Great Plains. They have smaller orange bills and pale lores. **HABITAT:** Brush, forest edges, thickets, gardens, parks; in winter, also farms, feeders.

HARRIS'S SPARROW *Zonotrichia querula*

Uncommon M459

7½ in. (19 cm). Large; size of Fox Sparrow. *Breeding adult: Black crown, face, and bib encircling pink bill. Nonbreeding adult:* Black crown scaled with gray, cheeks mostly tan-brown. *Immature:* Has *white on throat,* less black on crown, buffy brown on rest of head; blotched and streaked on breast. **VOICE:** Song has quavering quality of White-throated Sparrow: clear whistles on same pitch, or one or two at one pitch, the rest slightly lower. Alarm call *wink.* **HABITAT:** Stunted boreal forests; in winter, brush, hedgerows, open woods. May mix with White-crowned Sparrows in nonbreeding season.

GOLDEN-CROWNED SPARROW
Zonotrichia atricapilla

Vagrant

7¼ in. (18 cm). Note *dull yellow crown* bordered broadly with black. Immature usually with dull yellow suffusion on forehead. **VOICE:** Song three to five high whistled notes, coming down scale, *oh-dear-me.* Call a sharp *tsew.* **SIMILAR SPECIES:** Immature Golden-crowned Sparrow (casual in East) slightly larger than White-crowned Sparrow, has *duskier bill and underparts,* more muted head pattern, *dull yellowish forehead.* **RANGE:** Casual visitor from West, mostly in fall and winter. **HABITAT:** Boreal and subalpine scrub, willow thickets, stunted spruces; in winter, similar to that of White-crowned, but Golden-crowned favors denser shrubs.

SPARROWS

tan-striped
morph

immature

white-striped
morph

**WHITE-THROATED
SPARROW**

adult

immature

"Gambel's"

**WHITE-
CROWNED
SPARROW**

immature

adult

breeding
adult

immature

**GOLDEN-
CROWNED
SPARROW**

**HARRIS'S
SPARROW**

DARK-EYED JUNCO *Junco hyemalis*   Common M461

6–6½ in. (15–16 cm). This hooded sparrow is characterized by *white outer tail feathers* that flash conspicuously as it flies away. Bill and belly usually whitish. Male may have dark hood; female and immature duller. Juvenile in summer finely streaked on breast. Two subspecies occur in East:

"Oregon" Junco is widespread subspecies in West, uncommon east to Great Plains, and a very rare winter visitor farther east. Male has *rusty brown back* with *blackish hood* and *buffy or rusty sides.* Female duller, but note contrast between paler gray hood and brown back, convex shape to lower border of hood. Intergrades with "Slate-colored" occur.

"Slate-colored" Junco is the common northern and eastern subspecies. A gray junco with *gray back,* white belly. Female and immature duller gray tinged brownish. The more uniform coloration, lacking rusty areas, is distinctive. Some particularly brownish young birds may be confused with "Oregon" Junco. **VOICE:** Song a loose trill, suggestive of Chipping Sparrow but more musical. Call a light *smack;* also clicking or twittering notes. **HABITAT:** Coniferous and mixed woods. In nonbreeding season, open woods, undergrowth, roadsides, brush, parks, gardens, feeders; usually in flocks.

LARK BUNTING   Uncommon, local M445
Calamospiza melanocorys

7 in. (18 cm). A plump, short-tailed prairie bird. Gregarious in nonbreeding season. Note rather *heavy, blue-gray bill. Breeding male:* Black, with *large white wing patches. Female, immature, and nonbreeding male:* Brown, streaked with *whitish* or *buffy white wing patches* and *tail corners.* Adult males retain some black on face, wings, and belly. **VOICE:** Song, given in display flight, composed of cardinal-like slurs, unmusical chatlike *chug*s, piping whistles, and trills; each note repeated 3 to 11 times. Call a flat, mellow *heew.* **SIMILAR SPECIES:** Male Bobolink has yellow nape patch and white rump. Leucistic blackbirds — those showing odd patches of white in plumage, including wings — may be confused with male Lark Bunting. **HABITAT:** Plains, prairies; in winter, also weedy arid lowlands and farm fields.

SNOW BUNTING *Plectrophenax nivalis*   Uncommon M466

6¾ in. (17 cm). Snow Buntings often swirl over snowy fields or dunes in flocks, sometimes mixed with Horned Larks or Lapland Longspurs. No other eastern songbird shows so much white. In winter some individuals, especially females and immatures, may look quite brown, but when they fly their flashing *white wing patches* identify them. Overhead, Snow Bunting looks almost entirely white, whereas American Pipit and Horned Lark are mostly black-tailed. Breeding male has black back, contrasting with white head and underparts. **VOICE:** Call a sharp, whistled *teer* or *tew;* also a rough, purring *brrt,* both similar to Lapland Longspur's calls. Song a musical *ti-ti-chu-ree,* repeated. **SIMILAR SPECIES:** Albino landbirds — such as juncos — are sometimes mistaken for Snow Buntings. **HABITAT:** Prairies, fields, dunes, shores. In summer, tundra.

JUNCO AND BUNTINGS

♀

♂

"Oregon"

juvenile

DARK-EYED JUNCO

♀

♂

"Slate-colored"

LARK BUNTING

breeding ♂

♀
(nonbreeding
♂ similar)

Snow
Bunting

♀

♂

nonbreeding
♂

nonbreeding
♀

Snow
Bunting

breeding ♂

SNOW BUNTING

LAPLAND LONGSPUR
Uncommon to fairly common M463

Calcarius lapponicus

6¼ in. (16 cm). Lapland Longspurs — like Horned Larks, pipits, and other longspurs — are birds of open country; in flight, they appear to have shorter tail. In nonbreeding season, longspurs are often found in flocks of larks. *Breeding male:* Black face outlined with white is distinctive. Rusty collar. *Female and nonbreeding male:* Sparse black streaks on sides, dull rusty nape, and smudge across breast. Note *dark frame to rear cheek, rufous brown wing coverts,* tail pattern. **VOICE:** In flight, a dry rattle, also a musical *teew;* when perched, a soft *pee-dle.* Song in display flight is vigorous, musical. **SIMILAR SPECIES:** Smith's Longspur buffier below; note face pattern. Other longspurs have more white in tail. American Pipit and Horned Lark have thin bill, different plumage. **HABITAT:** In summer, tundra; in winter, fields, prairies, shores.

CHESTNUT-COLLARED LONGSPUR
Uncommon M465

Calcarius ornatus

6 in. (15 cm). *Breeding male:* Solid *black* below, except on throat and lower belly; nape *chestnut. Female and nonbreeding:* Adult males show dull black belly, but otherwise all are sparrowlike; best field mark is tail pattern — dark triangle on white tail — and flight call. **VOICE:** Song short, feeble, but musical; suggests Western Meadowlark. Call a finchlike *ji-jiv* or *kittle-kittle,* unique among longspurs. **SIMILAR SPECIES:** McCown's Longspur. **HABITAT:** Plains, native-grass prairies; generally prefers some cover, and winter flocks may disappear in grass until flushed.

MCCOWN'S LONGSPUR
Uncommon, local M462

Calcarius mccownii

6 in. (15 cm). *Breeding male:* Crown and breast patch black, tail largely white. Hindneck *gray. Female and nonbreeding male:* Rather plain; note tail pattern and *swollen-looking, fleshy bill.* **VOICE:** Song in display flight is clear sweet warbles, suggestive of Lark Bunting. Call a dry rattle, softer than Lapland Longspur's. Also a soft *pink.* **SIMILAR SPECIES:** Nonbreeding Chestnut-collared Longspur darker, more heavily marked below, has slightly smaller, darker bill, different call. **HABITAT:** Plains, prairies, short-grass and dirt fields.

SMITH'S LONGSPUR *Calcarius pictus*
Scarce, local M464

6¼ in. (16 cm). This secretive longspur prefers enough grassy cover to disappear in. It is *warm buff on entire underparts.* Tail edged with white, as in Vesper Sparrow and Lapland Longspur. *Breeding male:* Deep buff; ear patch with *white spot,* strikingly outlined by *black triangle. Female and nonbreeding:* Buffy breast lightly streaked; some males may show white shoulder patch. **VOICE:** Rattling or clicking notes in flight (has been likened to winding of a cheap watch). Song sweet, warblerlike, terminating in *WEchew.* Does not sing in flight. **SIMILAR SPECIES:** Lapland and Chestnut-collared longspurs, Vesper Sparrow, Sprague's Pipit. **HABITAT:** Prairies, fields, airports; in summer, tundra with scattered bushes.

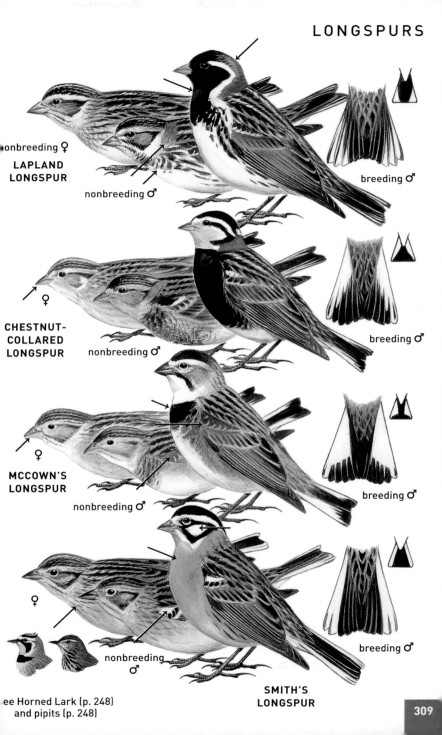

nonbreeding ♀
**LAPLAND
LONGSPUR**

nonbreeding ♂

breeding ♂

♀

**CHESTNUT-
COLLARED
LONGSPUR**

nonbreeding ♂

breeding ♂

♀

**MCCOWN'S
LONGSPUR**

nonbreeding ♂

breeding ♂

♀

nonbreeding
♂

breeding ♂

ee Horned Lark (p. 248)
and pipits (p. 248)

**SMITH'S
LONGSPUR**

CARDINALS, BUNTINGS, AND ALLIES
Family Cardinalidae

Medium-sized colorful songbirds with heavy bills. Songs loud and rich. **FOOD:** Seeds, fruit, insects. **RANGE:** New World.

BLACK-HEADED GROSBEAK
Uncommon, local M473

Pheucticus melanocephalus

8¼ in. (21 cm). *Male:* Breast, collar, and rump *dull orange-brown.* Otherwise similar to eastern counterpart, Rose-breasted Grosbeak. In nonbreeding plumage, head appears somewhat striped. *Female and immature:* Largely brown, with sparrowlike streaks above; head strongly patterned with light stripes and dark ear patch. Breast strongly *washed with butterscotch;* dark streaks on sides *fine,* nearly absent across middle of chest. Wing linings yellow. *Upper mandible dark.* **VOICE:** Song consists of rising and falling passages; resembles American Robin's song, but more fluent and mellow. Call a flat *ik* or *eek.* **SIMILAR SPECIES:** Rose-breasted Grosbeak. Rarely hybridizes with Rose-breasted where ranges come into contact. **HABITAT:** Deciduous and riparian woods; vagrant farther east, often at winter feeders.

ROSE-BREASTED GROSBEAK
Fairly common M472

Pheucticus ludovicianus

8 in. (20 cm). *Adult male:* Black and white, with large triangle of rose red on breast and thick pale bill. In flight, pattern of black and white flashes across upperparts. Wing linings rose pink. *Immature male:* In first-autumn plumage similar to female, but has touch of red on buffier breast. *Female:* Streaked, like a large sparrow or female Purple Finch; recognized by large grosbeak bill, broad white wing bars, striped crown, and broad white eyebrow stripe. Wing linings yellow. **VOICE:** Song consists of rising and falling passages; resembles American Robin's song, but given with more feeling (as if a robin had taken voice lessons). Call a squeaky, metallic *kick* or *eek.* **SIMILAR SPECIES:** Female told from female Purple Finch by larger size, boldly striped head, obvious wing bars, and pink bill. Differs from female and immature Black-headed Grosbeak in having *heavily streaked* breast, paler bill. **HABITAT:** Deciduous woods, orchards, groves, thickets, sometimes at feeders in spring.

CRIMSON-COLLARED GROSBEAK *Rhodothraupis celaeno* Vagrant

8½ in. (22 cm). *Male:* A blackish grosbeak with *dark red collar and underparts* encircling throat and chest. Red underparts often spotted or blotched with black. *Female and immature:* Similar to male, but *yellowish green* replaces red. **VOICE:** Song similar to Black-headed Grosbeak; a hoarse, bouncy warble, ending in up-slurred note: *zwee!* **SIMILAR SPECIES:** Female tanagers and orioles. **RANGE:** Mexican species, casual visitor (mostly in winter) to s. TX. **HABITAT:** Brushy woods, second growth.

GROSBEAKS

breeding ♂

♀

BLACK-HEADED GROSBEAK

breeding ♂

♀

ROSE-BREASTED GROSBEAK

♀

♂

CRIMSON-COLLARED GROSBEAK

NORTHERN CARDINAL *Cardinalis cardinalis* Common M470

8¾ in. (22 cm). *Male:* An *all-red* bird with pointed *crest* and black patch at base of heavy, *triangular reddish bill. Female:* Buff brown, with some red on wings and tail. *Crest, dark face,* and *heavy reddish orange bill* distinctive. *Juvenile:* Similar to female, but with blackish bill. **VOICE:** Song is clear, slurred whistles, repeated. Several variations: *what-cheer cheer cheer,* etc.; *whoit whoit whoit* or *birdy birdy birdy,* etc.; usually two-part. Call a short, sharp *tik.* **SIMILAR SPECIES:** Pyrrhuloxia. Male Summer Tanager also all red, lacks cardinal's crest. **HABITAT:** Woodland edges, thickets, towns, gardens, feeders.

PYRRHULOXIA *Cardinalis sinuatus* Uncommon, local M471

8¾ in. (22 cm). *Male:* A *slender, gray and red bird,* with *long, spiky crest* and *pale yellowish,* stubby, almost parrotlike bill (strongly curved upper mandible). *Female:* Has gray back, buff breast, and touch of red in wings. Always note spiky crest and *stubby yellow bill.* **VOICE:** Song a clear *quink quink quink quink quink,* on one pitch; also a slurred, whistled *what-cheer, what-cheer,* etc., usually not two-part like Northern Cardinal's song. **SIMILAR SPECIES:** Best told from female Northern Cardinal by bill color and shape, also by grayer color overall and spiky crest. **HABITAT:** Mesquite, thorn scrub, feeders.

BLUE GROSBEAK *Passerina caerulea* Uncommon M474

6¾ in. (17 cm). *Adult male:* Deep *dull blue,* with thick bill, *two broad rusty or chestnut wing bars.* Often *flips or twitches tail. Immature male:* A mixture of brown and blue. *Female:* About size of Brown-headed Cowbird; warm brown, slightly lighter below, with two *rusty buff wing bars;* rump or tail may be tinged with blue. **VOICE:** Warbling song, phrases rising and falling; suggests Purple or House finch, but slower, more guttural. Call a sharp *chink,* in flight a flat *bzzzt.* **SIMILAR SPECIES:** Female and immature Indigo Bunting also warm brown and have buffy, though weaker, wing bars, but they are smaller, and smaller billed. **HABITAT:** Thickets, hedgerows, riparian undergrowth, brushy hillsides, weedy ditches.

RED AND BLUE FINCHES

NORTHERN CARDINAL

♂

♀

juvenile

PYRRHULOXIA

♂

♀

BLUE GROSBEAK

breeding ♂

♀

BLUE BUNTING *Cyanocompsa parellina*   **Vagrant**
5½ in. (14 cm). *Male:* Blue-black; brighter blue on crown, shoulders, and rump. *Female:* Richer brown than female Indigo; no streaks; *bill blacker.* **VOICE:** Song a high, sweet jumble of warbled phrases. Call a metallic *chink!* **RANGE:** Mexican visitor, casual to s. TX, mostly in winter. **HABITAT:** Brushy woods with dense cover.

INDIGO BUNTING *Passerina cyanea*   **Common M476**
5½ in. (14 cm). *Male:* A small deep blue finch. In first spring, blue is blotchy. Nonbreeding male like female, but with some blue in wings and tail. *Female and immature:* A small, medium to warm brown finch; breast slightly paler with faint *blurry* streaks; wing bars weak or lacking. Like Blue Grosbeak, may flick or jerk tail sideways. **VOICE:** Song lively, high, and strident; measured phrases, usually paired: *sweet-sweet, chew-chew,* etc. Call a sharp *spit* and a dry buzz. **SIMILAR SPECIES:** Blue Grosbeak (larger) has rusty wing bars. See Lazuli Bunting. **HABITAT:** Overgrown brushy fields, riparian thickets, bushy wood edges.

LAZULI BUNTING *Passerina amoena*   **Rare M475**
5½ in. (14 cm). The western counterpart of Indigo Bunting. *Breeding male:* turquoise blue with burnt orangey breast and white belly, suggesting a bluebird, but with *two white wing bars. Nonbreeding male:* Brownish tips to feathers mute some of blue. *Female and immature:* Very similar to female Indigo but note *distinct buffy wing bars, unstreaked warm buffy breast, duller brown* upperparts. Juvenile may show fine breast streaks well into fall. Hybrids are regular where range overlaps that of Indigo. **VOICE:** Song similar to Indigo Bunting's, but faster. Calls similar. **HABITAT:** Like Indigo.

VARIED BUNTING *Passerina versicolor*   **Scarce, local M477**
5½ in. (14 cm). *Male:* A small dark finch with plum purple body (looks black at a distance). Crown, face, and rump blue, with *bright red patch on nape;* colored like an Easter egg. *Female:* Very similar to female Indigo but slightly duller brown with no breast streaks and slightly more curved upper edge to bill. **VOICE:** Song thin, bright, more distinctly phrased, less warbled than Painted Bunting's. **HABITAT:** Riparian thickets, mesquite and other scrub in washes and lower canyons.

PAINTED BUNTING *Passerina ciris*   **Uncommon M478**
5½ in. (14 cm). The most gaudily colored N. American songbird. *Male:* A patchwork of *blue-violet* on head, *green* on back, *red* on rump and underparts, red orbital ring. *Female and immature:* Electric green *above,* paling to lemon yellow below; *no other small finch is so green.* *Juvenile:* Grayer above with only tinge of green, duller below. **VOICE:** Song a wiry warble; suggests Warbling Vireo. Call a sharp *chip.* **HABITAT:** Riparian undergrowth, brushy hedgerows, woodland edges, stands of weedy grass.

BLUE FINCHES, ETC.

breeding ♂

molting ♂

♀

INDIGO BUNTING

♀

**BLUE
BUNTING**

LAZULI BUNTING

♀

breeding ♂

♀

♂

VARIED BUNTING

♀

♂

PAINTED BUNTING

DICKCISSEL *Spiza americana*   Fairly common M479
6¼ in. (16 cm). A grass- and farmland bird; migrants often travel in large flocks. *Male:* Suggests a miniature meadowlark (black bib, yellow chest). Has chestnut shoulder patch. In fall, bib obscure. *Female and immature:* Much like female House Sparrow, but with bolder stripe over eye (often tinged yellowish), touch of yellow on breast, and blue-gray bill. **VOICE:** Song a staccato *dick-ciss-ciss-ciss* or *chup-chup-klip-klip-klip.* Call a short, hard buzz, often given in flight. **HABITAT:** Fields, meadows, prairies.

OLD WORLD SPARROWS Family Passeridae

Old World sparrows differ from our native sparrows (which are in the Emberizidae family) in several subtle ways, including having a more curved culmen (ridge on bill). **FOOD:** Mainly insects, seeds. **RANGE:** Widespread in Old World, two species introduced in New World.

HOUSE SPARROW *Passer domesticus*   Common M511
6¼ in. (16 cm). Introduced from Europe in 1840. Familiar to many people. Sooty city birds often bear little resemblance to clean country males with *black throat, white cheeks, chestnut nape.* Much plainer female and young lack black throat, have dingy breast, and dull eye stripe *behind eye only;* note *single bold wing bar.* **VOICE:** Hoarse *chirp* and *shillip* notes, also a rising *sweep.* **SIMILAR SPECIES:** Female Dickcissel, buntings, sparrows, Eurasian Tree Sparrow. **HABITAT:** Cities, towns, farms, feeders.

EURASIAN TREE SPARROW   Uncommon, local M512
Passer montanus
6 in. (15 cm). Both sexes resemble male House Sparrow, but black throat patch smaller. Key mark is *black ear spot.* Crown brown. **VOICE:** Higher pitched than House Sparrow's. A metallic *chik* or *chup,* a repeated *chit-tchup.* In flight, a hard *tek, tek.* **HABITAT:** Farmland, weedy patches, locally in residential areas, feeders.

BLACKBIRDS AND ORIOLES Family Icteridae

Varied color patterns; sharp bills. Some black and iridescent; orioles are highly colored. Sexes unlike. **FOOD:** Insects, fruit, seeds, waste grain, small aquatic life. **RANGE:** New World; most in Tropics.

BOBOLINK *Dolichonyx oryzivorus*   Fairly common M480
7 in. (18 cm). *Breeding male:* Our only songbird that is *solid black below and largely white above.* Has buff-yellow nape. In spring, shows extensive brownish tips to dark feathering. *Female and nonbreeding male:* A bit larger than House Sparrow; rich buff-yellow, with dark striping on crown and back. Bill more like a sparrow's than a blackbird's. Note pointed tail feathers. **VOICE:** Song, in hovering flight and quivering descent, ecstatic and bubbling: starts with low, reedy notes and rollicks upward. Flight call a clear *ink,* often heard overhead in migration. **SIMILAR SPECIES:** Male Lark Bunting has white confined to wings. **HABITAT:** Hayfields, moist meadows, marsh edges.

OLD WORLD SPARROWS, DICKCISSEL, AND BOBOLINK

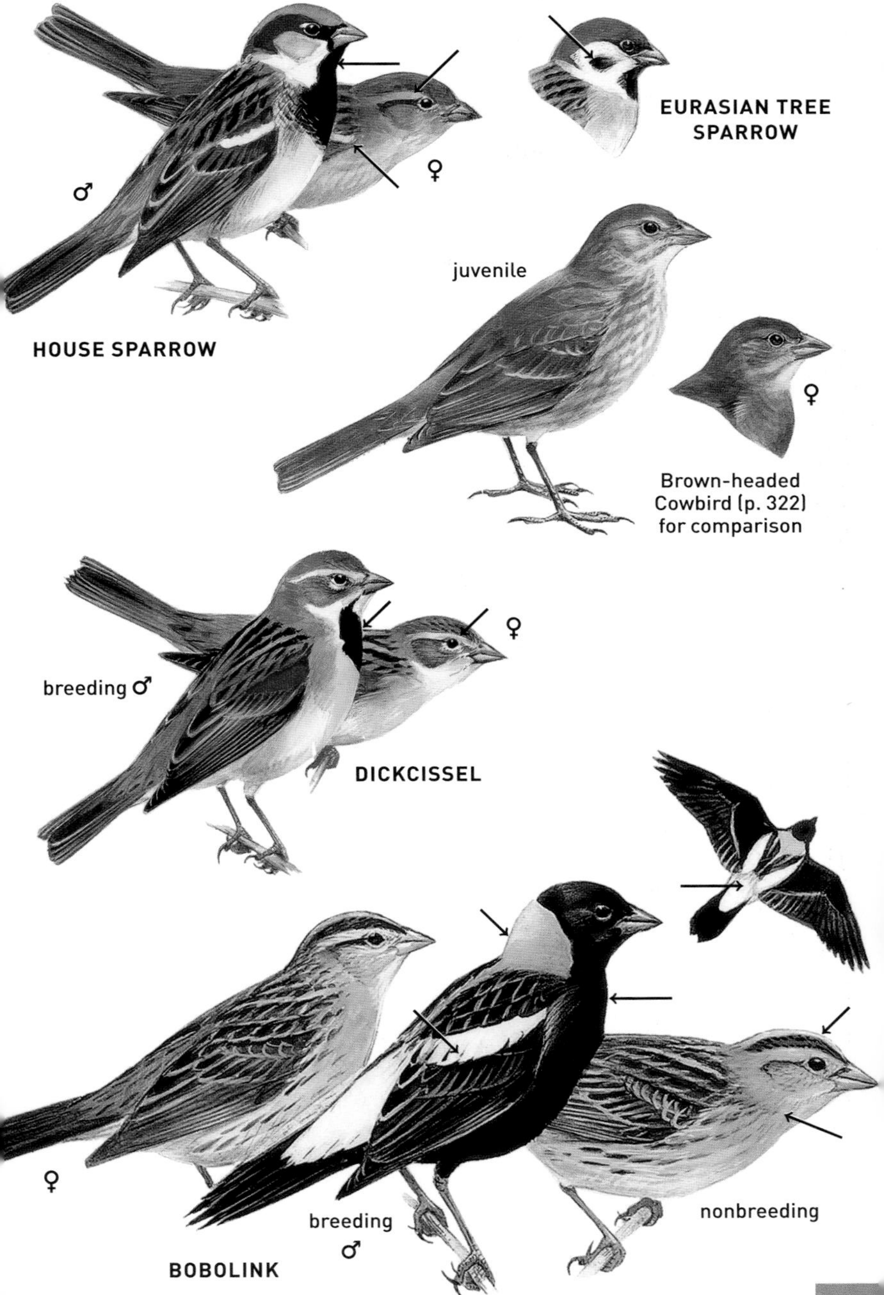
♂
♀
HOUSE SPARROW
EURASIAN TREE SPARROW
juvenile
♀
Brown-headed Cowbird (p. 322) for comparison
breeding ♂
♀
DICKCISSEL
♀
breeding ♂
nonbreeding
BOBOLINK

EASTERN MEADOWLARK   Uncommon to fairly common M482
Sturnella magna

9½ in. (24 cm). In grassy country, a chunky, brown, starling-shaped bird. When flushed, shows conspicuous white sides on short tail. Several shallow, snappy wingbeats alternate with short glides — like a Spotted Sandpiper. When bird perches on a post, chest shows bright yellow crossed by black V. Walking, it flicks tail open and shut. **VOICE:** Song composed of two clear, slurred whistles, musical and pulled out, *tee-yah, tee-yair* (last note slurred and descending). Call a rasping or buzzy *dzrrt;* also a guttural chatter. **SIMILAR SPECIES:** Western Meadowlark, Dickcissel. **HABITAT:** Open fields and pastures, meadows, prairies, marsh edges.

WESTERN MEADOWLARK   Uncommon to fairly common M483
Sturnella neglecta

9½ in. (24 cm). Very similar to Eastern Meadowlark, but paler above and whiter on flanks (Eastern's flanks washed with buff in fresh plumage); *yellow of throat invades malar area* behind bill. Crown stripes paler, more streaked with buff; wingbeats floppier, more starlinglike. Best identified by voice. **VOICE:** Song variable; 7 to 10 flutelike notes, gurgling and double-note, unlike clear whistles of Eastern Meadowlark. Calls *chupp* or *chuck* and a dry rattle. **SIMILAR SPECIES:** Eastern Meadowlark. **HABITAT:** Grasslands, cultivated fields and pastures, meadows, prairies, marsh edges.

RED-WINGED BLACKBIRD *Agelaius phoeniceus*   Common M481

8½–8¾ in. (22 cm). *Adult male:* Black, with *bright red or orange-red epaulets,* most conspicuous in breeding display. Much of the time red is concealed and only yellowish or off-whitish margin shows. *Immature male:* Sooty brown, mottled (like female), but with red shoulders. *Female:* Brownish, with sharply pointed bill, "blackbird" appearance, and *well-defined dark streaking* below; may have pinkish tinge to throat. Gregarious, traveling and roosting in flocks during nonbreeding season. **VOICE:** Calls a loud *check* and a high, slurred *tee-err.* Song a liquid, gurgling *konk-la-ree* or *o-ka-lay.* **SIMILAR SPECIES:** Other blackbird species. **HABITAT:** Breeds in marshes, brushy swamps, fields, pastures, roadsides; forages also in cultivated land, feedlots, towns, feeders, etc.

YELLOW-HEADED BLACKBIRD   Fairly common M484
Xanthocephalus xanthocephalus

9–9¾ in. (23–25 cm). Gregarious. *Adult male:* A robin-sized blackbird, with *yellow or orange-yellow head and breast;* in flight, shows *white wing patch. Female and immature male:* Smaller (female) and browner; most of yellow confined to throat and chest; lower breast streaked with white; white wing patch restricted or lacking. **VOICE:** Song consists of low, hoarse rasping notes produced with much effort; suggests rusty hinges. Call a low *kruck* or *kack.* **HABITAT:** Nests in freshwater marshes. Forages in farm fields, open country, feedlots. Often associates with other blackbirds in mixed flocks in fall and winter.

MEADOWLARKS AND BLACKBIRDS

EASTERN
MEADOWLARK

WESTERN
MEADOWLARK

red epaulets
hidden

♂

♀

RED-WINGED
BLACKBIRD

immature ♂

♂

♀

YELLOW-HEADED
BLACKBIRD

COMMON GRACKLE *Quiscalus quiscula*   Common M487
12½ in. (32 cm). *Male:* A large, *iridescent,* yellow-eyed blackbird, larger than a robin, with long, wedge-shaped or *keel-shaped (when breeding) tail.* In good light, iridescent purple-blue on head. *Female:* Somewhat smaller and duller, with less wedge-shaped tail. *Juvenile:* Sooty, with dark eyes. "Bronzed" Grackle (New England and west of Appalachians; deep bronze on back and belly) and "Purple" Grackle (seaboard south of New England; greener tinge to back) are separate, identifiable subspecies. **VOICE:** Call *chuck* or *chack.* "Song" a split rasping note. **SIMILAR SPECIES:** Boat-tailed and Great-tailed grackles, Brewer's Blackbird. **HABITAT:** Cropland, towns, parks, feeders, groves; swampy woods; often nests in conifers.

BOAT-TAILED GRACKLE   Fairly common, local M488
Quiscalus major
Male 16½ in. (42 cm); female 14½ in. (37 cm). *Male:* A very large blackbird of the coast; larger than Common Grackle, with longer, more ample tail. More rounded head than other grackles. Males of Atlantic Coast (except in FL) have yellow eyes; those of Gulf region and FL have brown eyes, but some may have dull yellowish eyes. *Female:* Smaller than male; much browner than female Common Grackle and with pale brownish breast. **VOICE:** Harsh *check check check;* harsh whistles and clucks. **SIMILAR SPECIES:** LA westward, see Great-tailed Grackle. **HABITAT:** Largely resident near salt water along coasts, marshes; more widespread habitats in FL.

GREAT-TAILED GRACKLE *Quiscalus mexicanus*   Common M489
Male 18 in. (46 cm); female 15 in. (38 cm). Like several other blackbirds, often found in large flocks. *Male:* A very large, purple-glossed blackbird, distinctly larger than Common Grackle and with longer, more ample tail. *Female:* Smaller than male; dark gray-brown above, warm brown below. Adults of both sexes have yellow eyes. **VOICE:** Harsh *check check check;* also a high *kee-kee-kee-kee.* Shrill, discordant notes, whistles, and clucks. A rapid, upward-slurring *ma-ree.* **SIMILAR SPECIES:** Common Grackle (smaller). Boat-tailed Grackle slightly smaller, with dark eyes (where ranges overlap), rounder crown (male), and slightly shorter, more rounded tail. **HABITAT:** Groves, farms, feedlots, towns, city parks, parking lots.

GRACKLES

"Purple" ♂

"Bronzed" ♂

COMMON GRACKLE

♀

♂ Atlantic Coast

♀

FL and Gulf Coast

♂

BOAT-TAILED GRACKLE

♂

♀

GREAT-TAILED GRACKLE

RUSTY BLACKBIRD *Euphagus carolinus*   Uncommon M485

9 in. (23 cm). Rusty only in fall and winter. *Breeding male:* A medium-sized blackbird with pale eye. Black head may show faint *greenish* gloss. *Breeding female:* Slate colored, with *light eye. Nonbreeding:* Variably washed with rusty, buffy eyebrow, narrow dark patch through eye. **VOICE:** Call *chack.* "Song" a split creak, like a rusty hinge: *kush-a-lee,* alternating with *ksh-lay.* **SIMILAR SPECIES:** Brewer's Blackbird, Common Grackle. **HABITAT:** Wooded swamps, muskeg, pond edges.

BREWER'S BLACKBIRD   Uncommon M486
Euphagus cyanocephalus

9 in. (23 cm). *Male:* All black, with whitish eye; in good light, *purplish* reflections on head, greenish reflections on body. *Female:* Brownish gray, with *dark* eye. **VOICE:** Song a harsh, wheezy, creaking *ksh-eee.* Call *chack.* **SIMILAR SPECIES:** Breeding male Rusty Blackbird flatter black with dull *greenish* head reflections (hard to see); bill slightly longer. Female Rusty has *light* eye. Brewer's do not acquire a rusty look in fall. See also Brown-headed Cowbird. **HABITAT:** Fields, prairies, farms, feedlots, lawns, parking lots.

BROWN-HEADED COWBIRD *Molothrus ater*   Common M492

7½ in. (19 cm). A rather small blackbird with short, sparrowlike bill. *Male:* Black with *brown head (may appear all black in poor light). Female:* Gray-brown with lighter throat; note short *finchlike bill. Juvenile:* Paler than female. Buffy gray, with soft breast streaking and pale scaling (edges) above; this plumage held into early fall. Often seen being fed by smaller birds whose nests have been parasitized. When flocking with other blackbirds, cowbirds look smaller and feed on ground with tails lifted high. **VOICE:** Flight call *weee-titi* (high whistle, two lower notes). Song a bubbly and creaky *glug-glug-gleeee.* **SIMILAR SPECIES:** Female told from female Brewer's Blackbird by its *stubby bill* and smaller size. Juvenile European Starling has longer bill, shorter tail. **HABITAT:** In nesting season, where passerine nest-hosts are numerous, a variety of forests and woodlands; also farms, fields, feedlots, lawns, feeders. Parasitizes a wide variety of smaller bird nests. Never builds its own nest.

BRONZED COWBIRD *Molothrus aeneus*   Uncommon M491

8½–8¾ in. (21–22 cm). *Male:* Slightly larger and more *bull-headed* than Brown-headed Cowbird. Does *not* have brown head. Bill longer. *Red eye.* Ruff on nape often conspicuous. *Female:* Smaller nape ruff; darker than female Brown-headed. **VOICE:** High-pitched mechanical creakings. Male's display very animated. **HABITAT:** Cropland, brush, semiopen country, towns, feedlots.

SHINY COWBIRD *Molothrus bonariensis*   Scarce, local M490

7½ in. (19 cm). *Male:* Black with violet gloss, thin pointed bill. *Female:* Warm brown, slightly thinner, blacker bill than Brown-headed. **VOICE:** Series of liquid burbles, ending in thin whistled note. **RANGE:** An invader to s. FL since 1985. Scattered records from as far north as NB and west to OK. **HABITAT:** Agricultural areas, disturbed habitats, suburban lawns, feeders.

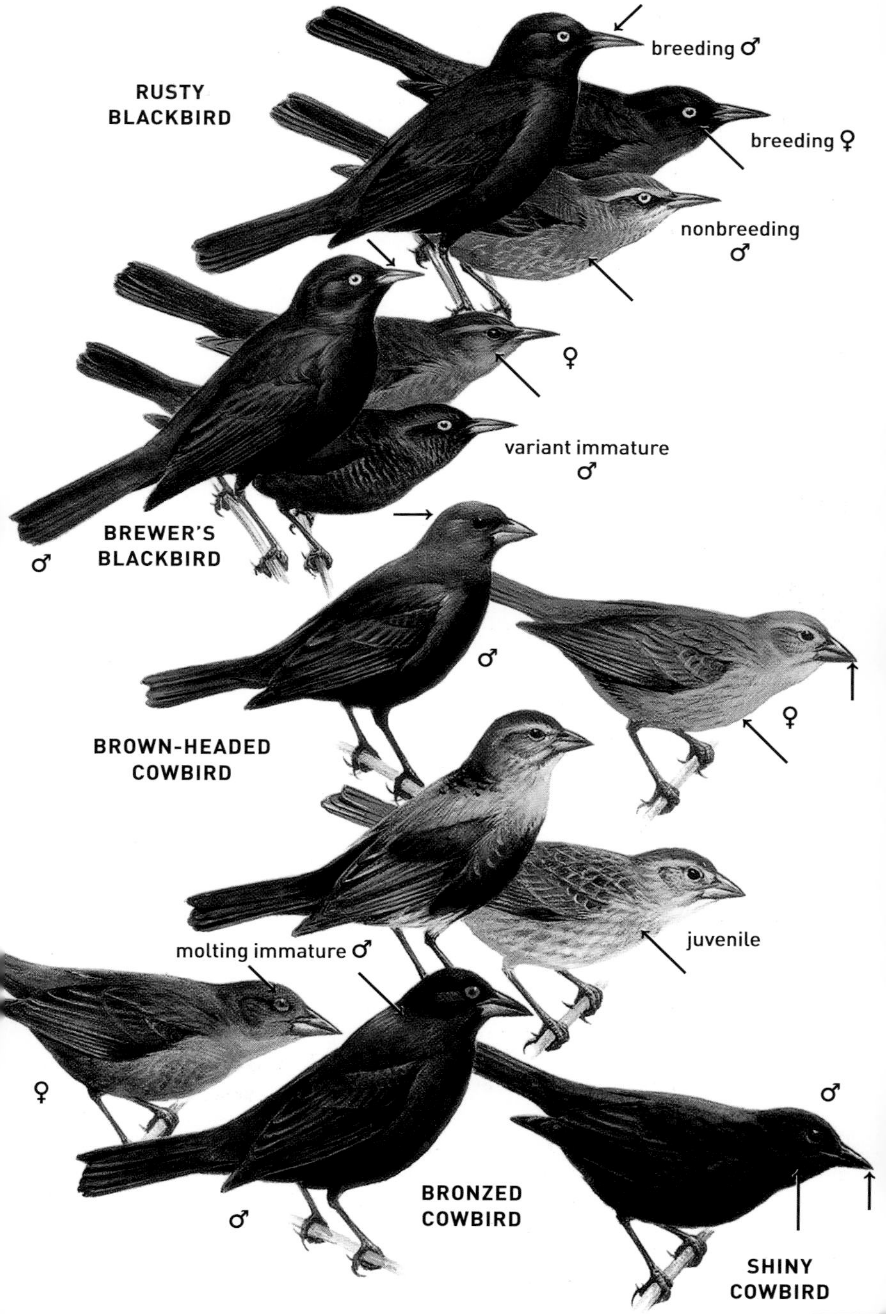

ICTERIDS (BLACKBIRDS, ETC.)

RUSTY BLACKBIRD

breeding ♂

breeding ♀

nonbreeding ♂

♀

variant immature ♂

BREWER'S BLACKBIRD

♂

BROWN-HEADED COWBIRD

♂

♀

molting immature ♂

juvenile

♀

♂

BRONZED COWBIRD

♂

SHINY COWBIRD

ORCHARD ORIOLE *Icterus spurius* Fairly common M493

7–7¼ in. (18 cm). A small, short- and straight-billed oriole. Often flicks tail sideways. *Male:* All dark; rump and underparts *deep chestnut. Female and immature:* Olive or greenish gray above, yellowish below; two white wing bars. First-spring male has black bib down to chest. **VOICE:** Song a fast-moving outburst interspersed with piping whistles and guttural notes. Suggests Purple or House finch. A strident slurred *wheeer!* at or near end is distinctive. Call a soft *chuck.* **SIMILAR SPECIES:** Some female and immature Baltimore Orioles have black throat (as do immature male Orchards), but are slightly larger and more orange. Female Scarlet and Summer tanagers lack wing bars, have different bill shape. Females and immatures difficult to tell from young Hooded Orioles but note Hooded's more curved bill, longer tail, and weaker wing bars. See voice. **HABITAT:** Wood edges, orchards, shade trees; more likely than other orioles to be seen in brushy areas.

BALTIMORE ORIOLE *Icterus galbula* Fairly common M499

8¼–8½ in. (21–22 cm). *Adult male:* Flame orange and black, with solid black head, orange sides to tail. *Female and immature:* Olive-brown above, burnt orange-yellow below; two white wing bars. Many adult females have traces of black on head, suggesting hood of male. Some immature females very dull, with grayer back, limited orange (mostly on breast), and whitish vent; much like female Bullock's Oriole. **VOICE:** Song rich, piping whistles. Call a low, whistled *hewli.* Chatter call not as rough as Bullock's. **SIMILAR SPECIES:** Female Orchard Oriole yellower than female Baltimore. Dull female Baltimore much like female Bullock's, but latter has more distinct dark eye line and yellowish supercilium, plain gray back lacking dark scalloping, and yellowish rather than orange undertail coverts. **HABITAT:** Open deciduous woods, shade trees; in winter, also at feeders.

BULLOCK'S ORIOLE *Icterus bullockii* Uncommon, local M495

8¼–8½ in. (21–22 cm). *Adult male:* Note *orange cheeks* and *dark eye line, large white wing patches,* and *black-tipped tail. Female:* Dark eye line, yellowish supercilium, plain gray back, *whitish belly. Immature male:* Similar to female, but slightly more orange and has black goatee. May hybridize with Baltimore Oriole. **VOICE:** Accented double notes and one or two piping notes. Calls include a rough chatter and low *churp.* **SIMILAR SPECIES:** Baltimore Oriole; also Hooded and Orchard orioles. **HABITAT:** Deciduous and riparian woods, shade trees, ranch yards; vagrant at eastern feeders in winter.

SPOT-BREASTED ORIOLE Uncommon, local M496
Icterus pectoralis

9¼–9½ in. (24 cm). Introduced from Central America in the 1940s. Note *orange crown,* black bib, and black spots on sides of breast. Much white in wing. **VOICE:** Song a long, melodic series of whistles, slower than other orioles. **SIMILAR SPECIES:** Baltimore Oriole. **HABITAT:** Flowering trees, residential areas.

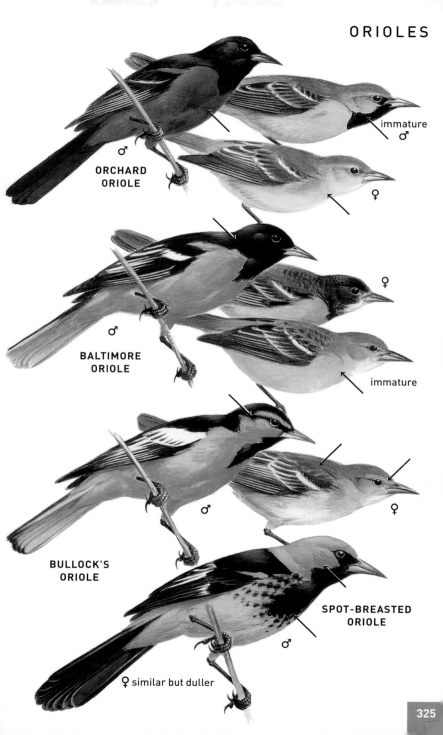

ORIOLES

ORCHARD ORIOLE
♂
immature ♂
♀

BALTIMORE ORIOLE
♂
♀
immature

BULLOCK'S ORIOLE
♂
♀

SPOT-BREASTED ORIOLE
♂
♀ similar but duller

325

HOODED ORIOLE *Icterus cucullatus*　　　Uncommon, local　M494
7½–8 in. (19–20 cm). *Male:* Orange and black, with black throat and *orange crown.* In winter, back obscurely scaled. *Female:* Similar to female Bullock's Oriole, but bill longer, slightly curved; more extensively yellow below; back olive-gray; head and tail more yellowish. Call different. *Immature:* Like female, with slightly shorter bill; much like female Orchard Oriole. **VOICE:** Song consists of rambling, grating notes and piping whistles: *chut chut chut whew whew;* opening notes throaty. Call an up-slurred, whistled *eek* or *wheenk.* **SIMILAR SPECIES:** Orchard, Bullock's, Baltimore, and Scott's orioles. **HABITAT:** Open woods, shade trees, towns, gardens.

ALTAMIRA ORIOLE *Icterus gularis*　　　Uncommon, local　M497
10 in. (25 cm). Similar to male Hooded Oriole, but larger, with thicker bill. Upper wing bar yellow or orange, not white. Sexes similar. **VOICE:** Song disjointed whistled notes. A harsh "fuss" note. **SIMILAR SPECIES:** Other orange orioles. **HABITAT:** Scrubby woodlands, often near water. Its name, in Spanish, means "look high." And this is often where this species is found — in treetops.

AUDUBON'S ORIOLE *Icterus graduacauda*　　Uncommon, local　M498
9½ in. (24 cm). A yellow oriole with black wings, head, and tail. Yellowish back distinctive. Other male orioles have black back. Sexes similar, but female duller. **VOICE:** Disjointed notes suggesting a child learning to whistle. **SIMILAR SPECIES:** Scott's Oriole. Green Jay at a distance looks yellow with a black head but has yellow outer tail feathers. **HABITAT:** Riparian woods.

SCOTT'S ORIOLE *Icterus parisorum*　　　　　Uncommon, local
8¾–9 in. (22–23 cm). *Adult male:* Solid black head and back and *lemon yellow* pattern distinguish it. *Female:* More greenish yellow below and more olivey gray and streaked above than other female orioles. Many have black on throat and face. **VOICE:** Song composed of rich fluty whistles; suggests Western Meadowlark. Call a harsh *chuck.* **SIMILAR SPECIES:** Female Hooded and Bullock's orioles. **HABITAT:** Dry woods and arid scrub.

ORIOLES

immature ♂

♂

♀

HOODED ORIOLE

ALTAMIRA ORIOLE

AUDUBON'S ORIOLE

♀

♂

immature

SCOTT'S ORIOLE

327

FRINGILLINE AND CARDUELINE FINCHES AND ALLIES Family Fringillidae

These birds have a seed-cracking bill, relatively short, notched tail, and somewhat undulating flight. Sexes usually unlike. Tend to be more arboreal than sparrows. **FOOD:** Seeds, insects, small fruit. **RANGE:** Worldwide.

BRAMBLING *Fringilla montifringilla*   Vagrant
6¼ in. (16 cm). *Breeding male:* Black head and back. *Female and nonbreeding:* Gray cheek bordered by dark. **VOICE:** Call a rising, whiny *zweee;* in flight, a distinctive nasal, hollow *eck.* **SIMILAR SPECIES:** Might be confused with Black-headed Grosbeak or Eastern Towhee. **RANGE:** Eurasian species; recorded casually in eastern N. America, mostly in winter, including at feeders.

RED CROSSBILL *Loxia curvirostra*   Uncommon, irregular M503
5¾–7 in. (14–17 cm). This erratic wanderer has a heavy head and short tail. Note *crossed mandibles* and *plain wings.* The sound when it cracks cones of evergreens often betrays its presence. Usually found in *flocks. Male:* Dull red, brighter on rump. Subadult males are more orange. *Female and immature:* Dull olive-gray to mustard yellow; yellowish on rump. *Juvenile:* Streaked above and below, suggesting a large Pine Siskin; note bill. Many subspecies vary slightly in bill size, body size, and color; most readily distinguished by flight call. **VOICE:** Call a hard *jip-jip* or *kip-kip-kip* (in some populations, *kwit-kwit* or *kewp-kewp*). Song consists of finchlike warbled passages, *jip-jip-jip-jeeaa-jeeaa;* trills, *chip*s. **SIMILAR SPECIES:** White-winged Crossbill. **HABITAT:** Variety of conifers; rarely at feeders. Erratic and irruptive wanderings, especially in fall and winter.

WHITE-WINGED CROSSBILL   Uncommon, irregular M504
Loxia leucoptera
6½ in. (17 cm). All plumages show *crossed mandibles, bold white wing bars,* and white tertial tips. *Male:* Dull rose pink. *Female and immature:* Olive-gray, with yellowish rump. *Juvenile:* Heavily streaked. **VOICE:** Calls a liquid *peet* and a dry *chif-chif.* Song a succession of loud trills on different pitches. **SIMILAR SPECIES:** Red Crossbill may show a single weak wing bar, but not two broad ones, and it lacks white tips to tertials. **HABITAT:** Spruce and fir forests, hemlocks; very rarely at feeders. Erratic and irruptive wanderings.

PINE GROSBEAK *Pinicola enucleator*   Scarce, irregular M500
8¾–9 in. (23 cm). Near size of a robin; a large, tame finch with dark, stubby bill, longish tail. Flight undulating. May be seen on dirt roads eating grit. *Adult male:* Dull rose red, wings dark with *two white wing bars. Female:* Gray, with two white wing bars; head and rump tinged with dull mustard yellow. *Immature male:* Similar to gray female, but with touch of russet on head and rump. **VOICE:** Song a rich, rapid warbling. Call a musical *pe-pew-pew.* **SIMILAR SPECIES:** Crossbills, Purple Finch. **HABITAT:** Conifers, larches; in winter, also mixed woods, crabapples and other fruiting trees, ashes. Erratic and irruptive wanderings, especially in winter.

FINCHES

♀

breeding ♂

nonbreeding
♂

BRAMBLING

♀

♂

**RED
CROSSBILL**

♂

♀

**WHITE-WINGED
CROSSBILL**

♀

♂

PINE GROSBEAK

PURPLE FINCH *Carpodacus purpureus* Uncommon M501

6 in. (15 cm). Like a sparrow dipped in raspberry juice. *Adult male:* Dull rose red, brightest on head, chest, and rump. Flanks unstreaked. *Female and immature:* Heavily streaked, brown; similar to female House Finch, but note *broad dark jaw stripe,* dark *ear patch,* broad light stripe behind eye, more deeply notched tail, undertail coverts with few or no streaks. **VOICE:** Song a fast lively warble; call a dull, flat, metallic *pik.* **SIMILAR SPECIES:** House Finch, Rose-breasted Grosbeak. **HABITAT:** Woods, groves, suburbs, feeders.

HOUSE FINCH *Carpodacus mexicanus* Common M502

5¾–6 in. (14–15 cm). Slimmer than Purple Finch with longer, more square-tipped tail. *Male:* Breast, forehead, stripe over eye, and rump vary from *red to orange to almost deep yellow* (diet related). Note *dark streaks* on sides and belly. *Female:* Streaked brown; separated from slightly larger female Purple Finch by its smaller head, bill, and *bland face.* **VOICE:** Song bright, loose, and disjointed; often ends in nasal *wheer.* Call suggests a House Sparrow's *chirp,* but more musical. **SIMILAR SPECIES:** Purple Finch. **HABITAT:** Cities, suburbs, farms, feeders. Bacterial infection of eyes has reduced numbers in some areas.

COMMON REDPOLL Uncommon, irregular M505
Acanthis flammea

5¼ in. (13 cm). Note *bright red forehead* and *black chin* of this little winter finch. Male has *pink breast;* female lacks this; juvenile heavily streaked and lacks red forehead. Usually found in flocks. **VOICE:** In flight, a rattling *chet-chet-chet.* Song a trill, followed by the rattling *chet-chet-chet.* **SIMILAR SPECIES:** Hoary Redpoll, Pine Siskin. Male House and Purple finches larger, redder, have red rump; lack black chin. **HABITAT:** Birches, tundra scrub. In winter, weeds, brush, thistle feeders.

HOARY REDPOLL *Acanthis hornemanni* Rare, irregular M506

5¼–5½ in. (13–14 cm). In nonbreeding season, often found in flocks of Common Redpolls. *Very similar.* Look for a "frostier" bird, with whiter rump containing *little or no streaking.* Also note *stubbier bill* and lighter streaking on flanks and undertail coverts. Some individuals *very difficult to identify.* **VOICE:** Much like Common Redpoll's. **SIMILAR SPECIES:** Common Redpoll, Pine Siskin. **HABITAT:** Birches, tundra scrub. In winter, weeds, brush, feeders.

RED FINCHES, ETC.

♂

♀

PURPLE FINCH

♂

orange variant

♂

♀

HOUSE FINCH

♀

COMMON REDPOLL

♂

HOARY REDPOLL

331

AMERICAN GOLDFINCH *Spinus tristis*   Common M509
5 in. (13 cm). Goldfinches are distinguished from other small, olive-yellow birds (warblers, etc.) by their short, conical bill and behavior. *Breeding male: A small yellow bird with black forehead and wings. Breeding female:* Dull yellow-olive; darker above, with blackish wings and conspicuous wing bars. *Nonbreeding:* Both sexes much like breeding female, but brownish; yellow on throat, bill dark. **VOICE:** Song clear, light, canary-like. In undulating flight, each dip is punctuated by *ti-DEE-di-di* or *per-chik-o-ree* or *po-ta-to-chip.* **SIMILAR SPECIES:** Lesser Goldfinch, Pine Siskin, Yellow Warbler. **HABITAT:** Patches of thistles and weeds, dandelions on lawns, sweet-gum balls, roadsides, open woods, edges; in winter, also feeders, often in flocks.

LESSER GOLDFINCH *Spinus psaltria*   Uncommon, local M508
4½ in. (11 cm). *Male:* A very small finch with *black cap,* black or greenish back, and yellow underparts; white on wings. Black cap retained in winter. Males may have *black* or *greenish* back. *Female:* Similar to nonbreeding American Goldfinch, but usually yellower below, has *less contrasting wing bars, yellowish* (not white) *undertail coverts,* and *dark rump.* Calls differ. **VOICE:** Sweet, plaintive, whiny notes, *tee-yee* (rising) and *tee-yer* (dropping). Song more phrased than American Goldfinch's; will imitate other bird calls. **SIMILAR SPECIES:** American Goldfinch. **HABITAT:** Open brushy and weedy country, open woods, wooded streams, towns, gardens, feeders.

PINE SISKIN *Spinus pinus*   Fairly common, irregular M507
5 in. (13 cm). Size of a goldfinch. A small, *heavily streaked* finch with deeply notched tail, sharply pointed bill. *A touch of yellow in wings* and *base of tail* (not always evident). Often first detected by voice, flying over. **VOICE:** Call a loud *chlee-ip;* also a light *tit-i-tit;* a buzzy *shreeeee.* Song suggests goldfinch, but coarser, wheezy. **SIMILAR SPECIES:** Nonbreeding American Goldfinch lacks streaks. Female House Finch has stubbier bill, longer tail. Common Redpoll has red forehead. All lack yellow in wings and tail. **HABITAT:** Conifers, mixed woods, alders, sweet-gum balls, weedy areas, feeders.

EUROPEAN GOLDFINCH *Carduelis carduelis*   Escapee
5½ in. (14 cm). Occasional reports, mostly at feeders. Assumed to be all or almost all escaped captive birds. Note red face, yellow wing patches.

EVENING GROSBEAK   Uncommon, irregular M510
Coccothraustes vespertinus
8 in. (20 cm). Size of a European Starling. A *chunky, short-tailed* finch with *very large, pale, conical bill* (tinged greenish). *Male:* Dull yellow, with darker head, *yellow eyebrow,* and black-and-white wings; suggests an overgrown goldfinch. *Female:* Silver gray, with white wing patches. Gregarious. In flight, overall shape and *large white wing patches* distinctive. **VOICE:** Song a short, uneven warble. Also a ringing, finchlike *clee-ip;* a high, burry *thew.* **SIMILAR SPECIES:** American Goldfinch (much smaller), female crossbills. **HABITAT:** Coniferous and mixed forests; in winter, box elders, fruiting shrubs, feeders.

YELLOW FINCHES, ETC.

nonbreeding ♂

breeding ♂

♀

AMERICAN GOLDFINCH

♂

♀

black-backed

LESSER GOLDFINCH

♂

green-backed

♂

♀

PINE SISKIN

EUROPEAN GOLDFINCH

♂

♀

EVENING GROSBEAK

MAPS

LIFE LIST

INDEX

RANGE MAPS

The maps on the following pages are approximate, giving the general outlines of the range of each species. Within these broad outlines may be many gaps—areas ecologically unsuitable for the species. A Marsh Wren must have a marsh, a Ruffed Grouse a woodland or a forest. Certain species may be extremely local or sporadic for reasons that may or may not be clear. Some birds are extending their ranges, a few explosively. Others are declining or even disappearing from large areas where they were formerly found. Winter ranges are often not as definite as breeding ranges. A species may exist at a very low density near the northern limits of its winter range, surviving through December in mild seasons but often succumbing to the bitter conditions of January and February. Varying weather conditions and food supplies from year to year may result in substantial variations in winter bird populations.

The maps are specific only for the area covered by this field guide. The Mallard, for example, is found over a large part of the globe. The map shows only its range in eastern North America.

The maps are based on data culled from many publications (particularly from monographs detailing the status and distribution of a state or province's avifauna, as well as from breeding bird atlases), from such journals as *North American Birds* (formerly *American Birds* and *Audubon Field Notes*), and from communication with many state and provincial experts from throughout North America.

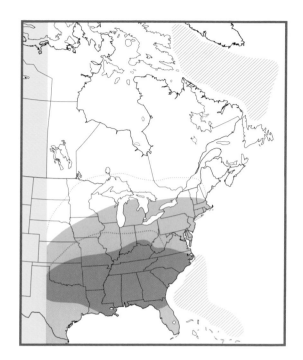

Many maps include comments on population increases and declines, extralimital occurrences, and regular winter or summer ranges outside North America. Migration routes are not depicted in these maps, but side notes sometimes include information on migration. Maps are likewise not filled in with solid color if the species is considered rare, very rare, casual, accidental, and/or a vagrant. Migrants can often be found in suitable habitat in those areas that lie between summering/breeding areas and wintering/nonbreeding areas.

Key to Range Maps

- Red: summer range
- Blue: winter range
- Purple: year-round range
  ⋯⋯ Red dash line: approximate limits of irregular summer range and/or post-breeding dispersal
  ⋯⋯ Blue dash line: approximate limits of irregular winter range
  ⋯⋯ Purple dash line: approximate limits of irregular year-round range
- Striped area: pelagic range

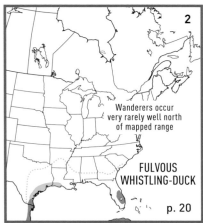

1

Wanderers occur
very rarely, well north
of mapped range, as
far as s. Canada

Recent population
increases and
expansion

**BLACK-BELLIED
WHISTLING-DUCK**

p. 20

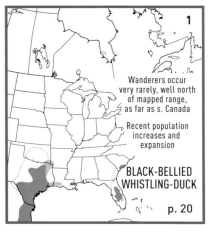

2

Wanderers occur
very rarely well north
of mapped range

**FULVOUS
WHISTLING-DUCK**

p. 20

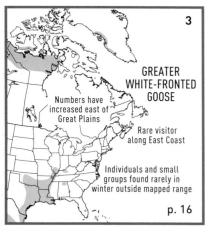

3

**GREATER
WHITE-FRONTED
GOOSE**

Numbers have
increased east of
Great Plains

Rare visitor
along East Coast

Individuals and small
groups found rarely in
winter outside mapped range

p. 16

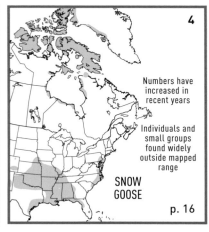

4

Numbers have
increased in
recent years

Individuals and
small groups
found widely
outside mapped
range

**SNOW
GOOSE**

p. 16

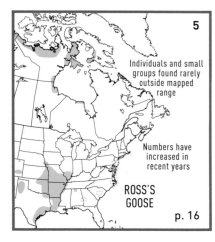

5

Individuals and small
groups found rarely
outside mapped
range

Numbers have
increased in
recent years

**ROSS'S
GOOSE**

p. 16

6

"Black" Brant
rare visitor
in East

Regular migrant on
e. Great Lakes

BRANT

Rare inland and
south to FL

p. 18

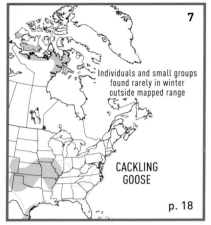

7

Individuals and small groups found rarely in winter outside mapped range

CACKLING GOOSE

p. 18

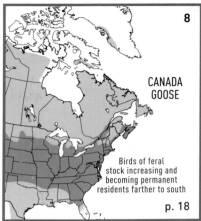

8

CANADA GOOSE

Birds of feral stock increasing and becoming permanent residents farther to south

p. 18

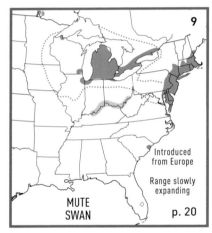

9

Introduced from Europe

Range slowly expanding

MUTE SWAN

p. 20

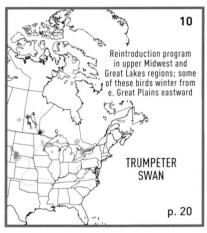

10

Reintroduction program in upper Midwest and Great Lakes regions; some of these birds winter from e. Great Plains eastward

TRUMPETER SWAN

p. 20

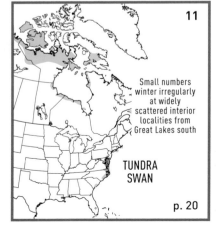

11

Small numbers winter irregularly at widely scattered interior localities from Great Lakes south

TUNDRA SWAN

p. 20

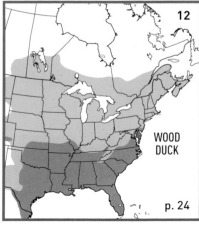

12

WOOD DUCK

p. 24

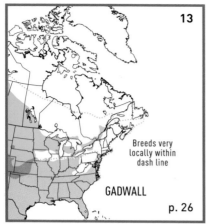

13

Breeds very locally within dash line

GADWALL

p. 26

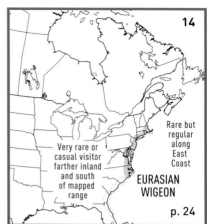

14

Very rare or casual visitor farther inland and south of mapped range

Rare but regular along East Coast

EURASIAN WIGEON

p. 24

15

AMERICAN WIGEON

p. 24

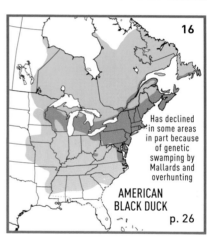

16

Has declined in some areas in part because of genetic swamping by Mallards and overhunting

AMERICAN BLACK DUCK

p. 26

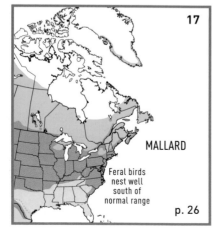

17

MALLARD

Feral birds nest well south of normal range

p. 26

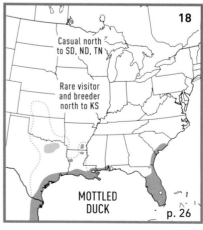

18

Casual north to SD, ND, TN

Rare visitor and breeder north to KS

MOTTLED DUCK

p. 26

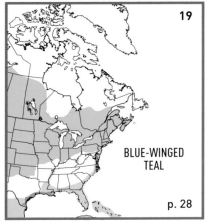

19

BLUE-WINGED
TEAL

p. 28

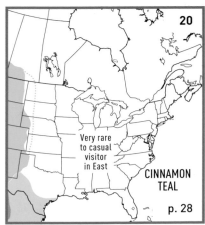

20

Very rare
to casual
visitor
in East

CINNAMON
TEAL

p. 28

21

NORTHERN
SHOVELER

p. 28

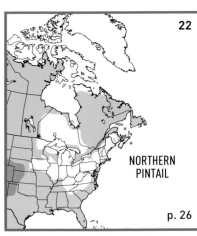

22

NORTHERN
PINTAIL

p. 26

23

Eurasian subspecies
rare but regular visitor
along Atlantic Coast,
casual well inland

GREEN-WINGED
TEAL

p. 28

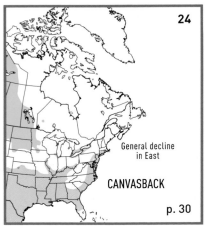

24

General decline
in East

CANVASBACK

p. 30

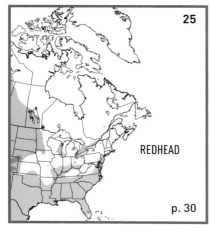

25

REDHEAD

p. 30

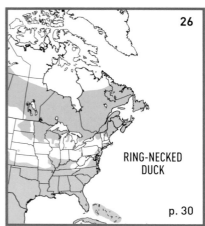

26

RING-NECKED
DUCK

p. 30

27

More common
winter scaup
in North

Rare but
regular
at many
inland
localities

GREATER
SCAUP

p. 30

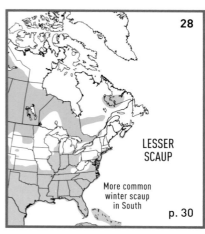

28

LESSER
SCAUP

More common
winter scaup
in South

p. 30

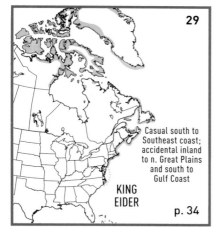

29

Casual south to
Southeast coast;
accidental inland
to n. Great Plains
and south to
Gulf Coast

KING
EIDER

p. 34

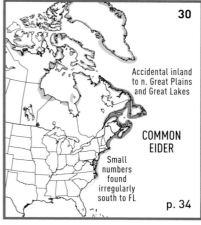

30

Accidental inland
to n. Great Plains
and Great Lakes

COMMON
EIDER

Small
numbers
found
irregularly
south to FL

p. 34

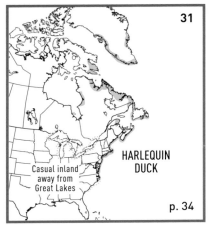

31

HARLEQUIN
DUCK

Casual inland
away from
Great Lakes

p. 34

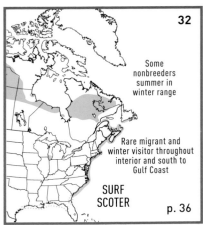

32

Some
nonbreeders
summer in
winter range

Rare migrant and winter visitor throughout
interior and south to
Gulf Coast

SURF
SCOTER

p. 36

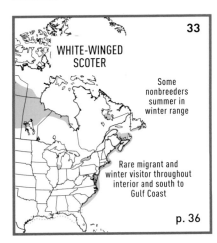

33

WHITE-WINGED
SCOTER

Some
nonbreeders
summer in
winter range

Rare migrant and
winter visitor throughout
interior and south to
Gulf Coast

p. 36

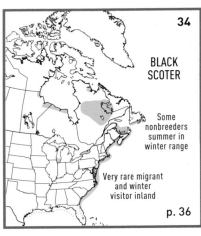

34

BLACK
SCOTER

Some
nonbreeders
summer in
winter range

Very rare migrant
and winter
visitor inland

p. 36

35

LONG-TAILED
DUCK

Rare migrant and
winter visitor throughout
interior and south to
Gulf Coast

p. 34

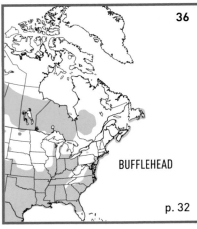

36

BUFFLEHEAD

p. 32

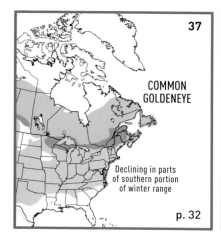

37

COMMON GOLDENEYE

Declining in parts of southern portion of winter range

p. 32

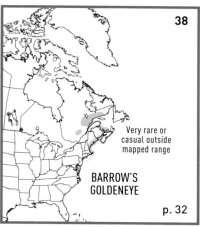

38

Very rare or casual outside mapped range

BARROW'S GOLDENEYE

p. 32

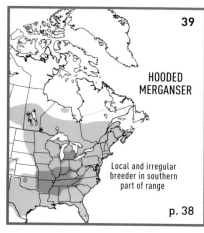

39

HOODED MERGANSER

Local and irregular breeder in southern part of range

p. 38

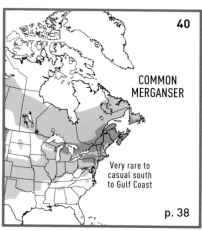

40

COMMON MERGANSER

Very rare to casual south to Gulf Coast

p. 38

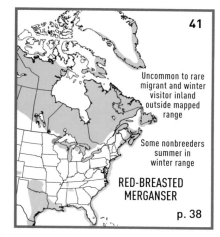

41

Uncommon to rare migrant and winter visitor inland outside mapped range

Some nonbreeders summer in winter range

RED-BREASTED MERGANSER

p. 38

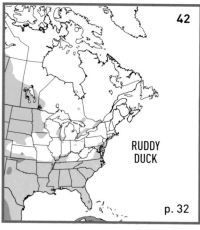

42

RUDDY DUCK

p. 32

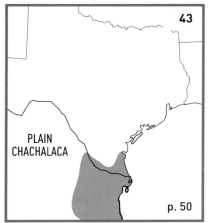

43

PLAIN
CHACHALACA

p. 50

44

SCALED
QUAIL

p. 56

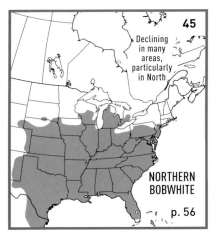

45

Declining
in many
areas,
particularly
in North

NORTHERN
BOBWHITE

p. 56

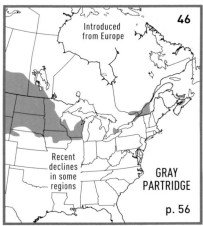

46

Introduced
from Europe

Recent
declines
in some
regions

GRAY
PARTRIDGE

p. 56

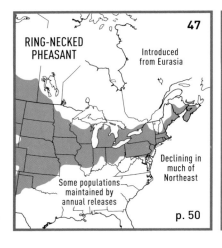

47

RING-NECKED
PHEASANT

Introduced from Eurasia

Declining in
much of
Northeast

Some populations
maintained by
annual releases

p. 50

48

Recent
declines
in East

RUFFED
GROUSE

p. 52

49

SPRUCE
GROUSE

p. 52

50

Irregular winter
movements to
slightly south of
mapped range

WILLOW
PTARMIGAN

Casual
south to
U.S. border

p. 52

51

Irregular winter
movements to
slightly south of
mapped range

ROCK
PTARMIGAN

Casual
south to
U.S. border

p. 52

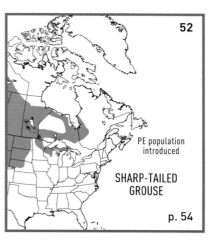

52

PE population
introduced

SHARP-TAILED
GROUSE

p. 54

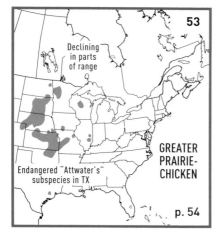

53

Declining
in parts
of range

GREATER
PRAIRIE-
CHICKEN

Endangered "Attwater's"
subspecies in TX

p. 54

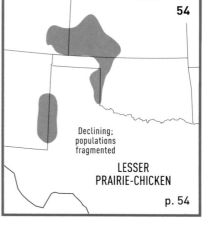

54

Declining;
populations
fragmented

LESSER
PRAIRIE-CHICKEN

p. 54

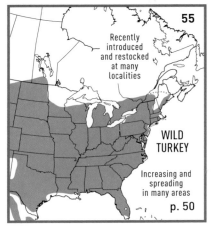

55

Recently introduced and restocked at many localities

WILD TURKEY

Increasing and spreading in many areas

p. 50

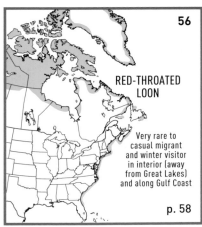

56

RED-THROATED LOON

Very rare to casual migrant and winter visitor in interior (away from Great Lakes) and along Gulf Coast

p. 58

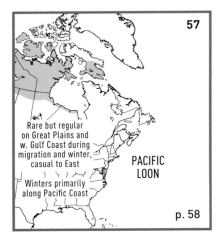

57

Rare but regular on Great Plains and w. Gulf Coast during migration and winter, casual to East

Winters primarily along Pacific Coast

PACIFIC LOON

p. 58

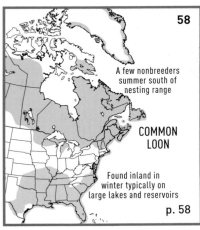

58

A few nonbreeders summer south of nesting range

COMMON LOON

Found inland in winter typically on large lakes and reservoirs

p. 58

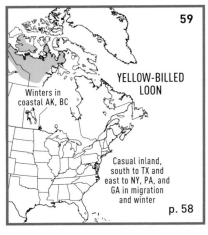

59

YELLOW-BILLED LOON

Winters in coastal AK, BC

Casual inland, south to TX and east to NY, PA, and GA in migration and winter

p. 58

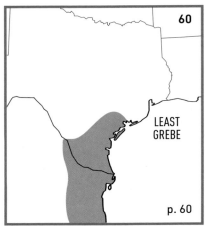

60

LEAST GREBE

p. 60

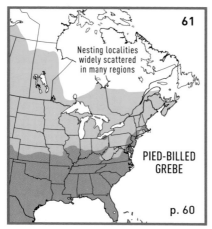

61
Nesting localities widely scattered in many regions

PIED-BILLED GREBE

p. 60

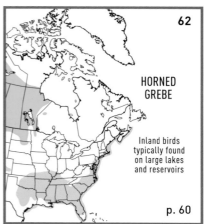

62
HORNED GREBE

Inland birds typically found on large lakes and reservoirs

p. 60

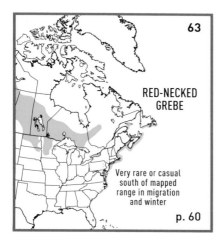

63
RED-NECKED GREBE

Very rare or casual south of mapped range in migration and winter

p. 60

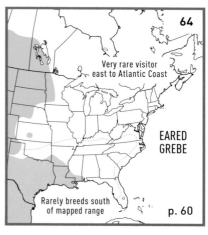

64
Very rare visitor east to Atlantic Coast

EARED GREBE

Rarely breeds south of mapped range

p. 60

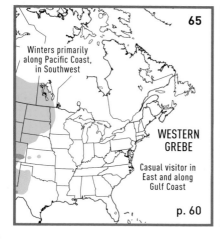

65
Winters primarily along Pacific Coast, in Southwest

WESTERN GREBE

Casual visitor in East and along Gulf Coast

p. 60

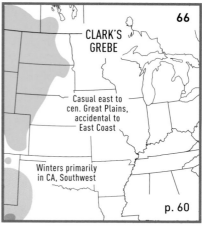

66
CLARK'S GREBE

Casual east to cen. Great Plains, accidental to East Coast

Winters primarily in CA, Southwest

p. 60

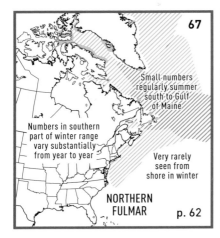

67

Small numbers regularly summer south to Gulf of Maine

Numbers in southern part of winter range vary substantially from year to year

Very rarely seen from shore in winter

NORTHERN FULMAR

p. 62

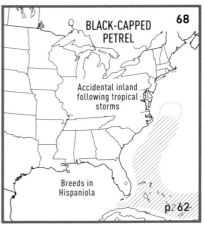

BLACK-CAPPED PETREL

68

Accidental inland following tropical storms

Breeds in Hispaniola

p. 62

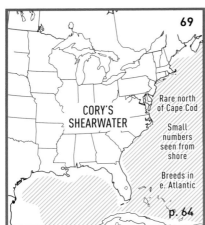

69

CORY'S SHEARWATER

Rare north of Cape Cod

Small numbers seen from shore

Breeds in e. Atlantic

p. 64

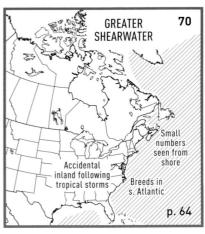

GREATER SHEARWATER

70

Accidental inland following tropical storms

Small numbers seen from shore

Breeds in s. Atlantic

p. 64

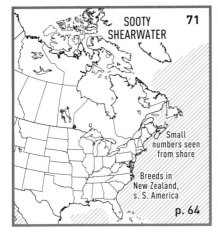

SOOTY SHEARWATER

71

Small numbers seen from shore

Breeds in New Zealand, s. S. America

72

Accidental in MI, Lake Ontario

Breeds mainly in Old World, probably in Maritimes, New England

MANX SHEARWATER

p. 64

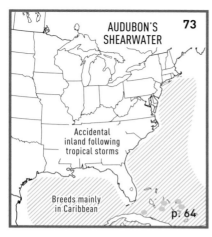

AUDUBON'S SHEARWATER 73

Accidental inland following tropical storms

Breeds mainly in Caribbean

p. 64

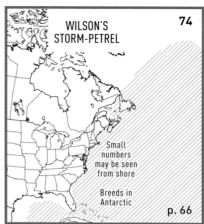

WILSON'S STORM-PETREL 74

Small numbers may be seen from shore

Breeds in Antarctic

p. 66

LEACH'S STORM-PETREL 75

Accidental inland, usually following tropical storms

Prefers deep water, only occasionally seen from shore, primarily during major storms

p. 66

BAND-RUMPED STORM-PETREL 76

Casual north to New England waters

Accidental inland after tropical storms

Nests in e. Atlantic

p. 66

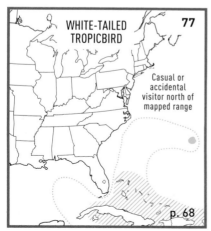

WHITE-TAILED TROPICBIRD 77

Casual or accidental visitor north of mapped range

p. 68

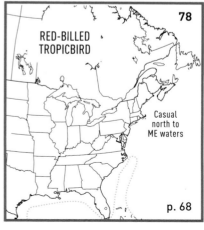

RED-BILLED TROPICBIRD 78

Casual north to ME waters

p. 68

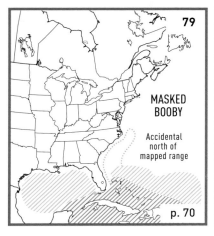

79

MASKED
BOOBY

Accidental
north of
mapped range

p. 70

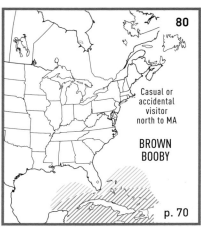

80

Casual or
accidental
visitor
north to MA

BROWN
BOOBY

p. 70

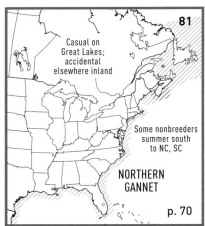

81

Casual on
Great Lakes;
accidental
elsewhere inland

Some nonbreeders
summer south
to NC, SC

NORTHERN
GANNET

p. 70

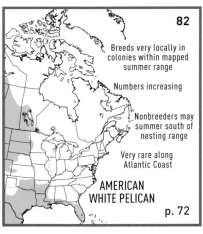

82

Breeds very locally in
colonies within mapped
summer range

Numbers increasing

Nonbreeders may
summer south of
nesting range

Very rare along
Atlantic Coast

AMERICAN
WHITE PELICAN

p. 72

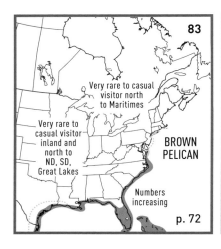

83

Very rare to casual
visitor north
to Maritimes

Very rare to
casual visitor
inland and
north to ND, SD,
Great Lakes

BROWN
PELICAN

Numbers
increasing

p. 72

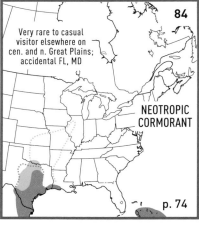

84

Very rare to casual
visitor elsewhere on
cen. and n. Great Plains;
accidental FL, MD

NEOTROPIC
CORMORANT

p. 74

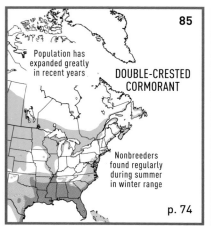

85

DOUBLE-CRESTED CORMORANT

Population has expanded greatly in recent years

Nonbreeders found regularly during summer in winter range

p. 74

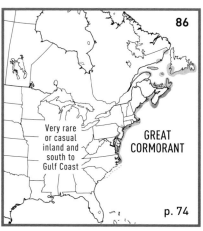

86

GREAT CORMORANT

Very rare or casual inland and south to Gulf Coast

p. 74

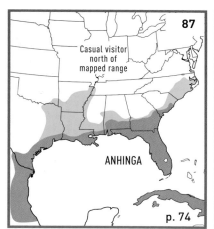

87

Casual visitor north of mapped range

ANHINGA

p. 74

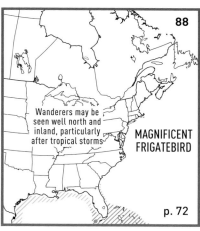

88

Wanderers may be seen well north and inland, particularly after tropical storms

MAGNIFICENT FRIGATEBIRD

p. 72

89

Major declines over most of range

Very local breeder

AMERICAN BITTERN

p. 80

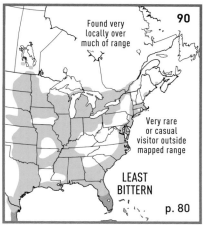

90

Found very locally over much of range

Very rare or casual visitor outside mapped range

LEAST BITTERN

p. 80

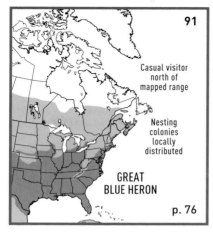

91

Casual visitor north of mapped range

Nesting colonies locally distributed

GREAT BLUE HERON

p. 76

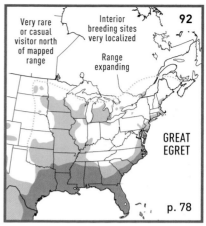

92

Very rare or casual visitor north of mapped range

Interior breeding sites very localized

Range expanding

GREAT EGRET

p. 78

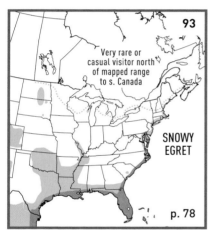

93

Very rare or casual visitor north of mapped range to s. Canada

SNOWY EGRET

p. 78

94

Very rare or casual visitor north to s. Canada

LITTLE BLUE HERON

p. 76

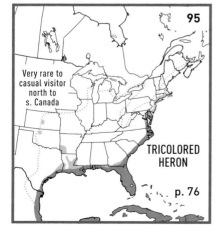

95

Very rare to casual visitor north to s. Canada

TRICOLORED HERON

p. 76

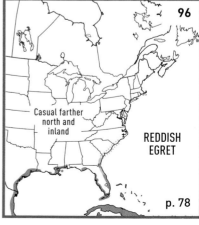

96

Casual farther north and inland

REDDISH EGRET

p. 78

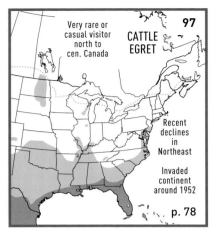

97 CATTLE EGRET

Very rare or casual visitor north to cen. Canada

Recent declines in Northeast

Invaded continent around 1952

p. 78

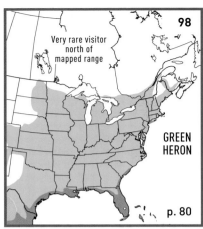

98 GREEN HERON

Very rare visitor north of mapped range

p. 80

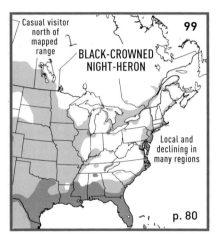

99 BLACK-CROWNED NIGHT-HERON

Casual visitor north of mapped range

Local and declining in many regions

p. 80

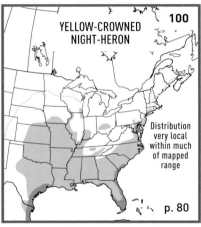

100 YELLOW-CROWNED NIGHT-HERON

Distribution very local within much of mapped range

p. 80

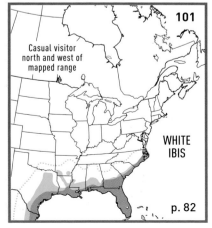

101 WHITE IBIS

Casual visitor north and west of mapped range

p. 82

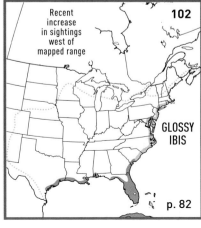

102 GLOSSY IBIS

Recent increase in sightings west of mapped range

p. 82

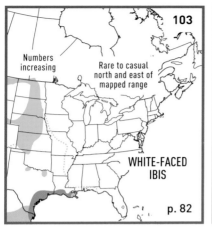

103

Numbers increasing

Rare to casual north and east of mapped range

WHITE-FACED IBIS

p. 82

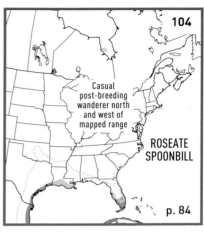

104

Casual post-breeding wanderer north and west of mapped range

ROSEATE SPOONBILL

p. 84

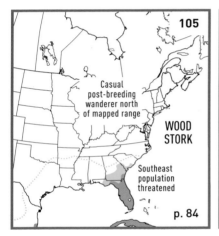

105

Casual post-breeding wanderer north of mapped range

WOOD STORK

Southeast population threatened

p. 84

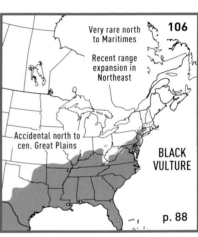

106

Very rare north to Maritimes

Recent range expansion in Northeast

Accidental north to cen. Great Plains

BLACK VULTURE

p. 88

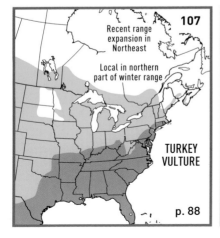

107

Recent range expansion in Northeast

Local in northern part of winter range

TURKEY VULTURE

p. 88

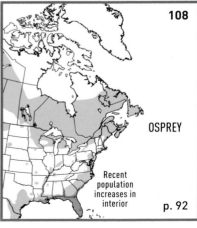

108

OSPREY

Recent population increases in interior

p. 92

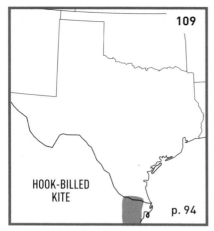

HOOK-BILLED KITE

109

p. 94

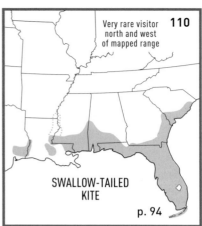

Very rare visitor
north and west
of mapped range

110

SWALLOW-TAILED KITE

p. 94

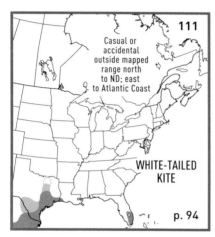

111

Casual or
accidental
outside mapped
range north
to ND; east
to Atlantic Coast

WHITE-TAILED KITE

p. 94

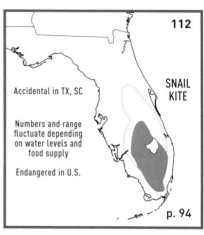

112

Accidental in TX, SC

Numbers and range
fluctuate depending
on water levels and
food supply

Endangered in U.S.

SNAIL KITE

p. 94

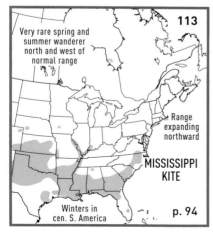

113

Very rare spring and
summer wanderer
north and west of
normal range

Range
expanding
northward

MISSISSIPPI KITE

Winters in
cen. S. America

p. 94

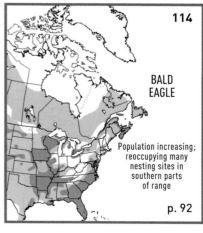

114

BALD EAGLE

Population increasing;
reoccupying many
nesting sites in
southern parts
of range

p. 92

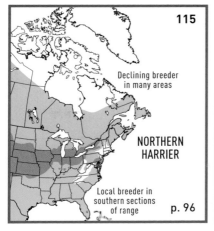

115

Declining breeder in many areas

NORTHERN HARRIER

Local breeder in southern sections of range

p. 96

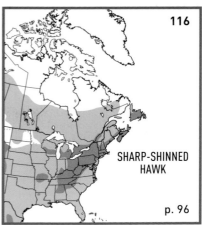

116

SHARP-SHINNED HAWK

p. 96

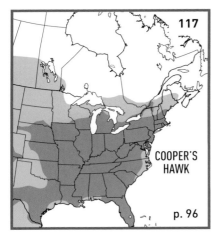

117

COOPER'S HAWK

p. 96

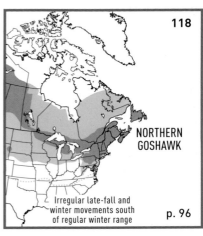

118

NORTHERN GOSHAWK

Irregular late-fall and winter movements south of regular winter range

p. 96

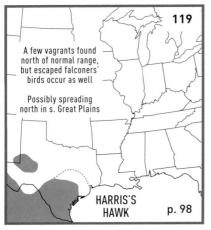

119

A few vagrants found north of normal range, but escaped falconers' birds occur as well

Possibly spreading north in s. Great Plains

HARRIS'S HAWK

p. 98

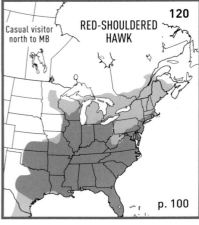

120

RED-SHOULDERED HAWK

Casual visitor north to MB

p. 100

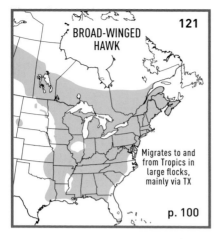

121

BROAD-WINGED HAWK

Migrates to and from Tropics in large flocks, mainly via TX

p. 100

122

Accidental in KS

GRAY HAWK

p. 98

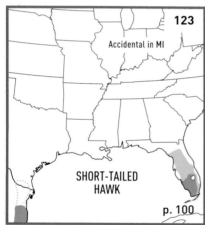

123

Accidental in MI

SHORT-TAILED HAWK

p. 100

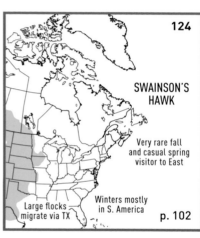

124

SWAINSON'S HAWK

Very rare fall and casual spring visitor to East

Winters mostly in S. America

Large flocks migrate via TX

p. 102

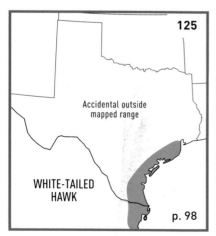

125

Accidental outside mapped range

WHITE-TAILED HAWK

p. 98

126

Accidental to NE, NS, FL

ZONE-TAILED HAWK

Rare but regular in winter in s. TX

p. 98

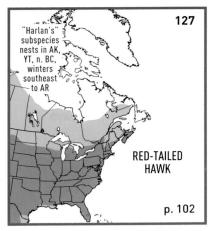

127

"Harlan's" subspecies nests in AK, YT, n. BC, winters southeast to AR

RED-TAILED HAWK

p. 102

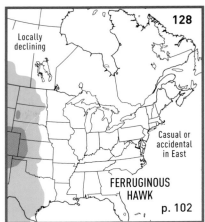

128

Locally declining

Casual or accidental in East

FERRUGINOUS HAWK

p. 102

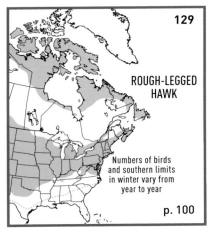

129

ROUGH-LEGGED HAWK

Numbers of birds and southern limits in winter vary from year to year

p. 100

130

Eastern breeding range poorly known

GOLDEN EAGLE

p. 92

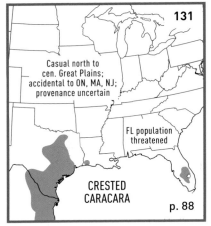

131

Casual north to cen. Great Plains; accidental to ON, MA, NJ; provenance uncertain

FL population threatened

CRESTED CARACARA

p. 88

132

Declining over parts of eastern range

AMERICAN KESTREL

p. 104

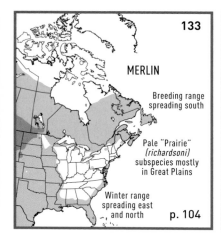

133

MERLIN

Breeding range
spreading south

Pale "Prairie"
(richardsoni)
subspecies mostly
in Great Plains

Winter range
spreading east
and north

p. 104

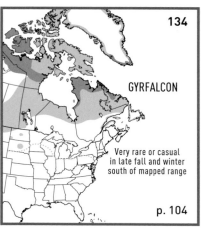

134

GYRFALCON

Very rare or casual
in late fall and winter
south of mapped range

p. 104

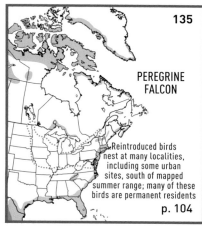

135

PEREGRINE
FALCON

Reintroduced birds
nest at many localities,
including some urban
sites, south of mapped
summer range; many of these
birds are permanent residents

p. 104

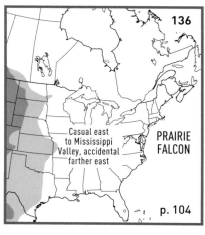

136

Casual east
to Mississippi
Valley, accidental
farther east

PRAIRIE
FALCON

p. 104

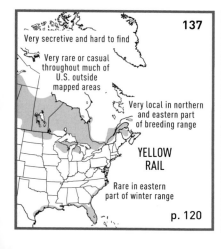

137

Very secretive and hard to find

Very rare or casual
throughout much of
U.S. outside
mapped areas

Very local in northern
and eastern part
of breeding range

YELLOW
RAIL

Rare in eastern
part of winter range

p. 120

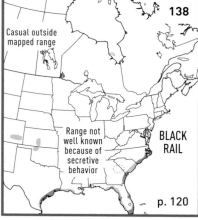

138

Casual outside
mapped range

Range not
well known
because of
secretive
behavior

BLACK
RAIL

p. 120

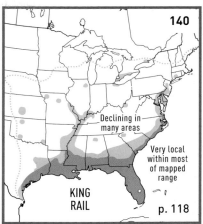

139

Very rare wanderer north of mapped range

CLAPPER RAIL

p. 118

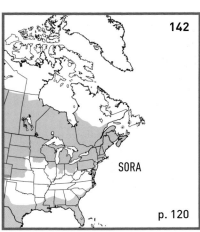

140

Declining in many areas

Very local within most of mapped range

KING RAIL

p. 118

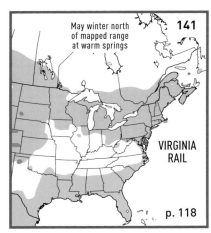

141

May winter north of mapped range at warm springs

VIRGINIA RAIL

p. 118

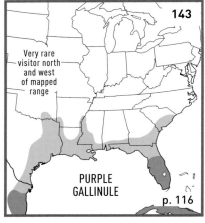

142

SORA

p. 120

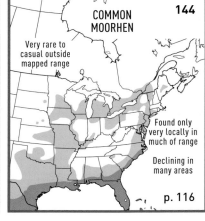

143

Very rare visitor north and west of mapped range

PURPLE GALLINULE

p. 116

COMMON MOORHEN

144

Very rare to casual outside mapped range

Found only very locally in much of range

Declining in many areas

p. 116

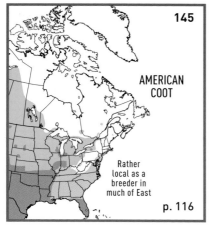

145

AMERICAN
COOT

Rather
local as a
breeder in
much of East

p. 116

146

Casual or accidental
north of
mapped range

LIMPKIN

p. 82

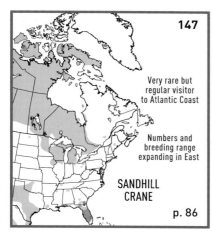

147

Very rare but
regular visitor
to Atlantic Coast

Numbers and
breeding range
expanding in East

SANDHILL
CRANE

p. 86

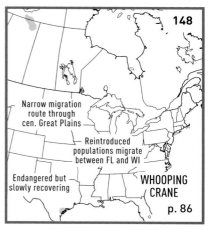

148

Narrow migration
route through
cen. Great Plains

Reintroduced
populations migrate
between FL and WI

Endangered but
slowly recovering

WHOOPING
CRANE

p. 86

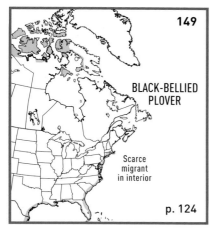

149

BLACK-BELLIED
PLOVER

Scarce
migrant
in interior

p. 124

150

AMERICAN
GOLDEN-PLOVER

Spring migration
mainly via Great
Plains and Midwest

Fall
migration
both inland
and down/off
Atlantic Coast

Winters in
S. America

p. 124

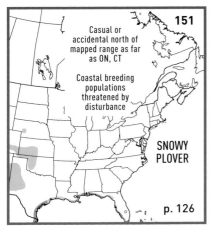

151

Casual or accidental north of mapped range as far as ON, CT

Coastal breeding populations threatened by disturbance

SNOWY PLOVER

p. 126

152

Casual north of mapped range and in interior

WILSON'S PLOVER

p. 126

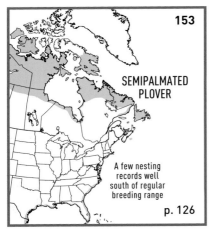

153

SEMIPALMATED PLOVER

A few nesting records well south of regular breeding range

p. 126

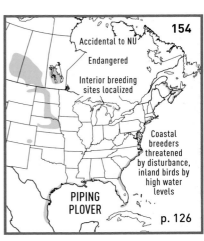

154

Accidental to NU

Endangered

Interior breeding sites localized

Coastal breeders threatened by disturbance, inland birds by high water levels

PIPING PLOVER

p. 126

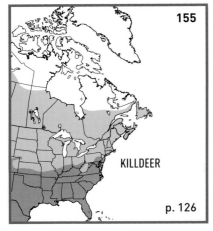

155

KILLDEER

p. 126

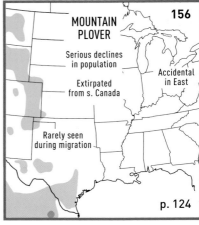

156

MOUNTAIN PLOVER

Serious declines in population

Extirpated from s. Canada

Rarely seen during migration

Accidental in East

p. 124

157

Recent range expansion in Northeast

Accidental inland

AMERICAN OYSTERCATCHER

p. 128

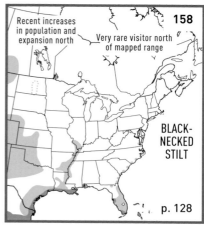

158

Recent increases in population and expansion north

Very rare visitor north of mapped range

BLACK-NECKED STILT

p. 128

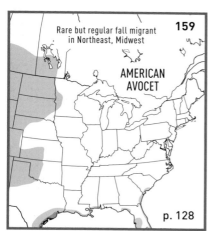

159

Rare but regular fall migrant in Northeast, Midwest

AMERICAN AVOCET

p. 128

160

SPOTTED SANDPIPER

p. 140

161

SOLITARY SANDPIPER

Winters mainly from W. Indies to S. America

p. 130

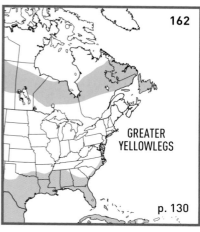

162

GREATER YELLOWLEGS

p. 130

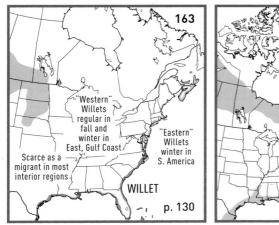

163

"Western" Willets regular in fall and winter in East, Gulf Coast

"Eastern" Willets winter in S. America

Scarce as a migrant in most interior regions

WILLET

p. 130

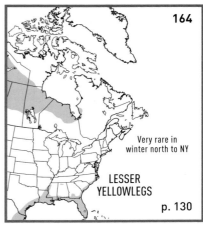

164

Very rare in winter north to NY

LESSER YELLOWLEGS

p. 130

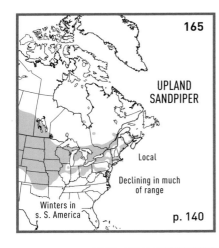

165

UPLAND SANDPIPER

Local

Declining in much of range

Winters in s. S. America

p. 140

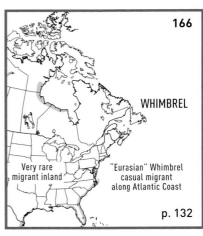

166

WHIMBREL

Very rare migrant inland

"Eurasian" Whimbrel casual migrant along Atlantic Coast

p. 132

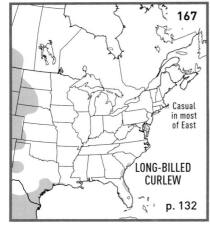

167

Casual in most of East

LONG-BILLED CURLEW

p. 132

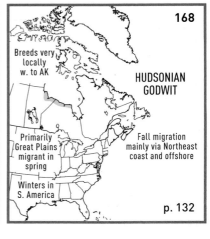

168

Breeds very locally w. to AK

HUDSONIAN GODWIT

Primarily Great Plains migrant in spring

Fall migration mainly via Northeast coast and offshore

Winters in S. America

p. 132

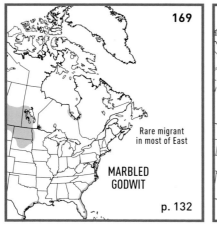

169

Rare migrant in most of East

MARBLED GODWIT

p. 132

170

Rare to very rare migrant inland

Regular migrant around Great Lakes

RUDDY TURNSTONE

p. 134

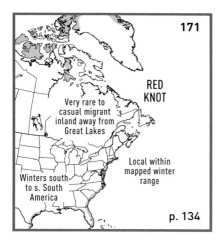

171

RED KNOT

Very rare to casual migrant inland away from Great Lakes

Winters south to s. South America

Local within mapped winter range

p. 134

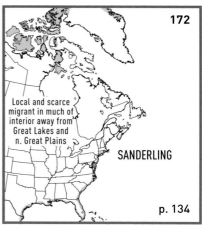

172

Local and scarce migrant in much of interior away from Great Lakes and n. Great Plains

SANDERLING

p. 134

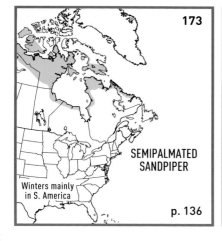

173

SEMIPALMATED SANDPIPER

Winters mainly in S. America

p. 136

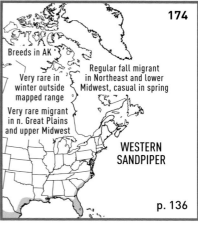

174

Breeds in AK

Regular fall migrant in Northeast and lower Midwest, casual in spring

Very rare in winter outside mapped range

Very rare migrant in n. Great Plains and upper Midwest

WESTERN SANDPIPER

p. 136

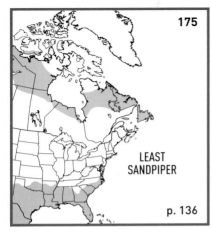

175

LEAST
SANDPIPER

p. 136

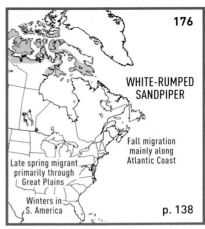

176

WHITE-RUMPED
SANDPIPER

Fall migration
mainly along
Atlantic Coast

Late spring migrant
primarily through
Great Plains

Winters in
S. America

p. 138

177

Scarce fall migrant
along Atlantic Coast

Primary migration
through Great
Plains

BAIRD'S
SANDPIPER

Winters in
S. America

p. 138

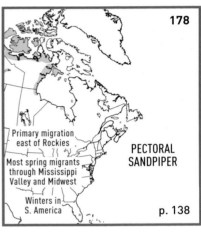

178

Primary migration
east of Rockies

Most spring migrants
through Mississippi
Valley and Midwest

PECTORAL
SANDPIPER

Winters in
S. America

p. 138

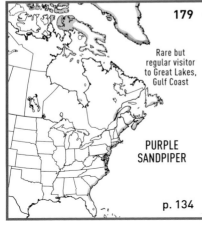

179

Rare but
regular visitor
to Great Lakes,
Gulf Coast

PURPLE
SANDPIPER

p. 134

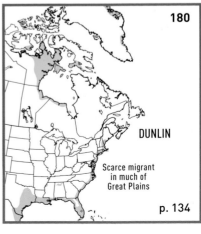

180

DUNLIN

Scarce migrant
in much of
Great Plains

p. 134

181

Scarce on East Coast and Great Lakes in spring; more numerous as a fall migrant

STILT SANDPIPER

Primary migration east of Rockies

p. 130

182

BUFF-BREASTED SANDPIPER

Primary migration through Great Plains

Small numbers of fall migrants in East

Winters in S. America

p. 140

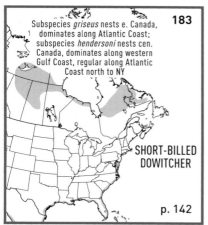

183

Subspecies *griseus* nests e. Canada, dominates along Atlantic Coast; subspecies *hendersoni* nests cen. Canada, dominates along western Gulf Coast, regular along Atlantic Coast north to NY

SHORT-BILLED DOWITCHER

p. 142

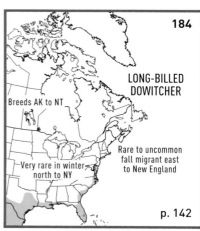

184

LONG-BILLED DOWITCHER

Breeds AK to NT

Rare to uncommon fall migrant east to New England

Very rare in winter north to NY

p. 142

185

WILSON'S SNIPE

p. 142

186

AMERICAN WOODCOCK

p. 142

187

WILSON'S
PHALAROPE

Rare but
regular
migrant
in East

Winters in
S. America

p. 144

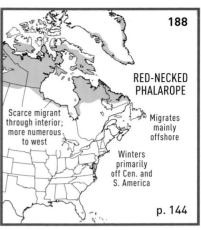

188

RED-NECKED
PHALAROPE

Scarce migrant
through interior;
more numerous
to west

Migrates
mainly
offshore

Winters
primarily
off Cen. and
S. America

p. 144

189

RED
PHALAROPE

Very rare to
casual migrant
inland, mostly
in fall

Migrates mainly
offshore, rare along
immediate coast,
most often
associated
with storms

Winters at sea
in irregular
numbers   p. 144

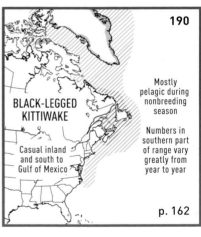

190

BLACK-LEGGED
KITTIWAKE

Casual inland
and south to
Gulf of Mexico

Mostly
pelagic during
nonbreeding
season

Numbers in
southern part
of range vary
greatly from
year to year

p. 162

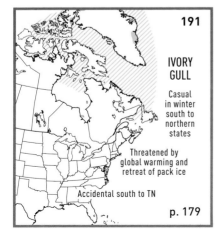

191

IVORY
GULL

Casual
in winter
south to
northern
states

Threatened by
global warming and
retreat of pack ice

Accidental south to TN

p. 179

192

SABINE'S
GULL

Most migrate
offshore

Very rare but
regular fall
migrant
through
interior and
off Atlantic
Coast (casual
in spring)

Accidental
in winter

Winters in
S. Hemisphere   p. 160

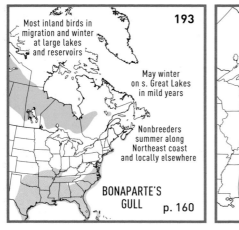

193

Most inland birds in migration and winter at large lakes and reservoirs

May winter on s. Great Lakes in mild years

Nonbreeders summer along Northeast coast and locally elsewhere

BONAPARTE'S GULL

p. 160

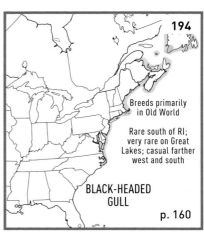

194

Breeds primarily in Old World

Rare south of RI; very rare on Great Lakes; casual farther west and south

BLACK-HEADED GULL

p. 160

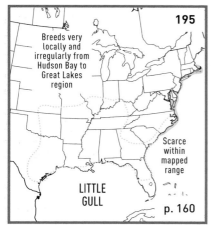

195

Breeds very locally and irregularly from Hudson Bay to Great Lakes region

Scarce within mapped range

LITTLE GULL

p. 160

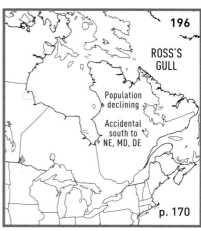

196

ROSS'S GULL

Population declining

Accidental south to NE, MD, DE

p. 170

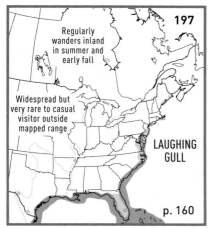

197

Regularly wanders inland in summer and early fall

Widespread but very rare to casual visitor outside mapped range

LAUGHING GULL

p. 160

198

Very rare but regular visitor east to Atlantic Coast

Winters off S. America

FRANKLIN'S GULL

p. 160

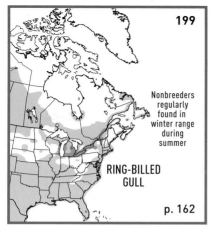

199

Nonbreeders regularly found in winter range during summer

RING-BILLED GULL

p. 162

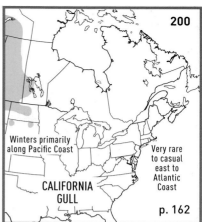

200

Winters primarily along Pacific Coast

Very rare to casual east to Atlantic Coast

CALIFORNIA GULL

p. 162

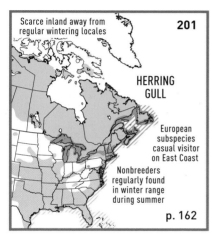

201

Scarce inland away from regular wintering locales

HERRING GULL

European subspecies casual visitor on East Coast

Nonbreeders regularly found in winter range during summer

p. 162

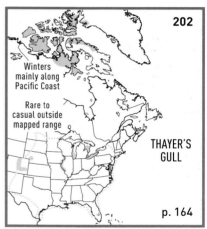

202

Winters mainly along Pacific Coast

Rare to casual outside mapped range

THAYER'S GULL

p. 164

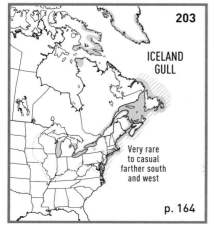

203

ICELAND GULL

Very rare to casual farther south and west

p. 164

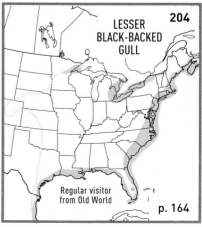

204

LESSER BLACK-BACKED GULL

Regular visitor from Old World

p. 164

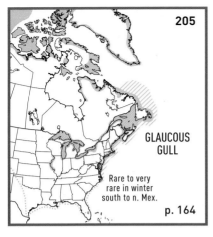

205

GLAUCOUS GULL

Rare to very rare in winter south to n. Mex.

p. 164

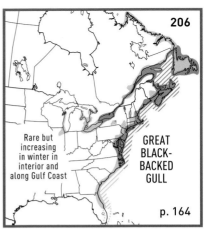

206

GREAT BLACK-BACKED GULL

Rare but increasing in winter in interior and along Gulf Coast

p. 164

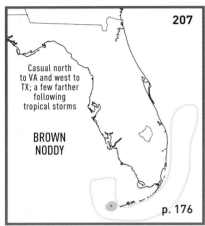

207

Casual north to VA and west to TX; a few farther following tropical storms

BROWN NODDY

p. 176

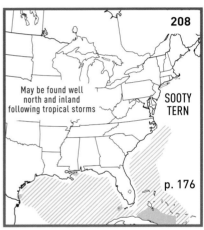

208

May be found well north and inland following tropical storms

SOOTY TERN

p. 176

209

BRIDLED TERN

May be found well north and inland following tropical storms

p. 176

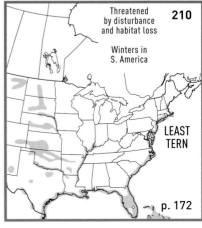

210

Threatened by disturbance and habitat loss

Winters in S. America

LEAST TERN

p. 172

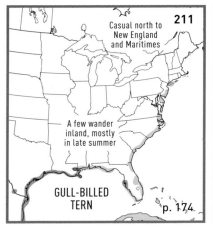

211

Casual north to New England and Maritimes

A few wander inland, mostly in late summer

GULL-BILLED TERN

p. 174

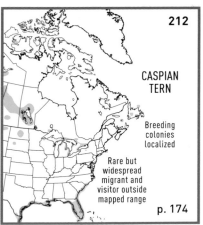

212

CASPIAN TERN

Breeding colonies localized

Rare but widespread migrant and visitor outside mapped range

p. 174

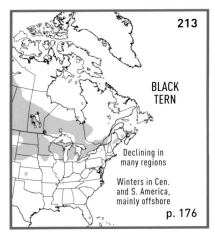

213

BLACK TERN

Declining in many regions

Winters in Cen. and S. America, mainly offshore

p. 176

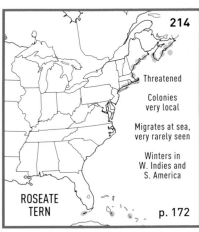

214

Threatened

Colonies very local

Migrates at sea, very rarely seen

Winters in W. Indies and S. America

ROSEATE TERN

p. 172

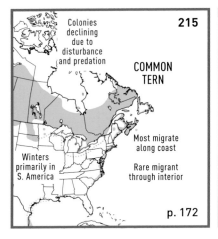

215

Colonies declining due to disturbance and predation

COMMON TERN

Most migrate along coast

Rare migrant through interior

Winters primarily in S. America

p. 172

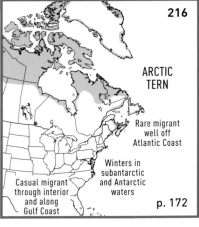

216

ARCTIC TERN

Rare migrant well off Atlantic Coast

Winters in subantarctic and Antarctic waters

Casual migrant through interior and along Gulf Coast

p. 172

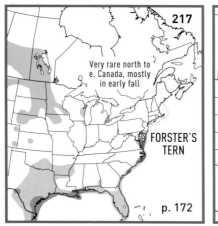

217

Very rare north to e. Canada, mostly in early fall

FORSTER'S TERN

p. 172

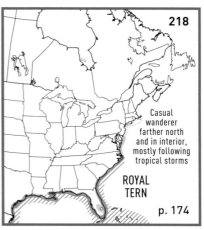

218

Casual wanderer farther north and in interior, mostly following tropical storms

ROYAL TERN

p. 174

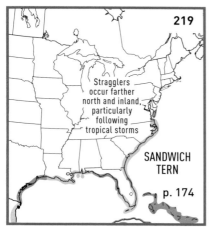

219

Stragglers occur farther north and inland, particularly following tropical storms

SANDWICH TERN

p. 174

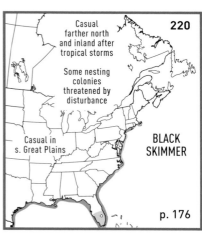

220

Casual farther north and inland after tropical storms

Some nesting colonies threatened by disturbance

Casual in s. Great Plains

BLACK SKIMMER

p. 176

221

GREAT SKUA

p. 178

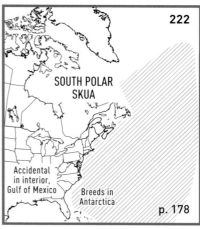

222

SOUTH POLAR SKUA

Accidental in interior, Gulf of Mexico

Breeds in Antarctica

p. 178

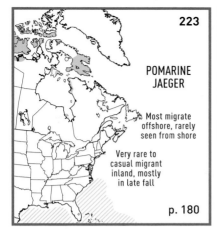

223

POMARINE JAEGER

Most migrate offshore, rarely seen from shore

Very rare to casual migrant inland, mostly in late fall

p. 180

224

PARASITIC JAEGER

Very rare to casual migrant inland, mostly in fall

Regularly seen from shore in small numbers

p. 180

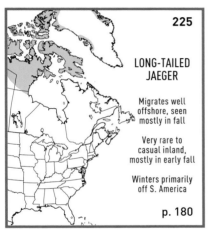

225

LONG-TAILED JAEGER

Migrates well offshore, seen mostly in fall

Very rare to casual inland, mostly in early fall

Winters primarily off S. America

p. 180

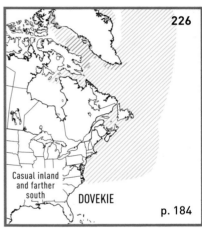

226

Casual inland and farther south

DOVEKIE

p. 184

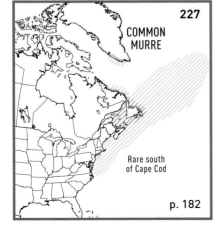

227

COMMON MURRE

Rare south of Cape Cod

p. 182

228

Winters north to leads (openings) in pack ice

THICK-BILLED MURRE

In winter, rarely seen from shore or south of New England

p. 182

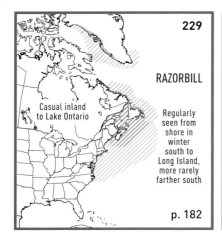

229

RAZORBILL

Casual inland to Lake Ontario

Regularly seen from shore in winter south to Long Island, more rarely farther south

p. 182

230

BLACK GUILLEMOT

Winters north to leads in pack ice

Threatened by retreat of pack ice

Accidental in Great Lakes, Prairie Provinces

Casual south of Long Island to SC

p. 184

231

In winter seen only casually from shore

Accidental inland to ON

ATLANTIC PUFFIN

Casual south to FL

p. 184

232

ROCK PIGEON

Introduced from Old World

p. 186

233

Accidental to w. FL, MS

WHITE-CROWNED PIGEON

p. 186

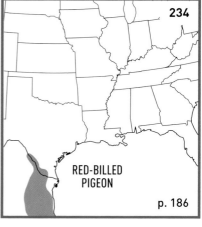

234

RED-BILLED PIGEON

p. 186

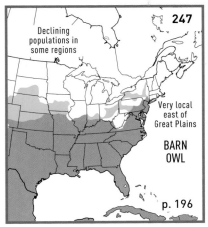

247

Declining populations in some regions

Very local east of Great Plains

BARN OWL

p. 196

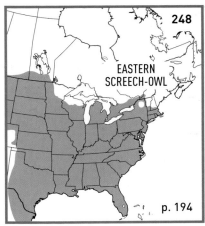

248

EASTERN SCREECH-OWL

p. 194

249

GREAT HORNED OWL

p. 194

250

SNOWY OWL

Irregular winter movements south to dash line

Casual south to Gulf Coast

p. 196

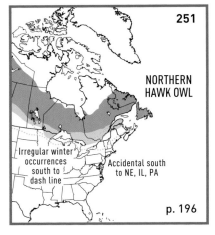

251

NORTHERN HAWK OWL

Irregular winter occurrences south to dash line

Accidental south to NE, IL, PA

p. 196

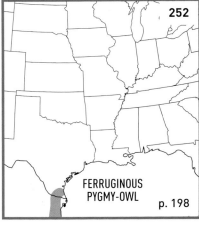

252

FERRUGINOUS PYGMY-OWL

p. 198

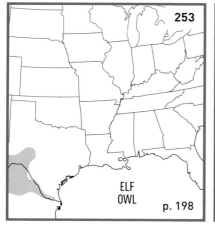

253

ELF
OWL

p. 198

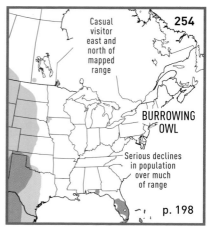

254

Casual
visitor
east and
north of
mapped
range

BURROWING
OWL

Serious declines
in population
over much
of range

p. 198

255

BARRED
OWL

p. 196

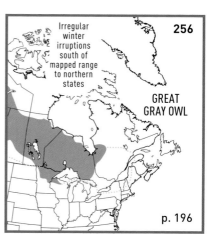

256

Irregular
winter
irruptions
south of
mapped
range to
northern
states

GREAT
GRAY OWL

p. 196

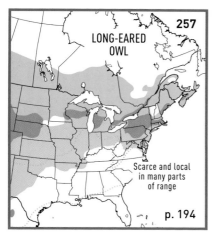

257

LONG-EARED
OWL

Scarce and local
in many parts
of range

p. 194

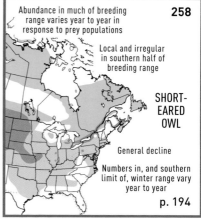

258

Abundance in much of breeding
range varies year to year in
response to prey populations

Local and irregular
in southern half of
breeding range

SHORT-
EARED
OWL

General decline

Numbers in, and southern
limit of, winter range vary
year to year

p. 194

259

BOREAL OWL

Irregular winter irruptions south to dash line and casually beyond

p. 198

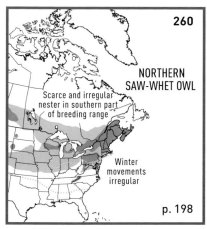

260

NORTHERN SAW-WHET OWL

Scarce and irregular nester in southern part of breeding range

Winter movements irregular

p. 198

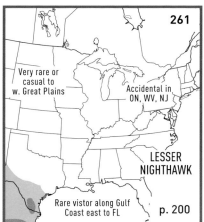

261

Very rare or casual to w. Great Plains

Accidental in ON, WV, NJ

LESSER NIGHTHAWK

Rare vistor along Gulf Coast east to FL

p. 200

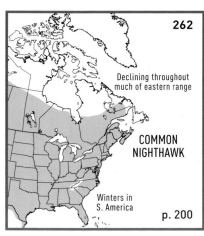

262

Declining throughout much of eastern range

COMMON NIGHTHAWK

Winters in S. America

p. 200

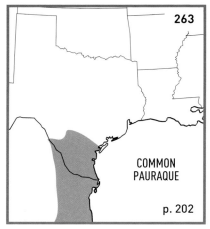

263

COMMON PAURAQUE

p. 202

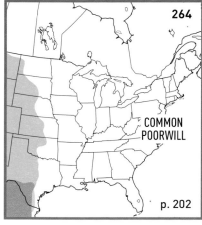

264

COMMON POORWILL

p. 202

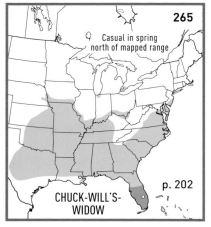

265

Casual in spring
north of mapped range

CHUCK-WILL'S-
WIDOW

p. 202

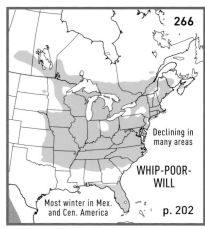

266

Declining in
many areas

WHIP-POOR-
WILL

Most winter in Mex.
and Cen. America

p. 202

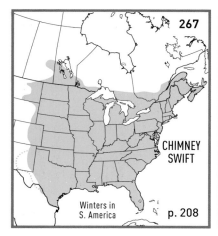

267

CHIMNEY
SWIFT

Winters in
S. America

p. 208

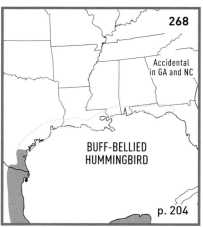

268

Accidental
in GA and NC

BUFF-BELLIED
HUMMINGBIRD

p. 204

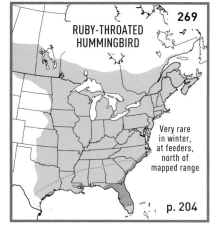

269

RUBY-THROATED
HUMMINGBIRD

Very rare
in winter,
at feeders,
north of
mapped range

p. 204

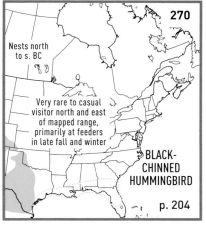

270

Nests north
to s. BC

Very rare to casual
visitor north and east
of mapped range,
primarily at feeders
in late fall and winter

BLACK-
CHINNED
HUMMINGBIRD

p. 204

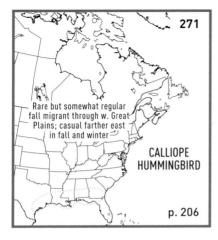

271

Rare but somewhat regular fall migrant through w. Great Plains; casual farther east in fall and winter

CALLIOPE HUMMINGBIRD

p. 206

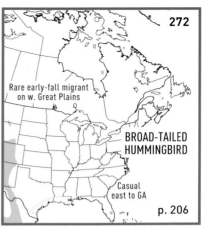

272

Rare early-fall migrant on w. Great Plains

BROAD-TAILED HUMMINGBIRD

Casual east to GA

p. 206

273

Breeds in Pacific Northwest

Regular fall migrant through w. Great Plains, very rare farther east

RUFOUS HUMMINGBIRD

Recent increases in small wintering population at southeastern feeders

p. 204

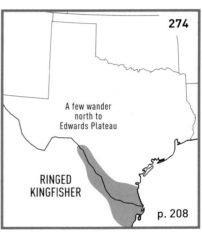

274

A few wander north to Edwards Plateau

RINGED KINGFISHER

p. 208

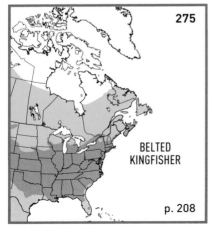

275

BELTED KINGFISHER

p. 208

276

GREEN KINGFISHER

p. 208

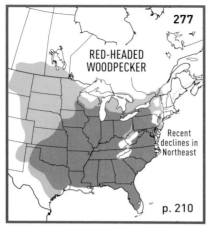

277

RED-HEADED WOODPECKER

Recent declines in Northeast

p. 210

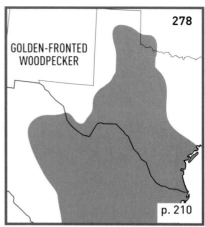

278

GOLDEN-FRONTED WOODPECKER

p. 210

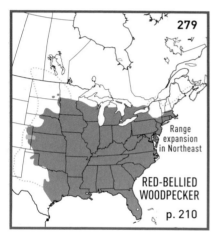

279

RED-BELLIED WOODPECKER

Range expansion in Northeast

p. 210

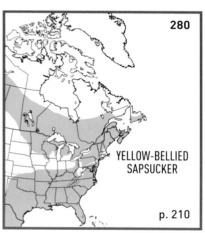

280

YELLOW-BELLIED SAPSUCKER

p. 210

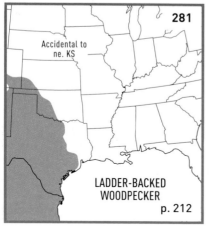

281

Accidental to ne. KS

LADDER-BACKED WOODPECKER

p. 212

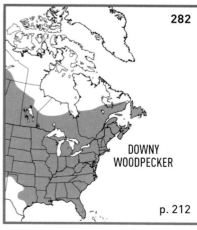

282

DOWNY WOODPECKER

p. 212

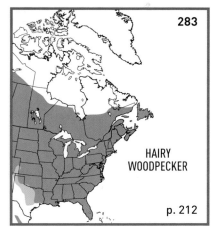

283

HAIRY WOODPECKER

p. 212

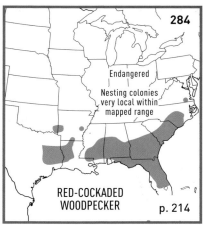

284

Endangered

Nesting colonies very local within mapped range

RED-COCKADED WOODPECKER

p. 214

285

AMERICAN THREE-TOED WOODPECKER

Casual in winter south of mapped range

p. 212

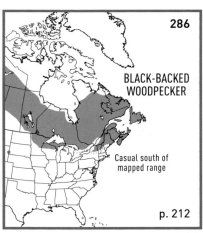

286

BLACK-BACKED WOODPECKER

Casual south of mapped range

p. 212

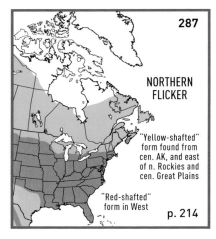

287

NORTHERN FLICKER

"Yellow-shafted" form found from cen. AK, and east of n. Rockies and cen. Great Plains

"Red-shafted" form in West

p. 214

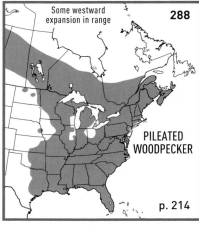

288

Some westward expansion in range

PILEATED WOODPECKER

p. 214

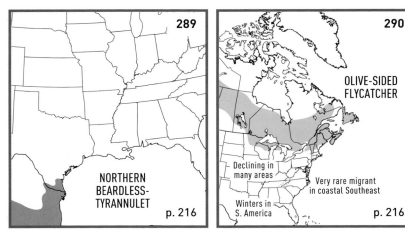

289

NORTHERN
BEARDLESS-
TYRANNULET

p. 216

290

OLIVE-SIDED
FLYCATCHER

Declining in
many areas

Very rare migrant
in coastal Southeast

Winters in
S. America

p. 216

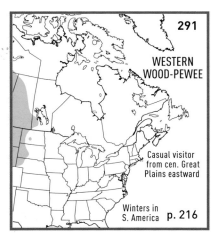

291

WESTERN
WOOD-PEWEE

Casual visitor
from cen. Great
Plains eastward

Winters in
S. America   p. 216

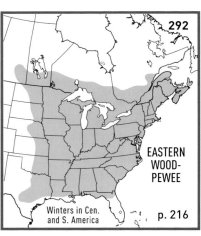

292

EASTERN
WOOD-
PEWEE

Winters in Cen.
and S. America   p. 216

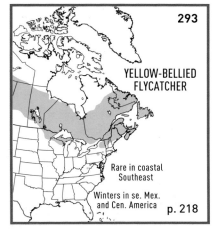

293

YELLOW-BELLIED
FLYCATCHER

Rare in coastal
Southeast

Winters in se. Mex.
and Cen. America   p. 218

294

ACADIAN
FLYCATCHER

Winters in Cen.
and S. America   p. 218

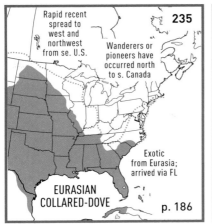

235

Rapid recent spread to west and northwest from se. U.S.

Wanderers or pioneers have occurred north to s. Canada

Exotic from Eurasia; arrived via FL

EURASIAN COLLARED-DOVE

p. 186

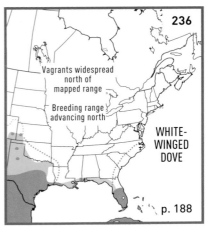

236

Vagrants widespread north of mapped range

Breeding range advancing north

WHITE-WINGED DOVE

p. 188

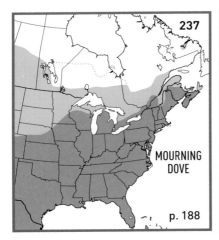

237

MOURNING DOVE

p. 188

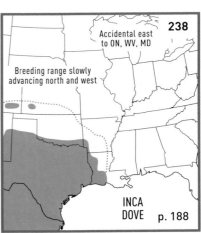

238

Accidental east to ON, WV, MD

Breeding range slowly advancing north and west

INCA DOVE

p. 188

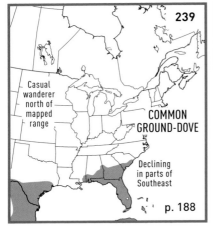

239

Casual wanderer north of mapped range

COMMON GROUND-DOVE

Declining in parts of Southeast

p. 188

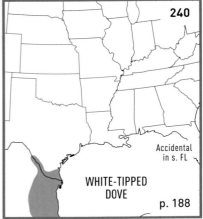

240

Accidental in s. FL

WHITE-TIPPED DOVE

p. 188

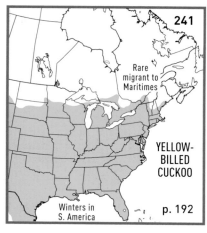

241

Rare migrant to Maritimes

YELLOW-BILLED CUCKOO

Winters in S. America

p. 192

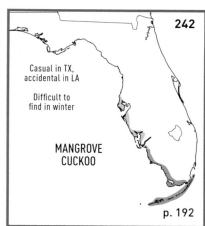

242

Casual in TX, accidental in LA

Difficult to find in winter

MANGROVE CUCKOO

p. 192

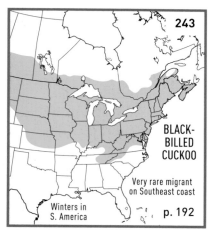

243

BLACK-BILLED CUCKOO

Very rare migrant on Southeast coast

Winters in S. America

p. 192

244

GREATER ROADRUNNER

p. 192

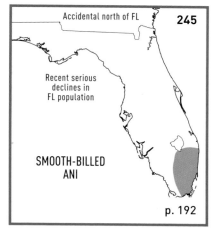

245

Accidental north of FL

Recent serious declines in FL population

SMOOTH-BILLED ANI

p. 192

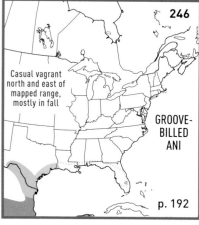

246

Casual vagrant north and east of mapped range, mostly in fall

GROOVE-BILLED ANI

p. 192

295

Migrates from
cen. Great Plains
eastward

**ALDER
FLYCATCHER**

Rare in coastal
Southeast

Winters in
S. America

p. 218

296

**WILLOW
FLYCATCHER**

Winters in Mex.
and Cen. America

p. 218

297

**LEAST
FLYCATCHER**

Winters in
Mex. and
Cen. America

p. 218

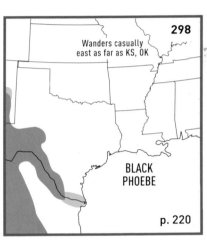

298

Wanders casually
east as far as KS, OK

**BLACK
PHOEBE**

p. 220

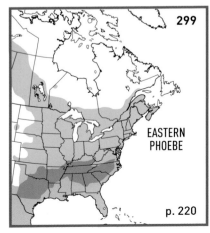

299

**EASTERN
PHOEBE**

p. 220

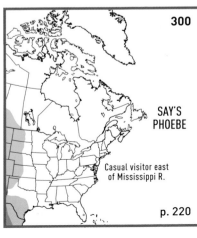

300

**SAY'S
PHOEBE**

Casual visitor east
of Mississippi R.

p. 220

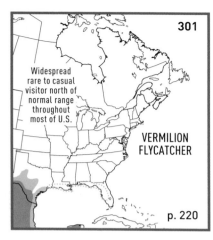

301

Widespread rare to casual visitor north of normal range throughout most of U.S.

VERMILION FLYCATCHER

p. 220

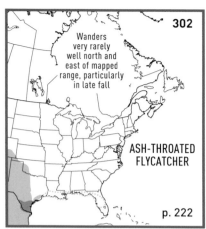

302

Wanders very rarely well north and east of mapped range, particularly in late fall

ASH-THROATED FLYCATCHER

p. 222

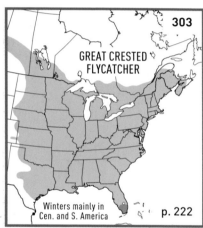

303

GREAT CRESTED FLYCATCHER

Winters mainly in Cen. and S. America

p. 222

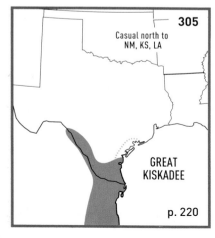

304

Very rare visitor east to s. FL

BROWN-CRESTED FLYCATCHER

p. 222

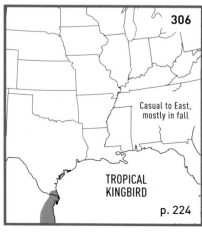

305

Casual north to NM, KS, LA

GREAT KISKADEE

p. 220

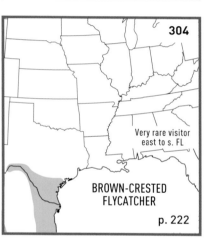

306

Casual to East, mostly in fall

TROPICAL KINGBIRD

p. 224

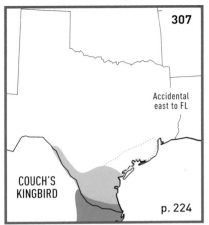

307

Accidental east to FL

COUCH'S KINGBIRD

p. 224

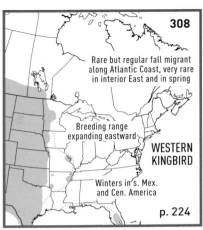

308

Rare but regular fall migrant along Atlantic Coast, very rare in interior East and in spring

Breeding range expanding eastward

WESTERN KINGBIRD

Winters in s. Mex. and Cen. America

p. 224

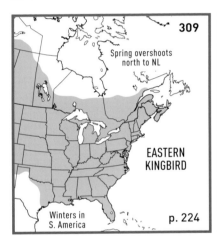

309

Spring overshoots north to NL

EASTERN KINGBIRD

Winters in S. America

p. 224

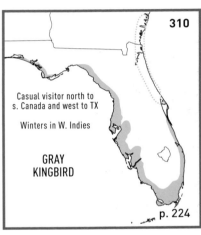

310

Casual visitor north to s. Canada and west to TX

Winters in W. Indies

GRAY KINGBIRD

p. 224

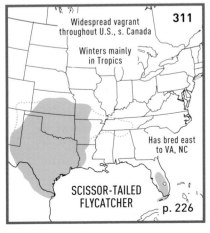

311

Widespread vagrant throughout U.S., s. Canada

Winters mainly in Tropics

Has bred east to VA, NC

SCISSOR-TAILED FLYCATCHER

p. 226

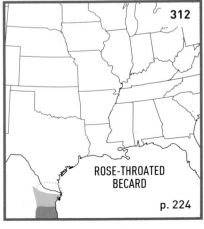

312

ROSE-THROATED BECARD

p. 224

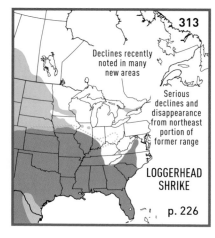

313

Declines recently noted in many new areas

Serious declines and disappearance from northeast portion of former range

LOGGERHEAD SHRIKE

p. 226

314

NORTHERN SHRIKE

Irruptive fall and winter visitor to dash line, very rarely beyond

Accidental to cen. TX

p. 226

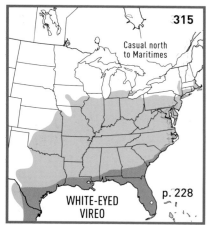

315

Casual north to Maritimes

WHITE-EYED VIREO

p. 228

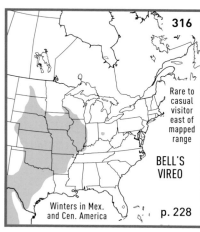

316

Rare to casual visitor east of mapped range

BELL'S VIREO

Winters in Mex. and Cen. America

p. 228

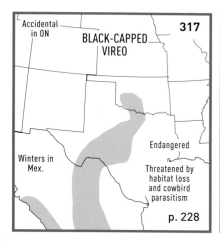

317

Accidental in ON

BLACK-CAPPED VIREO

Winters in Mex.

Endangered

Threatened by habitat loss and cowbird parasitism

p. 228

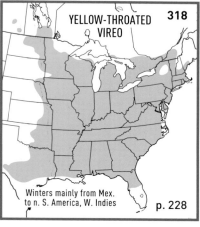

318

YELLOW-THROATED VIREO

Winters mainly from Mex. to n. S. America, W. Indies

p. 228

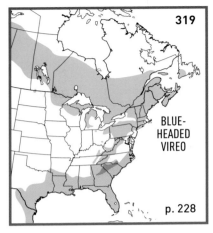

319

BLUE-HEADED VIREO

p. 228

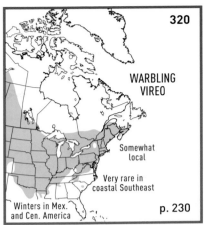

320

WARBLING VIREO

Somewhat local

Very rare in coastal Southeast

Winters in Mex. and Cen. America

p. 230

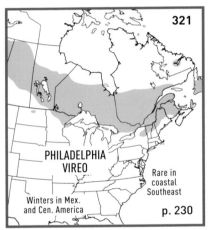

321

PHILADELPHIA VIREO

Rare in coastal Southeast

Winters in Mex. and Cen. America

p. 230

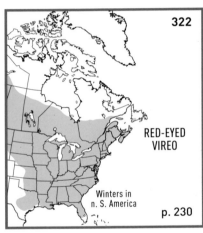

322

RED-EYED VIREO

Winters in n. S. America

p. 230

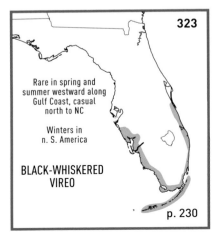

323

Rare in spring and summer westward along Gulf Coast, casual north to NC

Winters in n. S. America

BLACK-WHISKERED VIREO

p. 230

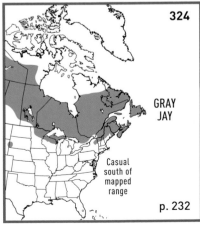

324

GRAY JAY

Casual south of mapped range

p. 232

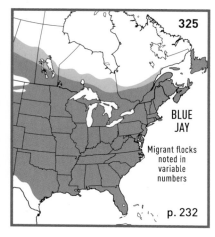

325

BLUE JAY

Migrant flocks noted in variable numbers

p. 232

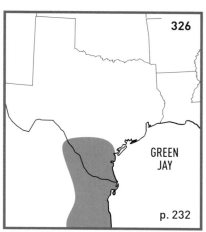

326

GREEN JAY

p. 232

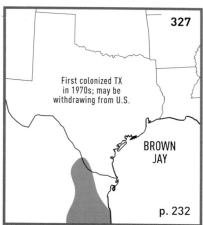

327

First colonized TX in 1970s; may be withdrawing from U.S.

BROWN JAY

p. 232

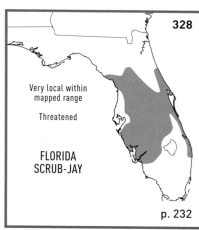

328

Very local within mapped range

Threatened

FLORIDA SCRUB-JAY

p. 232

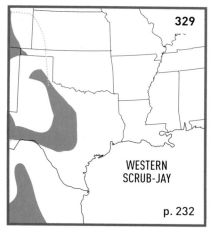

329

WESTERN SCRUB-JAY

p. 232

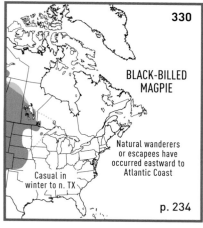

330

BLACK-BILLED MAGPIE

Natural wanderers or escapees have occurred eastward to Atlantic Coast

Casual in winter to n. TX

p. 234

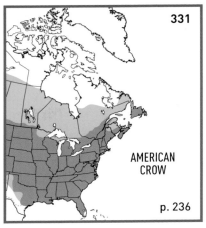

331

AMERICAN CROW

p. 236

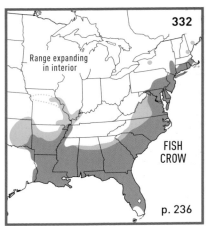

332

Range expanding in interior

FISH CROW

p. 236

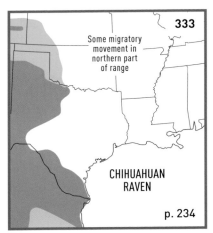

333

Some migratory movement in northern part of range

CHIHUAHUAN RAVEN

p. 234

334

COMMON RAVEN

Casual to Great Plains

Expanding range east and south

p. 234

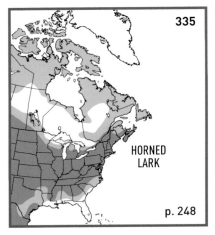

335

HORNED LARK

p. 248

336

PURPLE MARTIN

Winters in S. America

p. 240

337

TREE
SWALLOW

p. 238

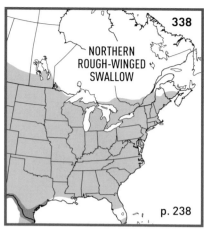

338

NORTHERN
ROUGH-WINGED
SWALLOW

p. 238

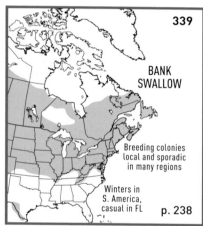

339

BANK
SWALLOW

Breeding colonies
local and sporadic
in many regions

Winters in
S. America,
casual in FL p. 238

340

CLIFF
SWALLOW

Range
expanding
southward

Winters in
S. America

p. 240

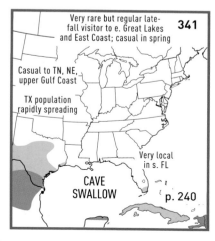

Very rare but regular late-
fall visitor to e. Great Lakes
and East Coast; casual in spring

341

Casual to TN, NE,
upper Gulf Coast

TX population
rapidly spreading

Very local
in s. FL

CAVE
SWALLOW   p. 240

342

BARN
SWALLOW

Winters mainly
in Cen. and
S. America

p. 240

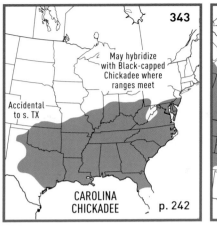

343

May hybridize with Black-capped Chickadee where ranges meet

Accidental to s. TX

CAROLINA CHICKADEE

p. 242

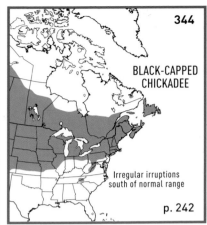

344

BLACK-CAPPED CHICKADEE

Irregular irruptions south of normal range

p. 242

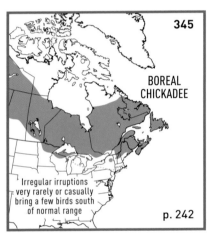

345

BOREAL CHICKADEE

Irregular irruptions very rarely or casually bring a few birds south of normal range

p. 242

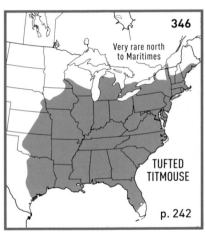

346

Very rare north to Maritimes

TUFTED TITMOUSE

p. 242

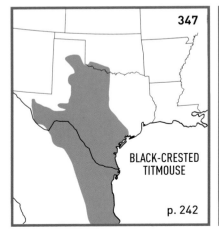

347

BLACK-CRESTED TITMOUSE

p. 242

348

VERDIN

p. 242

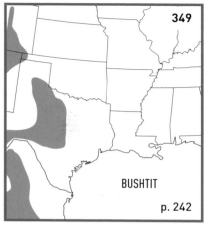

349

BUSHTIT

p. 242

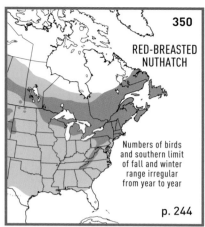

350

RED-BREASTED NUTHATCH

Numbers of birds and southern limit of fall and winter range irregular from year to year

p. 244

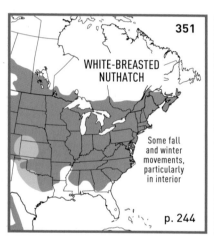

351

WHITE-BREASTED NUTHATCH

Some fall and winter movements, particularly in interior

p. 244

352

Accidental north to Great Lakes, NY

BROWN-HEADED NUTHATCH

p. 244

353

BROWN CREEPER

A few nest locally and irregularly south of mapped range

p. 244

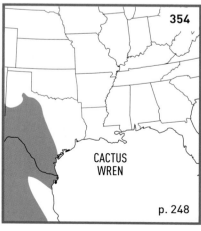

354

CACTUS WREN

p. 248

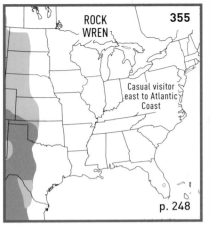

ROCK
WREN

355

Casual visitor
east to Atlantic
Coast

p. 248

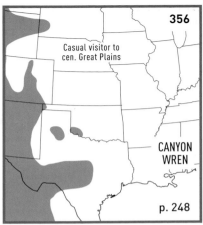

356

Casual visitor to
cen. Great Plains

CANYON
WREN

p. 248

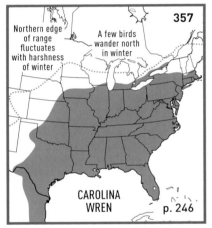

357

Northern edge
of range
fluctuates
with harshness
of winter

A few birds
wander north
in winter

CAROLINA
WREN

p. 246

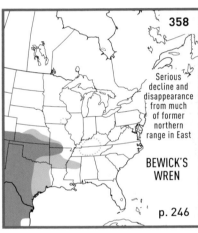

358

Serious
decline and
disappearance
from much
of former
northern
range in East

BEWICK'S
WREN

p. 246

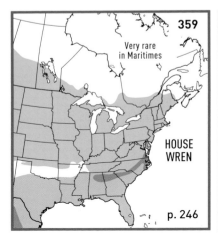

359

Very rare
in Maritimes

HOUSE
WREN

p. 246

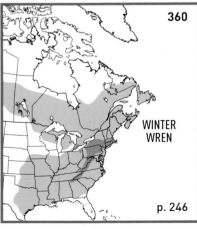

360

WINTER
WREN

p. 246

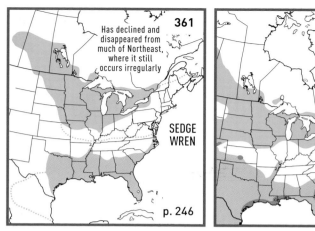

361

Has declined and disappeared from much of Northeast, where it still occurs irregularly

SEDGE WREN

p. 246

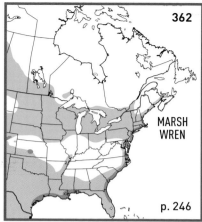

362

MARSH WREN

p. 246

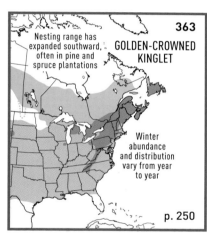

363

GOLDEN-CROWNED KINGLET

Nesting range has expanded southward, often in pine and spruce plantations

Winter abundance and distribution vary from year to year

p. 250

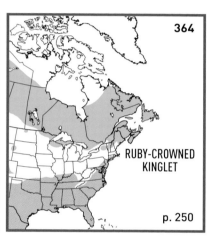

364

RUBY-CROWNED KINGLET

p. 250

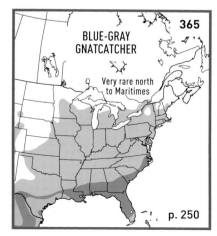

365

BLUE-GRAY GNATCATCHER

Very rare north to Maritimes

p. 250

366

BLACK-TAILED GNATCATCHER

p. 250

367

NORTHERN
WHEATEAR

Casual visitor in
remainder of
N. America,
mostly in fall

Winters in
Old World,
primarily in
Africa

p. 252

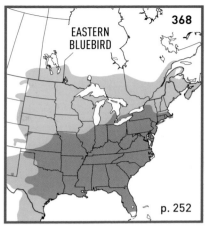

368

EASTERN
BLUEBIRD

p. 252

369

MOUNTAIN
BLUEBIRD

Casual visitor
outside mapped
range all the way
to East Coast,
mostly in fall and winter

Numbers of birds
and southern limit
of winter range
vary substantially
from year to year

p. 252

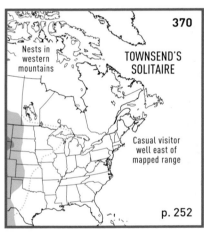

370

Nests in
western
mountains

TOWNSEND'S
SOLITAIRE

Casual visitor
well east of
mapped range

p. 252

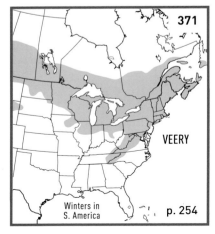

371

VEERY

Winters in
S. America

p. 254

372

GRAY-CHEEKED
THRUSH

Winters in
S. America

p. 254

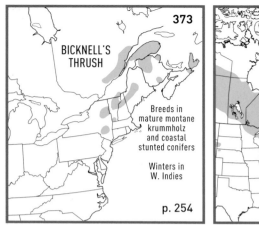

373

BICKNELL'S THRUSH

Breeds in mature montane krummholz and coastal stunted conifers

Winters in W. Indies

p. 254

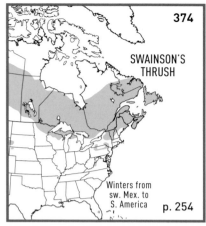

374

SWAINSON'S THRUSH

Winters from sw. Mex. to S. America

p. 254

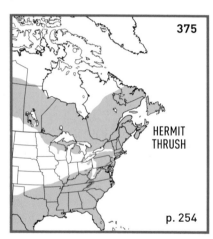

375

HERMIT THRUSH

p. 254

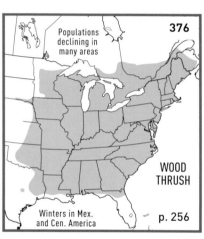

376

Populations declining in many areas

WOOD THRUSH

Winters in Mex. and Cen. America

p. 256

377

Winter populations may vary substantially from year to year depending on food supply

AMERICAN ROBIN

Recent breeding range expansion in southern regions

p. 256

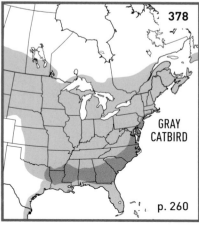

378

GRAY CATBIRD

p. 260

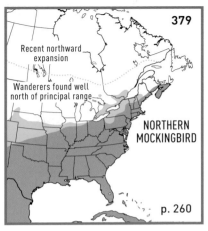

379

Recent northward expansion

Wanderers found well north of principal range

NORTHERN MOCKINGBIRD

p. 260

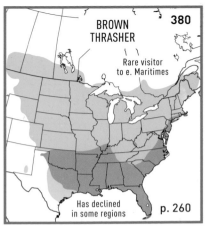

380

BROWN THRASHER

Rare visitor to e. Maritimes

Has declined in some regions

p. 260

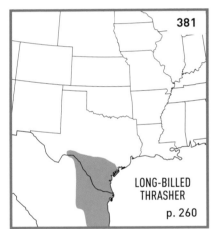

381

LONG-BILLED THRASHER

p. 260

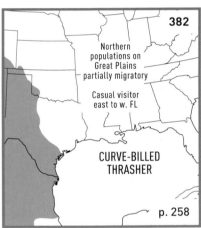

382

Northern populations on Great Plains partially migratory

Casual visitor east to w. FL

CURVE-BILLED THRASHER

p. 258

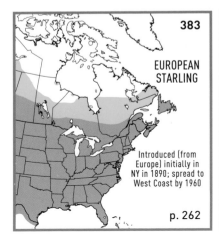

383

EUROPEAN STARLING

Introduced (from Europe) initially in NY in 1890; spread to West Coast by 1960

p. 262

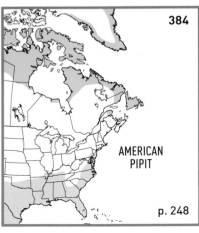

384

AMERICAN PIPIT

p. 248

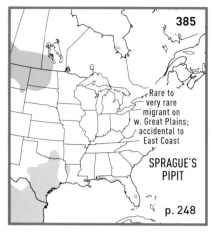

385

Rare to
very rare
migrant on
w. Great Plains;
accidental to
East Coast

SPRAGUE'S
PIPIT

p. 248

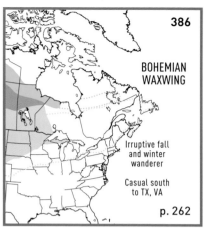

386

BOHEMIAN
WAXWING

Irruptive fall
and winter
wanderer

Casual south
to TX, VA

p. 262

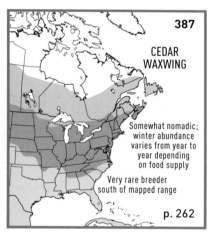

387

CEDAR
WAXWING

Somewhat nomadic;
winter abundance
varies from year to
year depending
on food supply

Very rare breeder
south of mapped range

p. 262

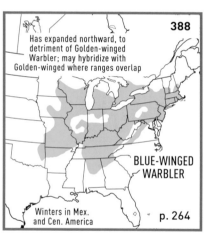

388

Has expanded northward, to
detriment of Golden-winged
Warbler; may hybridize with
Golden-winged where ranges overlap

BLUE-WINGED
WARBLER

Winters in Mex.
and Cen. America

p. 264

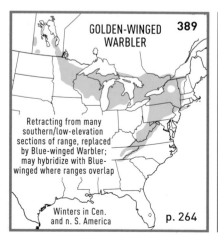

389

GOLDEN-WINGED
WARBLER

Retracting from many
southern/low-elevation
sections of range, replaced
by Blue-winged Warbler;
may hybridize with Blue-
winged where ranges overlap

Winters in Cen.
and n. S. America

p. 264

390

TENNESSEE
WARBLER

Recent overall
population
declines,
possibly cyclical

Winters from
Mex. to n. S. America

p. 266

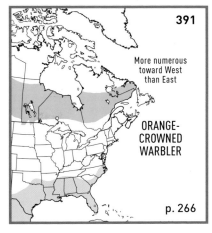

391

More numerous toward West than East

ORANGE-CROWNED WARBLER

p. 266

392

NASHVILLE WARBLER

Very rare in coastal Southeast

Winters mainly in Mex. and Cen. America

p. 266

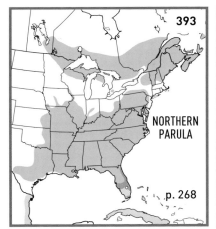

393

NORTHERN PARULA

p. 268

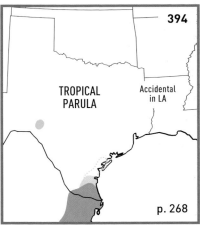

394

TROPICAL PARULA

Accidental in LA

p. 268

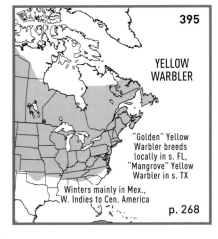

395

YELLOW WARBLER

"Golden" Yellow Warbler breeds locally in s. FL, "Mangrove" Yellow Warbler in s. TX

Winters mainly in Mex., W. Indies to Cen. America

p. 268

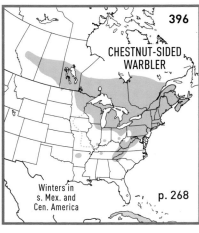

396

CHESTNUT-SIDED WARBLER

Winters in s. Mex. and Cen. America

p. 268

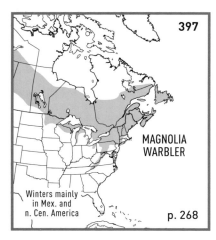

397

MAGNOLIA WARBLER

Winters mainly in Mex. and n. Cen. America

p. 268

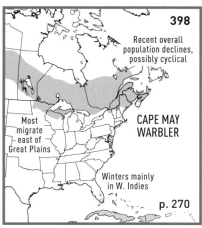

398

Recent overall population declines, possibly cyclical

CAPE MAY WARBLER

Most migrate east of Great Plains

Winters mainly in W. Indies

p. 270

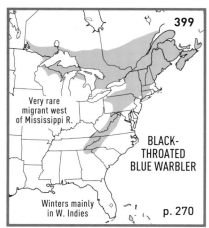

399

Very rare migrant west of Mississippi R.

BLACK-THROATED BLUE WARBLER

Winters mainly in W. Indies

p. 270

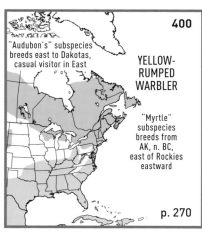

400

"Audubon's" subspecies breeds east to Dakotas, casual visitor in East

YELLOW-RUMPED WARBLER

"Myrtle" subspecies breeds from AK, n. BC, east of Rockies eastward

p. 270

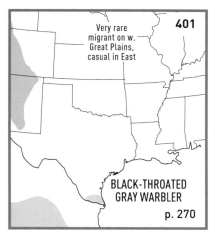

401

Very rare migrant on w. Great Plains, casual in East

BLACK-THROATED GRAY WARBLER

p. 270

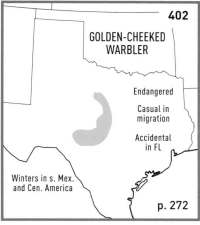

402

GOLDEN-CHEEKED WARBLER

Endangered

Casual in migration

Accidental in FL

Winters in s. Mex. and Cen. America

p. 272

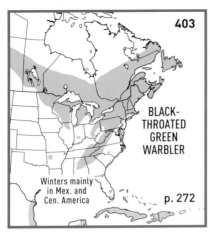

403

BLACK-THROATED GREEN WARBLER

Winters mainly in Mex. and Cen. America

p. 272

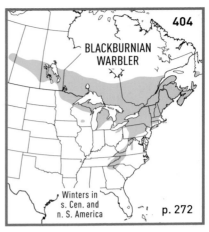

404

BLACKBURNIAN WARBLER

Winters in s. Cen. and n. S. America

p. 272

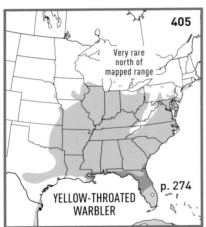

405

Very rare north of mapped range

YELLOW-THROATED WARBLER

p. 274

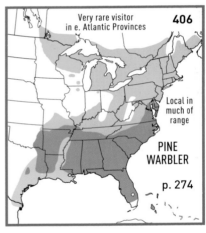

406

Very rare visitor in e. Atlantic Provinces

Local in much of range

PINE WARBLER

p. 274

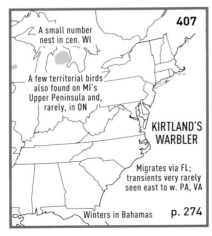

407

A small number nest in cen. WI

A few territorial birds also found on MI's Upper Peninsula and, rarely, in ON

KIRTLAND'S WARBLER

Migrates via FL; transients very rarely seen east to w. PA, VA

Winters in Bahamas

p. 274

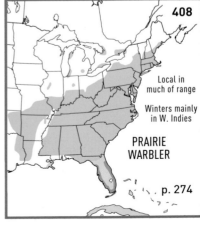

408

Local in much of range

Winters mainly in W. Indies

PRAIRIE WARBLER

p. 274

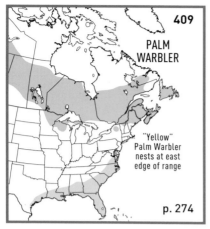

409

PALM
WARBLER

"Yellow"
Palm Warbler
nests at east
edge of range

p. 274

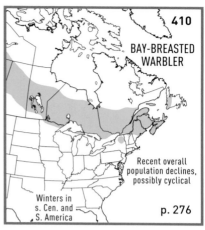

410

BAY-BREASTED
WARBLER

Recent overall
population declines,
possibly cyclical

Winters in
s. Cen. and
S. America

p. 276

411

BLACKPOLL
WARBLER

Most migrate
east of cen.
Great Plains

Winters in
n. S. America

p. 276

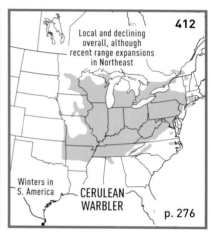

412

Local and declining
overall, although
recent range expansions
in Northeast

Winters in
S. America

CERULEAN
WARBLER

p. 276

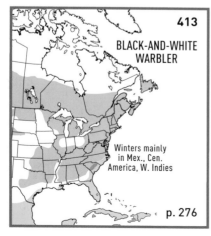

413

BLACK-AND-WHITE
WARBLER

Winters mainly
in Mex., Cen.
America, W. Indies

p. 276

414

AMERICAN
REDSTART

Winters in Mex.,
Cen. America, W. Indies

p. 276

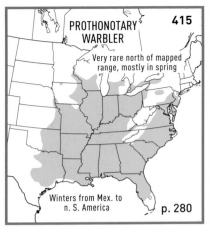

PROTHONOTARY WARBLER — **415**

Very rare north of mapped range, mostly in spring

Winters from Mex. to n. S. America

p. 280

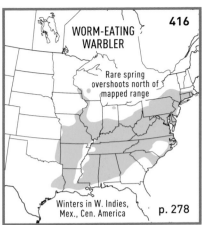

WORM-EATING WARBLER — **416**

Rare spring overshoots north of mapped range

Winters in W. Indies, Mex., Cen. America

p. 278

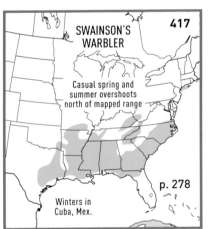

SWAINSON'S WARBLER — **417**

Casual spring and summer overshoots north of mapped range

Winters in Cuba, Mex.

p. 278

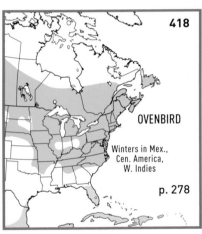

418

OVENBIRD

Winters in Mex., Cen. America, W. Indies

p. 278

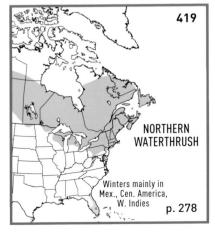

419

NORTHERN WATERTHRUSH

Winters mainly in Mex., Cen. America, W. Indies

420

LOUISIANA WATERTHRUSH

Winters in W. Indies, Mex. to n. S. America

p. 278

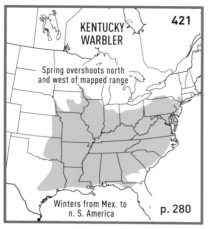

KENTUCKY
WARBLER
421
Spring overshoots north
and west of mapped range
Winters from Mex. to
n. S. America
p. 280

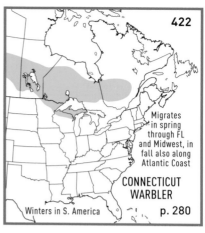

422
Migrates
in spring
through FL
and Midwest, in
fall also along
Atlantic Coast
CONNECTICUT
WARBLER
Winters in S. America
p. 280

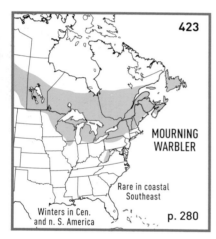

423
MOURNING
WARBLER
Rare in coastal
Southeast
Winters in Cen.
and n. S. America
p. 280

424
COMMON
YELLOWTHROAT
p. 282

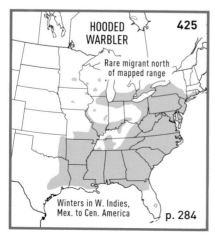

HOODED
WARBLER
425
Rare migrant north
of mapped range
Winters in W. Indies,
Mex. to Cen. America
p. 284

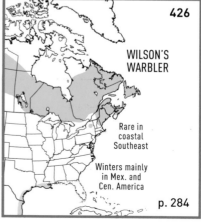

426
WILSON'S
WARBLER
Rare in
coastal
Southeast
Winters mainly
in Mex. and
Cen. America
p. 284

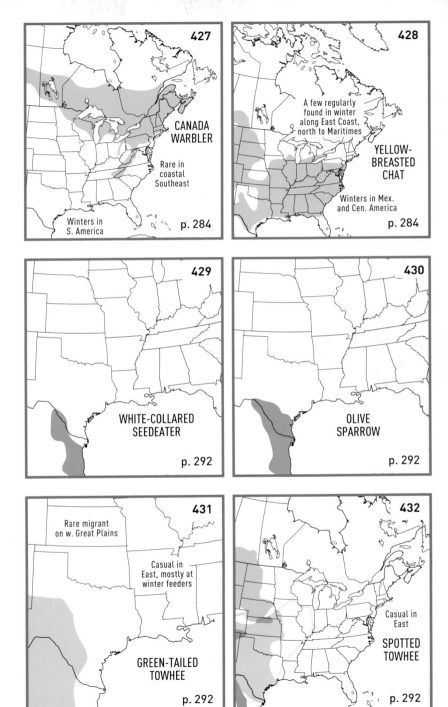

427

CANADA
WARBLER

Rare in
coastal
Southeast

Winters in
S. America

p. 284

428

A few regularly
found in winter
along East Coast,
north to Maritimes

YELLOW-
BREASTED
CHAT

Winters in Mex.
and Cen. America

p. 284

429

WHITE-COLLARED
SEEDEATER

p. 292

430

OLIVE
SPARROW

p. 292

431

Rare migrant
on w. Great Plains

Casual in
East, mostly at
winter feeders

GREEN-TAILED
TOWHEE

p. 292

432

Casual in
East

SPOTTED
TOWHEE

p. 292

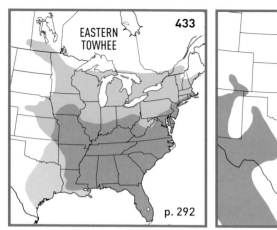

433 EASTERN TOWHEE

p. 292

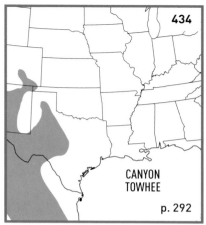

434 CANYON TOWHEE

p. 292

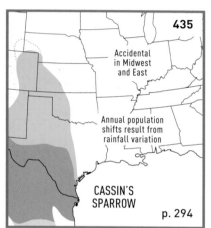

435

Accidental in Midwest and East

Annual population shifts result from rainfall variation

CASSIN'S SPARROW

p. 294

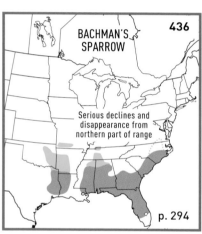

436 BACHMAN'S SPARROW

Serious declines and disappearance from northern part of range

p. 294

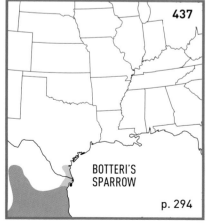

437

BOTTERI'S SPARROW

p. 294

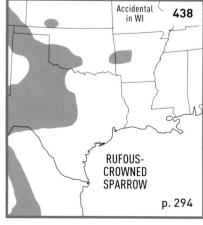

438

Accidental in WI

RUFOUS-CROWNED SPARROW

p. 294

439

AMERICAN TREE
SPARROW

Casual fall
visitor to
Gulf states

p. 296

440

Very rare to casual
in winter north of
mapped range

CHIPPING
SPARROW

p. 296

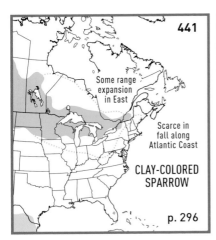

441

Some range
expansion
in East

Scarce in
fall along
Atlantic Coast

CLAY-COLORED
SPARROW

p. 296

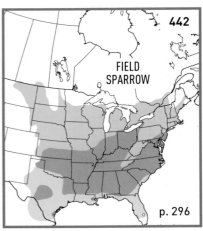

442

FIELD
SPARROW

p. 296

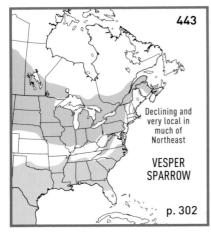

443

Declining and
very local in
much of
Northeast

VESPER
SPARROW

p. 302

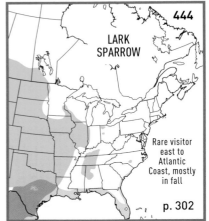

444

LARK
SPARROW

Rare visitor
east to
Atlantic
Coast, mostly
in fall

p. 302

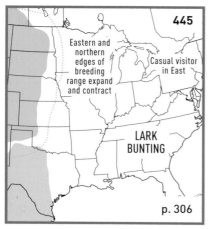

445

Eastern and
northern
edges of
breeding
range expand
and contract

Casual visitor
in East

LARK
BUNTING

p. 306

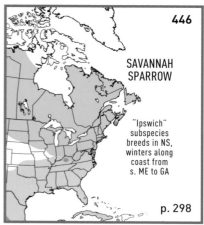

446

SAVANNAH
SPARROW

"Ipswich"
subspecies
breeds in NS,
winters along
coast from
s. ME to GA

p. 298

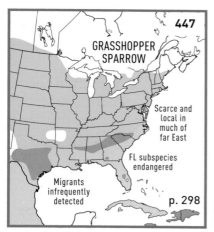

447

GRASSHOPPER
SPARROW

Scarce and
local in
much of
far East

FL subspecies
endangered

Migrants
infrequently
detected

p. 298

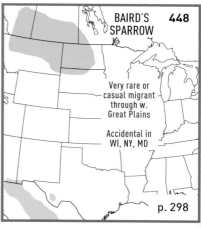

BAIRD'S
SPARROW

448

Very rare or
casual migrant
through w.
Great Plains

Accidental in
WI, NY, MD

p. 298

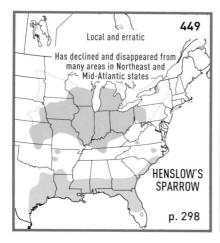

449

Local and erratic

Has declined and disappeared from
many areas in Northeast and
Mid-Atlantic states

HENSLOW'S
SPARROW

p. 298

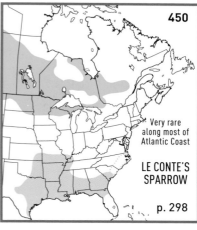

450

Very rare
along most of
Atlantic Coast

LE CONTE'S
SPARROW

p. 298

451

Scarce migrant through interior

NELSON'S SPARROW

p. 300

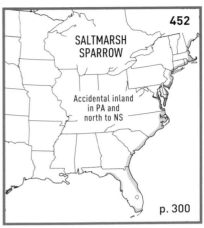

452

SALTMARSH SPARROW

Accidental inland in PA and north to NS

p. 300

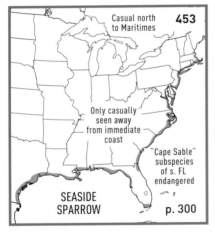

453

Casual north to Maritimes

Only casually seen away from immediate coast

"Cape Sable" subspecies of s. FL endangered

SEASIDE SPARROW

p. 300

454

Winters casually north to Great Lakes

FOX SPARROW

p. 302

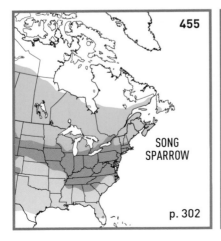

455

SONG SPARROW

p. 302

456

More numerous and easier to find in western half of range

LINCOLN'S SPARROW

p. 302

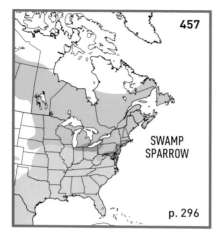

457

SWAMP
SPARROW

p. 296

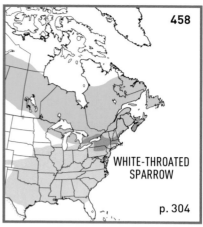

458

WHITE-THROATED
SPARROW

p. 304

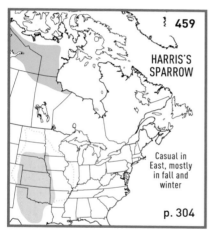

459

HARRIS'S
SPARROW

Casual in
East, mostly
in fall and
winter

p. 304

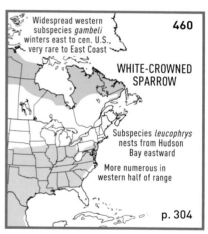

460

Widespread western
subspecies *gambeli*
winters east to cen. U.S.,
very rare to East Coast

WHITE-CROWNED
SPARROW

Subspecies *leucophrys*
nests from Hudson
Bay eastward

More numerous in
western half of range

p. 304

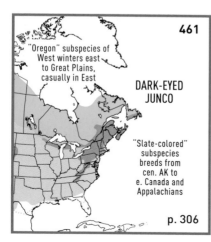

461

"Oregon" subspecies of
West winters east
to Great Plains,
casually in East

DARK-EYED
JUNCO

"Slate-colored"
subspecies breeds
from cen. AK to
e. Canada and
Appalachians

p. 306

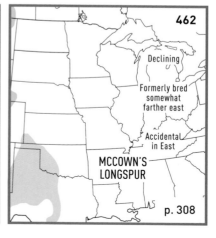

462

Declining

Formerly bred
somewhat
farther east

Accidental
in East

MCCOWN'S
LONGSPUR

p. 308

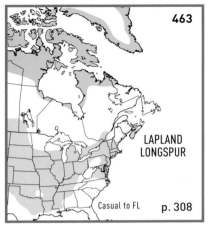

463

LAPLAND
LONGSPUR

Casual to FL

p. 308

464

SMITH'S
LONGSPUR

Rare spring
transient in
Midwest

Casual to
East Coast

p. 308

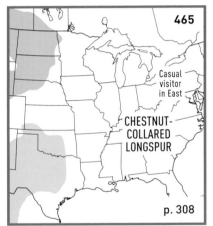

465

Casual
visitor
in East

CHESTNUT-
COLLARED
LONGSPUR

p. 308

466

SNOW
BUNTING

Accidental south
to s. TX, n. FL

p. 306

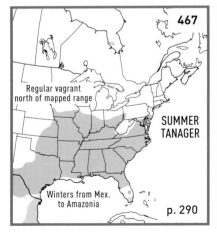

467

Regular vagrant
north of mapped range

SUMMER
TANAGER

Winters from Mex.
to Amazonia

p. 290

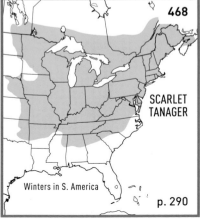

468

SCARLET
TANAGER

Winters in S. America

p. 290

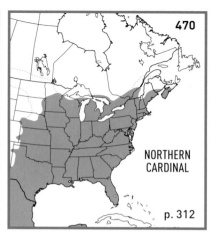

469

Casual east from cen. Great Plains to East Coast (where some visit winter feeders)

WESTERN TANAGER

Winters primarily in Mex. and Cen. America

p. 290

470

NORTHERN CARDINAL

p. 312

471

Accidental in ON

PYRRHULOXIA

p. 312

472

ROSE-BREASTED GROSBEAK

Winters primarily in Mex., Cen. America, W. Indies

p. 310

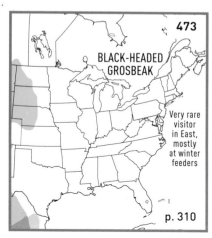

473

BLACK-HEADED GROSBEAK

Very rare visitor in East, mostly at winter feeders

p. 310

474

Rare visitor north to Maritimes

Some northward expansion in breeding range

BLUE GROSBEAK

Winters mainly in Mex., Cen. America

p. 312

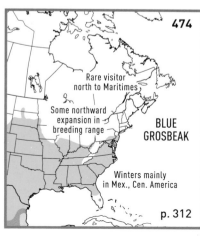

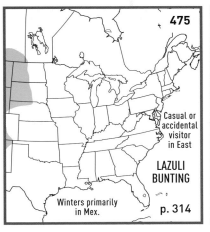

475

Casual or accidental visitor in East

LAZULI BUNTING

Winters primarily in Mex.

476

INDIGO BUNTING

Rare migrant in Maritimes

A few winter records along East Coast

Winters mainly in Mex., Cen. America, W. Indies

p. 314

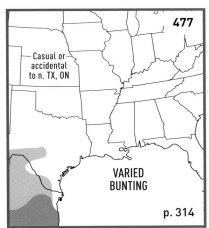

477

Casual or accidental to n. TX, ON

VARIED BUNTING

p. 314

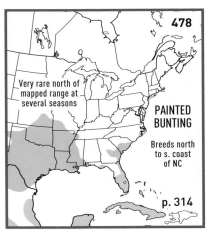

478

Very rare north of mapped range at several seasons

PAINTED BUNTING

Breeds north to s. coast of NC

p. 314

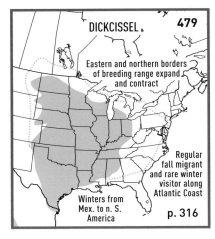

479

DICKCISSEL

Eastern and northern borders of breeding range expand and contract

Regular fall migrant and rare winter visitor along Atlantic Coast

Winters from Mex. to n. S. America

p. 316

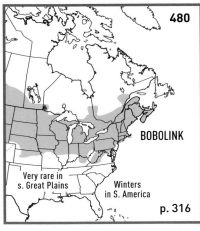

480

BOBOLINK

Very rare in s. Great Plains

Winters in S. America

p. 316

481

Accidental in NU

**RED-WINGED
BLACKBIRD**

p. 318

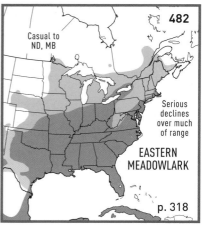

482

Casual to
ND, MB

Serious
declines
over much
of range

**EASTERN
MEADOWLARK**

p. 318

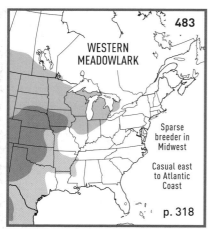

483

**WESTERN
MEADOWLARK**

Sparse
breeder in
Midwest

Casual east
to Atlantic
Coast

p. 318

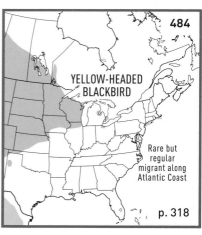

484

**YELLOW-HEADED
BLACKBIRD**

Rare but
regular
migrant along
Atlantic Coast

p. 318

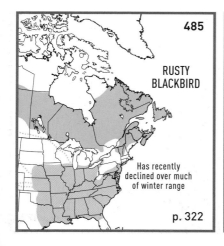

485

**RUSTY
BLACKBIRD**

Has recently
declined over much
of winter range

p. 322

486

**BREWER'S
BLACKBIRD**

Very rare visitor in
most areas east of
Mississippi R.

p. 322

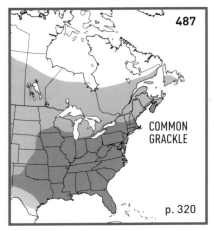

COMMON GRACLE

487

p. 320

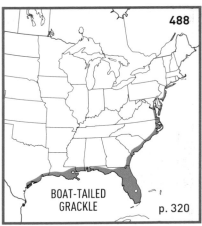

488

BOAT-TAILED GRACLE

p. 320

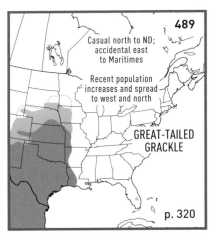

489

Casual north to ND; accidental east to Maritimes

Recent population increases and spread to west and north

GREAT-TAILED GRACLE

p. 320

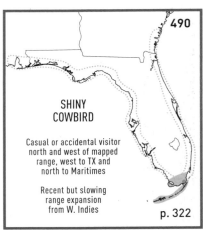

490

SHINY COWBIRD

Casual or accidental visitor north and west of mapped range, west to TX and north to Maritimes

Recent but slowing range expansion from W. Indies

p. 322

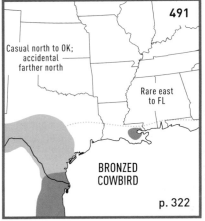

491

Casual north to OK; accidental farther north

Rare east to FL

BRONZED COWBIRD

p. 322

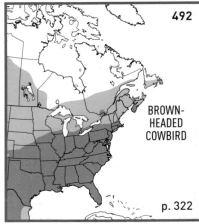

492

BROWN-HEADED COWBIRD

p. 322

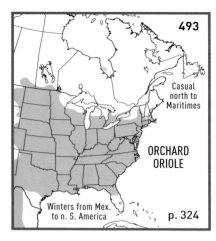

493

Casual north to Maritimes

ORCHARD ORIOLE

Winters from Mex. to n. S. America

p. 324

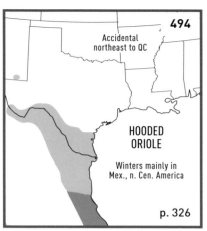

494

Accidental northeast to QC

HOODED ORIOLE

Winters mainly in Mex., n. Cen. America

p. 326

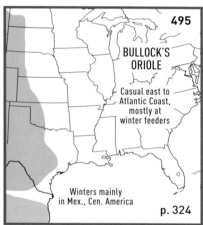

495

BULLOCK'S ORIOLE

Casual east to Atlantic Coast, mostly at winter feeders

Winters mainly in Mex., Cen. America

p. 324

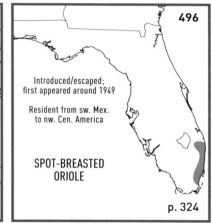

496

Introduced/escaped; first appeared around 1949

Resident from sw. Mex. to nw. Cen. America

SPOT-BREASTED ORIOLE

p. 324

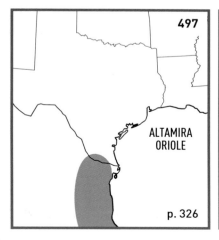

497

ALTAMIRA ORIOLE

p. 326

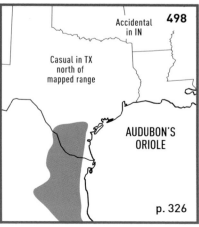

498

Accidental in IN

Casual in TX north of mapped range

AUDUBON'S ORIOLE

p. 326

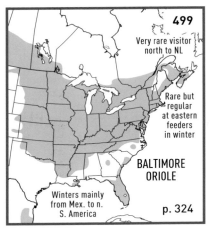

499

Very rare visitor north to NL

Rare but regular at eastern feeders in winter

BALTIMORE ORIOLE

Winters mainly from Mex. to n. S. America

p. 324

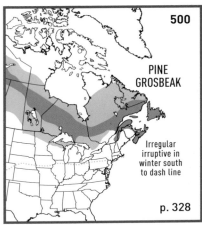

500

PINE GROSBEAK

Irregular irruptive in winter south to dash line

p. 328

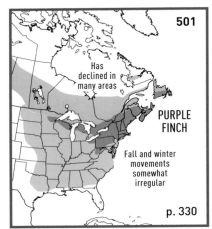

501

Has declined in many areas

PURPLE FINCH

Fall and winter movements somewhat irregular

p. 330

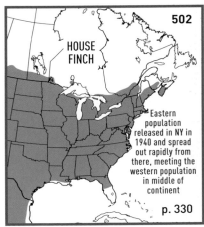

502

HOUSE FINCH

Eastern population released in NY in 1940 and spread out rapidly from there, meeting the western population in middle of continent

p. 330

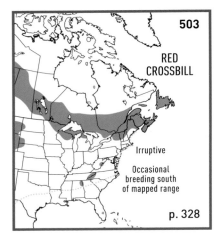

503

RED CROSSBILL

Irruptive

Occasional breeding south of mapped range

p. 328

504

WHITE-WINGED CROSSBILL

Irruptive

Rarely breeds south of mapped range

Irregularly irruptive in fall and winter south to dash line, casually farther

p. 328

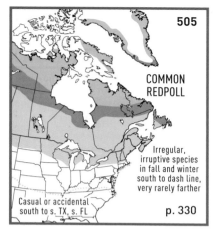

505

COMMON REDPOLL

Irregular, irruptive species in fall and winter south to dash line, very rarely farther

Casual or accidental south to s. TX, s. FL

p. 330

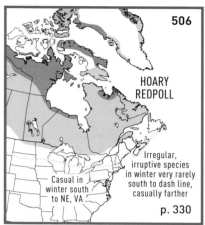

506

HOARY REDPOLL

Casual in winter south to NE, VA

Irregular, irruptive species in winter very rarely south to dash line, casually farther

p. 330

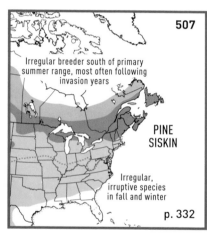

507

Irregular breeder south of primary summer range, most often following invasion years

PINE SISKIN

Irregular, irruptive species in fall and winter

p. 332

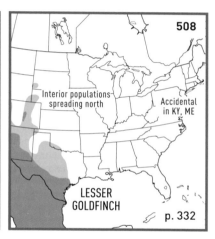

508

Interior populations spreading north

Accidental in KY, ME

LESSER GOLDFINCH

p. 332

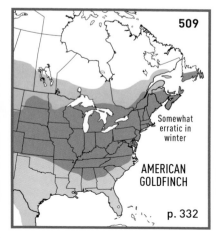

509

Somewhat erratic in winter

AMERICAN GOLDFINCH

p. 332

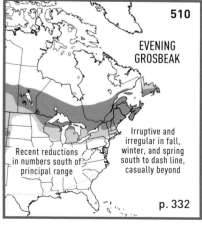

510

EVENING GROSBEAK

Irruptive and irregular in fall, winter, and spring south to dash line, casually beyond

Recent reductions in numbers south of principal range

p. 332

511

Introduced
(from Europe)
initially to
NY in 1840

HOUSE
SPARROW

p. 316

512

Accidental
to NE,
MB, MN

Some northward
range expansion
from initial
release around
St. Louis in 1870

EURASIAN
TREE SPARROW

p. 316

LIFE LIST

Keep a Life List. Check off the birds you have seen.

The list on the following pages includes all of the birds shown on the plates, except for some of the accidentals that have not been verified.

For a checklist of all the birds of North America, see the *ABA Checklist: Birds of the Continental United States and Canada,* compiled by the Checklist Committee of the American Birding Association, 4945 North 30th Street, Suite 200, Colorado Springs, CO 80919-3151 (www.aba.org/checklist). It lists every species that has occurred north of the Mexican border.

In the following list, birds are grouped first under orders (identified by the Latin ending *-formes*), followed by families (*-dae* ending), and then species. Sequencing of orders and families follows the American Ornithologists' Union's Check-list of North American Birds (1998 through the 50th supplement, from 2009), as do the scientific names for genus and species. Scientific names are not given below but can be found in the species accounts throughout the book.

Species marked with an asterisk are exotic and unestablished. Though not countable on official ABA lists, they are included here because birders may encounter them and wish to record their sightings.

ORDER ANSERIFORMES

Ducks, Geese, and Swans (Anatidae)
_____Black-bellied Whistling-Duck
_____Fulvous Whistling-Duck
_____Greater White-fronted Goose
_____Snow Goose
_____Ross's Goose
_____Brant
_____Barnacle Goose
_____Cackling Goose
_____Canada Goose
_____Mute Swan
_____Trumpeter Swan
_____Tundra Swan
_____Muscovy Duck
_____Wood Duck
_____Gadwall
_____Eurasian Wigeon

_____American Wigeon
_____American Black Duck
_____Mallard
_____Mottled Duck
_____Blue-winged Teal
_____Cinnamon Teal
_____Northern Shoveler
_____White-cheeked Pintail
_____Northern Pintail
_____Garganey
_____Baikal Teal
_____Green-winged Teal
_____Canvasback
_____Redhead
_____Ring-necked Duck
_____Tufted Duck
_____Greater Scaup
_____Lesser Scaup
_____King Eider
_____Common Eider
_____Harlequin Duck
_____Surf Scoter
_____White-winged Scoter
_____Black Scoter
_____Long-tailed Duck
_____Bufflehead
_____Common Goldeneye
_____Barrow's Goldeneye
_____Smew
_____Hooded Merganser
_____Common Merganser
_____Red-breasted Merganser
_____Masked Duck
_____Ruddy Duck

ORDER GALLIFORMES

Curassows and Guans (Cracidae)
_____Plain Chachalaca
New World Quail (Odontophoridae)
_____Scaled Quail
_____Northern Bobwhite
Partridges, Grouse, Turkeys, and Old World Quail (Phasianidae)
_____Chukar
_____Gray Partridge
_____Ring-necked Pheasant
_____Ruffed Grouse
_____Spruce Grouse
_____Willow Ptarmigan
_____Rock Ptarmigan
_____Sharp-tailed Grouse
_____Greater Prairie-Chicken
_____Lesser Prairie-Chicken
_____Wild Turkey

ORDER GAVIIFORMES

Loons (Gaviidae)
_____Pacific Loon
_____Common Loon
_____Yellow-billed Loon

ORDER PODICIPEDIFORMES

Grebes (Podicipedidae)
_____Least Grebe
_____Pied-billed Grebe
_____Horned Grebe
_____Red-necked Grebe
_____Eared Grebe
_____Western Grebe
_____Clark's Grebe

ORDER PHOENICOPTERIFORMES

Flamingos (Phoenicopteridae)
_____American Flamingo

ORDER PROCELLARIIFORMES

Albatrosses (Diomedeidae)
_____Yellow-nosed Albatross
_____Black-browed Albatross
Shearwaters and Petrels (Procellariidae)
_____Northern Fulmar
_____Herald Petrel
_____Bermuda Petrel
_____Black-capped Petrel
_____Fea's/Zino's Petrel
_____Cory's Shearwater
_____Greater Shearwater
_____Sooty Shearwater
_____Manx Shearwater
_____Audubon's Shearwater
Storm-Petrels (Hydrobatidae)
_____Wilson's Storm-Petrel
_____White-faced Storm-Petrel
_____European Storm-Petrel

_____Leach's Storm-Petrel
_____Band-rumped Storm-Petrel

ORDER PELECANIFORMES

Tropicbirds (Phaethontidae)
_____White-tailed Tropicbird
_____Red-billed Tropicbird
Boobies and Gannets (Sulidae)
_____Masked Booby
_____Brown Booby
_____Red-footed Booby
_____Northern Gannet
Pelicans (Pelecanidae)
_____American White Pelican
_____Brown Pelican
Cormorants (Phalacrocoracidae)
_____Neotropic Cormorant
_____Double-crested Cormorant
_____Great Cormorant
Darters (Anhingidae)
_____Anhinga
Frigatebirds (Fregatidae)
_____Magnificent Frigatebird

ORDER CICONIIFORMES

**Bitterns, Herons, and Allies
   (Ardeidae)**
_____American Bittern
_____Least Bittern
_____Great Blue Heron
_____Great Egret
_____Little Egret
_____Snowy Egret
_____Little Blue Heron
_____Tricolored Heron
_____Reddish Egret
_____Cattle Egret
_____Green Heron
_____Black-crowned Night-Heron
_____Yellow-crowned Night-Heron
**Ibises and Spoonbills
   (Threskiornithidae)**
_____White Ibis
_____Glossy Ibis
_____White-faced Ibis
_____Roseate Spoonbill
Storks (Ciconiidae)
_____Wood Stork

New World Vultures (Cathartidae)
_____Black Vulture
_____Turkey Vulture

ORDER FALCONIFORMES

**Hawks, Kites, Eagles, and Allies
   (Accipitridae)**
_____Osprey
_____Hook-billed Kite
_____Swallow-tailed Kite
_____White-tailed Kite
_____Snail Kite
_____Mississippi Kite
_____Bald Eagle
_____Northern Harrier
_____Sharp-shinned Hawk
_____Cooper's Hawk
_____Northern Goshawk
_____Harris's Hawk
_____Red-shouldered Hawk
_____Broad-winged Hawk
_____Gray Hawk
_____Short-tailed Hawk
_____Swainson's Hawk
_____White-tailed Hawk
_____Zone-tailed Hawk
_____Red-tailed Hawk
_____Ferruginous Hawk
_____Rough-legged Hawk
_____Golden Eagle
Caracaras and Falcons (Falconidae)
_____Crested Caracara
_____American Kestrel
_____Merlin
_____Aplomado Falcon
_____Gyrfalcon
_____Peregrine Falcon
_____Prairie Falcon

ORDER GRUIFORMES

Rails, Gallinules, and Coots (Rallidae)
_____Yellow Rail
_____Black Rail
_____Clapper Rail
_____King Rail
_____Virginia Rail
_____Sora
_____Purple Gallinule

_____Common Moorhen
_____American Coot
Limpkins (Aramidae)
_____Limpkin
Cranes (Gruidae)
_____Sandhill Crane
_____Common Crane
_____Whooping Crane

ORDER CHARADRIIFORMES

Lapwings and Plovers (Charadriidae)
_____Northern Lapwing
_____Black-bellied Plover
_____European Golden-Plover
_____American Golden-Plover
_____Pacific Golden-Plover
_____Snowy Plover
_____Wilson's Plover
_____Common Ringed Plover
_____Semipalmated Plover
_____Piping Plover
_____Killdeer
_____Mountain Plover
Oystercatchers (Haematopodidae)
_____American Oystercatcher
Stilts and Avocets (Recurvirostridae)
_____Black-necked Stilt
_____American Avocet
Jacanas (Jacanidae)
_____Northern Jacana
**Sandpipers, Phalaropes, and Allies
(Scolopacidae)**
_____Spotted Sandpiper
_____Solitary Sandpiper
_____Spotted Redshank
_____Greater Yellowlegs
_____Willet
_____Lesser Yellowlegs
_____Upland Sandpiper
_____Eskimo Curlew
_____Whimbrel
_____Long-billed Curlew
_____Black-tailed Godwit
_____Hudsonian Godwit
_____Bar-tailed Godwit
_____Marbled Godwit
_____Ruddy Turnstone
_____Red Knot

_____Sanderling
_____Semipalmated Sandpiper
_____Western Sandpiper
_____Red-necked Stint
_____Little Stint
_____Least Sandpiper
_____White-rumped Sandpiper
_____Baird's Sandpiper
_____Pectoral Sandpiper
_____Sharp-tailed Sandpiper
_____Purple Sandpiper
_____Dunlin
_____Curlew Sandpiper
_____Stilt Sandpiper
_____Buff-breasted Sandpiper
_____Ruff
_____Short-billed Dowitcher
_____Long-billed Dowitcher
_____Wilson's Snipe
_____American Woodcock
_____Wilson's Phalarope
_____Red-necked Phalarope
_____Red Phalarope
Gulls, Terns, and Skimmers (Laridae)
_____Black-legged Kittiwake
_____Ivory Gull
_____Sabine's Gull
_____Bonaparte's Gull
_____Black-headed Gull
_____Little Gull
_____Ross's Gull
_____Laughing Gull
_____Franklin's Gull
_____Black-tailed Gull
_____Mew Gull
_____Ring-billed Gull
_____California Gull
_____Herring Gull
_____Yellow-legged Gull
_____Thayer's Gull
_____Iceland Gull
_____Lesser Black-backed Gull
_____Slaty-backed Gull
_____Glaucous Gull
_____Great Black-backed Gull
_____Brown Noddy
_____Black Noddy
_____Sooty Tern

_____Bridled Tern
_____Least Tern
_____Gull-billed Tern
_____Caspian Tern
_____Black Tern
_____White-winged Tern
_____Roseate Tern
_____Common Tern
_____Arctic Tern
_____Forster's Tern
_____Royal Tern
_____Sandwich Tern
_____Black Skimmer

Skuas and Jaegers (Stercorariidae)
_____Great Skua
_____South Polar Skua
_____Pomarine Jaeger
_____Parasitic Jaeger
_____Long-tailed Jaeger

Auks, Murres, and Puffins (Alcidae)
_____Dovekie
_____Common Murre
_____Thick-billed Murre
_____Razorbill
_____Black Guillemot
_____Long-billed Murrelet
_____Ancient Murrelet
_____Atlantic Puffin

ORDER COLUMBIFORMES

Pigeons and Doves (Columbidae)
_____Rock Pigeon
_____White-crowned Pigeon
_____Red-billed Pigeon
_____Band-tailed Pigeon
_____Eurasian Collared-Dove
_____African Collared-Dove*
_____White-winged Dove
_____Mourning Dove
_____Inca Dove
_____Common Ground-Dove
_____Ruddy Ground-Dove
_____White-tipped Dove

ORDER PSITTACIFORMES

Lories, Parakeets, Macaws, and Parrots (Psittacidae)
_____Budgerigar
_____Monk Parakeet

_____Green Parakeet
_____Mitred Parakeet*
_____Black-hooded Parakeet*
_____White-winged Parakeet
_____White-fronted Parrot*
_____Yellow-chevroned Parakeet*
_____Red-crowned Parrot
_____Lilac-crowned Parrot*
_____Yellow-headed Parrot*
_____Red-lored Parrot*

ORDER CUCULIFORMES

Cuckoos, Roadrunners, and Anis (Cuculidae)
_____Yellow-billed Cuckoo
_____Mangrove Cuckoo
_____Black-billed Cuckoo
_____Greater Roadrunner
_____Smooth-billed Ani
_____Groove-billed Ani

ORDER STRIGIFORMES

Barn Owls (Tytonidae)
_____Barn Owl
Typical Owls (Strigidae)
_____Eastern Screech-Owl
_____Great Horned Owl
_____Snowy Owl
_____Northern Hawk Owl
_____Ferruginous Pygmy-Owl
_____Elf Owl
_____Burrowing Owl
_____Barred Owl
_____Great Gray Owl
_____Long-eared Owl
_____Short-eared Owl
_____Boreal Owl
_____Northern Saw-whet Owl

ORDER CAPRIMULGIFORMES

Goatsuckers (Caprimulgidae)
_____Lesser Nighthawk
_____Common Nighthawk
_____Antillean Nighthawk
_____Common Pauraque
_____Common Poorwill
_____Chuck-will's-widow
_____Whip-poor-will

ORDER APODIFORMES

Swifts (Apodidae)
_____Chimney Swift

Hummingbirds (Trochilidae)
_____Green Violetear
_____Green-breasted Mango
_____Broad-billed Hummingbird
_____Buff-bellied Hummingbird
_____Ruby-throated Hummingbird
_____Black-chinned Hummingbird
_____Calliope Hummingbird
_____Broad-tailed Hummingbird
_____Rufous Hummingbird
_____Allen's Hummingbird

ORDER CORACIIFORMES

Kingfishers (Alcedinidae)
_____Ringed Kingfisher
_____Belted Kingfisher
_____Green Kingfisher

ORDER PICIFORMES

Woodpeckers and Allies (Picidae)
_____Red-headed Woodpecker
_____Golden-fronted Woodpecker
_____Red-bellied Woodpecker
_____Williamson's Sapsucker
_____Yellow-bellied Sapsucker
_____Red-naped Sapsucker
_____Ladder-backed Woodpecker
_____Downy Woodpecker
_____Hairy Woodpecker
_____Red-cockaded Woodpecker
_____American Three-toed
          Woodpecker
_____Black-backed Woodpecker
_____Northern Flicker
_____Pileated Woodpecker
_____Ivory-billed Woodpecker

ORDER PASSERIFORMES

Tyrant Flycatchers (Tyrannidae)
_____Northern Beardless-Tyrannulet
_____Olive-sided Flycatcher
_____Western Wood-Pewee
_____Eastern Wood-Pewee
_____Yellow-bellied Flycatcher
_____Acadian Flycatcher
_____Alder Flycatcher

_____Willow Flycatcher
_____Least Flycatcher
_____Black Phoebe
_____Eastern Phoebe
_____Say's Phoebe
_____Vermilion Flycatcher
_____Ash-throated Flycatcher
_____Great Crested Flycatcher
_____Brown-crested Flycatcher
_____La Sagra's Flycatcher
_____Great Kiskadee
_____Tropical Kingbird
_____Couch's Kingbird
_____Western Kingbird
_____Eastern Kingbird
_____Gray Kingbird
_____Scissor-tailed Flycatcher
_____Fork-tailed Flycatcher
_____Rose-throated Becard

Shrikes (Laniidae)
_____Loggerhead Shrike
_____Northern Shrike

Vireos (Vireonidae)
_____White-eyed Vireo
_____Bell's Vireo
_____Black-capped Vireo
_____Yellow-throated Vireo
_____Blue-headed Vireo
_____Warbling Vireo
_____Philadelphia Vireo
_____Red-eyed Vireo
_____Yellow-green Vireo
_____Black-whiskered Vireo

Jays and Crows (Corvidae)
_____Gray Jay
_____Blue Jay
_____Green Jay
_____Brown Jay
_____Florida Scrub-Jay
_____Western Scrub-Jay
_____Black-billed Magpie
_____American Crow
_____Tamaulipas Crow
_____Fish Crow
_____Chihuahuan Raven
_____Common Raven

Larks (Alaudidae)
_____Horned Lark

Swallows (Hirundinidae)
_____Purple Martin
_____Tree Swallow
_____Violet-green Swallow
_____Northern Rough-winged
        Swallow
_____Bank Swallow
_____Cliff Swallow
_____Cave Swallow
_____Barn Swallow

Chickadees and Titmice (Paridae)
_____Carolina Chickadee
_____Black-capped Chickadee
_____Boreal Chickadee
_____Gray-headed Chickadee
_____Tufted Titmouse
_____Black-crested Titmouse

Verdin (Remizidae)
_____Verdin

Bushtits (Aegithalidae)
_____Bushtit

Nuthatches (Sittidae)
_____Red-breasted Nuthatch
_____White-breasted Nuthatch
_____Brown-headed Nuthatch

Creepers (Certhiidae)
_____Brown Creeper

Wrens (Troglodytidae)
_____Cactus Wren
_____Rock Wren
_____Canyon Wren
_____Carolina Wren
_____Bewick's Wren
_____House Wren
_____Winter Wren
_____Sedge Wren
_____Marsh Wren

Bulbuls (Pycnonotidae)
_____Red-whiskered Bulbul

Kinglets (Regulidae)
_____Golden-crowned Kinglet
_____Ruby-crowned Kinglet

Old World Warblers and Gnatcatchers (Sylviidae)
_____Blue-gray Gnatcatcher
_____Black-tailed Gnatcatcher

Thrushes (Turdidae)
_____Northern Wheatear
_____Eastern Bluebird
_____Mountain Bluebird
_____Townsend's Solitaire
_____Veery
_____Gray-cheeked Thrush
_____Bicknell's Thrush
_____Swainson's Thrush
_____Hermit Thrush
_____Wood Thrush
_____Fieldfare
_____Redwing
_____Clay-colored Thrush
_____Rufous-backed Robin
_____American Robin
_____Varied Thrush

Mockingbirds and Thrashers (Mimidae)
_____Gray Catbird
_____Northern Mockingbird
_____Bahama Mockingbird
_____Sage Thrasher
_____Brown Thrasher
_____Long-billed Thrasher
_____Curve-billed Thrasher

Starlings (Sturnidae)
_____European Starling
_____Hill Myna*
_____Common Myna

Wagtails and Pipits (Motacillidae)
_____American Pipit
_____Sprague's Pipit

Waxwings (Bombycillidae)
_____Bohemian Waxwing
_____Cedar Waxwing

Wood-Warblers (Parulidae)
_____Bachman's Warbler
_____Blue-winged Warbler
_____Golden-winged Warbler
_____Tennessee Warbler
_____Orange-crowned Warbler
_____Nashville Warbler
_____Northern Parula
_____Tropical Parula
_____Yellow Warbler
_____Chestnut-sided Warbler
_____Magnolia Warbler
_____Cape May Warbler
_____Black-throated Blue Warbler
_____Yellow-rumped Warbler
_____Black-throated Gray Warbler
_____Golden-cheeked Warbler
_____Black-throated Green Warbler

_____Townsend's Warbler
_____Blackburnian Warbler
_____Yellow-throated Warbler
_____Pine Warbler
_____Kirtland's Warbler
_____Prairie Warbler
_____Bay-breasted Warbler
_____Blackpoll Warbler
_____Cerulean Warbler
_____Black-and-white Warbler
_____American Redstart
_____Prothonotary Warbler
_____Worm-eating Warbler
_____Swainson's Warbler
_____Ovenbird
_____Northern Waterthrush
_____Louisiana Waterthrush
_____Kentucky Warbler
_____Connecticut Warbler
_____Mourning Warbler
_____Common Yellowthroat
_____Gray-crowned Yellowthroat
_____Hooded Warbler
_____Wilson's Warbler
_____Canada Warbler
_____Fan-tailed Warbler
_____Golden-crowned Warbler
_____Rufous-capped Warbler
_____Yellow-breasted Chat

Bananaquits
_____Bananaquit

Tanagers (Thraupidae)
_____Western Spindalis

Emberizids (Emberizidae)
_____White-collared Seedeater
_____Olive Sparrow
_____Green-tailed Towhee
_____Spotted Towhee
_____Eastern Towhee
_____Canyon Towhee
_____Cassin's Sparrow
_____Bachman's Sparrow
_____Botteri's Sparrow
_____Rufous-crowned Sparrow
_____American Tree Sparrow
_____Chipping Sparrow
_____Clay-colored Sparrow
_____Field Sparrow
_____Vesper Sparrow
_____Lark Sparrow

_____Black-throated Sparrow
_____Lark Bunting
_____Savannah Sparrow
_____Grasshopper Sparrow
_____Baird's Sparrow
_____Henslow's Sparrow
_____Le Conte's Sparrow
_____Nelson's Sparrow
_____Saltmarsh Sparrow
_____Seaside Sparrow
_____Fox Sparrow
_____Song Sparrow
_____Lincoln's Sparrow
_____Swamp Sparrow
_____White-throated Sparrow
_____Harris's Sparrow
_____White-crowned Sparrow
_____Golden-crowned Sparrow
_____Dark-eyed Junco
_____McCown's Longspur
_____Lapland Longspur
_____Smith's Longspur
_____Chestnut-collared Longspur
_____Snow Bunting

Cardinals, Saltators, and Allies (Cardinalidae)
_____Summer Tanager
_____Scarlet Tanager
_____Western Tanager
_____Crimson-collared Grosbeak
_____Northern Cardinal
_____Pyrrhuloxia
_____Rose-breasted Grosbeak
_____Black-headed Grosbeak
_____Blue Bunting
_____Blue Grosbeak
_____Lazuli Bunting
_____Indigo Bunting
_____Varied Bunting
_____Painted Bunting

Blackbirds (Icteridae)
_____Bobolink
_____Red-winged Blackbird
_____Eastern Meadowlark
_____Western Meadowlark
_____Yellow-headed Blackbird
_____Rusty Blackbird
_____Brewer's Blackbird
_____Common Grackle
_____Boat-tailed Grackle

_____Great-tailed Grackle
_____Shiny Cowbird
_____Bronzed Cowbird
_____Brown-headed Cowbird
_____Orchard Oriole
_____Hooded Oriole
_____Bullock's Oriole
_____Spot-breasted Oriole
_____Altamira Oriole
_____Audubon's Oriole
_____Baltimore Oriole
_____Scott's Oriole

Fringilline and Cardueline Finches and Allies (Fringillidae)
_____Brambling
_____Pine Grosbeak

_____Purple Finch
_____House Finch
_____Red Crossbill
_____White-winged Crossbill
_____Common Redpoll
_____Hoary Redpoll
_____Pine Siskin
_____Lesser Goldfinch
_____American Goldfinch
_____European Goldfinch*
_____Evening Grosbeak

Old World Sparrows (Passeridae)
_____House Sparrow
_____Eurasian Tree Sparrow

INDEX

SHORE SILHOUETTES

1 Forster's Tern
2 Black Tern
3 Herring Gull
4 Cormorant
5 Loon
6 Great Blue Heron
7 Mallard
8 Pied-billed Grebe
9 Marbled Godwit
10 Greater Yellowlegs
11 Dowitcher
12 Clapper Rail
13 Whimbrel
14 Black-bellied Plover
15 Turnstone
16 Night-Heron
17 Phalarope
18 Least Sandpiper
19 Semipalmated Plover
20 Sanderling
21 Spotted Sandpiper
22 Killdeer
23 Coot
24 Green Heron

FLIGHT SILHOUETTES

1 Barn Swallow
2 Cliff Swallow
3 Purple Martin
4 Chimney Swift
5 Starling
6 Common Grackle
7 Blackbird
8 Bluebird
9 Robin
10 Goldfinch
11 House Sparrow
12 Belted Kingfisher
13 Blue Jay
14 Flicker
15 Mourning Dove
16 Meadowlark
17 Bobwhite
18 Ruffed Grouse
19 Pheasant
20 Nighthawk
21 Crow
22 Sharp-shinned Hawk
23 Kestrel
24 Killdeer
25 Wilson's Snipe
26 Woodcock